# Service Management

"*Theory and Practice* is different from other books; it emphasizes value creation through interdependencies of systems, structures, processes and outcomes in service businesses. The book is a must read for executives not only in service businesses but also in manufacturing companies and for those taking courses in service management, both at universities and in executive development programs. It is also a must read for scholars who are searching for an overview of service management theory and practice."
—Bo Edvardsson, *Professor of Business Administration and Founder of Service Research Center (CTF), Karlstad University, Sweden*

"This new service management textbook provides timely information about the impact of artificial intelligence and the current pandemic on the opportunities and need for service innovation. The authors are well-known for their numerous contributions to the service research field, and this textbook draws on and synthesizes considerable recent service theory that is impacting service practice today. In sum, practitioners, students, and researchers can all benefit from reading this timely work and gain insights from the multiple perspectives on service theory and practice it offers for managing a service business."
—Jim Spohrer, *Cognitive Opentech Group (COG), IBM, San Jose, CA, USA*

John R. Bryson  •  Jon Sundbo
Lars Fuglsang  •  Peter Daniels

# Service Management

Theory and Practice

palgrave
macmillan

John R. Bryson
Department of Strategy and International
Business
The University of Birmingham
Edgbaston, UK

Lars Fuglsang
Roskilde University
Roskilde, Denmark

Jon Sundbo
Roskilde University
Roskilde, Denmark

Peter Daniels
The University of Birmingham
Edgbaston, UK

ISBN 978-3-030-52059-5      ISBN 978-3-030-52060-1    (eBook)
https://doi.org/10.1007/978-3-030-52060-1

This Palgrave Macmillan imprint is published by the registered company Springer Nature
Switzerland AG.
The registered company address is: Gewerbestrasse 11, 6330 Cham, Switzerland

# Preface

It is a very strange time to be working on a book on service management. The onset of the Covid-19 pandemic has meant that many people are practicing social distancing and that homeworking has become the new normal. Many service businesses that rely on face-to-face encounters have been temporarily closed; some will never reopen. Other service businesses have rapidly adopted homeworking as the new normal using online communication platforms including Skype for business or Zoom. All this highlights the need for a new approach to understanding the management of service businesses. The impacts related to Covid-19 have cut across all service processes—from human resource management to operations and marketing. This book develops a new integrated approach to understanding service businesses designed for those wanting to understand, establish and manage all types of service businesses. This focus includes a discussion of concepts, theories, tools and approaches. Our ambition has been to develop a 'smart' or 'intelligent' approach to understanding service management. Such an approach not only presents models and prescriptions that managers should explore but also considers the problems of managing service businesses.

The existing approaches to exploring services have a tendency to focus on one aspect, for example, a discussion of service operations or service marketing. At the centre of this book is a discussion regarding approaches to reading service businesses. We begin by asking the question: how should one read a service business? This question does not emphasize one aspect of service business, but rather the focus is on highlighting the interdependencies of business processes that occur within service businesses. Our answer to the question of how to read a service business resulted in the identification of 14 critical questions. Exploring these 14 questions has been the basis for this book's 14 chapters. For practitioners, responses to these questions include adaptation strategies to enhance business resilience, competitiveness or to adopt a more responsible approach to managing businesses. This book intends to encourage a more reflexive approach to management decisions founded on understanding the complex interrelationships between the 14 perspectives explored in this book. This approach is intended to develop a problem-based and intelligent approach to managing service business.

We begin by exploring service theory and business models before examining the 'upstream' aspects of the production of services (technology, operations and production) and then we consider the downstream aspects (customers and marketing). Our focus is on two types of services. First, the primary focus is on understanding the management of all types of service businesses. These include large international businesses and much smaller more locally oriented firms. Second, it is important to distinguish between service businesses and service functions within manufacturing firms, but also the enabling roles that services businesses have played to support internationalization. Thus, Chap. 11 explores the critical contribution that logistic service businesses have played in underpinning the development of an international economy. Chap. 12 explores services within manufacturing firms. This is not a book about servitization and manufacturing, but it is important to understand the shift within manufacturing companies towards the integration of services into goods.

Our approach has been not only to explore the more recent research but also to place this within a wider context. We are interested in providing an approach to reading service businesses that encourages readers to learn and reflect on the opportunities, possibilities and challenges of managing service businesses. Our ambition is that our integrated approach will enhance practitioner competencies. Reading service businesses initially focuses on the identification of the critical 14 questions and then to provide an analysis that will inform the development of context-based solutions. We are very much aware of the dangers of applying best practice solutions to business problems without engaging in local adaptations. Business practices are constantly changing. This means that it is important to identify the core questions and to develop approaches to crafting local solutions considering on-going quantitative and qualitative alterations that will continue to transform service businesses.

We have written this book for students, practitioners, researchers and other academics interested in the on-going transformation of service firms, work and service experiences and for managers involved in the everyday tasks of managing service businesses. This book has been an exercise in co-creation. The book proposal was reviewed by eight scholars from across the world. In addition, detailed feedback was provided by the editorial team at Palgrave Macmillan. The manuscript was then reviewed and revised. The authors met many times to review progress and to discuss ideas, but there have also been Skype meetings and innumerable emails. Every chapter has been read, developed and critiqued. Each chapter initially had a chapter lead author who developed an initial draft based on a detailed outline agreed by all authors. Then the chapter authorship was broadened to include all authors. Some chapters were also tested on our students. Writing this book also reflects many conversations, discussions and reflections with other scholars, students and business owners, managers and employees. These conversations have included discussions with scholars and practitioners in many different countries including all member states of the European Union, the US, Canada, China, India, Brazil, Dubai, Singapore, Australia, New Zealand and east Africa. These experiences are reflected in our analysis of service businesses.

This book has its origins in discussions between the co-authors about our many experiences of researching and teaching students about the shift towards service-led production systems. A distinction is often made between teaching and research-led teaching. This book has been guided and informed by the research experiences of the authors—our many published journal papers, book chapters and books, and, in this sense, this is a research-led text. Nevertheless, it has also been informed by our direct experiences of managing service businesses and providing consultancy advice to service businesses and to regional and national governments on service policy. We would also like to acknowledge the influence that our teaching and students have had on the development of this book. In this sense, this text is research-led, practice-led and teaching-led.

Other books on service management have been published. However, these were published some years ago and do not cover the latest aspects including digitalization, the platform economy and the GIG economy (self-employment, projects and temporary employment, etc.). Furthermore, they tend to avoid exploring the challenges and potential problems of managing service businesses. Several books have been published that present knowledge and prescriptive models about selected service fields including service marketing, innovation and internationalization, but this book is the first to develop an integrated approach to reading service businesses. This approach is based on the understanding that a business is a set of linked processes and practitioners need to develop an informed integrated understanding of the totality of processes that lie behind the creation of services. The 14 chapters are illustrated with short case studies that are positioned throughout the book. Nevertheless, in Chap. 14, we develop a set of integrated case studies that focus on the application of our approach to reading service businesses to a set of cases from different sectors and host economies.

Peter Daniels was one of the original authors of this book. In early April 2019, he was unable to continue to work on this book due to ill-health. On 8 July 2019, Peter wrote to us just before another round of chemotherapy and in this email he noted that 'I really feel guilty about the book but do not hesitate to chop about my drafts in whatever way appropriate!'. There was no need for Peter to feel guilty. We chopped and changed his text, but then all chapters have been transformed, chopped and changed, since April 2019. We very much enjoyed working with him on this book and appreciated the contributions he made to service scholarship. Peter was one of the greatest of service sector enthusiasts. We dedicate this book to commemorate Peter. Peter was Professor of Geography at the University of Birmingham, UK, and founding director of the *Service Sector Research Unit*. This was established in 1993 and was one of the very first research units to focus on services. He was also one of the founding members of RESER, the *European Association for Research on Services*. Prior to coming to Birmingham, he held posts at

Portsmouth and Liverpool. There is no question that he was one of the founding fathers of service science. Peter died of cancer on 3rd September 2019.
We miss him as a good colleague and an outstanding researcher. He also
played a critical role in shaping this book, drafting chapters and commenting
on chapters. We carry with us fond memories and the intellectual imprint of
our unforgettable colleague. We suspect that he would have liked the final
book, but we will never know for sure.

Edgbaston, UK                                                          John R. Bryson
Roskilde, Denmark                                                        Jon Sundbo
Roskilde, Denmark                                                      Lars Fuglsang
Birmingham, UK                                                         Peter Daniels
3 April 2020

# Contents

# About the Authors

**John R. Bryson** is Professor of Enterprise and Competitiveness, Birmingham Business School, University of Birmingham, UK. His research interests include understanding the growth and dynamics of knowledge-intensive service firms, innovation and services, the interactions between services and manufacturing and the impacts of robotics and artificial intelligence on services.

**Jon Sundbo** is Professor in Business Administration and Innovation, Roskilde University, Denmark. His research interests include service firms and the service economy, innovation, service processes, marketing and the management of service firms.

**Lars Fuglsang** is Professor at the Department of Social Sciences and Business, Roskilde University. He currently leads the research group on Innovation in Service and Experiences. His research interests include how institutional and organizational frameworks are created to deal with the impacts of innovation, technology and other forms of change on business and society.

**Peter Daniels** was Emeritus Professor of Geography in the School of Geography, Earth and Environmental Sciences, University of Birmingham, UK. His research focused on the geography of advanced business and professional services including a focus on services across Asia-Pacific.

# List of Figures

# List of Tables

# Reading and Managing Service Businesses

1

**Key Themes**

- What is a service business?
- What is a service?
- General trends in the rise of service businesses
- How to establish a service business
- Reading and managing service businesses
- The structure of this book

This book explores the challenges and problems of running and managing service businesses. It is not just about what works, but also about what does not work. The book's focus is on understanding and managing private sector service businesses. Nevertheless, it is also relevant for understanding and managing public services and service functions within manufacturing-orientated production systems.

Terminology and typologies are important. The focus of this book is on service businesses. This includes understanding the on-going shift towards the production and sale of all types of service products. The term '*service*' both characterizes the process of producing a service and also describes the outcome of this process. This outcome is a '*product*' or a '*service product*'. Product bundling occurs when a company combines different services together into a combined product or service package, for example, insurance policies or meal deals. A *good* is a '*tangible manufactured thing*'. Tangible goods are increasingly being combined with service products to produce hybrids. These are both goods and service products. Manufacturing firms, or firms that orchestrate the production of goods but are not directly engaged in production, are increasingly altering their position on the goods-service continuum to produce *product-service combinations* or product-service bundles.

The approach adopted in this book is to provide an overview of service research and theory (Chap. 2) before exploring strategy and operational issues (Chaps. 3, 4, 5, 6, and 7). This includes a discussion of service business models, operations and productivity and personnel management. The focus then shifts from process and product innovation (Chap. 7) to exploring marketing and customers (Chaps. 8 and 9) before exploring the internationalization of service firms (Chap. 10). The analysis then explores the role logistic services have made to underpinning internationalization and the shift within manufacturing companies towards the production of goods that are supported by services (Chap. 12). In Chap. 13, the measurement of company performance and customer satisfaction is explored before the book in Chap. 14 concludes with the development and application of an integrated case study approach to reading service businesses (Chap. 14).

**Electronic Supplementary Material** The online version of this chapter (https://doi.org/10.1007/978-3-030-52060-1_1) contains supplementary material, which is available to authorized users.

© The Author(s) 2020

J. R. Bryson et al., *Service Management*, https://doi.org/10.1007/978-3-030-52060-1_1

1

Managers, employees, students, academics and others interested in understanding and running service businesses will benefit from this book. It can be used as a reference book where selected topics and tools can be found in each chapter, or it can be read entirely. Each chapter explores core business and management processes as they relate to the creation of services and to running and managing service businesses. This chapter presents definitions of the core phenomenon—service and service business. Part of the challenge is how to read a business or to engage in an analytical process that informs management decisions.

Services play an important role in enabling all types of economic activities and in facilitating everyday living. Logistics, financial services and information services underpin all economic transactions and all economic activities. Service businesses matter. This book is targeted at those whose working lives will be predominantly focused on the management and delivery of services. It develops a holistic and integrated approach to understanding service businesses by highlighting and exploring the key elements and processes required to develop and manage service businesses. It is intended to provide the reader with an integrated or systemic understanding of service businesses and this understanding will inform the reader's ability to adopt, apply and use management and organizational tools. All businesses function through complex interactions between different but interrelated activity systems, or business domains, ranging from processes that focus on learning and development to monitoring and evaluation systems.

Firms are highly complex socio-technical systems formed by ever-shifting coalitions of people, technologies and organizational systems. To survive, such systems must contain adaptive capacity and must be open to new ideas and ways of organizing production. This book's object of study is the totality of systems and processes that come together in service businesses of all types. These processes include marketing, operations, innovation, customer satisfaction and human resource management, and each is explored in this book with a focus on identifying key challenges, opportunities and business and management tools. To establish and run a service business it is essential to understand each of these processes and how they are woven together inside firms to support the co-creation of services between service providers and consumers.

The first section of this chapter defines service businesses and the concept of 'service'. The next section then explores the development of service businesses by focusing on the shift towards service-led or service-dominated economies. The focus is on charting the rise of service businesses, activities and employment, but in relation to the whole economy. This section provides an overview of the history of the development of service firms, activities and employment. The final section explores the rationale and structure of this book with a focus on understanding how to read and manage service businesses.

## 1.1 Definitions

### 1.1.1 What Is a Service Business?

In principle, it is straightforward to define a service business as a commercial enterprise delivering work performed in an expert manner by an individual or team for the benefit of customers. The typical service business provides intangible products, such as accounting, banking, consulting, cleaning, landscaping, education, insurance, treatment and transportation services. Put another way, a service business helps in an organized, structured and skilled way to resolve problems experienced by its clients or customers. Look more closely at these statements and it rapidly becomes apparent that they incorporate some assumptions. For example, that a service business is a commercial enterprise, that it delivers work informed by expertise, that it delivers work to benefit customers or that it provides intangible products. You might be thinking that the notion of 'intangible products' is a contradiction; surely a product is a tangible (physical) object and it cannot be intangible. Yet, you will see plenty of references to 'service products' and this highlights the requirement to think more expansively about something that is produced—a commodity that has both a use and exchange value—alongside something that is marketed or sold as a commodity—a service.

Nonetheless, the distinction that is made in some official statistics between goods-*producing* and service-*providing* industries implies that there is a sharp distinction between these categories of business, but some further reflection may lead you to ask whether this distinction is actually very useful in understanding the production process.

### 1.1.2 What Is a Service?

The word service is very problematic as it has too many meanings and associations. The word comes from the Latin *servitium* or 'slavery'. The meaning of the term service has altered so that the act of serving is no longer associated with slavery. There are many types of 'service' including the occupation of a servant, a public or civil servant or religious associations based on church service, public worship or 'Divine Service' and serving God. The various meanings of the term service are all based on the concept of the 'act of serving'.

It is important to first establish what the term 'service' means. Much depends on whether the term is used as a noun, an adjective or a verb. As a noun, a 'service' could be the duties performed by a bartender, providing overnight accommodation for a traveller, delivering a package from an online store to a customer, any helpful act or activity, supplying utilities such as electricity or water, providing public transportation and so on. If an adjective, a 'service' includes supplying services rather than goods (such as services provided by teachers or doctors), supplying repair or maintenance (vehicle or computer service centres) and charging for a service (a tip provided after a restaurant meal). As a verb, 'service' is used in relation to an object, such as to service a vehicle, to meet monthly payments on a loan, or to supply information or aid to a third party. We also sometimes refer to being 'at someone's service' or to 'be of service'. The use of the word

'service' as a verb is a very recent development. In this context, Gowers noted that the verb 'service' 'is a useful newcomer in an age when almost everyone keeps a machine of some sort that needs periodical attention' (Gowers 1982, p. 46). It was only in 1925 that the term 'service' was first applied to describe 'expert advice or assistance given to customers after sale by manufacturers or vendors' (Oxford English Dictionary 1991, p. 1950).

These examples are not exhaustive, but it should be apparent that the meaning of 'service' is multi-dimensional. You can add to this the fact that what constitutes a 'service' also depends upon whether you look at this from the perspective of the individual user or customer, whether the supplier is a public institution or a private company, whether it is a single-person enterprise or a major multinational corporation or whether or not the user is in the same business as the supplier. Again, the possibilities are wide-ranging and suggest that a proscribed definition or meaning of 'service' is very hard to pin down.

The question 'what is a service?' therefore elicits almost as many responses as there are types of services.

### 1.1.3 Goods and Services

It is critical to answering our earlier question about whether the distinction between goods-*producing* and service-*providing* activities is useful (Table 1.1). Clients who ask what someone can make for them are thinking about a good, while those who ask what someone can do for them are thinking about a service. Famously, The Economist (2010) defined a service as the output from any activity that 'you can't drop on your foot'. This makes sense but what about digital products that are weightless apart from the physical media upon which they depend to exist? This neatly captures the ease with which exceptions to definitions of services are readily identified. It is not necessary here to consider all the possibilities, but we suggest that the following may be helpful.

**Table 1.1** Differences between marketing service products and goods

| Service products | Goods |
| --- | --- |
| Intangible—difficult to see and compare. For marketing purposes, there may be emphasis on branding, or some strategy to connect consumers with the service 'product'. | Tangible—can be seen, assessed and compared with one another. But may include services that are intangible. |
| An experience based on a relationship or a service encounter in which some transformation will have occurred—a change of state, but with no exchange of a physical artefact. | Satisfy a need or a want involving a physical exchange—the ownership of a good, a thing or an artefact. |
| Many different choices of provider, but the nature of the service might be the same. A visit to a general practitioner (GP) should produce the same outcome as any visit to any GP. | Many choices of artefacts—colour, style, size, fashion, raw materials. |
| Very difficult to assess quality without using some form of proxy—branding, third party referral. Never certain that the service will be the best that could be obtained. | Quality can be assessed through direct comparison of the physical good. A test drive of a car or the outcome from using a good. |
| Much harder to return a service as the service is consumed during the point of delivery. | A good can be returned for a refund or a replacement. |
| A service encounter cannot be stored. A service encounter that has no customer cannot be stored. Thus, a hairdresser or a lawyer with no client appointments is unable to store this time and sell it at some time in the future. A vacant hotel room is a service that can never be resold in the future. | Goods can be stored and sold at some later date. |

Source: Authors' own

A service has the purpose of solving a problem. It is an activity that includes the use of human (soft) resources and material (hard) resources. The balance between soft and hard resource use will vary according to the type of interaction or transaction involved, but common to both is the use, and application, of knowledge (the body of truths or facts accumulated over time) (see Grant 1996, for a useful discussion of

knowledge as residing within individuals). A business that offers a service is contributing to the solution of a problem of some kind. Sometimes the dimensions of the problem and how it can be solved is understood in advance; in other circumstances, the solution is not known in advance and the service is acquired on the basis that it will hopefully lead to a solution to a problem at some time in the future. If you reflect on these alternatives you may well conclude that a goods-*producing* business such as a white-goods manufacturer is actually providing a solution to a service problem, that is, how can individual households, or service businesses such as restaurants or hotels, manage the cleaning of significant quantities of linen or crockery in a timely and efficient manner. Likewise, when purchasing a new car (a product), the driver is simultaneously gaining access to services such as the use of the vehicle to travel to work, to send and receive telephone calls in transit or to plan the fastest routes avoiding traffic congestion using satellite navigation systems. You can probably construct your own examples based on other goods-providing businesses such as headphones, cameras, smartphones or computer chip manufacturers.

It seems, then, that services and goods can both be used to solve problems, but they achieve this in different ways. A service business can offer a customized solution that fits closely with a problem, much more so than a good where the fit is likely to vary given that it is based much more on a one-solution-fits-all approach. But this implies that the relative cost of providing a solution tends to be higher for a service than for a good unless the former can develop a standardized solution that can be applied to different problems. This explains why setting up a service business can be less attractive compared to establishing a manufacturing company; as a general rule, the ratio of revenue to enterprise value is lower for the former than the latter.

Manufacturing firms are evolving to provide services or good/service combinations. In the same way, some service firms evolve from producing customized service solutions to the provision of good/service solutions or a packaged service—a customized service that has become standardized. There is an on-going blurring of the services/goods distinction given the ability to transform customized services to packaged services and to transform goods into products that deliver service outcomes (see, e.g. Bryson and Daniels 1998). In a packaged service, the price of the service is based on value rather the hours of staff input so that profitability is improved. When service businesses consolidate expertise into the design, implementation, integration and management of the use of very desirable but complex goods, then these can be priced at a premium to create even higher margins. Alternatively, scaling service products provides revenue streams based on low margins combined with mass consumption. Innovations in app-based business models represent one way of packaging services for mass consumption.

On the opposite side of the coin, and as the examples above suggest, service-providing businesses often rely on the availability of suitable goods from goods-producing businesses for their services to be useful for solving problems; sophisticated payroll management software has little intrinsic value unless loaded on to an appropriately specified computer system. That said, a service does possess some attributes that are not present in a physical good. For example, a customer for a service must trust that the supplier is able to deliver the expected solution to a problem or can offer another way of dealing with the problem. There is also scope for differing assessments of whether a solution offered by a service has sufficiently resolved the customer's problem; the advice from a management consultant on the best way of re-organizing a failing business may be state of the art but implementation depends on the willingness or ability of the customer to implement the necessary actions. It is also possible for a service to change as it is delivered to the customer, perhaps because of the drafting in of new personnel or because of changes in the regulations or standards determining the type or quality of service that must be provided.

Although there are interdependencies between goods producers and service providers, a service is not a good. When acquiring a good, the purchaser can see beforehand exactly what it is;

there can be no negotiation between the goods provider and the customer about what it might comprise (as can happen for service) although the customer may be able to specify a bespoke configuration, for example, cars or laptops.

A key challenge is comparing and contrasting the characteristics of different types of service businesses. Many different approaches can be adopted to developing typologies of services. One approach is to group services by sector, for example, retailing, financial services, business and professional services and tourism. One difficulty is that within each of these service sectors, products, outputs or values can be delivered in very different ways. A retail service can be delivered through a face-to-face experience or via e-commerce, or legal services can be provided from a call centre or via face-to-face. This suggests that another type of classification would be based on differentiating between capital- and labour-intensive services. Nevertheless, as we have seen, the same type of service can be delivered by employing many people or by substituting labour with capital. Alternatively, it is possible to differentiate between knowledge-based services and more manual-based services, for example, contract cleaning. The difficulty is, for example, that contract cleaning is based on specialist knowledge.

The key challenge is the diversity of service businesses and the diversity of approaches to the delivery of services. An alternative approach is to classify services by the type of experience or output that is created (Table 1.2). These categories are not mutually exclusive. The important point to note is that the diversity of service types and functions makes it essential for students and practitioners of service businesses to identify the primary characteristics of a service business that adds value and provides competitiveness. This is one of the rationales behind this book's structure. The diversity of types, functions and values in service businesses makes it important to develop an integrated approach to understanding service businesses that includes an appreciation of different business models, technologies, innovation processes, operations, employee management, marketing and customers.

**Table 1.2** A typology of service businesses by service experiences

| Core service experience | Characteristic | Examples |
|---|---|---|
| Creative | Incorporate, represent or present ideas that are used to shape production, encourage consumption or interpret culture and identity. | Advertising services, design services, art galleries, museums, theatres, film production. |
| Enabling | Many services act as intermediaries in the sense that they enable other tasks or objectives. | Telecommunications services, public transport facilities, executive search consultants, employment agencies, contract lawyers. |
| Experiential | Requires presence of the customer or user who expects to experience something tangible or intangible. | Ballet or opera performance, massage, haircut, gastronomic meal at a restaurant, visit to a theme park. |
| Extending | Tasks intended to extend the life of a good, to maintain reliability, to encourage customer loyalty and repeat transactions. | Full replacement warranties for specified times or levels of use, other after sales services, consumer satisfaction services, installation and updating services, 'health' checks. |
| Entrusted | Undertaken on behalf of customers or clients at their request or as part of a contractual arrangement, usually without the need for the customer to be present. | Car servicing, watch or camera repair, financial portfolio management, return-to-base warranties. |
| Information | Decision making on a wide range of personal and corporate matters is facilitated by access to information; some is freely available, some can be accessed for a fee, some is privileged. | News agencies, data mining services, real estate agents, stockbrokers, travel agents, Internet search engines, electronic data base services, broadcasting. |
| Innovation | Highly dynamic and rapidly changing as yesterday's innovations are replaced by today's innovations. | Platform-enabled services; services based on predictive artificial intelligence (AI). |
| Problem solving | Individuals and firms are constantly confronted with financial, management, restructuring, staffing, infrastructure (cleaning and facilities) and many other problems. | Management consultants, tax consultants, marriage counselling, Citizens Advice Bureaux, IT consultants, engineering and planning consultants. Cleaning and rescue services. |
| Quality of life | Services that reflect availability of increased leisure time, opportunities to counteract illness or threats to things such as the environment. | Adult education services, health services, sports and recreation services, tourism services, waste disposal services, security services. |
| Regulation | Much of the economy (and indeed society) operates within a framework of rules and regulations that apply at all levels ranging from the local to the global. | Police services, patent agents, legal services, planning services, environmental services. |

Source: Authors' own

## 1.2　Trends in the Development of Service Businesses

### 1.2.1　Services: A Growing Business Sector

Since the 1960s, one of the most important transformations in the structure of national economies has been the shift towards various forms of service work. In developed market economies, more than 80% of all jobs involve some form of service work. Much of this work is directly related to final consumption including service activities related to retailing, tourism and hospitality management. In some interpretations, this shift towards service work has been considered to challenge the primacy of manufacturing as a source of innovation and economic growth. Against this, however, the fastest growth in services, in many national economies, has been in 'business and professional services' such as management consultancy, computer services and technical and financial services. To the extent that these activities are inextricably linked to, if not dependent on, manufacturing, this reflects not the decline of manufacturing, but the growing complexity of production functions and organizations.

Manufacturing is also being transformed as goods are increasingly incorporated into product-service systems with the emergence of service product/good combinations that are the outcome of a hybridization process of manufacturing and service tasks. A smartphone is simultaneously a physical product with materiality and a conduit for accessing services. Economic development, or growth, is all about the evolution of the division of labour combined with a continual process of creative destruction and reconstruction. Central to this process is the continual obsolescence of institutions, societal practices, economic practices, techniques, infrastructure, designs, business models, companies, professional practices, artefacts combined with globalization or on-going alterations in the relationships between places. Part of this process involves the destruction of jobs and their replacement with new forms of work.

The on-going debate on artificial intelligence (AI) and robotics heralds another stage of creative reconstruction, but it is only part of a continual cycle of replacing variable costs (labour) with fixed costs (machines). Flows of people, knowledge, components, goods and raw materials, including energy, continue as part of an on-going process of increased or deepening internationalization. There are two conflicting processes at work here. On the one hand, there is the on-going internationalization of economic activities that can be traced back to before the industrial revolution. On the other hand is the continual rebalancing of national economies towards services. There is a conflict here between the internationalization of manufactured goods and the very different and more localized geographies of services.

It is worth noting at the onset the common mistake of assuming that the transformation of economies towards services is a twentieth century phenomenon. In 1971, the economic historian R.M. Hartwell proclaimed that the service sector was the 'neglected variable' in the economic history of the industrial revolution compared to the dominance of research on manufacturing and agriculture. As the UK was becoming an industrialized society, it was simultaneously being transformed into a service economy; growth in manufacturing employment went hand-in-hand with the growth of service employment. In his analysis of Britain and the industrial revolution (1700–1850), Mokyr noted that 'Even if these sectors were rather modest in size compared to say, agriculture, they contributed disproportionately to the economy, much as a lubricant to a well-functioning engine' (2009, p. 199). Services play a critical role in Mokyr's account of the industrial revolution. There are two important points to make here.

The first is that 'no market economy can operate without an extensive service industry that supports trade and travel' (Mokyr 2009, p. 250). Innovations and investments in services underpinned the development of national economies and the wider processes of internationalization. The overemphasis placed on manufacturing in the literature on global value chains (GVC) or global production networks (GPN) obscures the catalytic role played by services functions, workers and businesses in the shift from national economies to a more internationalized economy. Innovations in logistics and financial services have been at the centre of internationalization. Second, the on-going evolution of market economies depends on generating, assembling, distributing and interpreting more and more information. The industrial revolution, to Mokyr, can be seen as the age of communication in which 'knowledge was placed in the public sphere, sometimes free of charge, sometimes sold' (2009, p. 250). This involved growth in specialists—all service workers—involved in creating and distributing knowledge (teachers, academics, journalists) and the emergence of new professions focused on the creation and application of technical expertise (engineers, accountants, consultants). All this information was then translated by entrepreneurs and speculators, and the outcome was a continual process of creative reconstruction.

## 1.2.2  Development of Different Service Industries

A forecast of the fastest growing businesses in the US between 2016 and 2026 is dominated by services (Table 1.3). This pattern is a symptom of the long-term shift in many countries from creating goods to providing services, especially in advanced economies, but also increasingly in emerging economies such as China, India or Brazil. In 1960, about 28% of workers in the US were in goods-producing activities (including manufacturing); by 2010, this share had fallen to just 14% as the share of service-providing activities increased from 60% to 86%.

What lies behind the growing share of service providers in most economies worldwide? (see, e.g. Bryson et al. 2004). As personal incomes have grown, initially in the advanced economies and more recently in the emerging economies, there has been more scope for income-elastic demand to take the form of consuming services. Increases in all kinds of legal, market, environmental and other regulations in response to the rise of globalization and the growth in international trade, for example, have led to an escalation in the division of labour and the spatial division of labour. Structural and demographic changes in economies, such as ageing or the shift to knowledge and expertise inputs as key to business success, have increased demand for education and for health-related services.

In most economies, employment in public services has expanded almost continuously for more than 70 years, creating additional employment as well as demand for private sector service businesses.

**Table 1.3**  Fastest growing business sectors, the US (2016–2026)

|  | Employment | | Change, 2016–2026 | |
| --- | --- | --- | --- | --- |
| Industry | 2016 | 2026 | Number | Percentage |
| Management occupations | 9533.1 | 10,340.4 | 807.3 | 8.5 |
| Business and financial operations occupations | 8066.8 | 8840.7 | 773.8 | 9.6 |
| Computer and mathematical occupations | 4419.0 | 5026.5 | 607.5 | 13.7 |
| Architecture and engineering occupations | 2601.0 | 2795.4 | 194.3 | 7.5 |
| Life, physical and social science occupations | 1299.5 | 1424.3 | 124.8 | 9.6 |
| Community and social service occupations | 2570.7 | 2942.6 | 371.9 | 14.5 |
| Legal occupations | 1283.3 | 1399.5 | 116.2 | 9.1 |
| Education, training and library occupations | 9426.5 | 10,315.4 | 888.9 | 9.4 |
| Arts, design, entertainment, sports and media occupations | 2772.9 | 2941.0 | 168.1 | 6.1 |
| Healthcare practitioners and technical occupations | 8751.5 | 10,088.1 | 1336.6 | 15.3 |
| Healthcare support occupations | 4315.6 | 5335.2 | 1019.6 | 23.6 |
| Protective service occupations | 3505.6 | 3663.8 | 158.2 | 4.5 |
| Food preparation and serving related occupations | 13,206.1 | 14,438.1 | 1232.0 | 9.3 |
| Building and grounds cleaning and maintenance occupations | 5654.1 | 6177.9 | 523.8 | 9.3 |
| Personal care and service occupations | 6419.7 | 7647.4 | 1227.6 | 19.1 |
| Sales and related occupations | 15,747.8 | 16,206.5 | 458.7 | 2.9 |
| Office and administrative support occupations | 23,081.2 | 23,230.8 | 149.6 | 0.6 |
| Farming, fishing and forestry occupations | 1060.1 | 1056.7 | −3.5 | −0.3 |
| Construction and extraction occupations | 6812.5 | 7560.0 | 747.6 | 11.0 |
| Installation, maintenance and repair occupations | 5905.4 | 6293.6 | 388.2 | 6.6 |
| Production occupations | 9356.9 | 8950.0 | −406.9 | −4.3 |
| Transportation and material moving occupations | 10,274.2 | 10,908.4 | 634.3 | 6.2 |

Source: Adapted from Lacey et al. (2017)

### 1.2.3    Relocation of Service Business: Outsourcing and Offshoring

Even though world trade flows are still dominated by goods, services have increasingly been involved, following a trend that is also evident for interregional trade within countries. One of the most important drivers is the outsourcing phenomenon whereby businesses choose to contract out some of their internal business processes to specialist providers of business services (Massini and Miozzo 2012). From the 1980s onwards, business process outsourcing has included domestic as well as foreign contracting and may also involve the physical relocation of some of a company's business functions to another country, known as offshoring (see Chap. 10). Outsourcing may be used for non-core activities (e.g. payroll, cleaning, transport or marketing services) or core activities (e.g. executive recruitment, computer maintenance services). Developments in information communications technologies (ICT) have enabled some services to be managed and delivered over considerable distances, such as call centres, website design, or Internet marketing and sales, and have also encouraged enterprises to focus on what they do best and to outsource the rest (Drucker 1989). Although there are risks, outsourcing enables enterprises to pay for only those services which they require; it allows greater budget flexibility and control, reduces the need to recruit and train specialized staff, brings in fresh expertise and reduces capital and operating expenses. In addition to peripheral or non-core functions, enterprises may also use outsourcing to minimize the impact of externalities such as taxes, energy costs or government regulation/mandates.

Whichever types of service activities are outsourced, external service providers tend to be predominantly located in the same region rather than elsewhere in the same country or overseas (Table 1.4). Service outsourcing is more of a local rather than international process reflecting the importance of both meeting local regulations, including non-tariff barriers, and delivering highly localized service inputs. Data from eight EU member states, for which data was available in 2003 for 14 types of services, shows that between 60% and 70% of external service providers were located in the same region as their clients with outsourcing to another country usually accounting for less than 1% of transactions (Alajääskö 2006).

The demand for services will continue to grow, especially for large manufacturing and service enterprises (250+ employees), and especially for business services, such as market research, human resource management, logistics, transport and computer software services including teleconferencing, which are now recognized as contributing to the competitiveness of users as well as of the wider economy (see also Table 1.4).

Service businesses have increasingly become more innovative. Not least, the development of IT platforms has led to the emergence of completely new service fields (e.g. Internet banking, goods and service assessment systems such as Trustpilot and sharing economy platforms such as Airbnb). This has created new opportunities for companies and consumers to acquire external expertise not previously available and it has stimulated the growth of additional jobs.

### 1.2.4    Small Businesses Dominate

While the growth of service multinational enterprises (MNEs), or translocal corporations (TLC), in banking, advertising, legal or accountancy services tends to dominate media coverage of service businesses, the reality is that the vast majority of service businesses (98%) are small- and medium-sized enterprises (SMEs). SMEs are non-subsidiary, independent firms that employ fewer than a specified number of employees (OECD 2010). National statistical agencies set the threshold at different levels, although probably the most frequently used is an upper limit of 250 employees. This is common across EU countries, but some countries set a lower limit at 200 employees and others, such as the US, consider SMEs to be firms with fewer than 500 employees.

**Table 1.4** Location of external service providers (2018; by number, all NACE activities)

|  | Total | Domestic sourcing | International sourcing | Function is not sourced |
|---|---|---|---|---|
| Bulgaria | 4949 | 71 | 28 | 4855 |
| Denmark | 3078 | 727 | 364 | 2152 |
| Germany (until 1990 former territory of the FRG) | 66,859 | 1462 | 1133 | 64,530 |
| Italy | 21,476 | 1067 | 709 | 19,870 |
| Latvia | 1600 | 64 | 17 | 1524 |
| Lithuania | 2511 | 61 | 22 | 2430 |
| Hungary | 4302 | 800 | 172 | 3421 |
| Netherlands | 8595 | 433 | 519 | 7743 |
| Austria | 1382 | 230 | 110 | 1089 |
| Poland | 18,094 | 1186 | 350 | 16,687 |
| Portugal | 6183 | 785 | 407 | 5254 |
| Romania | 9842 | 2444 | 364 | 7340 |
| Slovakia | 3061 | : | 90 | 1637 |
| Finland | 3545 | 1037 | 378 | 2314 |
| Sweden | 5602 | 402 | 385 | 4883 |
| Norway | 3715 | 239 | 239 | 3300 |

Source: Adapted from Eurostat (2018)

Many of these small firms are concentrated in the wholesale and retail trades, hotels and restaurants, communications and business services. SMEs predominate in the important business service subsectors including marketing, computer software and information processing, research and development, human resource management and business organization. The trend towards increased outsourcing by major manufacturing firms, alongside the availability of new technologies, has enabled knowledge-based service SMEs to fill market niches, reflected in a 10% annual growth in these services in recent years. The average firm size in strategic business services is many times smaller than the average size of firms in manufacturing or in the economy as a whole; this underlines the importance of SMEs in service business.

A service business is an attractive option for starting a business because the start-up costs, such as equipment or space requirements, are almost always lower than those for their manufacturing counterparts. They are also more flexible insofar as during the early stages of formation, the tasks involved can be fitted around other commitments or undertaken on a part-time basis. The dynamics of service businesses are down to entrepreneurs; they are central to the constantly changing landscape of births, expansion, contraction and deaths of firms (see, e.g. Hisrich et al. 2012). Entrepreneurs are individuals who cannot be neatly classified; some have never worked for anybody else; others are disillusioned about working for others, while some may have been identified as surplus to employers' requirements. Whatever the circumstances, they must use their accumulated knowledge or expertise to identify new business opportunities, possess a willingness to take risks, be creative or innovative and have a sense for what might constitute a promising service business opportunity. The one thing to note about the service economy is the diversity of business opportunities (Table 1.5).

The extent to which entrepreneurial opportunities are recognized and pursued varies between countries as well as across and within regions and cities within them. The economic, social, political, institutional and cultural milieu is key to the availability of resources and attitudes to risk taking that will encourage or discourage entrepreneurs (Salder and Bryson 2019). Obstacles such as unsupportive institutions, poor education and training, and unhelpful regulations will discour-

**Table 1.5**   115 Service business opportunities

| Service sub-group | Types of service business |
|---|---|
| Personal services | Mobile pet grooming; Beauticians; Collectibles search; Dry-cleaning pickup and delivery; Image consultancy; Mobile locksmith; Graffiti removal and abatement; Golf-club cleaning; Self-defence instructor; Adventure tours; Pet sitting; Mobile massage; Personal chef; Mobile mechanic; Seamstress/tailor; Court-paper serving; Porcelain repair; Cover letter/resume service; Mystery shopping; Tax-form preparation; Wedding-guide publishing; Mobile car-wash and detailing; Used-car inspection; Professional organizer; Tutoring; Power washing; Windshield repair; Private investigation |
| Business services | Business-plan consulting; Packing and unpacking service; Business travel management; Carpet dyeing; Hospital-bill auditing; Specialized staffing; Bookkeeping; Computer repair; Referral service; Video brochure; Executive search; Freight brokerage; Long-distance reselling; Computer consulting; Limousine service; Language translation; Office relocation service; Office plant maintenance; Professional office consultant; Miniblind cleaning; Office support service; Apartment prepping; Debt collection service; Restaurant delivery services; Catering; Seminar promotion; Window washing; Valet parking; Professional organizer; Power washing; Employee relocation services; Cyber Security; Teleconferencing services |
| Marketing and sales services | Sales-lead generation; Public relations agency; Copywriting and proofreading service; Direct mail/coupon; Public relations agency; Mailing services; Sales training; Welcoming service; Social media |

(continued)

**Table 1.5**   (continued)

| Service sub-group | Types of service business |
|---|---|
| Home services | Packing and unpacking service; Handyman services; Carpet dyeing and cleaning; Home entertainment installation; Mortgage/debt reduction service; Swimming pool services; Lawn care; Home inspection service, House painting; Local moving service; House-sitting; Home decorating; Miniblind cleaning; Pet food and supplies delivery; Custom closet systems; Window cleaning; Residential cleaning; Security services; ironing |
| Computers and technology services | Computer repairs; Computer consulting; Internet research; Website designer; cyber security |
| Children's services | Children's party planning; Child identification programme; Children's fitness; Children's transportation services; Babysitting; Computer training for children; Nanny placement; New mother/infant home care; Home tutoring |
| Event services | Photography; Errand runner/personal shopper; Family history video; Mobile disc jockey; Wedding planning service; Event planning; Limousine service; Photo birth announcements; Videotaping service; Reunion organizing |

Source: Authors' own

age new service business ventures from forming or the expansion of existing activities. Entrepreneurs need not necessarily rely on just their own ideas and resources but may also make use of opportunities to share information in localities where there are clusters of related services and other businesses; an excellent example is Silicon Valley (California), others include Digital Media City (Seoul), Paris-Saclay (south of Paris), Bangalore (India), Silicon Fen (Cambridge, UK) and Silicon Delta (Shenzhen, China). The nexus of social, cultural and intellectual capital typical of such business clusters not only stimulates entrepreneurial activity but also benefits small and micro firms, many of which will be service businesses that find it difficult to finance in-house services such as training, research or marketing. The competitive advantage of service businesses within clusters will also be enhanced with this success stimulating the emergence of new entrepreneurial firms. Service firms that are located in localized agglomerations, or clusters, are embedded in formal and informal institutional and firm networks. Embeddedness has a long history, but emphasis has been on socio-spatial embeddedness combining notions of social capital and networks. This sociologically informed analysis of embeddedness highlights that entrepreneurs are social agents who are situated within a wider structure of socio-economic relationships (Salder and Bryson 2019).

There is also a gender dimension as the number of women entrepreneurs is rising with the number of women-owned businesses in some countries, such as Canada, growing faster than the growth of new businesses in general (McAdam 2013). While women-owned businesses account for about one-third of the worldwide population of businesses, there are still obstacles such as access to finance, sex discrimination, education and training opportunities, and attitudes towards women managing their own businesses.

New business service start-ups, as well as established SMEs, constantly scan the customer environment for new opportunities. This is often broadly characterized as innovation and although SMEs are on average less likely to be innovators because of the constraints imposed by their size and financial capabilities, in business services about 40%–60% will be in this category (OECD 2010). Research and development (R&D) is mainly the prerogative of larger service firms, with business service SMEs focusing more on refining, improving, diversifying, enhancing pre-existing processes and products. Examples include enhancing productivity by introducing different organizational arrangements, re-engineering existing or creating new business models, in response to changing market requirements, or devising new techniques for increasing sales.

SMEs that innovate most successfully are classified as 'gazelles', or all enterprises up to five years old with average annualized growth greater than 20% per annum over a three-year period, and with ten or more employees at the beginning of the observation period (Eurostat-OECD 2007). Research on the total number of 'gazelles' by sector has revealed that the share of service 'gazelles' exceeds the share of manufacturing 'gazelles' (Kubičková et al. 2018). Firms that are identified as 'gazelles' grow rapidly compared to their counterparts or so-called elephants—large companies employing many thousands, but which do not create significant numbers of new jobs. The problem with the 'gazelle' concept is that the focus is on employment rather than productivity. Thus, 'sleeping gazelles' have been defined as enterprises which have experienced high growth rates in profits over a three-year period, but without any corresponding increase in employment (Grundström et al. 2012). Managing a service business is an exercise that should focus primarily on value and productivity rather than on rapidly creating new employment opportunities.

The performance of service business 'gazelles' is not just about their capacity for innovation, but it is also likely that they will be more outward looking. There is a perception that SMEs, especially those offering services, largely engage with domestic markets. Many will continue to do so but others are active in international markets, and often the most successful will grow faster than their domestic equivalents. Here it is important to appreciate the role that online platforms can play in the emergence of service business models that can be scaled up and internationalized including companies like Tencent, Uber and Airbnb (see Chaps. 3 and 4).

The benefits from clustering are again relevant in that service businesses can use their local networks to collaborate with other SMEs, or larger service multinationals, to fulfil customer needs or to link into international networks used by their clients (Salder and Bryson 2019). Combined with the opportunities offered by advances in ICT, service businesses can set up joint ventures, strategic alliances or licensing agreements with partners outside their home country. It is important to differentiate between service firms that focus on providing services to local clients and those that have become international businesses (see Chap. 10). Service internationalization involves local investment either to support local face-to-face service experiences or the localization of online platforms and related infrastructure.

## 1.2.5   IT and Social Media and the Emergence of New Service Businesses

There has been a dramatic shift from an analogue to a digital economy transforming everyday living. In the 1970s, an office worker would be woken by an analogue alarm clock which might switch on a cable analogue radio. On their way to work, they would read the printed edition of a newspaper. Once at work, they would open letters and then work perhaps with a typewriter or a very early form of word processor. Communications involved physical letters and landlines. By 2020, all this had changed. Digital alarms on smartphones have replaced alarm clocks. The news and weather are provided by a smart speaker—a digital assistant—Amazon Alexa, Google Assistant or Siri from Apple. Travel to work might be via a taxi hailed by an app. At work they log in and check e-mail, but they will have already checked all their accounts before arriving at the office and the most recent e-mails will have been read via smartwatches. This office worker might be a virtual assistant, an independent contractor, providing various administrative services to businesses or individuals from their home and via the Internet to access required documents and shared calendars. Global positioning systems (GPS) play a critical role in underpinning everyday living. GPS is an invisible utility that links customers with providers of services including bank payments, stock markets, power grids, digital television, cloud computing, just-in-time logistics systems, farming, construction, fishing, surveying, container cranes at ports and emergency services (Billing and Bryson 2019). In 2020, with Covid-19 and lockdown, it is worth appreciating the telecommunication innovations that have transformed everyday living and have facilitated the rapid transition to homeworking.

Businesses within market economies are in a continual process of becoming as they respond to endogenous and exogenous change. Radical revolutionary change is unusual, and much change is the outcome of an on-going accumulation of incremental adaptations by individuals, firms and societies. There are times of radical and rapid change, for example, the rapid adaptations to Covid-19 by individuals, businesses and governments.

The shift towards service-dominated economies and internationalization is an on-going gradual change. Nevertheless, there are times when disruptive innovation occurs that destroys existing business models and companies. On 9 January 2007, Steve Jobs introduced a new product that transformed lifestyles, societies and economies. This was the iPhone, the first smartphone. From 2007, individuals could carry a miniature computer with them everywhere and use this to access information, but also existing services and new services. It is extremely unusual for a new product to be introduced that then becomes an essential artefact for the majority of people to carry at all times; clothing was the first such product, followed perhaps by the watch and then the smartphone.

The smartphone represents one of the most important recent cultural or technological inflection points, or a major turning point, facilitating radical societal, cultural and economic transformations. The smartphone has played an important role in the on-going transformation of service businesses by revolutionizing the ways in which individuals interact with place and space, with government and with businesses. It has destroyed and disrupted existing business models and has facilitated the on-going shift towards e-commerce, but also the emergence of companies like Uber, DiDi, WeChat, Twitter and Airbnb. All these developments in IT and social networks have created new opportunities to establish new service-based business models (Chap. 4).

## 1.2.6   Increasing Customer Expectations

Wider socio-economic trends enable purchasers and users of a wide range of services or products to be much better informed about their statutory rights, about how to identify the relative merits of similar offers by different service providers or about the attributes of good customer service. Consumer expectations are rising exponentially and present challenges to service businesses in relation to service quality or achieving a level for outcomes that exceeds that achieved by competitor service businesses. Waiting on a telephone line for a call centre operative to answer, or long and complicated menus to wade through before (possibly) reaching a human operative to respond to a problem, is now widely condemned as poor-quality service. This is already far removed from the time not so long ago when customers were expected to wait several days, or even weeks, for service businesses to respond to customers. Failure to address pressures on customer response times, given the ease of finding and contacting alternatives, is easily rectified by potential customers identifying a service business that does fulfil escalating customer expectations.

Alongside the challenge of providing comprehensive and well-organized solutions to clients, there is also the challenge of identifying and even anticipating their future requirements (perhaps even before they themselves are aware that they need them). Learning from, and interacting with clients on a regular basis, whether using social media, e-mail or face-to-face, requires investment in time and staff resources but does allow a service business to try to persuade its clients that it is still the best choice for solving their problem(s). It is a challenge for smaller service businesses to juggle such activities alongside preparing and delivering solutions for clients, especially when the outcome from being client-aware is never guaranteed.

## 1.3 Reading and Managing Service Businesses

### 1.3.1 A Holistic Approach

This book emerged from an on-going discussion that commenced in the 1980s regarding the rise and role of service businesses and the contributions that they made to employment, management and the nature of work and to local and national economic development. This discussion included a focus on understanding innovation in service businesses, the creation of service experi-

ences, the creation and management of new service businesses, the internationalization of services, service operations including learning and productivity, service business models and the evolving spatial divisions of labour within the service economy. We have been engaged in a process of reading service businesses (Bryson et al. 2018). This has included exploring the ways in which service businesses form, evolve, innovate and are managed. There is an issue of scale here. We appreciate the importance of micro-processes that occur within service businesses and in shaping service encounters and experiences. Nevertheless, it is important to understand inter-firm relationships and the on-going internationalization of service businesses.

These discussions led to this book. This book has been a journey of discovery in which we have focused on developing a more integrated understanding of the management of service businesses. This approach to reading service businesses builds upon the debate over the emergence of a specialist service science. This is to argue that service tasks and businesses are complex and require the development of multidisciplinary approaches that break down the existing rather siloed approaches to understanding business. The literature on the service economy continually highlights that the service sector is heterogeneous. We do not disagree with this statement, but it is worth considering that heterogeneity also exists across manufacturing.

In this book, the primary object of study is service businesses with a focus on understanding the interplay and interactions between different processes and activity systems. Existing approaches to understanding service businesses have tended to emphasize marketing, operations, innovation and other specific topics. Our approach is very different; establishing and running a service business involves developing a holistic approach to management and we have tried to mirror this in the structure of this book. We argue that the primary aim of the social scientist interested in firms and businesses is to develop approaches to reading businesses and these approaches must appreciate the complex interactions between different processes that occur within and between firms and institutions and in place and across space and time.

## 1.3.2 Reading Service Businesses

Managing a business involves understanding a firm or company and an economic sector; intervention, strategy formulation, alterations to business models and adaptations within a firm all must be preceded and followed by a process based on analysis leading to understanding. This process is similar to reading. Reading is a mental process involving written signs—words—that are structured into sentences and paragraphs. Reading results in comprehension or understanding of texts. Our texts are service businesses of all types. These businesses are structured as they contain different, but related, activity systems.

Reading a business is a process in which the reader—the student, the company analyst or the manager—needs to identify and understand the structures, systems and processes that lie behind the creation of all forms of value. It is only then that effective management can occur. The process of reading to comprehend and understand a business is a capability that is applied before, during and after interventions. But this should be an on-going process in which managers continually observe and read the business, and then act. This is a process of continual strategic reflexivity that informs minor and major interventions including incremental adaptations to routines, but also alterations to the values-in-use that are co-created with customers. Service employees, during the service encounter with customers, must continually read these encounters to make minor adjustments to enhance the quality of the service experience. This includes on-going diagnostics to identify problems and to identify possible innovations and refinements.

This action of reading is critical for managers and employees of service businesses. A manager must engage in a continual process of reading the business. This includes measurement based on key performance indicators, but also understanding how to manage employees and how to maximize the creation of value for consumers. Reading is a process of continual analysis and must precede and follow any intervention. In this account, the emphasis is on an evidence-based informed view of the managerial process that is based on collecting information, understanding business processes and appreciating the interplay between a firm's business model, operational processes, employees and the co-creation of value with customers.

Reading service businesses is both a necessary pre-condition and a tool for managing service businesses. This approach to reading service businesses provides a more nuanced account of the management of service companies. It presents tools to run service companies, but it also prepares managers and other practitioners for the difficulties and challenges that this can imply.

How does one read a business? This is a question that is rarely asked. The answer is complex. Any reading of a business will suffer from information asymmetry or information that can never be accessed. There is a real danger that business is considered to be a very rational process with informed entrepreneurs and managers making correct decisions. This is not the case—too often business decisions must be made rapidly and there is never sufficient information to make a completely informed decision. The development of a science of business has had a tendency to ascribe too much rationality to what is a people-centric, highly politicized and culturally inflected process.

## 1.3.3 Fourteen Questions as the Foundations to Reading Service Businesses

Reading a business involves developing answers to 14 questions. These are high-level questions, and each reflects a series of business processes and activities. These questions have informed the structure of this book, with each chapter focusing on one core question. However, it is worth noting that some of these questions cut across chapters, highlighting the interdependencies that exist between business activity systems. The first question—on value—is one example of a cross-cutting question. The questions and their relationship to the book's structure are as follows:

1. How is value created and what types of values are created by service businesses? (Chaps. 3, 5, 7, and 14)
2. Which business models and strategies do service firms adopt and develop? (Chap. 3)
3. How are new technologies, particularly digitization, altering service business models? (Chap. 4)
4. How are service operations organized, and how is productivity growth achieved? (Chap. 5)
5. How is the management of service personnel organized? (Chap. 6)
6. How do service firms innovate new services and processes? (Chap. 7)
7. What role do customers play in service businesses? (Chap. 8)
8. How do service firms sell their services to customers? (Chap. 9)
9. How do service firms internationalize—can they export? (Chap. 10)
10. What role do service businesses play in global supply chains? (Chap. 11)
11. What role do services play within manufacturing firms and their products? (Chap. 12)
12. What measurement instruments have been developed to control and manage service businesses and how are they used by firms? (Chap. 13)
13. What theories have been developed to understand the rise, role and management of service businesses and how do these contribute to understanding services? (Chap. 2)
14. How do different business activity systems interact within and between service businesses? (Chap. 14)

The first question is critical. The focus may just be on profit or on the return on invested capital and time or it might include wider societal and environmental values. The 'what' aspect tends to be ignored or relegated as a matter of secondary importance, with the focus of much academic enquiry being on the 'how' (operations and innovation), the 'where' and market positioning. In many respects, these 14 questions are central to any reading of a business as an integrated business model (see Chap. 3). A business model is developed based on the identification of a prob-lem that requires a solution, resulting in some type of revenue generation process. A business model highlights strategy rather than operational processes; it simultaneously enhances the understanding of business strategy whilst obscuring the importance of other business processes. A business model-based analysis is thus only one dimension of reading a business.

These 14 questions are interrelated (Fig. 1.1). These are a set of questions that reflect drivers of change and transformation. These include new business models, new forms of competition, new technologies and socio-economic changes (Questions 2, 3, 7). These transformations create opportunities that may result in new service products. Service businesses alter existing operations, develop new approaches to managing employees, engage in process and product innovation, internationalize and measure the performance of the business (Questions 5, 6, 8, 9, 10, 12). Finally, a set of outcomes are produced. These include the creation of all forms of value, including value-in-use, service experiences, productivity enhancement, new forms of work and the application of services to manufacturing (Questions 1, 7, 4, 6, 11). Understanding service business also involves engaging with service theory as these assist managers in understanding how to create value-in-use and service experiences (Question 13).

Reading service business naturally leads to managing service businesses and to identifying, developing and implementing changes to enhance value. This process of management involves identifying new business opportunities and engaging in incremental or radical alterations to existing processes. At the centre of this process is understanding the management of processes that create value, and especially, value-in-use. It also involves appreciating the interactions between value creation and different business activity systems including operations, management of employees, understanding customers, co-creation of value with customers, and measurement and monitoring.

There are three recurrent cross-cutting themes in this book. These highlight some of the central management challenges facing the managers of service businesses.

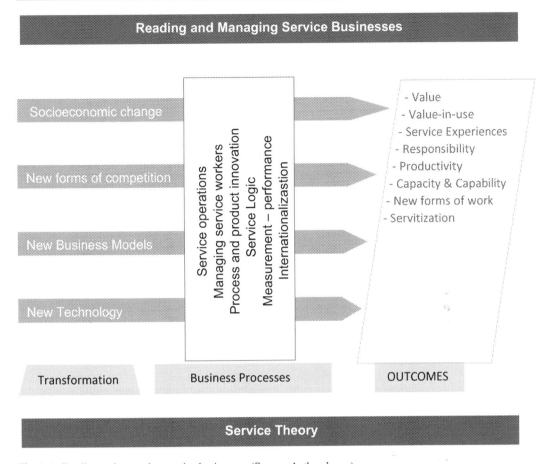

**Fig. 1.1**  Reading and managing service businesses. (Source: Authors' own)

The first is about value. There are different forms of value explored through this book including value for customers, value for employees and wider societal values. There is also value that is created through the interplay between a firm's business model(s), operational processes, employees and customers.

Second is the role of technological development and its impacts on service businesses and service work. This includes the rise of platform-based business, gig style work, AI and many different forms of algorithm.

Third are the interdependencies between different business activity systems. A technological innovation may lead to an alteration in a business model impacting service employment and lead-

ing to the co-creation of new form of value-in-use for customers. Here it is worth highlighting the symbiotic relationship between technological innovations and process innovations in service businesses. Managing innovation within a service business must include innovations that occur at the interface between technological innovation that occurs elsewhere in the economy and process innovation within service businesses. Internet-enabled online platforms, for example, represent bundles of operational processes that have been designed to create service value. Moreover, the interrelationships between the Internet, platforms and smartphones are reconfiguring capitalism and one outcome are new forms of work, service business and lifestyle.

## 1.4    Structure of the Book

Our approach to reading and managing service businesses unfolds over 14 chapters.

The first chapter sets out our approach to reading and managing service businesses and highlights the role that service work and businesses play in the wider economy. In Chap. 2, the focus is on service theory. Here the approach is chronological and the intent is both to review the ways in which theory has been developed to inform understanding of services, but also to provide a guide to theory that can be used to inform debates that are explored elsewhere in this book. It is important to note that all chapters engage with theory and that not all theories explored in this book are contained within Chap. 2.

Chapter 3 focuses on the emergence of service-based or -orientated business models. The focus is very much on exploring strategy and service businesses by identifying the emergence of different types of business model. In Chap. 4, the analysis shifts to focusing on technological developments, including the rise of AI and robotics, and the impacts on, or consequences for, service businesses. Chapters 3 and 4 should be considered together. Technological development opens up possibilities for the development of new service business models.

Productivity plays an important role in competitiveness and is currently considered to be a critical policy topic for developed market economies. Chapter 5 combines a focus on exploring service operations with understanding the productivity challenge experienced across all types of service businesses. People, and the interface between people, process and technology, play an important role in service operations and productivity. These topics are considered in Chap. 6, which explores service workers and their management.

Innovation plays an important role in destroying existing business models and operational solutions and enabling new forms of business to develop. For services, both process and technological innovations matter. These are explored in Chap. 7.

It is difficult to isolate customers from the marketing of services. The development of customer relationships is examined in Chap. 8 and service marketing in Chap. 9. Service delivery and customer relationship marketing must be explored as a distinct feature of service businesses and this must be combined with exploring more conventional approaches to marketing services.

Most service businesses are small local enterprises. This is not to argue that they are disconnected from the international economy as they will be directly and indirectly woven into complex flows that link places together. Nevertheless, there are extremely important and large international service businesses, and service internationalization is explored in Chap. 10. Chapter 11 explores service supply chains and the role service logistics firms play in lubricating global value chains or global production networks.

Manufacturing continues to matter, but manufacturing has been transformed. Here it is important not to overstate the development of product-service systems or servitization. This process has been on-going for many decades and can be traced back to the early years of the industrial revolution. Manufacturing firms have always sold services. Both production-related and product-related services are explored in Chap. 12.

Business is about attending to detail and in understanding the day-to-day operations of business processes. For smaller firms, the owner can keep track of processes and is able to identify and respond to problems as they arise. Larger firms must monitor and track processes, and this requires the development and application of approaches to measuring and monitoring business processes and customers; these are explored in Chap. 13.

The final chapter, Chap. 14, develops a set of integrated case studies to highlight the complexity of managing service businesses. These case studies are indicative. By this, we mean that we highlight and explore key features rather than develop comprehensive case studies. This chapter is meant to encourage debate, but also further research to extend the case studies. We are conscious that a case study represents an assessment of a business in the past rather than in the present. Business, if it is about anything, is about adaptation and this means that all case studies should be in a process of continual development. Cases are used across the 14 chapters to illustrate points and to explore problems.

## 1.5    Wrapping Up

Reading and managing service businesses is an exercise in identifying challenges being experienced by firms and in identifying and exploring adaptation strategies. These strategies may include alterations to business models, to operational processes, to supply chains, to logistics and to customer relationship management. Here it is important to develop a more holistic approach to reading and managing service businesses. This approach should recognize that establishing and managing a business is partly an art and partly a science. Nevertheless, all managers and specialists in reading businesses should expect the unexpected and identify outcomes that emerge from strategic interventions—or best practice management—combined with chance or serendipity.

All firms, and their employees, will have developed idiosyncratic routines that reflect the interplay between people, business and place. These idiosyncratic routines may be just as important, perhaps even more important, than best practice routines; idiosyncratic routines will be known, unknown and will often be inimitable. Part of the challenge of reading and managing businesses is to accept that all firms are different in their own way and that these differences matter.

**Learning Outcomes**
• A service has the purpose of solving a problem. It is an activity that therefore includes the use of human (soft or intangible) resources and material (hard or tangible) resources.
• The meaning of 'service' is multi-dimensional, and it includes production and operational

problems as well as delivery systems and customer care.
• The typical service business provides intangible products, such as accounting, banking, consulting, cleaning, landscaping, education, insurance, treatment and transportation services.
• New service businesses are evolving, particularly connected to ICT and social networks. Here, tangible elements become more dominant.
• Service is a growing industry.
• Reading service businesses naturally leads to managing service businesses.

## References

Alajääskö, P. (2006). The Demand for Services: External But Local Provision. In *Statistics in Focus* (pp. 1–7). Luxembourg: Eurostat.

Billing, C. A., & Bryson, J. R. (2019). Heritage and Satellite Manufacturing: Firm-level Competitiveness and the Management of Risk in Global Production Networks. *Economic Geography, 95*(5), 423–44.1.

Bryson, J. R., & Daniels, P. W. (1998). *Recipe Knowledge and the Four Myths of Knowledge-Intensive Producer Services*. Birmingham: Service Sector Research Unit and Department of Geography, University of Bristol.

Bryson, J. R., Daniels, P. W., & Warf, B. (2004). *Service Worlds: People, Organisations, Technologies*. London: Routledge.

Bryson, J. R., Andres, L., & Mulhall, R. (Eds.). (2018). *A Research Agenda for Regeneration Economies: Reading City-Regions*. Cheltenham: Edward Elgar.

Drucker, P. F. (1989). Sell the Mailroom in Wall Street Journal. *Wall Street Journal*.

Eurostat. (2018). *International Sourcing Statistics, Survey 2018*. Retrieved April 3, 2020, from https://ec.europa.eu/eurostat/web/structural-business-statistics/global-value-chains/international-sourcing.

Eurostat-OECD. (2007). *Manual on Business Demography Statistics*. Luxembourg and Paris: Eurostat and OECD.

Gowers, E. (1982). *The Complete Plan Words*. Harmondsworth: Penguin.

Grant, R. M. (1996). Toward a Knowledge-Based Theory of the Firm. *Strategic Management Journal, 17*(Suppl., Winter), 109–122.

Grundström, C., Sjöström, V., Uddemberg, A., & Rönnbäck, A. (2012). Fast-Growing SMEs and the Role of Innovation. *International Journal of Innovation Management, 16*(3). https://doi.org/10.1142/S1363919612400038.

Hartwell, R. M. (1971). *The Industrial Revolution and Economic Growth*. London: Methuen.

Hisrich, R., Peters, M., & Shepherd, D. (2012). *Entrepreneurship*. New York: McGraw Hill.

Kubičková, V., Krošláková, M., Michálková, A., & Benešová, D. (2018). Gazelles in Services: What Are the Specifics of Their Existence in Slovakia? *Management & Marketing. Challenges for the Knowledge Society, 13*(2), 929–945.

Lacey, T. A., Toossi, M., Dubina, K. S., & Gensler, A. B. (2017, October). Projections Overview and Highlights, 2016–26. *Monthly Labor Review,* U.S. Bureau of Labor Statistics. Retrieved from https://doi.org/10.21916/mlr.2017.29

Massini, S., & Miozzo, M. (2012). Outsourcing and Offshoring of Business Services: Challenges to Theory, Management and Geography of Innovation. *Regional Studies, 46*(9), 1219–1242.

McAdam, M. (2013). *Female Entrepreneurship*. London: Routledge.

Mokyr, J. (2009). *The Enlightened Economy: Britain and the Industrial Revolution 1700–1850.* (London: Penguin).

OECD. (2010). High Growth Enterprises: What Governments Can Do to Make a Difference. In *OECD Studies on SMEs and Entrepreneurship*. Paris: OECD.

Oxford English Dictionary. (1991). *The Shorter Oxford English Dictionary*. Oxford: Clarendon Press.

Salder, J., & Bryson, J. R. (2019). Placing Entrepreneurship and Firming Small Town Economies: Manufacturing Firms, Adaptive Embeddedness, Survival and Linked Enterprise Structures. *Entrepreneurship and Regional Development, 31*, 806–825.

The Economist. (2010). *Economics A–Z*. London: The Economist.

## Further Reading

Bryson, J. E., & Daniels, P. W. (Eds.). (2015). *Handbook of Service Business*. Cheltenham: Edward Elgar.

Gershuny, J., & Miles, I. (1983). *The New Service Economy*. London: Pinter.

OECD. (2000). *The Service Economy*. Paris: Business and industry policy forum, OECD.

## Useful Websites

http://www.businessdictionary.com/definition/service-business.html#ixzz3cCqXvZcr.

http://www.entrepreneur.com/article/80684.

# Service Research and Service Theory

**Key Themes**

- What theories have been developed to understand the rise and role and management of service businesses and how do these contribute to understanding services?
- How is value created and what types of values are created by service businesses?
- Economic view on services
- Service management and service marketing
- Service industrialization and operations
- Service-dominant logic
- The E-service and AI challenge to service theory

The field of service business has been the object of research and theorizing as academics have tried to understand, for example, the nature of service work, service firms, operations, service innovation, marketing and the geography of services. Service theories have been developed by different academic disciplines from operations to innovation studies to marketing. It is important to understand the different theoretical positions which have developed over time and which have focused on different aspects of services.

Service research used to be a niche research area, but this academic sub-field has developed comprehensive approaches to researching services with the emergence of specialist scientific journals (e.g. *Journal of Service Management*, *Journal of Service Research*, *Service Industries Journal*). Service research and theory are fundamental to developing a practical understanding of service businesses.

Reading, establishing and managing service businesses is informed by understanding service theory. The theory highlights key processes amongst the complexity of the real world. A theory is 'a statement of relations among concepts within a set of boundary assumptions and constraints' and the function of a theory is to 'organize (parsimoniously) and to communicate (clearly)' (Bacharach 1989, p. 496). A theory is a simplification of reality that tries to illuminate key processes enhancing understanding. All chapters in this book incorporate and engage with service theory. Nevertheless, it is important to bring these theories together and to explore the evolution of service theory and its diversity. This chapter can be used as a work of reference or it can be read in its entirety to gain insights into the different theoretical positions that have been developed to understand service businesses.

The approach adopted in this chapter is to explore the development of service theory chronologically, starting with the first theoretical focus and concluding with the most recent contributions. All these theoretical contributions remain relevant today and will be referred to throughout this book. The chronological presentation identifies how each new theory builds upon previous

---

**Electronic Supplementary Material** The online version of this chapter (https://doi.org/10.1007/978-3-030-52060-1_2) contains supplementary material, which is available to authorized users.

theory. Theory evolves as the economy and the society change. Problems with existing theories are identified, modifications proposed but the theory may no longer be viable. New theory is also being developed that has the potential to transform the ways in which we understand service businesses, tasks and work.

## 2.1    The Economic View on Services as Residual

The first service theory emerged in the discipline of economics. Economists began to study the contributions made to the economy of different industrial sectors and discovered services as a large and growing sector. This sector was labelled the third sector, or tertiary sector, and was seen as additional to the primary (agriculture, fisheries, etc.) and the secondary (manufacturing) sectors. This third sector was considered to be a kind of 'residual'—it included all activities that were not included in the primary or secondary sectors. All three sectors can be measured statistically, but there were problems in quantifying services. The primary sector could be measured as activities involving the extraction of raw materials from the earth and the secondary sector as activities that transform raw materials into goods. The difficulty was that the tertiary sector involved no material stream that could be followed and measured. The third sector contains many different activities and the academic debate noted that the service part of the economy was heterogeneous. Nevertheless, slowly researchers and theorists began to identify common characteristics in the third sector and a debate emerged on how to conceptualize the third sector. The overarching concept was 'service' (Illeris 1996).

### 2.1.1    Classic Economists' View on Services as Unproductive

The first economists to explore services considered service activities as necessary for business and society, but that they were *unproductive*

activities. In this account, services were considered as activities which do not contribute to the creation of wealth and, moreover, productivity improvements were impossible given the labour intensity of service activities. In 1776, Adam Smith (1723–1790), known as the father of economics, argued that services were unproductive when he proclaimed that:

> The labour of some of the most respectable orders in the society is, like that of menial servants, unproductive of any value, and does not fix or realize itself in any permanent subject; or vendible commodity, which endures after that labour is past, and for which an equal quantity of labour could afterwards be procured. The sovereign, for example, with all the officers both of justice and war ... the whole army and navy, are unproductive labourers. ...In the same class must be ranked, some both of the gravest and most important, and some of the most frivolous professions: churchmen, lawyers, physicians, men of letters of all kinds; players, buffoons, musicians, opera-singers, opera-dancers, etc. .... Like the declamation of the actor, the harangue of the orator, or the tune of the musician, the work of all of them perishes in the very instant of its production. (1977 [1776], pp. 430–431)

It is important to understand this approach to conceptualizing services for two reasons. First, this explains the relative neglect of services by academics and policymakers until the 1960s. Second, this was the first conceptual approach to appreciate that service products and production systems have different characteristics compared to goods.

In 1857, the German statistician Ernst Engel (1821–1896) developed a theory on services, known as Engel's law, which stated that services have high-income elasticity. Wealthier people consume more services than poorer people. This implies that during times of economic crises when peoples' relative income falls, service consumption will fall. In this way, services were defined as a residual: services are activities that are consumed when an economic surplus is produced after fundamental needs have been fulfilled. In this account, services were classified as luxuries whose outputs were unnecessary for everyday survival compared to the outputs from the primary and secondary sectors. In this theory, services were considered to be unproductive activities.

In this account, services did not involve innovation, and there was no significant application of technology to create value. Part of this argument hinged on the assumption that productivity in services cannot be increased given their labour intensity. In 1967, the classic economist William Baumol introduced the concept of the *'cost-disease'* as another characteristic of services. In this account, Baumol identified 'progressive' services (those oriented towards the application of technology in production and which can therefore achieve improved rates of output per capita) from 'non-progressive' services (for which substitution of technology for labour is impossible). In relation to the latter, the nature of the production process determines that the work done (such as a ballet or an opera, a consultancy) cannot be speeded up or abbreviated in the interests of improved productivity (by reducing the number of dancers or performers, devoting less time to researching and preparing a consultancy report). This would be unacceptable to those watching or listening to the performance or those paying to obtain the best advice from a consultant. There is limited scope for productivity improvements of the kind possible in 'progressive' services where innovation, economies of scale or developments in information communications technologies (ICT), for example, can be adopted to enhance productivity. The overall implication is that over time, services become more costly relative to goods. If it is assumed that the demand for services is inelastic to price, but that demand will continue to increase as living standards rise, then there will be a steady transfer of employment from the progressive to the non-progressive parts of the economy. The result is not only a general shift of employment from manufacturing to services, but also a shift from the progressive to the non-progressive sectors within services.

One of the classical assumptions of economic theory is the belief that some economic activities function as 'motors' of economic growth. This assumption, derived from economic base theory, divides an economy into two sectors: basic activities, which produce goods that are consumed outside the area or region, and 'dependent' or service activities, which provide services (retailing, banking, etc.) to the local population. The total regional or national employment is a product of these two types of activities. According to this theory, service growth is dependent on the expansion of 'basic' activities.

For the classic economist, services were considered to be a necessary evil. Economic growth required economies to be dominated by sectors that could experience productivity gains through the application of process innovations. Services were identified with extra and unproductive activities in pre-industrial societies including servants and court jesters.

## 2.1.2   Discovery of Services as the Largest Economic Sector

In the 1980s, a new perspective on services and their importance for economic development emerged. Analysis of economic sectors revealed that not only was the service sector the largest sector in employment terms, but that it was also the fastest growing. During this period, the third sector or the service economy was expanding, whilst the primary and secondary sectors were declining. This decline reflected an absolute growth in service employment and output, an absolute decline in manufacturing and agricultural employment, but a relative decline in output.

Developed market economies were restructuring towards service activities combined with productivity improvements in manufacturing and agriculture. Two economic sociologists, Jonathan Gershuny and Ian Miles (1983), made important contributions to this debate. Economists had already in the 1930s expanded Engel's theory to include the assumption that the richer a society becomes the more services will be consumed. As societies became richer during the twentieth century, services grew and became a dominant economic sector. To Gershuny and Miles, the growth of the service sector could be explained by the continued application of the division of labour within the primary and secondary sectors and particularly within manufacturing. Functions such as accounting, management with the growth of management consultancy, security, transport and cleaning, which had previously been internalized within manufacturing companies, were outsourced or externalized to specialized business service companies. This was a period in which companies were encouraged to focus on their core activities and to outsource contributory activities to specialist service providers.

After this initial discovery, several studies were undertaken in different countries (for a review see Illeris 1996). These studies identified that the service sector (including public services) accounted for between two-thirds and three-quarters of the total economy, whether it was measured in terms of the contribution service activities made to gross national product (GNP) or in employment terms (cf. Chap. 1). This appreciation of the size of the service economy led to the development of new theoretical approaches to understanding services. The focus was on different generic types, for example, business services, or producer services, as providers of intermediate inputs to other companies and consumer services.

Different typologies were produced (see Chap. 1). A distinction was made between knowledge-intensive services involved in selling information and knowledge (e.g. lawyers and consultancy), manual services (e.g. transport and cleaning) and people-related services based on the provision of social care (e.g. health care service and hairdressers) (Djellal and Gallouj 2008). The key dimension used in this classification of services was between producer services providing intermediate inputs to companies and consumer services, and furthermore between those services that were more knowledge-intensive compared to those which were more capital-intensive and relied more on goods to deliver services. There are complications here; accountants or lawyers provide producer and consumer services. The producer services can be classified in to different different categories, cf. Table 2.1.

The discovery of services as an independent economic sector led to the development of a new set of theories. These were a reaction to the previously dominant industrial or manufacturing accounts of national economies. Concepts such as 'post-industrial', 'information' and 'service' society were introduced to characterize this new society that had begun to emerge during the twentieth century. Services, including information and knowledge production, were considered as the most dynamic economic sector and the sector that would in the future create the most employment. Nevertheless, not all agreed with the claims regarding a shift towards a service society where service firms and the service sector would continue to expand. Jonathan Gershuny (1978), for example, argued that what was emerging was a 'self-service society'. He argued that the service economy was based on growth in households carrying out service activities with the assistance of machines. Examples include washing machines and dishwashers, transport to work and the application of self-service to retailing. These machines were manufactured and thus societies were industrial with manufacturing activities accounting for the majority of economic activities and GNP. Although there is some truth in Gershuny's theory, these views were not accepted, and research did not support this claim.

### 2.1.3   Services and the Extended Division of Labour

The concept of a division of labour has played an important role in understanding the evolution of labour markets and the organization of economic activity. This concept can be traced back to Plato's Republic, a Socratic dialogue written around 380 BC. In this dialogue, Plato discusses with Adeimantus the benefits associated with a division of labour and specialization. In this account, the origins of the state are grounded in inequalities between people and this inequality is embodied in the division of labour. This division of labour results in the development of specialization within labour markets. There is a very large literature on the division of labour with the concept attributed to Adam Smith (1776).

**Table 2.1** Classifying producer services

| Producer services | Business-related services | Knowledge-intensive business services (KIBS) | Professional services | •Accountancy<br>• Legal services |
|---|---|---|---|---|
| | | | • Personnel training, headhunting<br>• Management consultancy<br>• Market research<br>• Tax advisors<br>• Technical services (engineering)<br>• Computer services<br>• Industrial design | |
| | | Goods-related services | • Distribution and storage of goods, wholesalers, waste disposal, transport management<br>• Facility management<br>• Installation, maintenance and repair of equipment<br>• Administration, bookkeeping<br>• Security services<br>• Catering services<br>• Couriers/telecommunications | |
| | | Financial and insurance services | | |
| | | Consumer services that provide services for both final and intermediate consumption (health services, personal travel and accommodation) | | |

Source: Authors' own

Nevertheless, Smith was not the first 'modern' analyst of this process as William Petty developed this concept in his book on political arithmetic published in 1678.

The division of labour has not been extensively studied in the economics and management theory since Adam Smith's account in The Wealth of Nations (1776). In this book, he explored his well-known example of the division of labour and associated productivity impacts in a factory manufacturing pins. This includes breaking the production of pins down into smaller steps. The division of labour also unpinned the development of approaches to scientific management in the early twentieth century and the application by Henry Ford of assembly lines in the early twentieth century to the manufacture of cars. These theories were mostly about the application of the division of labour to work processes to enhance efficiency. In addition, social scientists began to identify the emergence of new divisions of labour in companies including service tasks and service work, and the division of labour was used to counter approaches that overemphasized the shift towards a service economy.

In the 1980s and 1990s, geographers and historians refined the concept of a division of labour. A new theory of the division of labour emerged in 1985 with the work of Michael Pioré and Charles Sabel under the concept of 'the second industrial divide'. This refers to a new and flexible division of labour amongst smaller companies that tied them into larger scale production. This new division of labour was enabled by the introduction of new numerically controlled machine tools (i.e. computer technology in manufacturing) that facilitated new types of collaboration across small and large firms that was labelled as a process of flexible specialization. Small companies could collaborate with larger firms by producing spare parts and providing services services to support the production, marketing and sales of mass-produced consumer goods. Furthermore, this debate revitalized the concept of industrial districts that had been developed by Alfred Marshall (1842–1924). The second industrial divide was considered to take place in local communities or places with a shared culture and traditions across manufacturing and services.

This reading of flexible specialization has been largely rejected, but geographers continued to work on exploring the division of labour and the shift towards service-dominated societies. In this account, the outsourcing of service functions, and the creation of new types of service occupations, may represent an increase or extension of the division of labour. An increasing division of labour reflects both increasing specialization of activity with a resultant increase in the complexity of production and alterations in the ways in which production is organized. Here the important point is the extended labour process (Walker 1985), which is work that occurs before and after goods and services are physically produced. Thus, research and development, design, market research, trial production, product testing, marketing, customer care and sales are all essential parts of the production process. The fact that they can be separated in both time and space from the actual production process does not necessarily imply that they are not an integral part of the manufacturing sector of the economy. Ultimately, this means that the dramatic growth in business service employment reflects alterations in the ways in which manufacturing production is organized, rather than the development of a service or knowledge economy.

Walker (1993) more generally speaks about a 'new social economy' emerging as a result of growing specialization in the economy and, at the same time, the need for more sophisticated ways of developing a more integrated approach to understanding the economy; this is where services come into the picture. On the one hand, our economy is becoming increasingly specialized. A growing number of goods/products are produced, many of them highly specialized and sold only business-to-business, and each good consists of many components produced in different places as part of complex value chains. These goods/products are part of a complicated 'flux of circulation' where goods and services are constantly moved around in complex interactions. To be effective in practice, this requires extensive exchanges of information and multi-level coordination undertaken by service workers within and between companies and coordination at the level of governance and policy.

At the same time, increasing specialization emerged as consumer behaviour was transformed. Many activities that previously were undertaken at home have been transformed into tradable services including food production, clothing and entertainment. Many of these activities were undertaken within families, but consumer behaviour altered shifting the balance between home provision and provision outside the home. Services emerged provided by specialist service providers that substituted for activities that most households used to provide as part of a process of self-service. Additional services were developed to inform consumers about the availability of goods and services and also about service quality, for example, social media including bloggers, vloggers and influencers and review sites.

Supporting all these activities, according to Walker, is an expanding sector consisting of the provision of 'social services' in education, health, military/police and the judicial system. As a result of this development, the economy is becoming increasingly 'social' (Walker 1993). The implication is that no one can produce or consume on their own, but everyone is now dependent on services that coordinate consumer behaviour including the exchange of knowledge and continuous adjustment to new innovations in science and technology. This type of society only works based on continuous social interactions and increasing social investments in services.

For managers of companies and organizations, it becomes a daily challenge to develop strategies and practices which integrate knowledge and services. The production of goods and services requires effective regulation, including common social standards at the societal level, and the ability to plan for change within and across firms. Furthermore, the ability to obtain knowledge about and to understand consumer behaviour becomes a key factor in shaping the competitiveness of firms. These discoveries led to the development of theories that specifically attempted to understand the types of logics that were emerging in services and in the development of service businesses.

## 2.2   Industrialization of Services and Service Operations

The first more recent theoretical development was based on a fundamental assumption that service tasks and work would eventually be industrialized, or in other words, mass produced, standardized and rationalized. This assumption was based on the understanding that an industrial logic is the driving imperative behind operational efficiency and productivity gains; industrial logic is part of the ways in which societies and economies are imagined in the media and elsewhere. In 1972, Levitt argued that service production should be organized by developing approaches that had been applied in manufacturing—services should be industrialized (see Chap. 5 for a discussion of service operations). Service companies should attempt to standardize services to rationalize and reduce costs and that this logic should drive productivity improvements in service businesses. This theoretical observation was based on observations of empirical tendencies towards standardization and mass production in services. These included the emergence of self-service in supermarkets and retailing more widely and the application of approaches to standardization in a range of services including cleaning and banking.

This industrial approach to understanding services led to the development in the management literature of a practice-oriented field of service research called service operations (Johnston and Clark 2004). This field introduced models and methods for enhancing operational performance of service firms including organizational principles for production and delivery ensuring service quality. Many of the later aspects of service theory, including quality and delivery processes, were introduced in this literature, but formulated from an engineering or design perspective. Topics, for example, including capacity planning, human resource planning, technology and operations control, were emphasized in these debates.

The aim was to develop an understanding of service companies as production entities thus following an industrial logic.

## 2.3   Service Management and the Importance of Frontline Personnel

The next development in service theory shifted the debate from a macro-economic perspective to explore micro behaviour within companies. This shift emerged directly in opposition to the industrial logic approach. A new search to identify and conceptualize the essence of 'service' emerged including a focus on what drives service businesses. The first suggestions emphasized that, unlike goods, services cannot be stored. A service cannot be purchased, consumed and then transferred to another person. A service is produced during the moment of consumption; some theorists talk about prosumption, which combines the processes of production and consumption. This has two important implications. One is that the user, or customer, unavoidably must be involved in prosumption. The other is that the customer encounters service personnel during the service delivery process.

These two implications led to the development of two streams of theory that became the basis for an emerging service theory. The first implication led to a new marketing theory, and the second to a new human resource management theory. We will treat the second theory first; the new marketing theory became the basis for later theory development. Thus, the analysis of this new marketing theory must come second as it led to subsequent theory development that underpins further advances in service theory.

### 2.3.1   The Service Encounter as Critical

In the 1980s, books were published that emphasized the special role played by frontline personnel in services (Norman 1984; Carlzon 1985). They emphasized customers' satisfaction with a service and particularly the importance of the service delivery process. Customers' satisfaction was critical for ensuring that consumers were willing to pay high prices for services and ensuring that they returned to purchase services from the same provider. Customer satisfaction and customer loyalty were connected.

Customer satisfaction was identified as being dependent on the service packet or on all the elements in the service that the customer encounters. The service packet includes the concrete service (e.g. being transported by airplane from A to B), other elements that are necessary for this service to be delivered (e.g. repairs and checking the aircraft, luggage handling and cleaning, ticketing) and the personnel involved in service delivery. The concept of peripheral services was also developed, which includes services that are not necessary for the delivery of the primary service, but which nevertheless enhance service quality. It may, for example, consist of the provision of free champagne and a service-minded airplane steward or supermarket checkout assistants packing goods. Peripheral services were considered as a means of creating satisfied and loyal customers and of service differentiation from competitors.

## 2.3.2  Management of Frontline Personnel

Another important factor in customer satisfaction and loyalty are frontline personnel and their behaviour towards customers. If they appear to be very service oriented towards customers, for example, by providing information and showing interest in customers, then this will increase customer satisfaction and loyalty. This occurs during the 'moment' at which the service is created during the encounter between the service provider and the service consumer and this was termed 'the moment of truth' (Carlzon 1985).

Because the 'moment of truth', and frontline personnel behaviour, is so decisive, then the most important management issue in a service company is the management of frontline personnel. Norman (1984) and Carlzon (1985) emphasized

that management's most important task was to support frontline personnel, including motivating them and enhancing their well-being. They developed human resource management models including the reversed pyramid in which service firm managers are not considered to be powerful leaders sitting at the top of an organizational hierarchy giving orders. Instead, the reversed pyramid emphasized that managers, in a service organization, should be completely dedicated to supporting frontline personnel and the 'moment of truth'.

Part of this debate also included an appreciation that service work was a form of emotional labour. Emotional labour describes the management of employees' feelings during social interaction in the work process (Hochschild 1983) (see Chap. 6 on service workers, Sect. 6.2.1). Hochschild reveals that much face-to-face interactive service work (flight attendants, debt collectors, waitresses, secretaries, fast food operations) involves the presentation of the 'right', managerially prescribed, emotional appearance or mask to customers, and that this involves real labour. In these occupations, workers are faced with the dilemma of how to identify with their work role without it becoming part of their identity. Service employees depersonalize the work by 'surface-acting' and 'deep acting'. In emotional labour, a smile becomes attached to the feelings that a company wishes to project rather than being attached to its usual function—to show sincere feelings (Hochschild 1983, p. 127).

Deep acting involves persuading employees to be sincere 'to go well beyond the smile that's just "painted on"' (Hochschild 1983, p. 33). Unprecedented efforts are being made by employers to control employees not simply in terms of what people say and do at work, but also how they feel and view themselves. In deep acting, the disjunction between displayed emotions and private feelings is severe and potentially psychologically damaging. The danger is that deep acting becomes part of the worker's personality and is used beyond the workplace.

In this service theory, human resource management became the most important service discipline (cf. Chap. 6). The care for, particularly, frontline personnel was centred not only on employee well-being, but also on organizational profitability. In this account, frontline service delivery employees that engaged directly with customers were considered to be the most important service employees and back-office personnel were considered to be less important.

## 2.4 Service Marketing and Service Quality

The first implication, that customers must be involved in prosumption, led to marketing theory developing a specialist sub-field that considered service production and delivery from a marketing perspective. The focus was on shifting the research focus to understanding service users, or customers (e.g. Lovelock 1984). This approach led to the development of a completely new marketing theory (cf. also Chap. 9).

### 2.4.1 The Service Marketing Theory

A new, service marketing theory was developed in the 1980s and 1990s (e.g. Grönroos 1990). Customers are present at the moment of service delivery and service firms sell services directly to customers. This means that service businesses are able to monitor and ensure that customers are satisfied. This is person-to-person marketing and not mass marketing involving the type of marketing and advertising campaigns associated with selling goods. Frontline personnel still play an important role in this process, but the emphasis in this approach shifts from service personnel towards customers. Everything became centred on the customer in terms of their demands, needs and degree of satisfaction with the service delivery process. Not only is the service considered in this theory to be important, but also the ways in which the service is delivered including the behaviour of frontline or customer-facing personnel.

This new marketing theory not only provided a theory for understanding service sales and marketing but also resulted in the creation of a new marketing paradigm within general marketing theory, known as Relationship Marketing (e.g. Gummesson 2000). Personal interactions between employees and customers were considered to be the foundations for marketing and customer satisfaction, in addition to price. This became a new way of thinking about marketing, and this approach has been successfully applied to industrial marketing. This approach is considered to be more effective than the old approaches to mass marketing. The marketing debate shifted towards understanding customers, their wishes and the development of a total life approach to understanding consumer behaviour. Service marketing theory has become the dominant approach for exploring service production processes over the last 25 years.

The arguments for applying service marketing theory to understand service encounters are strong, but the focus on customers may sometimes be exaggerated. The success of personal interactions between customers and service providers depends on the activities of frontline personnel; sometimes service marketing theory tends to forget the role played by service employees in creating customer service experiences. Furthermore, the production of mass-produced services, and particularly e-services, does not involve direct employee-customer interactions. Yet, such technologically mediated services are sold successfully. Therefore, it is important to challenge the hegemony and dominance of this service marketing theory for understanding service businesses. Perhaps, the solution is the development of an 'eclectic' service paradigm that acknowledges the importance of customers, employees, technology and the application of capital- rather than labour-intensive solutions to the creation of services. The challenge is that service marketing theory is not able to explain the sales of all types of services and is unable to explain the application of new technological innovations to the relationship between producers and consumers. One response to the limitations of this approach has emerged within service marketing. This is an extension of the service marketing paradigm to the service economy as a whole. What has emerged is perhaps more of a general sociological theory under the label *Service-Dominant Logic*. We consider this approach in Sect. 2.6.

## 2.4.2  Service Quality

Service marketing theory led to theories that focused on service quality (e.g. Brown et al. 1991). Quality was not defined based on manufacturing approaches that highlighted product failure or the provision of long-lasting goods. Instead, the service quality literature focused on perceptions of service quality. Customer perception of service quality plays a critical role in service transactions, and this perception emerges in real time during the delivery of a labour-intensive service. Perceived quality depends on the technical qualities of the service—whether it solves the problem—and the functional qualities—the ways in which the service is delivered. This implies that service businesses can increase the customer's perceived quality. Strategies involve ensuring that frontline employees are perceived as pleasant and customer focused, but it also involves providing peripheral services, which can increase sales without altering the technical quality of the service. Customer perception of service quality is assumed to be dependent not only on service delivery, but also on customer expectations (cf. Chap. 8). This is expressed in models that relate perceived service quality with the actual service that is delivered and then compared with the expected service (See for example Fig. 8.2).

Service firms wanting to enhance perceived service quality and customer satisfaction to increase sales have two options: increase the quality of the service or reduce customer expectations.

## 2.5  Other Topics Introduced to Service Theory

Frontline personnel and marketing are not the only issues and problems encountered by service businesses. Therefore, since the 1990s, research on specific topics has been undertaken leading to the development of what can be considered to be niche or very focused service theories.

*Innovation* was one of the first topics to be explored by service researchers. This debate speculated on whether service firms innovate and, if they do, does service innovation follow a similar approach to manufacturing companies. A special service innovation model emerged from this debate. This model emphasized the importance of practice-based innovation in service businesses rather than innovation processes based around science and technology. In service businesses, employees and consumers play important roles in innovation processes including behavioural alterations and incremental improvements rather than more radical innovations. These service innovation theories positioned themselves in relation to both service theory and more general or manufacturing-orientated innovation theories. Service innovation theories are explored in Chap. 7.

*Internationalization* (which is explored in Chap. 10) was another topic that was incorporated into debates on the development of service-informed theory. The internationalization of service firms and international trade in services was considered to be associated with special conditions that distinguished this type of internationalization from manufacturing. This led to the emergence of service internationalization theory. Traditional customer-facing services cannot be exported because they are produced and consumed at the same time and in the same place. Service exports are, therefore, difficult but not impossible. The primary way for exporting services is via the establishment of a network of local service delivery centres or by web-based platforms. The chain metaphor theory that has been developed to explore globalization has focused on understanding the internationalization of manufacturing activities with the emphasis on understanding the mass production of consumer goods. Both the Global Value Chain (GVC) and Global Production Networks (GPN) approaches have yet to adequately incorporate service internationalization into their conceptual frameworks. One challenge is the incorporation of service quality and localization into these frameworks and another is to understand the servitization of manufacturing.

*Productivity* is central to economics and to debates on operational management. Approaches to measuring productivity within manufacturing are well-developed but there are many challenges in measuring productivity across the service sector (Djellal and Gallouj 2008). Baumol's 'cost disease' has been rejected on the grounds that it is possible for service firms to enhance productivity through process innovations and the substitution of labour by capital. Productivity must be measured differently within services compared to the production of goods. Service productivity must be measured not only as labour productivity (income per work hour or income in relation to costs), but customers' perceptions of service quality must also be taken into consideration; an increase in service quality can increase income without reducing costs. Furthermore, service businesses can introduce technology, increasing productivity. We explore productivity and services in Chap. 5.

A particular theoretical focus has been directed towards the role *knowledge-intensive business services play in the whole economy*. Knowledge-intensive business services transmit knowledge from one company to another and this includes all types of private and public sector organizations. They provide knowledge that can form the basis for innovation and development in client firms. Thus, knowledge-intensive business services play a core role in facilitating economic and social change. For example, accountancy and consultancy firms support and encourage their existing local clients to internationalize.

From the year 2000, service theory has been extended from a primary focus on private sector services towards explaining service development in the *public sector*. It was emphasized in the first phase of service theory building during the 1970s and 1980s that the public sector delivers services, but these services were largely ignored by service researchers until this century. The topic was re-introduced with developments in New Public Sector Management theory that emphasized that the public sector provided services and that user satisfaction was extremely important. This realization that citizen expectations and satisfaction with service quality was important led to the application of service theory to the public sector. Developments in service theory including research on the importance of frontline personnel, user satisfaction, productivity and innovation can be applied to the public sector, but not all aspects of service theory are applicable. The public sector operates under conditions in which there are differences compared to private sector or market-orientated services. For example, the management system may be different because of the role played by a democratic political system in shaping public sector delivery; there is no price, or at least no cost-based price, for public services, and the tradition and pressures for public service innovation have been relatively low. These differences call for the development of a special theory to explain the production and delivery of public sector services. Recently, even public-private collaborations in public service delivery have been emphasized requiring further theory development.

## 2.6   Service Relations and Service-Dominant Logic

The service marketing approach—relationship marketing—was further developed in the 2000s. New elements and understandings have been introduced to this approach. Value has become a central concept and the theory has been developed into a more general theory of service value. It is arguable that this approach has transformed from a marketing-based approach to a more general economic or sociological theory.

## 2.6.1  Value as the Basis for Service Relationships

Services have been theorized as an economic sector, but increasingly this has shifted to developing theory that focuses on services as an approach. A key element of this approach is the service relationship or, to be more precise, the relationship between a service provider and a service customer. Theories have developed in service marketing that theorize this relationship. In particular, this has given rise to an alternative perspective on value creation. Traditionally, the marketing literature understands value creation as based on the creation of a good by a company that is sold to a customer and this process involves the exchange of a specific value. Value is understood as price and as an objective economic value. Furthermore, when customers acquire goods and consume them, then this value is destroyed (Skålén 2018). From the moment a new car is purchased and driven away from the car dealership, then the car begins to lose value. A process of devaluation has commenced.

But, the alternative theory of value (Grönroos and Voima 2013) turns value creation on its head; value is created by users during the process of product consumption. Thus, driving a car creates additional values including values related to transportation. It is only through use that these use values emerge. These values are values-in-use, and the focus of research now includes a research agenda on understanding how these values are created.

Value is not only created by users in isolation, but this process of value-in-use creation is also influenced by family, friends, networks and ultimately the culture into which a customer is embedded. Thus, if we like to drink coffee, then this reflects the values that we have learnt about drinking coffee in social situations. There are multiple values associated with drinking coffee—from the purchase of the coffee to the much broader values that emerge from drinking coffee in social situations.

Sometimes a service company is able to influence the service experience and the value-in-use creation process through interactions with customers. In this case, a customer invites the company to participate in the value creation sphere (Grönroos and Voima 2013). The company can thereby both influence perceived values and learn from the interactions with customers. This learning can be a basis for further innovation through which the company develops new value propositions and introduces them to customers. The company facilitates the customer's value creation process, but it is still the customer that, from this perspective, creates the value.

The value-in-use approach has much in common with the ways in which Marx conceptualized production. Production, distribution, exchange and consumption are the key features of a capitalist economy, but these are not separate processes. To Marx 'production is also immediately consumption' (Marx 1973, p. 90), and the term 'productive consumption' should be used to describe the relationships between these activities. Marx provided a number of examples to highlight his belief that the 'act of production is … in all of its moments also an act of consumption' (Marx 1973, p. 90). Eating is a form of consumption in which the consumer produces their own body. This is also true of all types of consumption which in 'one way or another produces human beings in some particular aspect' (Marx 1973, p. 91). Without production there is no consumption and without consumption no production. It is only through the process of consumption that commodities become real objects. Thus, a pair of jeans becomes a real pair of jeans only through the act of being worn. Consumption is the final part of the process of production.

## 2.6.2  Service-Dominant Logic

Considering 'service' as an approach, with the service relationship at the centre, has led to the development of the Service-Dominant Logic approach (as opposed to a Goods-Dominant

Logic) (Vargo and Lusch 2016) and the Service Logic approach (Grönroos and Voima 2013). It is not just an approach but an institutional logic that governs business relationships. This approach was developed by Vargo and Lusch and originally defined as follows:

> In a service-centered model, humans both are at the center and are active participants in the exchange process. What precedes and what follows the transaction as the firm engages in a relationship (short- or long-term) with customers is more important than the transaction itself. Because a service-centered view is participatory and dynamic, service provision is maximized through an iterative learning process on the part of both the enterprise and the consumer. (Vargo and Lusch 2004, p. 12)

> Our argument is that value obtained in conjunction with market exchanges cannot be created unilaterally but always involves a unique combination of resources and an idiosyncratic determination of value [...] and thus the customer is always a co-creator of value. (Vargo and Lusch 2008, p. 8)

This approach has implications for the roles assigned to value creation and value co-creation in service relationships. The importance of value creation by customers rather than providers is emphasized, alongside the role companies can play in customer value co-creation, for example, through customer interaction and by better understanding the context of the service encounter and the customer's situation (Helkkula et al. 2012; Grönroos and Voima 2013). Not only service companies but also manufacturing companies and public service organizations can decide to focus more on the development of a service mindset. Such a service mindset involves a company placing more importance on the service relationship with their users and users' own value creation processes. This shifts the focus away from just focusing on the planning and preproduction of a service as a readymade entity. For activities that are strongly dependent on professional knowledge, such as health or legal services, this transition can be challenging to implement. It is also the case that, because of the uncertainty and costs of servitization, some companies decided to apply a 'deservitization' process that involves separating out service tasks and

processes into a separate business area (Kowalkowski et al. 2017).

Vargo and Lusch's (2004, 2016) generic concept of a Service-Dominant Logic consists of a much-quoted integration perspective on service activities whereby 'service' is seen as the fundamental basis for economic exchange. People exchange 'service' for 'service'. Value is created by the beneficiary, and co-created by multiple actors, that in some ways influences beneficiaries (family, school, service provider etc.). All actors' actions are tied into and co-developed as part of a service ecosystem of mutual influences regulated by institutions. In this perspective, all actors become resource integrators combining and integrating resources around them to create value. Value is created by the consumer rather than being consumed or destroyed by the consumer though consumption. Innovation in service is the development of new value propositions that customers integrate (or not) into their value creation processes. The practical consequence of this perspective is that companies must place value propositions and value co-creation at the centre of their sales and innovation efforts.

On the one hand, the service logic approach in marketing, especially as developed by Grönroos and Voima (2013), highlights how users invite providers into their value creation processes. Thus, face-to-face interactions between providers and users are considered to be critical. The knowledge and experiences gained from these interactive processes provide inputs into innovation processes and the development of new value propositions. On the other hand, Service-Dominant Logic theory has developed into a grand theory that has been incorporated into other approaches. The development of the Service-Dominant Logic approach is thus affiliated with attempts to develop a more general service science, while the service logic approach is more specifically focussed on understanding service relationships. The service logic of Grönroos has also been applied to public services (amongst others by Osborn 2018) to understand how public services, through management and governance, can become more outward focused and more oriented towards service users while not losing sight of their special role as providers of public services.

## 2.7    Service Science

The more engineering and operational approach to services was also revived in the 2000s parallel to, and to some degree in collaboration with, the introduction of Service-Dominant Logic theory. IBM, the American technology company, played an important role in encouraging the development of service science as a new multidisciplinary academic discipline whose object of study would be everything connected to understanding the production and co-creation of services. IBM had redefined itself as a service company and this led to this company supporting the development of service science as a special field that would bring together theories and methods from many different disciplines to deal systematically with issues which were considered to be unique to the service sector and to the service approach (Maglio and Spohrer 2007).

The focus of this new science should be on an integrated understanding of service systems to promote systematic service innovation as an essential task, as service innovation is of central importance for the survival and development of companies (Maglio and Spohrer 2007). Service is defined in a new way as 'the application of competences for the benefit of another' (ibid.). That is, service actually covers all economic activities in manufacturing and services, but they are understood from a service perspective as *service*. *Service* is often used here in the singular form to signal that this is not a sector but an approach.

The call to establish a distinctive discipline of service science reflected the on-going extension of the division of labour that places new demands on understanding the processes of value creation involving many stakeholders. Service systems are theorized in a new way as 'value-co-creation configurations of people, technology, value propositions connecting internal and external service systems, and shared information' (Maglio and Spohrer 2007). Service science is the study of such service systems. It is argued that many different disciplines have accumulated knowledge about *service* that are relevant for this program, for example, in law, marketing, geography, operations or computer science. Nevertheless, the idea was to integrate these approaches into a unifying theory. This would enable the systematic analysis of the many facets that were and had emerged with the development and evolution of more service-orientated production systems. The emphasis was on applying this scientific knowledge to design, improve and scale up service systems benefitting both business and society (Maglio and Spohrer 2007).

## 2.8    The Relationship Between Services and Manufacturing in Service Theories

Services potentially achieve a new role in the economy, not only as a sector, but also as an approach that can be applied to other economic sectors, particularly manufacturing (Daniels and Bryson 2002) (see Chap. 12). The relationships between service, services and manufacturing have recently been the focus of innovations in service theory.

### 2.8.1    Servitization

As a consequence of this development, a new theory of servitization has been developed that explores the application of service-based approaches by manufacturing companies. This represents a paradigm shift involving the application of service approaches to all types of economic activities. Services have become important to manufacturing both as inputs, or production-related services (accounting, financing, marketing, knowledge), and also as outputs, or product-related services (cf. Chap. 12). It is important to appreciate that service outputs are concerned not just with after-sales, but also with the perception that manufacturing companies deliver integrated product-service systems (see Chap. 14). This more service-informed approach of manufacturing is important for the competitiveness and survival of manufacturing companies. Manufacturing companies have always incorporated services into their production processes, but service tasks have moved beyond a factory-led culture focussing on goods and production.

A service-informed approach to manufacturing transforms manufacturing firms into service firms. An automotive manufacturer is involved not just with the design and fabrication of cars, but also with the creation and co-delivery of integrated service systems. For automotive companies, this includes leasing arrangements, finance packages and service content to support the driving experience. They begin to think about the development of transport machines (e.g. trains) as service systems that include a wide range of goods and services which are delivered to customers. The key challenge for companies is to integrate these components into effective product-service systems.

The theory of servitization (starting with Vandermerwe and Rada 1988) focusses on how manufacturing companies develop into more service-orientated businesses. It shows how the boundaries between manufacturing and service companies have become increasingly blurred. Manufacturing companies produce bundles of products and services, but increasingly services play a central and often leading role in this process. This phenomenon has also been labelled as service growth or service infusion (Kowalkowski et al. 2017), indicating that this is a process with many barriers and constraints. This literature has a conceptual and empirical focus, describing different degrees of development of service-oriented business models; from small incremental steps towards offering services, to paradigmatic shifts from product/good-centric to service-centric approaches (see Chap. 14 for two case studies).

### 2.8.2  Manufacturing Still Matters

It is important to critically review the relationship between services and manufacturing as seen within service theories. These theories are often too one-sided as well as being under-developed.

In this context, there are two important points to make about the academic literature on services.

First, it overstates the shift towards service-dominated economies and away from manufacturing. Manufacturing still matters and continues to play an important role in developed market economies. Similarly, emerging economies are also becoming more service orientated. It is important to define what we mean by 'service orientated'. In this analysis, there is an on-going shift in employment towards services and away from manufacturing, but output from manufacturing continues to increase. Thus, there is an absolute increase in service employment and an absolute decline in manufacturing employment. But there has only been a relative shift in output terms towards services; services have grown at a faster rate than manufacturing, but output in manufacturing has continued to increase. All this is explained by productivity improvements in manufacturing and the challenges of enhancing productivity in labour-intensive services.

In 1994, Paul Krugman proclaimed that

> Productivity isn't everything, but in the long run it is almost everything. A country's ability to improve its standard of living over time depends almost entirely on its ability to raise its output per worker.

This quotation has become a cliché to support debates on the importance of productivity in national and regional economies. It is, of course, incorrect or perhaps one should argue partially incorrect. There is no question that productivity differentials between manufacturing and services are behind the shift in the structure of national labour markets towards various types of service employment. Nevertheless, what is overlooked in Krugman's account is the other part of this statement. If productivity is 'almost everything', then what is the other part of the analysis. The key issue here is innovation; it is process and product invention and innovation that lies behind a country's ability to improve its standard of living. Krugman's statement should be rewritten: 'Invention and innovation isn't everything, but in the long run it is almost everything in facilitating productivity improvements.' The problem is one of causality; productivity improvements are an output of invention and innovation. Invention and innovation create new business models and unlock new ways of creating wealth combined with facilitating productivity improvements. Business models are also interconnected, with innovation in one sector facilitating innovation in another. This type of approach highlights the importance of adopting an integrated approach to understanding services businesses.

Second, service businesses are extremely varied. The academic literature continually highlights that the service part of national economies is heterogeneous (Daniels 1982, 1985). Building on this literature, Pla-Barber and Ghauri noted that:

> the heterogeneity of services implies considerable differences between sub-sectors in a range of factors including competitiveness and patterns of geographical distribution and internationalization. (2012, p. 1007)

This statement is both correct and also misleading. There is no question that the service economy is extremely variegated including complex international providers of financial services, on the one hand, and hairdressers and nail salons on the other. Every service sub-sector will have many distinctive business models, operational procedures and different relationships between invention/innovation, competitiveness and productivity. The problem is that there is the same degree of heterogeneity in manufacturing. In manufacturing, on the one hand, there are complex international corporations producing many types of extremely complex goods and services and hybrid goods. On the other hand, are small single-site manufacturing companies that specialize in the production of customized goods and parts. Within manufacturing, there are many different sub-sectors with distinctive business models and geographies.

There are a number of major challenges in any attempt to understand economic activities and, in particular service business. These challenges include a debate on the object of study. Is this a firm, a site within a firm, a task, process or good/product/service within a firm? Is the focus on understanding internationalization, or operations, or placing the firm, or parts of a firm, in a regional

setting? Is the focus on strategy, operations or employment? Should the focus be on invention, innovation and/or productivity? There is another challenge. This is to differentiate between timeless processes or processes that can be applied to all firms, or to a specific sub-sector of firms. Is it possible to identify and explore a set of generic processes that have meaning for all firms or a group of firms? The problem is that a firm includes more generic processes combined with idiosyncratic processes that might only occur in that firm. The danger is that academics focus on identifying the generic processes and ignore or under-emphasize the importance of more firm-based idiosyncratic processes. This type of debate challenges the ways in which academics conceptualize firms and economic activities.

## 2.9  E-Service, Robots and AI (Artificial Intelligence): The Need for a New Theory

Current developments in information technology are radically transforming service production and delivery processes. In services delivered by IT networks—e-services—there is no direct service personal customer encounter. Customer encounters that occur on an IT platform, for example, a web page, still represent producer-consumer interactions that create value. The perceived quality of this type of encounter might play an important role in a customer's decision to consume. Furthermore, knowledge-intensive services are being radically changed by the application of AI and this is changing professional knowledge service employees' work and their interface with consumers. Professional knowledge services are becoming more self-service in orientation in which customers produce knowledge services themselves by the application of IT systems. In manual services, robots are changing production conditions with a reduction in labour intensity related to a corresponding increase in capital-intensity. Manual services are also being transformed by the 'internet of things' in which machines are linked to service centres which monitor performance identifying when repairs or interventions are required. This is another type of servitization of manufactured goods. Chapter 4 explores innovations in information technology and service businesses.

These developments require new theory to understand the ways in technological innovation is altering service relationships, service business models and service businesses. Such a theory is emerging although not yet fully developed. There have been empirical investigations into the impacts of the application of IT on service users' encounters and what this means for customers' perceived quality, but no real new theory has been developed. The role robots play in some economic relationships has been theorized. Differences in the characteristics of service robots compared to service employees have been identified and a model of the differences between physical service robots (manual services) and virtual service robots (knowledge services) has been developed (Wirtz et al. 2018). The greatest difference is that robots do not have emotions, empathy and social intelligence compared with employees. Therefore, the most optimal service production systems combine robots with employees. The application of AI for knowledge service production has also attracted increased theoretical awareness. Again, AI systems can manage technical tasks efficiently reducing the cost of knowledge-intensive services. AI is able to produce analytical inputs that are of high technical quality, including no errors, and these inputs are beginning to transform professional knowledge-intensive services such as consultancy, law and accountancy. Some high-cost professional service work is being commoditized and transformed into a standardized mass self-service system. Nevertheless, AI systems cannot feel empathy or the often-unconscious feelings that employees' develop regarding customers' requirements compared to what the customer considers that they require. One theory, therefore, suggests that AI systems will take over information processing and even thinking tasks and that the role of the professional knowledge-intensive service worker will be focused on the feelings and empathy aspects of service work (Huang et al. 2019).

What still needs more theorizing is the ways in which e-services change the economic conditions for service firms and the macro-economy. Will e-services mean that the service sector contributes more or less to economic growth and dynamism in the future? How will service business production processes be organized? Will these organizations be similar to manufacturing or will e-service firms develop new forms? Will e-service lead to standardization and will price competition become dominant? One implication is that the importance given to extra-sales and loyal customers by service marketing theory becomes increasingly unrealistic. How will consumers and companies react to e-service systems? These reactions have not yet been included in service research. How will customers evaluate services and service experiences? Will they lose or increase their interest in how their problems are solved by service companies? If customers lose interest, then service businesses will have great difficulty in persuading service customers to pay high prices.

The economy and businesses are in a continual process of change as new technologies and business models emerge, combined with alterations in consumer lifestyles and behaviours. This means that theory needs to alter to keep up with these changes. On the one hand, there are more timeless theories that play a fundamental and continual role in understanding economic activities. Such theories include the division of labour. On the other hand, there is a need for theory that focuses on understanding one alteration, or one stage in capitalism's on-going transformation.

## 2.10 Wrapping Up

The development of service theory emerged in the discipline of macro-economics in the eighteenth century with the emphasis placed on services as activities that were non-productive and a necessary evil. In the 1980s, new insights began to emerge in response to the realization that service sub-sectors were amongst the largest and fastest growing economic sectors in developed market economies. The focus of theory was on trying to explain the growth in service firms and in service work. Later, the focus shifted to the micro level—firms and management. The emphasis here was on the realization that a service must be consumed at the moment of production and the customer encounter played a decisive role in service transactions. Initially, the focus was on frontline personnel and their management. Later, the focus shifted towards marketing, and this has remained the dominant focus of academic debate.

Since the 1990s, service theory has been subdivided into distinct branches including innovation, internationalization, productivity, operations and servitization of manufacturing firms. Currently, the development of e-services, service robots and AI calls for new developments in service theory to explain what these innovations mean for management, marketing, exports and customer reactions in service businesses. For example, can the Internet of Things (e.g. household equipment such as refrigerators, boilers, burglar alarms and televisions, which are connected to the Internet) facilitate the delivery of manual services over distance, making it possible to export manual services? AI is also impacting the co-creation of knowledge-intensive services including developments in self-services. AI and robotics are challenging existing service business models and operational procedures, and these innovations need to be reflected in service theory. A new wave of service theory building has only just commenced that is trying to develop frameworks for understanding the implications of new digitized technologies on service business, tasks and work.

**Learning Outcomes**

- The service encounter plays an important role in the development of theory designed to understand service businesses and service relationships.
- Service marketing is the dominant field within service theory.
- Service marketing theory has developed into a more general theory of value co-creation

based on Service-Dominant Logic.
- The service approach has also been applied to theories that explain the on-going servitization of manufacturing firms.
- E-services, service robots and AI challenge traditional service theory and new service theories are emerging.
- Manufacturing also matters. The relationship between services and manufacturing needs to be further explored in service theory.

## References

Bacharach, S. B. (1989). Organizational Theories: Some Criteria for Evaluation. *Academy of Management Review, 14*(4), 496–515.

Baumol, W. (1967). Macroeconomics of Unbalanced Growth: The Anatomy of Urban Crisis. *American Economic Review, 3*(June), 415–426.

Brown, S., Gummesson, E., Edvardsson, B., & Gustavsson, B.-O. (1991). *Service Quality*. Lexington: Lexington Books.

Carlzon, J. (1985). *Moments of Truth*. Cambridge, MA: Ballinger.

Daniels, P. W. (1982). *Service Industries: Growth and Location*. Cambridge: Cambridge University Press.

Daniels, P. W. (1985). *Service Industries: A Geographical. Appraisal*, London: Methuen.

Daniels, P. W., & Bryson, J. R. (2002). Manufacturing Services and Servicing Manufacturing: Knowledge-Based Cities and Changing Forms of Production. *Urban Studies, 39*(5–6), 977–991.

Djellal, F., & Gallouj, F. (2008). *Measuring and Improving Productivity in Services*. Cheltenham: Elgar.

Gershuny, J. (1978). *After Industrial Society? The Emerging Self-Service Economy*. London: Macmillan.

Gershuny, J., & Miles, I. (1983). *The New Service Economy*. London: Pinter.

Grönroos, C. (1990). *Service Management and Marketing*. Lexington: Lexington Books.

Grönroos, C., & Voima, P. (2013). Critical Service Logic: Making Sense of Value Creation and Co Creation. *Journal of the Academy of Marketing Science, 41*(2), 133–150.

Gummesson, E. (2000). *Total Relationship Marketing*. Oxford: Butterworth-Heinemann.

Helkkula, A., Kelleher, C., & Pihlstrom, M. (2012). Characterizing Value as an Experience: Implications for Service Researchers and Managers. *Journal of Service Research, 15*(1), 59–75.

Hochschild, A. R. (1983). *The Managed Heart: Commercialization of Human Feeling*. London: University of California Press.

Huang, M.-H., Rust, R., & Maksimovic, V. (2019). The Feeling Economy: Managing the Next Generation of Artificial Intelligence (AI). *California Management Review, 61*(4), 43–65.

Illeris, S. (1996). *The Service Economy*. London: Wiley.

Johnston, B., & Clark, G. (2004). *Service Operations Management*. Englewood Cliffs, NJ: Prentice Hall.

Kowalkowski, C., Gebauer, H., Kamp, B., & Parry, G. (2017). Servitization and Deservitization: Overview, Concepts, and Definitions. *Industrial Marketing Management, 60*, 4–10.

Krugman, P. (1994). *The Age of Diminishing Expectations*. Boston: The MIT Press.

Levitt, T. (1972). Production-Line Approach to Service. *Harvard Business Review, 50*(September), 41–52.

Lovelock, C. H. (1984). *Services Marketing*. Englewood Cliffs, NJ: Prentice Hall.

Maglio, P. P., & Spohrer, J. (2007). Fundamentals of Service Science. *Journal of the Academy of Marketing Science, 36*(1), 18–20.

Marx, K. (1973). *Grundrisse*. Harmondsworth: Penguin.

Norman, R. (1984). *Service management*. New York: Wiley.

Osborn, S. (2018). From Public Service-Dominant Logic to Public Service Logic: Are Public Service Organizations Capable of Co-Production and Value Co-Creation? *Public Management Review, 20*(2), 225–231.

Pla-Barber, J., & Ghauri, P. N. (2012). Internationalisation of Service Industry Firms: Understanding Distinctive Characteristics. *Service Industries Journal, 32*(7), 1007–1010.

Skålén, P. (2018). *Service Logic*. Lund: Studentlitteratur.

Smith, A. (1977 [1776]). *The Wealth of Nations*. Harmondsworth: Penguin Books.

Vandermerwe, S., & Rada, J. (1988). Servitization of Business: Adding Value by Adding Services. *European Management Journal, 6*(4), 314–324.

Vargo, S. L., & Lusch, R. F. (2004). Evolving to a New Dominant Logic for Marketing. *Journal of Marketing, 68*(1), 1–17.

Vargo, S. L., & Lusch, R. F. (2008). Service-Dominant Logic: Continuing the Evolution. *Journal of the Academy of Marketing Science, 36*(1), 1–10.

Vargo, S. L., & Lusch, R. F. (2016). Institutions and Axioms: An Extension and Update of Service Dominant Logic. *Journal of the Academy of Marketing Science, 44*(1), 5–23.

Walker, R. (1985). Is there a Service Economy? The Changing Capitalist Division of Labour. *Science and Society, 49*(1), 42–83.

Walker, R. (1993). The Hidden Dimension of Industrialization. *Futures, 25*(6), 673–693.

Wirtz, J., Patterson, P., Kunz, W., Gruber, T., Lu, V., Paluch, S., & Martins, A. (2018). Brave New World: Service Robots in the Frontline. *Journal of Service Management, 29*(5), 776–808.

## Further Reading

Bryson, J., & Daniels, P. (2015). *Handbook of Service Business. Management, Marketing, Innovation and Internationalization*. Cheltenhem: Elgar.

Delaunay, J.-C., & Gadrey, J. (1992). *Services in Economic Thought*. Boston: Kluwer.

Heskett, J. L., Sasser, W. E., & Hart, C. (1990). *Service Breakthroughs*. New York: Free Press.

Pioré, M., & Sabel, C. (1984). *The Second Industrial Divide. Possibilities for Prosperity*. New York: Basic Books.

## Useful Websites

https://www.reser.net/.
https://www.servsig.org/.
https://www.kau.se/en/ctf/about-ctf/ctf/seminars-events/quis.

# Business Models and Service Strategy

**Key Themes**

- Which business models and strategies do service firms adopt and develop?
- How is value created and what types of value are created by service businesses?
- From strategy to improvisation
- Business models
- Disruptive innovation and the emergence of new service-orientated business models
- Key elements of service-orientated business models
- Service value propositions
- From dyadic to multi-sided service business models
- Financialization and multi-sided service business models
- Service business models and the rise of the platform economy

Firms are established and then evolve through processes of gradual and sometimes radical or rapid adaptation or transformation. Central to all firms are processes of exchange involving giving and receiving. This process of exchange may occur between two people or between groups of people and involve exchanges of goods, services, information, knowledge or experiences or some combination. In a business sense, processes of exchange are shaped by some type of strategic intent reflecting the interests, intended purpose,

capacities and capabilities of those involved in production processes. The term strategy implies that this process of exchange is driven by some defined aim or purpose. This aim will be a response by an individual or a group to some identifiable need. This is a path-dependent process as previous experiences, decisions and investments will shape current and future decision-making. Part of this process of path dependency will be driven by sunk costs that take many forms including investments in buildings, processes, technologies, employees and brands, but also relationships with clients or customers and suppliers. Path dependency limits or restricts innovation and may eventually reduce the ability of a firm to cope effectively with alterations in market demand or with the emergence of new forms of competition.

The term strategy must be used with care. The origins of this term are associated with generalship and in the reproduction of hierarchically organized social relationships (Knights and Morgan 1990). There are two important points to make about strategy. First, firms are established and must try to survive. Both these processes—of establishment and survival—involve decision-making in response to internal and external challenges or endogenous and exogenous processes. Second, this decision-making involves information asymmetry and bounded rationality. The implication is that strategy often results in some degree of failure combined with unexpected or perverse outcomes. Firms and individuals also

**Electronic Supplementary Material** The online version of this chapter (https://doi.org/10.1007/978-3-030-52060-1_3) contains supplementary material, which is available to authorized users.

engage in processes of post-rationalization in which confused, and often disorganized, decision-making is reclassified as the outcome of an organized process of rational decision-making. Business strategy has evolved into a debate on business models. Reading and managing service businesses involves understanding different types of service-led or service-informed business model and their management.

This chapter explores service business and organizational or service strategy focusing on the on-going debate on business models. Exploring business models and service strategy is complicated by the heterogeneity of service businesses (see Chap. 1). Thus, a service business may be extremely capital intensive or involve very limited capital investment. It may be a locally owned and focused firm with no international clients, or it might be a large complex international business (see Chap. 10). It might also be a manufacturing firm in which the provision of services makes an important contribution to the firm's business (see Chap. 12).

## 3.1    From Strategy to Improvisation

A concern with strategy in the private and public sectors emerged out of discussions on organizational planning and an appreciation that managers should consider future opportunities as part of a more formal process of strategic planning (Alford and Greve 2017). This was part of a 'rational-comprehensive' approach to managing firms that was extremely influential in shaping the strategy debate in the business and management literature (Mintzberg 1988). Nevertheless, this approach was challenged for the overemphasis placed on rational decision-making. In 1959, Lindblom argued that organizational strategy was more like an exercise in the 'science of muddling through' rather than a process of rational decision-making (Lindblom 1959). An alternative account is found in the more recent literature on improvisation (Di Domenico et al. 2010) (see Chap. 7). Central to the critiques of the 'rational-comprehensive' approach to strategy was a con-

cern that they underestimated the complexity and turbulence of the environments within which organizations operated (Clegg et al. 2019).

A firm is the outcome of an accumulation of many micro- and macro-decisions. On the one hand, some of these decisions have longer-term outcomes that shape the direction of a business. These are the more strategic decisions involving the allocation of resources and the types of services that will be created and provided. On the other hand, other decisions reflect everyday decisions required to provide services including overcoming problems, obtaining and retaining clients and recruiting and motivating employees. There is a tension between these two types of decisions. The everyday decisions reflect immediate distractions that may prevent a firm from addressing more longer-term strategic and operational challenges. This is a major problem for smaller service firms that have limited time to consider the firm's longer-term strategic direction.

The term strategic direction requires some clarification. A strategic direction may initially be the outcome of some process involving the management of inputs and outputs, or supply and demand. Nevertheless, all firms are semi-rational, goal-directed organizations that are also cultural, social, political and knowledge-processing entities. Firm-based incremental decision-making is affected by the external environment including decisions made by governments about taxation, employment legislation and service/product standards, but also by decisions made by suppliers and competitors. This decision-making process is undertaken in the context of asymmetric information; not all information that should be known to inform a decision can be known. The implication is that organizational decision-making is an exercise in bounded rationality.

There are at least two ways of conceptualizing organizational strategy. First, as the outcome of a formal process involving accessing all available information and the development of an informed decision. This is a very formal and academic definition. Second is a definition of strategy associated with the work of Henry Mintzberg, who argued that an organization's strategy should be conceptualized as a realized strategy because 'strategy is a pattern, specifically a pattern in a stream of actions' (1988, p. 14). This is to move away from a definition of strategy as something that is based on a deliberate plan that is conceived in advance (Mintzberg 1978). Similarly, Watson building on Mintzburg argued that 'we can conceptualize an organization's strategy *as the pattern to be seen emerging over time as actions are taken to enable the organization to continue into the future*' (1994, p. 87). This pattern might be the outcome of a deliberate strategy and, in this case, the pattern would reflect what Mintzburg called an 'intended strategy' (Mintzberg 1988). Nevertheless, bounded rationality, asymmetric information and unpredictability imply that there will be some mismatch between the realized strategy, the pattern and the intended strategy.

Developing and enacting a strategy is a process based on information capture, assessment and interpretation. All this suggests that this is an uncertain process. There is an alternative way of conceptualizing strategy as a process of improvisation or spontaneous actions in response to whatever is available (Baker et al. 2003; Weick 1993). This adds another dimension to understanding strategy as a much more fluid and responsive process. Strategy development and enactment is simultaneously a proactive and reactive process that is both planned and unplanned and improvised. In this context, improvisation 'is associated with adapting standard ways of working and creative thinking in order to counteract environmental limitations' (Di Domenico et al. 2010, p. 694).

## 3.2 Business Models

The debate on organizational strategy has evolved into one that is exploring the design and implementation of business models. The assumption is that all organizations, either explicitly or implicitly, deploy some form of business model that defines the process of value creation, delivery and appropriation (Teece 2010). The primary driver behind a business model is a definition of the values that an organization will provide to customers. The business model approach provides a framework for comparing and contrasting different types of business models. The emphasis placed on values created for customers suggests that this approach makes an important contribution to understanding the development and evolution of service-led or service-centred business models. Thus, for a service business, a business model should include values that are co-created or shaped by interactions between producers and consumers. Central to many service business models will be a focus on the co-creation of service experiences (Sundbo and Sørensen 2013).

The business model construct is ambiguous and imprecise, and this imprecision reflects the origins of the concept. The term 'business model' was first used in an article published in 1957 that developed a business simulation game designed for executive training (Bellman et al. 1957). The focus was on modelling business. In 1960, the first academic paper that used the term in both the title and the abstract was published providing an account of business models in the context of information systems (Jones 1960). Much of the early literature on business models focussed on business modelling. It is only in the 1990s, with the emergence of e-commerce and the dot-com boom, that the term gained wider applicability (Teece 2010; Zott et al. 2011). From the 1990s, the term 'business model' has been used to describe innovative ways of practicing or doing business with an emphasis on information communication technologies, the Internet and e-commerce.

The term 'business model' describes the ways in which a firm engages in business activities (Chesbrough and Rosenbloom 2010) or describes the processes by which firms try to create value (Wirtz 2011). To Teece 'the concept of a business model lacks theoretical grounding in economics or in business studies. Quite simply there is no established place in economic theory for business models' (2010, p. 175). This difficulty reflects the focus in economics and business studies on price. Similarly, Zott et al. (2011) noted that there is no widely accepted language to examine business models. The term business model is used in four ways in the literature. First, in many instances, the concept is used to frame an empirical analysis without being defined (Zott et al. 2011). Second, business models are often directly related to firms that typify an approach to business—the Apple business model compared to the Samsung model (Baden-Fuller and Morgan 2010, p. 157). Third, there are scholars who relate the business model concept to debates over strategy informed by the adoption of new technology (Zott and Amit 2008). Fourth, an alternative approach is to adopt the construct to develop a comparative approach to understanding business behaviour and performance (Teece 2010; Baden-Fuller and Morgan 2010).

A business model contains many different elements, these include governance, a set of products and services, the resources and capabilities of a firm, the organization of a firm and its activities, a revenue generation model, an investment model, customer engagement, value delivery, target market segments and monetization or the value proposition that is provided or offered to customers, the firm's network with external organizations that support value creation and the organization's strategy including motivations. It should not be assumed that profit is the central motivation behind the activities of all firms. Many firms are satisfiers and are not driven by a desire to grow; a firm may also blend a search to create profit with other forms of value creation including the creation of social benefits.

A review of the academic literature on business models, supplemented by an analysis of 500 business models, identified five approaches to using the business model concept (International Integrated Reporting Council 2013, p. 4):

*Organizational Overview*: The term business model in these accounts describes what an organization does, how it is structured and governed and its organizational geography.

*Business Strategy*: The emphasis is on identifying and understanding critical aspects of a firm's strategy.

*Value Chain*: The analysis highlights a firm's proposition and role within value chains and includes a focus on various forms of dependency.

*Financial Performance*: An analysis of the relationship between a firm's business models, revenue generation and profitability.

*Value Creation*: The focus is on understanding the relationship between a firm's inputs (land, labour, raw materials, finance and organization), value creation and other required impacts or outcomes.

This review developed a broad and inclusive definition of the term that is applicable across industries and sectors:

> Business model: **The organization's chosen system of inputs, business activities, outputs and outcomes that aims to create value over the short, medium and long term**. (International Integrated Reporting Council 2013, p. 6)

The literature on business models tends to apply this concept at the level of the firm, but the concept may also be used beyond the boundaries of a firm to explore inter-organizational relationships or production chains or networks that create value (Zott and Amit 2008). The concept can also be applied within a firm on the understanding that many firms are involved with the management and delivery of many different types of business model.

A business model can never be static but must evolve to meet alterations in demand and new forms of competition. This involves a process of continual innovation in which firms try to develop an approach to capturing value from customers that may be difficult to copy. The business model construct has six advantages:

1. It combines a narrative or story of doing business with a financial model. This encourages academics, practitioners and policymakers to consider the complexity and variety of approaches to value capture in an era of ever-increasing competition.

2. The construct may be used to undertake a comparative analysis of different business models intended to deliver similar products and services to clients, but with different narratives and forms of monetization. This highlights the importance of understanding differences in the processes and strategies that lead to value creation.

3. Exemplar case studies of new business models can be developed and used to understand alterations in the interplay between new or emergent narratives and financial models.
4. The business model construct can be applied at the level of the firm, but also within firms. Many firms will include different business models reflecting different forms of demand and market conditions.
5. The business model approach highlights the different forms of value (financial, social and environmental) that may be created by a firm.
6. Unusual and inimitable business models have emerged, but business models are also models, or simple recipes, that can act as learning tools for practitioners and policymakers (Baden-Fuller and Morgan 2010, p. 165)

An important advantage of the business model construct is that it enables academics and practitioners to explore models that have been developed to meet the needs of industrial sectors.

## 3.3   Disruptive Innovation and the Emergence of New Service-Orientated Business Models

Technological development, including process innovations, can involve disruptive innovation (Bower and Christensen 1995) that may destroy existing markets or create entirely new markets. Disruptive innovation may create a new business model with a different type of value proposition and value network that displaces established firms, networks and value propositions. Not all innovations are disruptive as they create new markets rather than destroying existing markets.

The emergence of new forms of service-orientated rather than product/good-orientated business model represents a form of disruptive process innovation that may be combined with technological innovation. All goods provide service. A continuum exists between business models that sell the ownership of a good outright and those that provide a service (see Chaps. 12 and 14 for an analysis of product/good ser-

vice systems). Music can be provided in the form of a compact disc or record and in this case ownership of the recording medium is transferred to the consumer, but with copyright restrictions limiting copying and playing in public places. Alternatively, music can be accessed by listening online by paid subscription. Spotify Technology S.A., the Swedish entertainment company, is a music streaming service providing a freemium service. A basic service is provided free to consumers but with restrictions and advertising. Additional features, including no advertising, are offered via a paid subscription revenue model. With a product/good-orientated business model, a recording artist receives a fixed fee per album sold. Spotify is, however, a service-orientated business model in which artists do not sell a physical copy, or a download, but receive royalties based on the number of times their material is streamed as a proportion of total songs that are streamed.

The freemium pricing strategy represents a form of disruptive innovation in terms of pricing or revenue appropriation. This approach to pricing involves a consumer being granted access to digital material—software, music, film, games and other web-enabled services—that is provided free of change, but often comes with advertising content. There is thus an advertising revenue stream created to support free service provision. Nevertheless, a premium can be paid to obtain access to additional services or features.

It is possible to identify three categories of business model—product/good-orientated, use-orientated and results-orientated (Table 3.1). Both use- and results-orientated models are service-orientated business models. In the development of a holistic approach to the development of new business models for electric vehicles, Kley et al. (2011) review these three types of business model as they might apply to the provision of electric cars. The product/good-orientated business model for the provision of automotive services represents the classical business model in this sector in which the consumer purchases a vehicle to access mobility services. An alternative service-orientated business model would be to access mobility services by using a pay-as-you go taxi service or some form of public transport. In the

**Table 3.1** Different types of business model

| Type | Characteristics | Revenue generation | Examples |
|---|---|---|---|
| Product/ good-orientated | Purchase of good with legal ownership transferred from producer to consumer | Profit on the sale of the good, but additional products and services can be offered to the consumer. | Outright purchase of car. |
| Use-orientated | Access to the service when required, but without a long-term contractual relationship. | Revenue generated on a transaction-by-transaction basis. Limited opportunities to sell additional goods and services | Taxi services |
| Results-orientated | The good is no longer considered to be a good, but a provider of services. Ownership of the good is retained by the manufacturer and a result-orientated contact agreed. | Revenue based on the result-orientated contract guaranteeing users with access to the product/good-related service. | Car-sharing scheme, leasehold schemes, mobility clubs. |

Source: Authors' own

classical product/good-orientated business model, additional services can be offered by manufacturers including financialization, insurance, breakdown or recovery services and inspection and repair services. The company's focus is on the sale of a core good—a car—and additional service-based business models are developed as supportive instruments (Table 3.1).

The alternative service-orientated business models are very different as 'the core product is no longer the focus, but rather a contractually guaranteed performance after delivery, which is provided with the help of the core product' (Kley et al. 2011, p. 3394). The car company's primary product is no longer a physical good—the car—but a mobility service. In this case, a certain value is promised which might include mobility guarantees that might include car-sharing or access to mobility services without having to own a vehicle. In the results-orientated business model, the final customer would always be able to travel from A to B with the assistance of the service provider. The consumer does not need to own a vehicle and a guarantee is provided to ensure that they are able to travel a specified distance at any time. This is different to the classical taxi business model because, in this case, the mobility services are provided by the manufacturer.

It is important to appreciate the ways in which product/good-orientated business models have altered. Manufacturing still matters within developed market economies. It is important not to underestimate the sophistication and knowledge-intensity of many manufacturing activities. To Fingleton, 'those who advocate post-industrialism overestimate the prospects for post-industrial services, but they greatly underestimate the prospects for manufacturing. A major problem with the argument of post-industrialists is that they do not understand how sophisticated modern manufacturing truly is' (1999, p. 3). Manufacturing has been transformed. This transformation was highlighted by Livesey when he noted that:

> manufacturing has evolved but our understanding of it has not, manufacturing firms turn ideas into products and services. In today's globally competitive landscape manufacturers are inventors, innovators, global supply chain managers and service providers. What was once seen just as production is now production, research, design, and service provision. (Livesey 2006, p. 1)

Traditionally, manufacturing was understood as a relatively simple process that focussed on the transformation of raw materials into completed goods. This is no longer the case. Manufacturing has become technologically sophisticated, but it is also a production process that includes many knowledge-based services. It is important to remember that all production processes consist of a number of elements: manufacturing or fabrication, the provision of services that support fabrication and customer-targeted services. There is a danger that manufacturing is equated with production rather than conceptualized as one element of a much more complex production process. The production of goods and services should be conceptualized as a process that consists of a complex and evolving blending of manufacturing and service processes or tasks. Some of these service functions/tasks directly support the manufacturing or fabrication process (production-related services, e.g. design, testing, marketing, procurement, logistics), whilst others support the consumption process (product/good-related services, e.g. servicing, aftercare).

The key point is that disruptive innovation can occur anywhere within a business model. Disruption may be driven by a technological breakthrough that destroys an existing technology, for example, the replacement of feature phones by smartphones. Feature phones are mobile phones that may be able to access the Internet and store and play music but do not have the advanced functionality that comes with a smartphone. Disruption may be driven by the replacement of an existing approach to revenue appropriation with a disruptive alternative. Disruptive innovation may destroy existing product/good-based business models by replacing them with service-oriented approaches.

## 3.4   Key Elements of Service-Based Business Models

Central to the debate on business models is one of the fundamental questions that lies at the core of business strategy—how to create and maintain sustainable competitive advantage? (Teece 2010, p. 173). Developing a successful business model is only the first stage of a very complex process. The challenge is to develop a business model that is inimitable or difficult to copy. A business model is an approach, a narrative and a concept rather than being just a business' financial model.

All business models include three important interrelated elements:

1. *Value proposition* or the use values that a firm will create for customers.
2. *Value network* or the set of firms or suppliers that are co-ordinated or controlled by the business model to create and deliver the value proposition.

3. *Value-capturing* or a revenue appropriation mechanism.

These three should result in the development of a differentiated business model that is targeted at the creation of a set of use values that are intended to meet the needs of a defined group of actual or potential customers. This process involves identifying the market segments that the business model will target and in exploring operational processes that will support the processes of value creation, delivery and capture. It is important to explore each of these elements in turn.

### 3.4.1   Service Value Propositions and Property Rights

The value proposition, or transaction content (Zott and Amit 2008), is the distinctive contribution made by an organization in the value creation process. This includes the types of solutions provided or promised by the organization to its customers or beneficiaries. There are many different types of value propositions ranging from the sale of a good in which ownership is transferred from producer to consumer to the sale of experiences. This highlights a key difference between a goods-based value proposition compared to one based on the delivery of services.

It is important to differentiate between product/good versus service propositions by drawing upon the theory of property rights. Thus, all economic transactions are exchanges of bundles of property rights. Thus, in legal terms 'it is not the physical property itself but the rights to certain aspects of that property that are exchanged' (Kim and Mahoney 2010, p. 810). This is to distinguish between an artefact or physical good and legal rights. This distinction is especially important for the production and sale of all types of services and service experiences. Thus, the provision or supply of a service and its consumption reflect a special form of exchange of property rights involving rights of access rather than outright ownership. This reflects the emphasis Coase placed on markets versus hierarchies in the definition of a firm (1937). A firm can use its assets to produce the services it needs inside the firm using the firm's hierarchy or can purchase services from external providers. This is an argument about the boundaries of a firm which are defined legally in terms of the right to negotiate and sign contracts but also in terms of the ownership titles held by the firm to key assets including land, machines, inventories and intellectual property. For firms, the theory of property rights suggests that firms should have ownership rights to those elements of their value creation processes that provide them with critical forms of inimitability and outsource other service elements that are less critical. This explains the growth in client demand for information, knowledge and expertise provided by business and professional service firms (Ehret and Wirtz 2015).

For individuals, services are consumed by paying directly or indirectly for access, but they are never owned outright. This reflects another form of the non-ownership of value that is created by service producers and consumed by clients (Ehret and Wirtz 2015, p. 138). Attending a music concert or a festival provides the consumer with the rights to participate in an experience but does not transfer ownership of any physical good. The same is true for all services that cannot be stored but only experienced.

### 3.4.2   Value Networks

A value network involves the identification, creation, co-ordination and management of interconnected relationships, or interfirm relationships, that form a nexus of interactions or a local or national value chain or, in some cases, a global value chain or a global production network. This includes the firms, or partners, involved in the delivery of the value proposition. The competitiveness of a value proposition may be founded within the composition of the value network. This transfers competition from the arena of the firm to the identification and co-ordination of a value network that has been assembled to deliver, or manage the delivery, of a product or service. This shift from firm to network reflects the ability of the network to access sources of financial capi-

tal, to spread risk across the network, to access specialist expertise and to draw upon established private/public sector relationships.

There are three types of organizations involved in a value network (Ehret and Wirtz 2015, p. 141). First, there is the *network architect* (the entrepreneur, the manager or management team) who is responsible for defining the value proposition and for identifying and co-ordinating those organizations which will be included in the value network. Second are *hybrid contributors* who contribute to the attractiveness or distinctiveness of the value proposition by providing key inputs. These inputs may be technological or the provision of additional services. For example, for restaurants providing takeaway food, the British online food delivery company Deliveroo operates as a hybrid contributor by providing couriers to transport orders from restaurants to customers. Apple, the provider of consumer electronics and related services, has developed and controls the Apple network by defining the network's personality, setting and regulating technical standards and governing the network. Nevertheless, Apple is supported by a complex ecosystem of hybrid contributors including App developers (Merchant 2017). For Apple, the App developers contribute to enhancing the appeal of Apple's products, but they also provide Apple with an additional revenue stream. Thus, Apple receives 30% of the value of all sales made in the App Store and this revenue stream comes from just providing and managing a platform (Merchant 2017, p. 174). Third are *technology providers* who are responsible for providing and managing infrastructure and facilities. Apple is the technology provider for App developers involved in creating mobile apps that are distributed via Apple's App Store.

### 3.4.3   Value-Capturing Mechanisms

The primary aim of a business model is to engage in a monetization process. This is often labelled as a value-capturing mechanism or revenue model designed to monetize a value network's value proposition. The revenue model describes the various ways in which a firm monetizes the value proposition. This can take many forms including the sale of products and related services as well as revenue obtained from providing aftersales services including servicing and repairs, training and additional content.

The revenue, or value-capturing part of a business model, is critical as it underpins capital investment and the network architect's ability to cover the costs related to financialization and the delivery of the value proposition to customers (Table 3.2). A sustainable business model can perhaps be defined as one that creates more value for customers than is captured by the value-capturing mechanism. This would reflect the development of a compelling value proposition.

Some business models are developed primarily to create social benefits by focusing on the creation of a double or triple bottom line. In the late 1980s, there was a rise in awareness of the impact of non-financial (primarily social) matters on financial performance. Socially Responsible Investment (SRI) funds were established that screened potential investments by sector (often no alcohol or tobacco products), workforce diversity and corporate governance, and eventually screening was extended to include a firm's environmental record or liabilities. The language of a double bottom line (DBL) was developed to refer to the requirement for firms increasingly to balance non-financial objectives against profit maximization. In the three decades since, SRI investment indices have consistently outperformed their mainstream equivalents (Miller 2001), which is indicative of the impact non-financial issues may have on financial performance. With the rise of the concept of sustainable development, often used interchangeably with sustainability, in the 1990s, businesses concentrated on integrating environmental issues into decision-making. In 1997, Elkington proposed the construction of a 'triple bottom line' in alignment with the three pillars of sustainability—economic, social and environmental (Elkington 1997). At the level of the firm, it is worth noting that a constant tension exists between each of these bottom lines and this tension must be balanced on a project-by-project basis (Bryson and Buttle 2005; Bryson and Lombardi 2009).

**Table 3.2** Value-capturing mechanisms and business models

| Type | Characteristics |
|---|---|
| Sale of good or service. | Price based on product/service cost plus a margin to cover overheads and with a profit. |
| Access to goods/services provided for no payment by the user. | Multi-sided business models in which revenue comes from advertisers or from selling big data. Requires a network effect based on a critical mass of users to be successful. |
| Freemium model. | A free version of the service is available to all, but users can pay for a premium service. This always requires a critical mass of users. |
| Price calculated on the basis of the average value provided to customers. | Price based on some saving or benefit obtained by customers from using this service/good rather than being directly related to the relationship between the cost of providing the service and price. |
| Recurring low subscriptions (monthly or annual). | Provides continual access to services with a predictable revenue scheme based on customer retention. |
| Tiered pricing based on volume of use. | Price set by the amount users consume, but in tiered bands. |
| Revenue based on a percentage of every transaction. | An approach used by platforms including e-commerce in which the platform receives a small fee on every final sale made by a customer. |
| Low product/good prices, but additional services/goods require additional payment. | Product/good prices are kept low, but additional fees required for customization, training, installation and other services. |
| Low product/good price but additional features available for additional cost. | A version of the freemium model but based on an initial low access fee to which additional features can be added for additional cost. |
| Low price, but revenue generated on the sale of consumables—the razor-blade model | The base unit is sold at or below cost with the expectation of on-going revenue from the sale of consumables. This requires consideration upfront investment. |

Source: Authors' own

Profitability tends to dominate these decisions but may be mediated though discussions in which social and sustainability issues are taken into consideration. All this is part of a much wider debate on corporate social responsibility (CSR) and responsible business.

## 3.5    Service Business Models

The three critical dimensions of a business model—value proposition, value network and value-capturing mechanism—are all primary decision-making points in the development and management of a business model (the diamonds in Fig. 3.1). The development of a new business model can commence at any decision-making point. Any change in a primary decision point affects decisions that are made at other decision-making points. This is also the case for an existing business model. Any alteration in the value proposition may alter the value-capturing mechanism in some way and also the structure of the value network. A complex iterative negotiation process occurs between the value proposition, value network and value-capturing mechanism. The interactions between these decision-making points results in the creation of a business model that might create value and might be sustainable (Bryson et al. 2018).

In a review of the relationship between business models, business strategy and innovation, Teece identified a number of business model innovations in traditional industries and in information/Internet industries (Teece 2010). The argument is that business models are an important essential feature of market-oriented economies based on consumer choice, competition, transaction costs and consumer and producer heterogeneity. The primary drivers behind business model innovation, and consequently the ever-changing diversity of business models, are consumer choice, competition and process and product innovation. The variegated nature of consumer demand is a primary driver behind the emergence of new value propositions.

For business model innovation in traditional industries, Teece (2010, p. 117) identified the emergence of containerization as a radical disruptive technology that transformed logistics and which was an important driver behind the fragmentation and internationalization of value chains (see Chap. 11). In 1955, Malcolm McLean, the owner of a large US trucking company, hired an engineer to design a road trailer body that could be detached from a chassis and loaded on to a ship. This led to the development of the container and all the infrastructure innovations related to containerization including container ports. This innovation also meant that

> shipping costs no longer offered shelter to high-cost producers whose great advantage was physical proximity to their customers; even with customs duties and time delays, factories in Malaysia could deliver blouses to Macy's in Herald Square more cheaply than could blouse manufacturers in the nearby lofts of New York's garment district. (Levinson 2006, p. 3)

It is possible to argue that it was the development of a standardized box—the container—that was a key driver behind the development of global value chains and of globalization more generally. To promote the adoption of this innovation, McLean made the patents for this cellular container system available royalty free to the International Standards Organization (ISO). The introduction of the container reduced the costs of shipping goods and raw materials and in so doing 'changed the shape of the world economy' as the container became the core element 'of a highly automated system for moving goods from anywhere, to anywhere, with a minimum of cost and

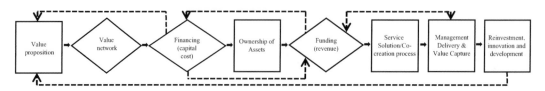

**Fig. 3.1**  The elements of a service-oriented business model. (Source: Authors' own)

complication on the way' (Levinson 2006, p. 2). At the same time, it destroyed the many service jobs that were involved in loading and unloading and in logistic administration.

Other innovations in traditional industries, according to Teece, include low-frill airlines, the 'razor-razor blade' model, sponsorship in the sports apparel business and new business models that have emerged in the music industry (2010, p. 177). The 'razor-razor blade' model is a classic example of a revenue-based business model. This operates by pricing razors, or computer printers, inexpensively but placing higher margins on consumables—razor blades or printing ink. Sponsorship is a core element of the business models of firms involved in the production of sporting apparel. These firms obtain market share and, more importantly, royalties from the sale of replica products.

For business model innovation in information/ Internet industries, Teece (2010, p. 178) highlighted the collapse of the DVD rental market and its replacement by online provision. Companies like Netflix have developed revenue models based on monthly fees. An important feature of the development of digital or Internet-enabled business models is the transfer of revenue models between sectors and products. Thus, the freemium model was adopted by Adobe to provide access to PDF readers and by Skype and Zoom to provide online telephony including teleconferences. What is interesting about this 2010 analysis is how dated this account of Internet business models appears today. This highlights another important feature of Internet-enabled business models. This is the rapid escalation and acceleration in the introduction of disruptive business models that are enabled by the Internet and, in particular, the development of Web-based platforms.

Platforms like Amazon or Alibaba provide companies with access to online platforms that remove the need to invest in purchasing, operating and maintaining computer servers or in developing their own platforms. These platforms transform capital-intensive business models to variable cost models. This transfer reduces the barriers to entry and has encouraged the growth

of new platform-enabled business models with access paid for based on a result-orientated business model (Table 3.1). A core part of this new innovation ecosystem has been the emergence of the smartphone as a dominant technology combined with the adoption of standard configurations for mobile devices. It is the adoption of smartphones by consumers that is behind the emergence of many new disruptive service business models. It is perhaps worth noting that it was only in 2013 that sales of Internet-connected smartphones exceeded those for more basic handsets (Cecere et al. 2015, p. 162).

Business model innovation occurs within and between different industrial sectors as innovations in business models are transferred and applied from one sector to another. Business model innovation is a core aspect of the evolution of a firm. Thus, Microsoft has shifted from selling a long-term licence to access software to a business model based on accessing a Cloud-based version of the software or by selling time-limited access. A very different example is found in Lieberman's detailed analysis of the evolution of Steinway & Sons, the German and American piano manufacturer. From 1853, the firm sold its products in different ways. Initially, the firm sold pianos on the quality of the instrument and on piano innovations that flowed from New York to Europe. From the 1860s, the company produced hundreds of new patents. During the twentieth century, innovation involved new models, new glues and finishes and new manufacturing processes. These innovations were also reflected in the company's marketing that in the nineteenth century was based on winning medals at exhibitions and from artists' endorsements. During the 1920s, the firm's marketing highlighted that a Steinway was a piece of art rather than a machine and by the

> late 1960s, technology had come to be regarded with suspicion. What people were now asking was not what was new about the piano being shown to them, but whether it was the traditional Steinway. As a result, patents are no longer used to sell Steinway pianos, and the recent marketing plans call for a limited number of new instruments, based on nineteenth-century models. (Lieberman 1995, p. 6)

Steinway's evolution is one in which different resources and capabilities are emphasized at different times to maintain market position. This represents a shift from selling based on innovation to a focus on cost reduction and then on tradition or heritage.

## 3.6    From Dyadic to Multi-sided Service Business Models

In service industries, new business models are emerging that represent new relationships between service producers and consumers. It is important to differentiate between dyadic-based business models and what are termed 'multi-sided business models', two-sided business models or triadic business models. A dyadic-orientated business model involves the co-creation of a service between a consumer and a producer. An example would be a haircut in which a hairdresser transforms a customer's hair in return for payment. This is a simple dyadic exchange. Individuals engage with other individuals in dyadic encounters rather than as part of a network. A dyad is a group of two individuals interacting with one another in some way. A dyad is the smallest possible group. A dyad includes all types of one-to-one encounters—family, friendships, employment, business transactions—and, like all relationships, experiences different forms of asymmetry. This includes asymmetric information, but also visible and less visible forms of power imbalance. Dyads may be unstable relationships as one party to a dyad may engage in activities that alter the balance of power or enhance some other form of asymmetry. This may include the trust-based element of a dyad failing.

A 'multi-sided business model', two-sided business model or triadic business model is very different as it is based on interrelationships between three or more parties to a transaction. A dyadic-based relationship is at the centre of this relationship but the encounter between consumer and producer involves another set of parties to the transaction. These are multi-sided or two-sided business models as there are two economic rela-

tionships within the same business model—between the consumer and the producer and between the producer and another set of organizations or customers who are paying to support or fund the service encounter between the producer and the initial consumer (Fig. 3.2). A more formal definition is provided by Rochet and Tirole when they note that:

> Two-sided (or, more generally, multi-sided) markets are roughly defined as markets in which one or several platforms enable interactions between end-users and try to get the two (or multiple) sides "onboard" by appropriately charging each side. That is, platforms court each side while attempting to make, or at least not lose, money overall. (Rochet and Tirole 2006, p. 645)

The value proposition of a multi-sided business model is to create, deliver and capture value provided to consumers, but that value is monetarized by different actors. For example, research on business models within Formula One racing has identified the operation of a multi-sided business model. In this case, one model is focused on developing and selling technology to competitors and another on trading human resources (Aversa et al. 2015).

Excellent examples of such business models are search engines like Google or social media sites such as Facebook. By the second quarter of 2018, Facebook had 2.23 billion monthly active users who were indirectly contributing to developing a dataset on consumer behaviour. This information—big data—is then monetarized as customers purchase access to this data for marketing and advertising purposes. Businesses also pay fees to Facebook to advertise their products/goods and services to consumers that fit defined market segments.

Google provides free search to all. This is an expensive process involving the development of complex algorithms combined with capital investment in a global network of linked computer servers. Google monetarizes the search process by obtaining revenue from retailers and advertising. These are multi-sided or triadic business models as there are at least two parts to the model—producer to consumer relationships and producer to customer (retailer/advertiser) rela-

**Fig. 3.2** Multi-sided
business models.
(Source: Authors' own)

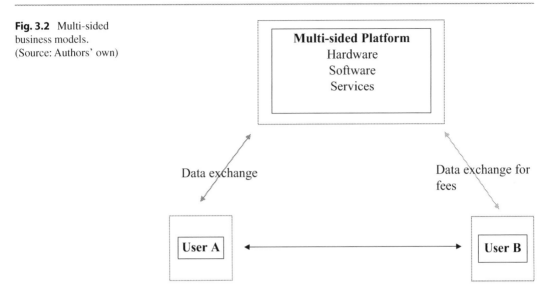

tionships. The largest group involved with these business models are the consumers—those using social media or search engines rather than customers—the buyers of access to consumers and/or information created by the interactions between the platform and the consumers. The customers are a much smaller group compared to the consumers and it is this group that are the target of the business model's value-capturing mechanism. Consumers 'pay' to access free services, but this payment takes the form of a derivative currency (Komatsu et al. 2017) or payment that is derived from the consumer's attention and routine usage of the service provided by the business model.

Business model innovation results in the creation of different forms of value—for consumers and for customers. A process of hybridization has occurred in which dyadic and multi-sided business models have been combined. This results in a service-provider-consumer relationship combined with a service-provided-customer relationship. Each party to this hybridized business model obtains different values. It is worth noting that a freemium business model is not a multi-sided business model. Instead, this is a service-orientated business model with two modes of access, but with the freemium model operating to encourage consumers to upgrade to obtain access to all the services provided by premium access.

## 3.7   Financialization and Multi-sided Business Models

Another form of multi-sided business model can be identified with the emergence of the debate on financialization (Epstein 2005; Bryson et al. 2017). These business models are perhaps most associated with transnational manufacturing firms as well as with the financialization of infrastructure (Bryson et al. 2018). Financialization is closely associated with the on-going transformation of the world economy, or with the process of internationalization or globalization. In a review of this debate, Epstein argues that 'this changing landscape has been characterized by the rise of *neoliberalism, globalisation* and *financialization*' (Epstein 2005, p. 3). The term financialization has many meanings. On the one hand, it is equated with the ascendancy of shareholder value and, on the other hand, with the development of new financial instruments.

In a review of the history and definition of financialization, Greta Krippner uses the term to refer to a 'pattern of accumulation in which profit making occurs increasingly through financial channels rather than through trade and commodity production' (Krippner 2004, p. 14). Financialization includes companies that allocate a proportion of their profits to share buy-backs to increase share prices. This is a process that also impacts on the value of stock options and corporate pay. In this case, profit is invested to increase the value of a company without investing in process or product innovation that would contribute directly to value creation over a long period. The application of financialization to business models results in another form of multi-sided business model. In these business models, products are produced and sold, but there are two moments of revenue value capture or two value-capturing mechanisms in place. The first comes from manufacturing and selling the goods/products including the sale of spare parts and increasingly software upgrades. The second comes from financial products that are provided to consumers. This type of financialized business model reflects the financialization of the production sector, but it is also another form of servitization in which a production-oriented business model is hybridized with a service-oriented model (Chap. 12). Mazzucato's analysis of value is especially useful in exploring this process. She notes that:

> In the 2000s … the US arm of Ford made more money by selling loans for cars then by selling the cars themselves. Ford sped up the car's transformation from physical product to financial commodity by pioneering the Personal Contract Plan (PCP), which allowed a 'buyer' to pay monthly instalments that only covered the predicted depreciation, and trade up to a new model after two or three years. (Mazzucato 2018, p. 162)

The development of PCPs and their adoption by car manufacturers led to another financial innovation. The PCP contracts could be bundled together, securitized and then resold as a financial product. In essence, financialization involves the action of money on money to produce additional value. The key question is the relationship between this type of financial value and wealth created by manufacturing goods and providing services including service experiences.

## 3.8 Service Business Models and the Rise of the Platform Economy

It is possible to argue that 'the Internet is arguably the most significant technology of the inter-millennial era, the leading technology of the fifth Kondratiev wave' (Malecki 2002, p. 399). The Internet can be classified as a disruptive technological innovation that defines an era because it is a general-purpose technology that creates opportunities for socio-economic innovation. The Internet is the platform behind all online platforms (Kenney and Zysman 2020). In a recent review of the rise of the platform economy, Kenney and Zysman note that: 'Platforms and the cloud, an essential part of what has been called the "third globalization", reconfigure globalization itself' (Kenney and Zysman 2016, p. 61). Central to this reconfiguration is the role played by online platforms in enabling the development of new forms of service-orientated business model included multi-sided models (Hagiu and Wright 2015). It is possible to argue that the impact that the platform economy will have on reconfiguring capitalism and service businesses has just commenced.

The development of the Amazon and Alibaba platforms has transformed the world of consumer retailing. This, combined with other e-commerce platforms, is hollowing out the high street and is partly responsible for the collapse of many capital-intensive multi-site retailers. The emergence of the Uber and Didi taxi platforms has challenged existing taxi business models and, at the same time, transformed employment terms and consumer accessibility to taxi services. In a similar way, Airbnb has emerged as a challenger provider of leisure accommodation. There are many dimensions of the platform economy. On the one hand, the combination of smartphones with platforms has enabled individuals and households to monetarize underutilized assets—their cars or spare rooms. This can be conceptualized as a process that is part of what has been termed the sharing economy. It is also another type of financialization in which assets acquired for their use value are converted into assets that have exchange values. On the other hand, the rise of platforms is challenging the established architecture of national and international economies, and it is this process that is reconfiguring capitalism.

There are six important features of the platform economy that need to be considered in relation to service business:

1. Platforms provide the primary platforms, or business model, on which other secondary platforms may be developed. A platform like Amazon or an App Store enables other secondary business models to be developed that are then hosted by the primary platform.
2. Platform operations have unprecedented control and, in many cases, represent a form and degree of concentrated capital or monopoly capitalism that has never been experienced before. A dominant platform enables new business opportunities to emerge, but it also operates as a barrier. A platform should be considered as a form of monopolistic disruptive innovation.
3. Platforms have created an alternative mechanism for monetarizing human effort (Google and searches, Facebook and social networks, LinkedIn and professional networks). This monetarization takes many forms and includes the creation of derivative currencies but also the conversion of use values into exchange values in platforms that are based on some form of asset sharing.
4. New forms of working relationships are developing across the platform economy that are transforming the nature and condition of some service work and employment.
5. Platforms, rather than corporations, will play an increasingly important role in the organization of production and work.
6. Platforms experience network effects based on incremental benefits that accrue by adding additional users to the network. The more consumers there are, the harder it is for any one consumer to leave the network as they have too much to lose. In addition, platforms can work together, making it very difficult for new platforms to displace established platforms.

It is worth noting that in 2019, Alphabet Inc, the holding company for the Google search platform, employed 118,899 and had a net income of US$34.34bn and assets valued at US$275.9bn. In 2018, the Ford Motor Company employed 199,000 and had a net income of US$7.7bn and assets valued at US$256.540bn. Creating a car is a complex process involving the development and organization of complex global value chains. Developing a platform-based business requires a very different skill set and global value chain. What is apparent is that the platforms are becoming dominant in developing or controlling critical business models that deliver services to consumers and add value to customers. It is also apparent that some of the platforms employ fewer people and make greater returns compared to some of the more production-orientated business models.

The network effect experienced by platforms includes direct and indirect effects. WeChat was established in China by Tencent in 2011 and has evolved into China's dominant lifestyle platform with over 850 m active users. WeChat is an all-embracing lifestyle platform that combines the types of services provided by, for example,

**Table 3.3** Services available via the WeChat app

| |
|---|
| Messaging, voice messaging, voice and video calls |
| Share updates and photographs with family and friends |
| Share real-time location with family and friends |
| Find people located nearby |
| Search for anything published and shared on WeChat |
| Read articles through Public Accounts owned by traditional media and online outlets and blogs. |
| Transfer money and pay in stores through the Wallet feature. |
| Access third-party services including ride-hailing, online shopping and food delivery through the WeChat Wallet |
| Check friends' updates and rankings in Tencent-owned mobile computer games |
| Repay credit cards, pay utility bills, top up mobile phones or buy wealth management products |
| Access public services including booking medical appointments, applying for visas and checking driving records. |
| Send virtual red envelopes filled with real money to family and friends |

Source: Authors' own

Facebook, WhatsApp, Messenger, Venmo, Amazon, Apple Pay and Uber (Table 3.3). This has resulted in the creation of an exceptionally strong network effect. Chinese consumers cannot afford not to engage with this app. WeChat's direct network effects revolve around the dominance of the platform and the role it has developed in linking network members together irrespective of their location. The Chinese diaspora use WeChat to remain connected with friends and family. Indirect network effects include the ways in which WeChat has permitted and encouraged third-party developers to provide services that are accessed via the WeChat platform. This produces positive feedback loops that persuade more people to use WeChat and the platforms hosted by WeChat. China's three dominant platforms—Baidu, Alibaba and Tencent—have developed linkages between their platforms that makes it difficult, perhaps impossible, for alternative platforms to disrupt the status quo.

## 3.9    Wrapping Up

The focus of this chapter has been on a discussion of strategy and the development of the ongoing debate on business models. The debate on business models provides a useful structure for comparing different approaches to creating value by the development of new or alternative forms of service-orientated business model. The chapter has highlighted the three primary elements that form a business model: value propositions, value networks and a value-capturing or revenue-appropriation mechanism. Innovation can occur anywhere within or between these three elements. This review of service business models has raised three important points that underpin the discussion of service business.

First, disruptive innovation continues to transform service business. It destroys existing business models and also develops new business models. This is a critical point. The pace of disruption continues to increase, reflecting an escalation in the velocity of change. This increase is partly the consequence of innovations that have transformed the wider framework conditions that

support service business. The most important alteration has been the emergence and continued development of the platform economy and all types of Internet-enabled business process.

Second, central to the development of new service-based business models are innovations in monetarization or in revenue- or value-capture mechanisms. Multi-sided business models, or triadic business models, represent one form of innovative value capture based on the monetarization of derivative currencies. This, however, is only one form. Globalization has led to intensified competition that has driven innovation in business models but also service operations. It must be noted here that this chapter needs to be read alongside Chaps. 5 and 11. Chapter 5 explores service operations and productivity, and Chap. 11 supply chains. Another important dimension of innovation in service business models is reflected in operational innovations and in innovations in the management and co-ordination of supply chains. Both these innovations reflect attempts to reduce the costs of providing services to customers. There is a danger in isolating a discussion of strategy and business models from an analysis of operational innovations and alterations in the management of supply chains.

Third, financialization is an on-going process. For service businesses, financialization is part of a process that is transforming many production-orientated business models into service-oriented models (see Chap. 12). Perhaps the best way of conceptualizing such models is as hybrid models that combine production and service elements. They are also another form of multi-sided business model.

It is important to conclude this chapter by noting that a firm may be formed to deliver a single type of business model. Nevertheless, many firms have within them many related and sometimes unrelated business models. This is a critical point. A firm is a blend or combination of many different linked and sometimes unrelated business models. Let us consider one example. A law firm may have within it at least three business models. First, there is a business model that provides the law firm with administrative support. This is an operational business model that is funded by profits made by providing legal services. In some firms, this administrative function may generate profit, in its own right, by providing administrative support to other firms or individuals. Second, there are legal services that are very price sensitive. These are services often funded by some form of legal aid. The business model that supports the delivery of these services is one based on operational efficiency. Third, there are legal services that involve the provision of innovative, highly customized and high value-added services, for example, problems being experienced by platforms or in the application of taxation regulations to platform providers. These represent a very different form of legal service based on a process of continual innovation. Many law firms will contain all three types of legal service business model. The profitability and long-term sustainably of a legal practice is based on the blend of models combined with their operational efficiency and effectiveness. There is another critical dimension; at the centre of a law firm's business model are the reputations of individual lawyers combined with their client networks.

Overall, the business model literature provides the student of service businesses and service practitioners with an essential toolkit for understanding the emergence and management of new ways of creating services. At the centre of this analysis is a concern with a process of value creation. There have been many types of value explored in this chapter—from the value created by consuming services—or the value proposition—to the value created by the monetarization of service use values. It is always worth noting that a sustainable service business model is created by providing consumers with value that is both desirable and inimitable, but also with values that can be monetarized.

**Learning Outcomes**

- Organizational strategy involves exploring the design and implementation of business models.
- A business model describes the ways in which a firm engages in business activities (or

describes the processes by which firms try to create value).

- All business models include three important interrelated elements: *a value proposition, a value network and a value-capturing* or revenue-appropriation mechanism.
- Disruptive innovation may create a new business model with a different type of value proposition and value network that displaces established firms, networks and value propositions.
- A dyadic-orientated business model involves the co-creation of a service between a consumer and a producer.
- A 'multi-sided business models', two-sided business model or triadic business model is very different as it is based on interrelationships between three or more parties to a transaction.
- Online platforms are reconfiguring capitalism enabling the development of new forms of service-orientated business model including multi-sided models.

## References

Alford, J., & Greve, C. (2017). Strategy in the Public and Private Sectors: Similarities, Differences and Changes. *Administrative Science, 7*(4), 35–47.
Aversa, P., Furnari, S., & Haefliger, S. (2015). Business Model Configurations and Performance: A Qualitative Comparative Analysis in Formula One Racing, 2005–2013. *Industrial and Corporate Change, 24*(3), 655–676.
Baden-Fuller, C., & Morgan, M. (2010). Business Models. *Long Range Planning, 43*(2–3), 156–171.
Baker, T., Miner, A. S., & Eesley, D. T. (2003). Improvising Firms: Bricolage, Account Giving and Improvisational Competencies in the Founding Process. *Research Policy, 32*(2), 255–276.
Bellman, R., Clark, C., Craft, C., Malcolm, D. G., & Ricciardi, F. (1957). On the Construction of a Multi-stage, Multi-person Business Game. *Operations Research, 5*(4), 469–503.
Bower, J. L., & Christensen, C. M. (1995). Disruptive Technologies: Catching the Wave. *Harvard Business Review, 73*(1), 43–53.
Bryson, J. R., & Buttle, M. (2005). Enabling Inclusion through Alternative Discursive Formations: The Regional Development of Community Development

Loan Funds (CDLFs) in the United Kingdom. *The Service Industries Journal, 25*(2), 273–286.

Bryson, J. R., & Lombardi, R. (2009). Balancing Product and Process Sustainability against Business Profitability: Sustainability as a Competitive Strategy in the Property Development Process. *Business Strategy and the Environment, 18*(2), 97–107.

Bryson, J. R., Mulhall, R. A., & Song, M. (2017). Urban Assets and the Financialisation Fix: Land Tenure, Renewal and Path Dependency in the City of Birmingham. *Cambridge Journal of Regions, Economy and Society, 10*(3), 455–469.

Bryson, J. R., Mulhall, R. A., Song, M., Loo, B. P. Y., Dawson, R., & Rogers, C. D. F. (2018). Alternative-Substitute Business Models and the Provision of Local Infrastructure: Alterity as a Solution to Financialization and Public-Sector Failure. *Geoforum, 95*, 25–34.

Cecere, G., Corrocher, N., & Battaglia, R. D. (2015). Innovation and Competition in the Smartphone Industry: Is there a Dominant Design? *Telecommunications Policy, 39*(3–4), 162–175.

Chesbrough, H., & Rosenbloom, R. (2010). The Role of the Business Model in Capturing Value from Innovation: Evidence from Xerox Corporation's Technology Spin-off Companies. *Industrial and Corporate Change, 11*(3), 529–555.

Clegg, S. R., Kornberger, M., Pitsis, T. S., & Mount, M. (2019). *Managing and Organizations: An Introduction to Theory and Practice*. London: Sage.

Coase, R. H. (1937). The Nature of the Firm. *Economica, 4*(16), 386–405.

Di Domenico, M., Haugh, H., & Tracey, P. (2010). Social Bricolage: Theorizing Social Value Creation in Social Enterprises. *Entrepreneurship Theory and Practice, 34*(4), 681–703.

Ehret, M., & Wirtz, J. (2015). Creating and Capturing Value in the Service Economy: The Crucial Role of Business Services in Driving Innovation and Growth. In J. R. Bryson & P. W. Daniels (Eds.), *Handbook of Service Business*. Cheltenham: Edward Elgar.

Elkington, J. (1997). *Cannibals with Forks: The Triple Bottom Line of 21st Century Business*. Oxford: Capstone Publishing.

Epstein, G. A. (2005). Financialization and the World Economy. In G. A. Epstein (Ed.), *Financialization of the World Economy*. Cheltenham: Edward Elgar.

Fingleton, E. (1999). *In Praise of Hard Industries: Why Manufacturing, Not the New Economy, Is the Key to Future Prosperity*. London: Orion.

Hagiu, A., & Wright, J. (2015). Multi-Sided Platforms. *International Journal of Industrial Organization, 43*, 162–174.

International Integrated Reporting Council. (2013). *Business Model: Background Paper for Integrated Reporting*. London: International Integrated Reporting Council.

Jones, G. M. (1960). Educators, Electrons, and Business Models: A Problem in Synthesis. *Accounting Review, 35*(4), 619–626.

Kenney, M., & Zysman, J. (2016). The Rise of the Platform Economy. *Issues in Science and Technology, 32*(3), 61–69.

Kenney, M., & Zysman, J. (2020). The Platform Economy: Restructuring the Space of Capitalist Accumulation. *Cambridge Journal of Regions, Economy and Society.* https://doi.org/10.1093/cjres/rsaa001.

Kim, J., & Mahoney, J. T. (2010). A Strategic Theory of the Firm as a Nexus of Incomplete Contracts: A Property Rights Approach. *Journal of Management, 36*(4), 806–826.

Kley, F., Lerch, C., & Dallinger, D. (2011). New Business Models for Electric Cars – A Holistic Approach. *Energy Policy, 39*(6), 3392–3403.

Knights, D., & Morgan, G. (1990). The Concept of Strategy in Sociology: A Note of Dissent. *Sociology, 24*(3), 475–483.

Komatsu, T., Deserti, A., Rizzo, F., Celi, M., & Alijani, S. (2017). Social Innovation Business Models: Coping with Antagonistic Objectives and Assets. In S. Alijani & C. Karyotis (Eds.), *Finance and Economy for Society: Integrating Sustainability*. Bingley: Emerald.

Krippner, G. (2004). What Is Financialization. In *mimeo*. California: Department of Sociology, UCLA.

Levinson, M. (2006). *The Box: How the Shipping Container Made the World Smaller and the World Economy Bigger*. Princeton: Princeton University Press.

Lieberman, R. K. (1995). *Steinway & Sons*. New Haven: Yale University Press.

Lindblom, C. E. (1959). The Science of "Muddling Through". *Public Administration Review, 19*(2), 79–88.

Livesey, F. (2006). *Defining High Value Manufacturing*. Cambridge: Institute for Manufacturing.

Malecki, E. J. (2002). The Economic Geography of the Internet's Infrastructure. *Economic Geography, 78*(4), 399–424.

Mazzucato, M. (2018). *The Value of Everything*. London: Allen Lane.

Merchant, B. (2017). *The One Device: The Secret History of the iPhone*. New York: Little Brown and Company.

Miller, H. (2001). A Moral Victory? *Director*, May, 58–62.

Mintzberg, H. (1978). Patterns in Strategy Formation. *Management Science, 24*(9), 934–948.

Mintzberg, H. (1988). Opening Up the Definition of Strategy. In J. B. Quinn, H. Mintzberg, & R. M. James (Eds.), *The Strategy Process*. Englewood Cliffs: Prentice-Hall.

Rochet, J. C., & Tirole, J. (2006). Two-Sided Markets: A Progress Report. *RAND Journal of Economics, 37*(3), 645–667.

Sundbo, J., & Sørensen, F. (Eds.). (2013). *Handbook on the Experience Economy*. Cheltenham: Edward Elgar.

Teece, D. (2010). Business Models, Strategy and Innovation. *Long Range Planning, 43*(2–3), 172–194.

Watson, T. J. (1994). *In Search of Management: Culture, Chaos & Control in Managerial Work*. London: ITP.

Weick, K. E. (1993). Organizational Redesign as Improvisation. In G. P. Huber & W. H. Glick (Eds.), *Organizational Change and Redesign: Ideas and Insights for Improving Performance* (pp. 346–379). Oxford: Oxford University Press.

Wirtz, B. W. (2011). *Business Model Management: Design – Instruments - Success Factors*. Heidelberg: Gabler Verlag.

Zott, C., & Amit, R. (2008). The Fit between Product Market Strategy and Business Model: Implications for Firm Performance. *Strategic Management Journal, 29*(1), 1–26.

Zott, C., Amit, R., & Massa, M. (2011). The Business Model: Recent Developments and Future Research. *Journal of Management, 37*(4), 1019–1042.

## Further Reading

Bryson, J. E., & Daniels, P. W. (Eds.). (2015). *Handbook of Service Business*. Cheltenham: Edward Elgar.

Foss, N. J., & Saebi, T. (Eds.). (2015). *Business Model Innovation: The Organizational Dimension*. Oxford: Oxford University Press.

Krippner, G. R. (2005). The Financialization of the American Economy. *Socio-Economic Review, 3*(2), 173.

## Useful Websites

https://mooc-book.eu/index/learn-more/key-areas/business-models/.

https://hbr.org/2015/01/what-is-a-business-model.

https://www.feedough.com/what-is-a-business-model/.

https://investmentbank.com/business-models/.

# Techno Service Worlds?
# Digitization of Service Businesses

**Key Themes**

- How are new technologies, particularly digitization, altering service business models? Technology and service businesses
- Digitization of service businesses
- Industrialization of service businesses and technology
- Disadvantages of technology for services businesses
- Business process management
- Self-service technology, Internet of Things, big data, robotics, artificial intelligence

Technology and service business have long been allies. During the nineteenth century, the emphasis was on the transformation of manufacturing following the invention of technologies for iron smelting, the steam engine or the rapid expansion of railway networks. This was entirely justified but should not be taken to mean that service businesses were excluded from the costs and benefits of developments in technology; indeed the invention of the electric telegraph not only reduced the friction of distance on effective communications between service firms and their clients but also changed the way in which they operated and created new types of occupations and business models.

**Electronic Supplementary Material** The online version of this chapter (https://doi.org/10.1007/978-3-030-52060-1_4) contains supplementary material, which is available to authorized users.

This has recently been likened to a 'Victorian Internet' that was a precursor to the Internet following the invention of the World Wide Web in 1989 (Standage 2014). As recently as 1993, the Internet was the communication medium used for only 1% of the information flowing through two-way telecommunications networks; this had changed to 51% by 2000 and to more than 97% by 2007 (Hilbert and López 2011). This has dramatically changed the environment within which service businesses now function, an environment in which digital media have almost totally replaced the analogue media that dominated a much smaller volume of digitized information during the mid-1980s. Often referred to as 'digitization', there are very few service businesses that do not make use of computers and telecommunications devices; the level and intensity of use will depend on the kind of service being offered—the needs of a hairdressing salon will differ markedly from those of the currency dealing floor of an international bank. This chapter should be read with Chap. 5 as the digitization of service business is part of the on-going debate on service operations and productivity.

But whatever the type of service business, in order to acquire the benefits from technology, there is a requirement to adapt to and change infrastructure and practices. Some service businesses are much better at this than others. Hair and beauty salons, for example, rely on information management programmes for accounting, payroll, financial reporting, inventory control, scheduling and customer relationship management. But, in addition, more innovative salons have adopted hairstyle and cosmetic imaging software programs that can be used to enable clients to consider different styles before any treatments are applied. These programs come with a standard database of hairstyles and makeup options and can be customized to meet the needs of a particular salon or stylist.

Consumers are playing a critical role in the development of the digital economy. In the US, household consumption and business investment each account for 45% of the ICT sector's output and government spending accounts for the rest. Household digital consumption has led the ongoing digital transformation of the US economy with innovations targeted at households rather than intended to enhance business or public sector productivity (Manyika et al. 2015, p. 26). An analysis of 22 industry sectors in the US identified the 'haves' and 'have-mores' in digitization (Manyika et al. 2015). Not unexpectedly, sectors such as ICT, professional services and media are highly digitized relative to several dimensions grouped into assets, usage and labour. At the other end of the spectrum, government, healthcare, hospitality and construction services, many of which are prominent at the local scale, lag significantly in all dimensions. This is not unimportant, in that government and healthcare in particular account for about 25% of employment and GDP of the US, whereas the most digitized sectors account for around 10%. Between these extremes, there are groups of services, especially small- and medium-sized enterprises (SMEs), that have yet to fully develop digitization of customer transactions (education, retail trade, entertainment and recreation, personal and local services). Services that are oriented more towards business-to-business (B2B) transactions, such as real estate, utilities, wholesale trade, also fall into an intermediate group that have yet to fulfil the potential for digital engagement with customers. Here, it is worth considering the disruptive impacts of Covid-19 as sectors, companies and households had to rapidly embrace service digitization including a rapid switch by schools and

universities to online provision and with churches introducing virtual religious services. Manyika et al. note that between 1997 and 2013, the most digitized service sectors show the largest growth of assets (2.0x), usage (almost 5.0x) and labour (7.9%). It is important to emphasize that digitization is a general-purpose technology that represents another form of transformational, technological inflection. Thus, innovations in digitization are transforming socio-economic relationships by underpinning process and product innovation throughout the economy.

In this chapter, the focus is on exploring the role that technological innovation has played in the emergence of new service business models and in new forms of service business and work. The emphasis is on the digitization of service operational processes and their impacts. This chapter should be read with Chap. 3 on business models, Chap. 5 on operations and productivity and Chap. 11 on supply chains and logistics. All chapters in this book explore the impacts of technological innovation and digitization on service businesses. Thus, reading and managing service businesses must include an appreciation of the ways in which technological innovation is transforming the management of service businesses.

## 4.1  What Is 'Technology'?

Technology can be defined as 'a means to fulfil a human purpose' (Arthur 2009, p. 28). There is a task to be undertaken and a way needs to be found for completing it, often taking into account parameters such as time, cost, ease of delivery, processing of raw materials, quality or consistency. An individual, or a group, may be able to accommodate these parameters and successfully complete this task, but to do so in a regular and consistent way to fulfil repeat demand, for example, it is more feasible if a set of tools or machines can be devised to create value from completing the task. These tools and/or machines may be material or immaterial; for many service businesses, computer software, teleconferencing and the use of business methods to improve services to clients are critical immaterial (or virtual) technologies that in some cases rely upon or comple-ment material technologies such as computer hardware or robot-controlled product-picking systems in large retail warehouses.

The techniques used by service businesses and their employees to organize production, or the user-friendliness of their services, for example, involves the application of technology including digitization. The deployment of techniques to solve problems, fulfil needs or satisfy wants often occurs by harnessing the physical forms of tech-nology such as computers that are now as ubiqui-tous as paper or pens in the business environment. Both types of technology rely upon the informa-tion, knowledge and skills of entrepreneurs and employees to develop, design or implement changes to existing applications or to develop and introduce new or state-of-the-art technologies. This is usefully summarized as the purposeful application and analysis of information, often big data, in the design, production and utilization of goods and services and in the organization of human activities. The types of technological solutions available, although not necessarily used, by service businesses are summarized in Table 4.1.

The rise of the digitization of information, particularly since the start of the twenty-first cen-tury, is perhaps the single most important event that has ensured a dependence between technol-ogy and service businesses that has superseded their age-long dependence on paper, film or face-to-face meetings for communications internally and with clients/customers.

Central to digitization are developments in access to data and the development of extremely large dataset, or big data. Big data, combined with developments in computer programmes, provides one of the drivers behind the emergence of artificial intelligence (AI) and robotics (see Chap. 5, Sect. 5.3.2). The interaction between big data and computer science has transformed social and economic activity by the application of com-plex algorithms. We are currently experiencing another form of industrial revolution in which algorithms become critical in shaping social and economic outcomes. Algorithms increasingly

**Table 4.1** Information technology services

| Technology | Characteristics |
|---|---|
| Cloud computing platforms | Data management, including data analytics, that can be accessed from any location. |
| Software applications | Designed for specific purposes and can be customized. |
| Platforms | Developed to manage customized applications including e-commerce platforms, logistics and supply-chain platforms and company information management platforms. |
| Application program interface (API) | A set of functions, routines, protocols and procedures allowing the creation of applications that access the features or data of an operating system, application or other service. |
| Networks | Intra and internet. |
| Data storage | Storage in localized server or on a cloud-based platform. |
| Data synchronization | Synchronization of data across many devices. |
| Databases including data analytics | Assembling, storing and analytics often in real time. |
| Content management tools | Enabling documents to be controlled and shared in a secure environment. |
| Content delivery | Publishing content automatically to a website or platform. |
| Transaction processing | Platforms that process business transactions including payment. |
| Workflow | Automated systems to manage, control and monitor workflow including supporting business models that are based on charging by the hour for services delivered. |
| Process automation | Tools to automate work tasks including e-commerce chatbots based on machine learning. |
| Event processing | Managing events including ticketing. |
| Monitoring | Monitoring business systems of all types. |
| Business automation | Platforms that can identify and compare business inputs and make purchasing decisions based on set parameters. |
| Robotics | Automated systems, including robotic workers—both actual and virtual. |

(continued)

**Table 4.1** (continued)

| Technology | Characteristics |
| --- | --- |
| Internet of Things | Physical artefacts linked to the Internet and monitored and supported by software services. |
| Artificial Intelligence | Automated systems that can made decisions and engage in continual learning. |

Source: Authors' own

underpin everyday living. This includes mobile phones and apps, laptops, email, social networking, accessing and viewing online entertainment, ordering taxis and food. Nearly all products and services have been co-created through the application of directly or indirectly linked algorithms. This book has been written using a word processing package that operates through a set of linked algorithms. Banks deploy machine-learning-based algorithms to scrutinize client purchasing activity in real time to identify fraud. Machine learning can be applied to AI to develop systems that automatically learn and improve from experience without being explicitly programmed. Machine-learning algorithms have been applied to finance, including lending decision-making processes and insurance, the legal sector, the criminal justice system, education and healthcare. They have also been applied to core business processes including recruitment and targeting adverts on social media.

The term algorithm needs some elaboration. An algorithm is a carefully structured set of logical instructions that informs a computer to undertake a set of tasks in a defined order. Conventional algorithms are often confused with machine learning, but they are a much more restricted form. Algorithms learn from example by analysing data and experiences to search for patterns and perhaps rules. Conventional algorithms are fully coded in which the programming controls the outcomes or alternatively machine-learning algorithms are partially coded with the emphasis placed on the algorithm's objectives. Most algorithms that support everyday living include legacy code or code that was written by computer programmers who are no longer employed by the firm using the algorithm and perhaps code that

was created with computer languages that are no longer widely used. Major problems can occur based on decisions made in the past as these decisions remain embedded in existing computer programmes. Algorithms require precisely crafted sets of logical instructions. Once these instructions have been written, and a computer code becomes functional, then the algorithm will continue to function. Algorithms are extremely effective in scaling up a solution to a problem; once an algorithm has been developed to solve a problem, then the solution can be made widely available. One of the primary drivers behind the shift towards an algorithm-based society is the drive towards efficiency through automation of tasks via the development of new algorithms.

It is worth reflecting on the computer programme as a task and central to this task is a continual process of debugging. In an account of the coding process, Thompson describes the process of debugging a piece of code in the following way:

> Debugging a piece of code is more than just staring at those few lines and trying to figure out why they're wrong. No, it often requires thinking about the enormous hairball of the entire system: how those few lines interact with dozens of hundreds of other modules of code—each one passing bits of data back and forth. You start with one function; see what other pieces of code it talks to; figure out which pieces of code *those* functions talk to. Slowly, slowly, you can begin to build up a mental picture of the many-nested-interrelations. (Thompson 2019, pp. 108–109)

The algorithms that support everyday living and economic activity are extremely complex—code building upon code.

Scale is critical as it leads to 'networking effects' that lock consumers into companies that are providing algorithm-enabled services (see Chap. 3). Once a social network becomes large enough, for example, WeChat or Facebook, then it becomes extremely difficult for customers to close their accounts, because all their friends are participating in the network. The search for scale is partly driven by venture capitalists who place key performance indicators (KPIs) based on the number of users on technology companies in which they have financial interests. This means that a key metric for obtaining start-up finance for a new platform are predictions regarding scale and also the potential for a firm's products to rapidly create a networking effect.

## 4.2    Why Not Industrialize Service Business?

Technology such as computers, including artificial intelligence (AI), are now widely used by service businesses to create their 'products'. This raises the important issue regarding the substitution of service workers with technology and raises the question of can service businesses adopt an industrialization approach to service provision? Industrialization involves identifying and removing redundancies in systems, standardization of processes wherever possible and automation. Industrialization developed through the application of this approach to manufacturing and agriculture in response to enhanced competition and the requirement to reduce the cost base of firms and, at the same time, to reconsider the value creation process.

Industrialization involves operational decisions that focus on the replacement of variable costs with fixed costs through the application of technology. This substitution of labour with capital takes two forms. First is the direct substitution of a task that was previously performed by an employee with a technological solution. This substitution might increase the speed of task delivery. Second is the application of technology to a task that completely transforms the task. This is much more than substitution but reflects a qualitative transformation in the delivery of the task. Thus, any discussion of the substitution of variable costs with capital investment must include an analysis of alterations in task production and delivery. This is to distinguish between qualitative versus quantitative alterations in the creation of service tasks.

The application of technology to tasks that leads to qualitative alterations—the task has been transformed—highlights that labour substitution by technology may be a discontinuous process; a new task is developed that transforms the tasks

that it displaces. The shift from analogue to digital represented a dramatic qualitative transformation. The application of AI, machine learning and robotics to the delivery of service tasks is also transformational, creating new types of services. Existing service tasks are being displaced by automated systems. This is an on-going process that involves job destruction combined with the creation of new types of employment.

By the middle of the twentieth century, industrialization had been incorporated into business models widely used by manufacturing businesses to achieve consistent product quality control and to improve employee productivity. In the early 1970s, when the growth and diversification of service businesses was beginning to attract attention, it was suggested that compared with manufacturing, service businesses were inefficient (productivity was poor) and suffered from variability in quality (Levitt 1972). It was proposed that the provision of services could follow the industrial model by investing in technology that was systematically deployed with careful planning to optimize service creation delivery and with consistency in quality. The merits of this approach are clear to see in the case of service businesses that are oriented towards mass markets, such as Starbucks, McDonalds, KFC, Pizza Express, Tim Hortons, CNHLS, Da Niang Dumpling, LEM hamburger and numerous other national market and international market providers. This business model emphasizes standardization of customer experiences (environment, product quality, predefined choice of items and ingredients), timeliness of delivery and low prices. Employees were also expected to make the service encounter a personable and enjoyable experience. This is the antithesis of assembly-line production where the emphasis on time, speed, accuracy of customer order receipt and delivery leaves little scope for personalizing or customizing service delivery. As a result, mass service providers experienced high staff turnover, poor morale and a reduction in service quality (see Chap. 6). They also tended to focus on the provision of low-value but high-frequency service products.

While standardization of services remains at the forefront of some service business models, it has also helped to highlight the significant part played by the personal touch in service delivery and the customization of the service experience. Material technology can be deployed using assembly-line models but irrespective of its impact on costs or product consistency, the ultimate success of a service business, and its efforts to create value and profitability, relies heavily on the human element. And this is not just on the delivery side of the equation; in fast food restaurants, for example, customers are expected to return trays, redundant packaging and unconsumed food to strategically located trash cans and storage, thereby helping to maintain the appearance of the service space and reducing the time and staff required to perform the task. Such self-service is also a feature of other service businesses such as banking that extensively use material technologies such as ATMs that can be used 24/7 by customers, bypassing expensive, staffed branch-based banking facilities (many of which also have ATMs inside). You might think that the bank example points to lowered expectations of personal service, but it also depends on the nature of the service business/customer interface. The most highly rated telephone banking services in the UK achieve high score for the attitudes, helpfulness and knowledge of banks' call centre employees. This highlights two points: first, that even where material technology (servers, computers, telephones, smartphones) are the core platform for a service, the human interface is a critical element for the delivery of successful service encounters, and second, that because supplying and sharing knowledge is at the heart of many services, in many cases, it will be impossible to use standardization of provision. Mass customization of marketing or call centres is aided by material and immaterial technology; computers are the hardware and computer software is customized to the requirements of the service provider enabling a degree of flexibility or customization. This is not the same as standardization and, ultimately, there is still a necessity for personnel at the interface between the service

business and the customer to mediate a transaction and the service experience.

## 4.3   How Can Technology Assist Service Businesses?

Developments in technologies that could be applied to service businesses were a very gradual process—from the telegraph to the telephone and the typewriter—until the early 1980s when the first desktop and the early 1990s when email, networked computers and the Internet became generally available (Table 4.2). For both employers and employees, these very quickly became very powerful tools for conducting business; emails could be transmitted more or less instantly irrespective of the distance between communicators, large quantities of data and information could be gathered, stored, processed and exchanged using desktop or handheld devices with the capacity and processing power of computers that formally required the space of a large room. It is important to appreciate the impacts that these technologies had on households and consumers. This transformed consumption, but also converted consumers into content producers including the growth in e-publishing but also the rise of social media influencers and, in particular, vloggers.

A computer should not be considered as a stand-alone device. This is especially the case with on-going developments in the Internet of Things (IoT) in which computing devices are embedded in everyday objects, enabling them to send and receive data. A computer has the potential to be connected to any other computer and is able to store, share and process information rapidly. The emergence of integrated networks of computers, including especially smartphones, provided opportunities for the creation of new services and for the transformation of existing services.

**Table 4.2** Successive waves of innovation that have impacted on service businesses

|  | 1960s | 1970s | 1980s | 1990s | 2000s | 2010s |
|---|---|---|---|---|---|---|
| Innovation | Mainframe and databases | Desktop and personal computing | Business software | Internet, platforms including e-commerce | Mobile broadband, social media, social media, smartphones and apps | Big data |
| Technologies | Modern programming languages, advances in algorithms | Desktops and PCs, basic office software, games and visual graphics | Enterprise software | Internet technologies, personal computing | GPS, Wi-fi, 2G/3G, laptops, mobile phones | Smart devices and sensors, predictive algorithms, machine learning |
| Business impacts | Business calculations, database management systems | Document processing, file storage | Efficient and automated business processes | B2B and B2C e-commerce, Email, chatrooms | Remote work and 24/7 connectivity, digital advertising and marketing | Predictive analytics, natural languages, big data, Internet of Things |
| Consumer impacts | Limited | Individuals with computers in larger firms, gaming and document processing | Creative destruction of jobs | Email, e-chatting and VoLP, e-commerce, remote work via VPNs | Connected anytime, anywhere, multiple devices per person, individuals as content creators | Data generation, content creation, digital devices everywhere |

Source: After Manyika et al. (2015, p. 23)

## 4.3.1   Business Process Management

Information technology involves the application of computers, telecommunication systems and online platforms to store and share information that has some utility for the conduct of service business. Some examples include email, online customer support software (including chatbots and data bases that contain information that may be directly accessed by customers, e.g. to answer queries or to help resolve technical problems without the need to speak directly with an employee), software for enterprise resource management (ERP) or customer relationship management (CRM), software for streamlining sales processes or electronic shopping carts of the kind used by online retailers (Table 4.1).

## 4.3.2   Productivity

Productivity management has long been challenging for service businesses (see Chap. 5). The tools made available by technological innovation, including AI, data analytics and robotics, offer a real prospect for significant advances, especially as tasks, such as planning, co-ordination, collaboration or design, can be performed more rapidly and reliably. This is the case for both tasks internal to service businesses and outward-facing activities including processing customer orders, customer software queries and updates, or service delivery via email, Skype, web forums, online chat rooms or the telephone. Service businesses can use social media to raise their visibility to potential clients including text messaging, online advertisements and online mapping packages, for example, Google Maps. Google Maps provides users with access to satellite mapping, ground-level photography and information about nearby businesses. Google Maps is based on the application of Global Positioning Systems (GPS) to identify the location of GPS-enabled devices. GPS underpins a set of tools developed to explore the ways in which people and products move through space. This enables new services to be created, but also productivity improvements to be identified (Milner 2016, p. 191). It is important, however, not to use technology as a catch-all for enhancing productivity; rather the most effective and efficient tools should be adopted according

to a careful evaluation of the outcomes required from a particular task.

The on-going application of digitization to service business has the potential to enhance productivity (Table 4.3). There are three impacts here to consider. First, digitization will enhance labour productivity including the application of online recruitment or talent platforms and the development of digitally enabled flexible work. Second, the Internet of Things (IoT) will continue to link assets with performance and monitoring systems, leading to enhanced asset utilization. This will also reduce energy consumption, facilitating the on-going development of the responsible business agenda. Third, companies investing in big data analytics and in IoT technologies will continue to contribute to enhancing multifactor productivity. This includes developments in applications that connect employees in the field and machine and facility or building monitoring systems. It has been estimated that the combined impacts of digitization on labour, capital and multifactor productivity in the US could generate a combined annual impact of between $1.6 and $2.2 trillion by 2025 and this would increase GDP by between 6% and 8% (Manyika et al. 2015, pp. 12–13).

**Table 4.3** Effects of digitization on service businesses productivity

| Effect | Outcomes |
| --- | --- |
| Labour: increased supply and productivity, including accessing labour remotely | Increased labour force participation including inclusion. Recruitment platforms better able to match applicants with jobs including an increase in speed. Increased labour productivity. |
| Capital: enhanced asset efficiency | Increased utilization of assets. Preventative maintenance based on sensors reducing downtime and maintenance costs with impacts on productivity. |
| R&D: process and product development | Data analytics of big data facilitates process and product innovation. Escalation in the speed of product development cycles. Virtual development and testing using computer-aided design systems. |
| Operations and supply-chain optimization | Real-time monitoring and control of supply chains. Path optimization and prioritization of logistic routing. Enhanced energy efficiency through optimization. |
| Resource management | Enhanced energy efficiency through intelligent facility management. Decreased waste of time and raw materials including recycling. Increased fuel/water efficiency. |

Source: After Manyika et al. (2015: 13)

### 4.3.3   Communication

Many improvements in productivity are linked with telecommunications technology (Tables 4.2 and 4.3). Many service businesses supply smartphones to employees in communication-intensive roles: sales, marketing, promotions, after-sales, delivery of services at customers' homes or at business premises, amongst others. Employees with smartphones can also keep in regular touch with managers, exchanging emails, information and applications in ways that keep them abreast of customers' requirements, providing prompt solutions for unexpected customer queries, or receiving 'just in time' guidance on the next client to contact or which address to go to for the next service repair or delivery. For some service businesses, it is vital to maintain active networking; smartphones enable text and social messaging to be conducted 24 hours a day, seven days a week.

Smartphones have disrupted existing service operational delivery models and led to the emergence of new services. This has led to developments in marketing and promotional campaigns targeted at smartphones, but also new services. For some users, smartphones have replaced watches, audio players and cameras. Different technologies have been captured and incorporated into smartphones—the implication being that many service businesses communicate with customers via their smartphones (Table 4.4).

### 4.3.4   Digitization and the Marketing Mix

Marketing is the lifeblood for many service businesses and this includes a focus on the '8Ps' that are part of the marketing mix approach: Product,

**Table 4.4** Smartphones and the rise of mobile commerce

| Task | Characteristics |
| --- | --- |
| Mobile money transfer | Mobile devices used to transfer money and to make cash or bank card payments. |
| Mobile ticketing | Replacement of paper tickets with digital tickets |
| Mobile vouchers/loyalty cards | Distribution of vouchers/coupons and loyalty cards via an app. |
| Purchase of content and delivery | Downloads for payment including apps, games, music, ring tones, wallpapers and video. |
| Local based services | Place-based marketing including local discount codes, weather forecasts, tracking and monitoring people |
| Information services | News, stock market information, sports results, financial analysis, traffic news. |
| Mobile banking | Accessing account information and making transactions |
| Mobile brokerage | Stock market services accessed via a mobile app |
| Auctions | Participating in online auctions |
| Purchasing | Accessing e-commerce |
| Mobile marketing | Advertising targeted at smartphone devices. |

Source: Authors' own

Price, Place, Promotion, People, Processes, Physical Evidence and Productivity and Quality (Zeithaml et al. 2006). Printed brochures, flyers and advertisements in newspapers and magazines have long been staple marketing tools and continue to have a role, but only alongside email, messaging and social media that can reach existing and potential customers rapidly and over much larger geographical areas.

Advertising, information, sales, technical support and updates and upgrades can all be promoted via the Internet while text messaging, pop-ups embedded in web browsers and in smartphone apps, including mapping apps, are just some of the ways of targeting customers or of promoting brand loyalty. The key point is that innovations in digitization have transformed the application of key elements of the marketing mix and this includes big data analytics to create highly targeted marketing campaigns with personalized communications (see also Chap. 9 on marketing).

### 4.3.5   Customer Service

Tangible and intangible technology has also 'raised the game' as well as customer expectations with respect to customer services provided by service businesses. Customer satisfaction is multi-dimensional; it includes the quality and price of a service, technical support following a purchase, consistency, reliability, access to help, advice and guidance from sales or service teams, the time required to reach sales or technical support via the telephone or email, access to chat services to resolve technical problems or answer queries about the suitability of one product compared to another. Speed of access to information has been transformed by a combination of telecommunications and software such that customer expectations with respect to service business response times have escalated. For example, efficient software-based routing of incoming calls, text messages or emails to the appropriate individual or group that can handle the query or problem identified by the customer is vital. This equipment and software is often expensive and sophisticated but this does not guarantee customer satisfaction; this will be determined by the extent to which the technical support or other staff responding to customers are trained in how to use the technology and in customer service techniques.

### 4.3.6  Working Practices in Service Businesses

The outward-facing impacts and opportunities afforded to service businesses by tangible and intangible technology are numerous. But it also has impacts on internal operations, practices and the costs of service businesses. Apart from employee salaries, one of the other unavoidable costs for service businesses arises from the requirement for office space. Some start-ups and on-going service businesses will be able to minimize this overhead by using a room at home as an office but most have to factor in substantial rents and service charges for office space supplied by a third party and only a few will be able to invest in custom-built office or warehouse space. Smartphones, intranets and video conferencing apps, for example, GoToMeeting, Zoom, Google Meet and Skype, provide opportunities for employees to work from home, whilst travelling or in clients' premises.

In the case of office space, historically it has been assumed that all employees require a space (in an open plan or as individual offices), five days a week. This requirement has been reassessed in the light of innovations in telecommunications technology; it has allowed greater flexibility in relation to where, and how, employees perform their day-to-day tasks, and interact with one another or with customers. They no longer need to be in their offices every working day; communications technology allows employees to work from home, from vehicles, from trains or aircraft for all or part of the working week and as needs dictate. Mobile computing, text messaging, emails and software (including cloud services) enable remote collaboration between colleagues and with customers. Practices such as hot-desking then enable service businesses to

reduce their office space needs and related overheads while still being able to use technology that allows them to monitor when, where and how employees are working.

Apart from encouraging changes in employee working practices and the ways in which service businesses use working spaces, technology has also transformed the ways of doing business. The role of face-to-face interaction has not, as some expected, been usurped by telecommunications technology; rather, it is now complemented by time and cost savings enabled by telephone, video or web conferencing for tasks undertaken within service businesses (especially those with operating units located nationwide or globally) and between them and their customers wherever they may be located (see, e.g. Duffy and McEuen 2010). Depending on the method used, participants can hear and/or see others, as well as share presentations and exchange documents in real time. One of the principal benefits for service businesses is a reduction in meeting costs, including the time taken by travelling.

In 2020, Covid-19 and the lockdown transformed the adoption of Internet-based teleconferencing and online services. This included established legal firms shifting to complete online provision, virtual church services and online teaching introduced for core provision of teaching by schools and universities. For many service businesses and their workers, remote working was relatively unusual, but Covid-19 forced rapid adoption by all service businesses able to substitute face-to-face service provision with online provision.

### 4.3.7  Boost to Profit Margins

Digitized service firms have the potential to capture more business opportunities and are more likely to be involved in internationalization including exports and attracting foreign visitors. Investing in digital technology is a high-risk but also high-reward activity. On the one hand, it may be essential for the survival of a firm. This is the case for high-street retailers who have had to establish effective online e-commerce platforms.

For many retailers, their largest store has become their e-commerce store. On the other hand, the emergence of the digital economy has created new business opportunities.

Going online also impacts profitability and there is a direct relationship with productivity. Data for US businesses reveals that post-tax profit margins improved by 60% between 1993 and 2013 for highly digitized firms in IT and business services and in media services well ahead of all other sectors for which data was available (Manyika et al. 2015, p. 21). Healthcare and retail services, which had low levels of overall digitization, showed little or no improvement in profit margins over this period.

## 4.4   Disadvantages of Technology for Services Businesses

Although technology has revolutionized the ways in which service businesses operate and innovate, the rush to embed technology into their activities exposes them to risks and challenges.

### 4.4.1   Costs of Technology Adoption

Whether a start-up or a well-established service business, a headlong rush into embedding technology, as part perhaps of a business plan, is not advisable. This is not to suggest that a service business should not adopt technology but it is vital, amongst other things, to consider: the stage reached in the development of the business, the identification of technology that is appropriate to the tasks to be performed, to weigh up the costs and benefits of leasing versus the purchase of hardware and/or software or accessing services via cloud-based solutions, the anticipated costs of depreciation and replacement of hardware/software as well as service maintenance packages, whether and at what cost training will be required for employees expected to use the technology, and the consequences for employee wages and/or job descriptions. The details will vary according to the type of service business, size and configuration.

In most service businesses, the necessary expertise for evaluating and implementing a technology 'strategy' will not be available in-house; the costs of commissioning external expertise, including that required for employee training, will also need to be incorporated into the equation. For many service businesses, especially start-ups, the costs of embedding technology can be daunting and are certainly a major hurdle to cross before the expected benefits materialize. Here it is important to appreciate that Covid-19 was an inflection point for all service businesses, forcing them to rapidly innovate and to shift to online provision.

### 4.4.2   Consequences for Employees

Ultimately, service businesses embed technology with a view to automating transactions and routine tasks undertaken by employees (Frey and Osborne 2013; Brynjolfsson and McAfee 2011). Computers and telecommunications substitute for employees in relation to cost estimates provided to customers, invoicing, chasing debtors, company budgeting, salaries and pensions, taxes and inventory management. Receptionists can be replaced by automated telephone answering systems and virtual receptionists. Incoming telephone call management and routing at call centres can be used to reduce the number of employees required to provide a service. The employee displacement effects of technology will vary depending on the type of service business; some tasks are more vulnerable than others but there is no doubting the scope for job losses, revised job descriptions, changes to working hours and salaries and deskilling.

In some circumstances, embedding technology does not only displace jobs in situ, it may also enable service businesses to relocate all or part of their activities to other parts of the country or even other parts of the world, whether to access untapped markets or perhaps because employee costs will be lower. Companies may employ receptionists located in low-wage economies but linked via online systems enabling customers located in high-wage locations to access their services. Ultimately, of course, most successful service businesses rely on attracting and retaining committed and effective employees; sensitive handling of technology adoption will, therefore, be at least as important as a careful assessment of the costs of the necessary hardware, software, expert advice, employee training, cyber security and system maintenance.

### 4.4.3 Keeping the Service Business Secure

Perhaps the most important downside of technology adoption by service businesses is the constant threat of digital security breaches. These are now so commonplace that, unless they affect the very largest firms, they hardly warrant a mention in the business press. Firms are most vulnerable if they rely on the Internet. Developing and maintaining secure systems is an on-going difficult and highly specialized task. For smaller firms, it is difficult to keep up with developments that might undermine their firm's digital or cyber security. The level of cyber threats has increased exponentially with the dependence on information systems. Both proprietary and other information owned by a service business, as well as its confidential customer databases, which may include credit card details and other sensitive information, are targets for security breaches. The possibilities are numerous but the most common digital breaches involve covert amendments or drawing down of business records without the knowledge of the service business, infecting databases with 'trojans' that enable hackers to draw down whatever information they need as and when they want or even to totally or selectively delete records at a predefined time (Table 4.5).

Distributed denial of service (DDoS) attacks that work by overloading websites or other online services with traffic so that they go offline increase year-on-year. Digital security is a universal threat with potentially significant costs for all service businesses. The most vulnerable are small- and medium-sized firms that do not have

**Table 4.5** Service business and the largest cyber security data breaches

| Company | Date | Number of user files (m) | Details of the data breach |
|---|---|---|---|
| LinkedIn | 2012 | 117 | Email addresses and encrypted passwords |
| eBay | 2014 | 145 | Passwords, email addresses, birthdates and physical addresses |
| Equifax | 2017 | 145.5 | Names, birthdates, social security numbers, driver's licence numbers and addresses of 144.5 million Americans along with 200,000 credit card numbers |
| Under Armour | 2018 | 150 | Usernames, emails, encrypted passwords |
| Exactis | 2018 | 340 | Religion and hobbies |
| Myspace | 2016 | 360 | 427,484,128 passwords and 360,213,024 email addresses |
| AdultFriendFinder | 2016 | 412 | Encrypted passwords, email address, date of last visit and membership status |
| Yahoo | 2014 | 500 | User personal information |
| Marriott International | 2014 | 500 | Discovered in Sept. 2018. Names, email address. Mailing address, phone number, birthdates, passport numbers |

Source: Adapted from Malwarebytes, https://www.malwarebytes.com/data-breach/, accessed 30 November 2019

the fiscal resources or the expertise to set up or maintain digital security systems that will minimize the threat of security breaches. Nonetheless, every service business has no option but to ensure that arrangements are in place for protecting data and information since a security breach is not only very costly to rectify but also risks significant reputational damage with consequences for the future viability of the business.

In many ways, the requirements for creating a secure business are daunting. They are not only multi-dimensional but are also highly dynamic, requiring constant monitoring, updating and where appropriate training to ensure that everybody in the business understands the vital importance of digital security. This starts at the top of the service business; managers must map where (inside the business, on external servers or in 'the cloud') information and data is stored, on what kinds of device, who is authorized to access it, the security controls that are in place and whether they comply with any legal requirements, and whether there is a disaster recovery plan in place proportionate to the likely risks. The latter does not just arise from digital breaches or failures but also the consequences of 'acts of God' such as earthquakes, fires or floods.

An employee acceptable-use policy, defining how employees should behave online at work, how data is to be shared and restricted, and whether monitoring of their online activities takes place is necessary. This includes guidance on the use of company and/or individual laptops, tablets and smartphones, especially outside the office when doing business or at home. The value of training employees in how to identify and counter potential cybercrime, such as email, search engine, deceptive and malware-based phishing, should not be underestimated. The risks arising when employees web-surf beyond the sites really necessary to undertake the work of the business (and therefore known and trusted) are also important. To some extent, depending on the type of service business, it may be necessary to conduct background checks on prospective employees (in some cases, these will be required by law) to establish whether there is any criminal history or whether their public social media use might be a cause for concern.

Then there are all the actions that employers need to ensure are in place to minimize the exposure of employees and the business to cybercrime; firewalls, encryption, password authentication, conforming to data privacy requirements, ensuring that software updates and patches are installed as soon as they are made available and seeking external technical support (or perhaps using managed security on a contract basis) to counter malware or Trojan attacks. Since service businesses will invariably rely to some extent on third-party technology providers, it will also be necessary to be aware of their digital security arrangements, the backup arrangements, their fitness for purpose and their responsibilities should their systems fail to the detriment of clients.

## 4.5   Disruptive Digitization?

The potential for a cyber-attack is an ever-present possibility for all service businesses but another source of disruption is digitization itself. Although analysed from the perspective of large, established companies, Dawson et al. (2016) explores how digitization changes the nature of supply or demand (or both). On the supply side, digital technology brings into play sources that may in the past have been uneconomic or impossible to access, while on the demand side, distortions are reduced by digitization as customers can access more complete information about aspects of services that may have previously been bundled with products for the convenience of a supplier. As Dawson et al. (2016, p. 5) put it: 'The newly exposed supply, combined with newly undistorted demand, gives new market makers an opportunity to connect consumers and customers by lowering transaction costs while reducing information asymmetry'. They cite two examples: Airbnb uncovering demand that always existed for greater variety in accommodation choices and prices, and Uber increasing the chances of hiring a taxi by improving the utilization of vehicles already on the road.

Companies providing tickets for major entertainment and sporting events, or airline companies, deploy digitally determined dynamic ticket pricing to more closely connect daily, or even hourly, fluctuations in supply and demand (see Chap. 5, Sect. 5.3.2).

Demand has become less distorted as consumers (as well as business-to-business relationships) use connectivity, technology and apps to obtain information about exactly what they want, where and when it is available, and with the best delivery times and prices. The ways in which services are offered alter as well as how customers prefer or want to use them, and this, in turn, raises consumer expectations of what to expect from a service and gives them a greater sense of empowerment over scheduling where exactly and at what time they choose to consume a service— even better if the service is free (such as deliveries by online retailers such as Amazon). All this is a source of disruption that service firms cannot overlook because, if they do not respond, it is very likely that other firms will find ways to do so. Your service business could be vulnerable if

> your customers have to cross-subsidize other customers; your customers have to buy the whole service for the one bit that they want; your customers can't get what they want where and when they want it; your customers get a user experience that doesn't match global best practice. (Dawson et al. 2016, p. 6)

The effect of digitization on supply is that it allows new sources of service products and labour to enter markets in ways that were previously more difficult. Some of the indicators of disruption to service businesses triggered by previously inaccessible sources of supply include 'customers use the product only partially; production is inelastic to price; supply is utilized in a variable or unpredictable way; fixed or step costs are high' (Dawson et al. 2016, p. 7).

More extreme disruptions can be initiated by digitization. This may be the result of new or significantly enhanced value propositions for customers, a re-imagination of business systems, or entirely new value chains and ecosystems, taking the form of the appearance of businesses from adjacent markets or companies with very differ-

ent business objectives but exacting 'collateral damage' on existing players (Dawson et al. 2016). This may have an impact on profits and introduce new control points for value, making established companies vulnerable even if they believe that they can rely for protection from things like regulatory requirements or the costs of investing in any necessary physical infrastructure. Regulations can be reconfigured in line with user demand, ways will be found by firms to collaborate in the use of costly infrastructure or other disruptive mechanisms will emerge. It will be important for different types of service businesses to take account of changes in the forces of supply and demand that are specific to their industry or ecosystem.

## 4.6 Cautious Digitization?

Given the ubiquity of technology, combined with an accelerating rate of change in its characteristics in a very short period (30 years), it is tempting to think that every type of service business cannot overlook digitization. The bottom line is that digitization is appealing because it has already delivered cost efficiencies and annual growth rates enhancing profitability. Yet a study examining the digitization challenges facing 150 large businesses worldwide suggests that their digital maturity (expressed as a Digital Quotient [DQ]) reveals a large range of digital performances (Catlin et al. 2015; see also Olanrewaju et al. 2014). Indeed, the number of corporations with a below-average DQ far exceeds the number of 'emerging leaders' and 'established leaders'. The DQ incorporates 18 'practices' and Catlin et al. (2015) found that digital strategy showed the greatest variation between the corporations in their study. Digitization based on following the established leaders is risky unless firms develop the correct digital strategy; for most businesses, it is necessary to make a 100% commitment rather than applying it to only selected parts of a firm's activities.

The universal application of a corporate digital strategy then requires investment in appropriate digital capabilities. Service businesses should not overlook the ways in which digitization has impacted the ways in which customers identify, search, evaluate and make purchasing decisions; successful digitization incorporates and fulfils internal objectives and outward-facing demands. Catlin et al. (2015) also identifies the importance of an adaptive culture within businesses as another key variable, especially where technical requirements such as analysing big data or digital content management are beyond the reach of all but the largest corporations. Finally, businesses should always evaluate/monitor the delivery of a chosen digital strategy using appropriately specified key KPIs, organizational structures and employee development programmes aligned to digitization needs. As Catlin et al. put it:

> Collectively, these lessons represent a high-level road map for the executive teams of established companies seeking to keep pace in the digital age. Much else is required, of course. But in our experience, without the right road map and the management mind-set needed to follow it, there's a real danger of travelling in the wrong direction, travelling too slowly in the right one, or not moving forward at all. (Catlin et al. 2015, p. 2)

While there may be a consensus about the risks of failing to engage with digital technology, Fitzgerald et al. (2014) concluded that employees find the adoption process slow and complex, often because many company managers still lack urgency and fail to engage with their employees in a vision of the ways in which dig-

ital technology can transform a business. All this must be placed in the context of Covid-19 that forced all service businesses to explore the application of digital solutions to service delivery.

## 4.7 Digitization Is Not Just for Larger Service Businesses

Larger service businesses have been in the vanguard for the implementation of digital technology as they are more likely to possess the required human and fiscal resources. Nevertheless, smaller service businesses can now also make this transition more easily. This follows from the relatively recent growth in the number of digital platforms with a global reach that are readily accessible to all service businesses as well as their clients/consumers. Facebook, Twitter, LinkedIn, Skype, Alibaba, WeChat, eBay and Amazon are just some of the digital platforms that connect service businesses and individuals across international borders. The emergence of platforms has led to a rapid and radical reconfiguring of capitalism. In 2008, the ten largest global companies included oil and gas companies. By 2018, these firms had been replaced by seven platform-based businesses (Table 4.6). The creation of digital communities and marketplaces allowing different groups to interact and transact has enabled companies like Tencent and Amazon to grow rapidly. For platforms, the network effect

**Table 4.6** The dominance of platform businesses: The eight largest global companies (2008 vs 2018)

| 2008 | | | | 2018 | | | | |
|------|---------|---------|------|------|-----------|-----------------------------|---------|------|
| Rank | Company | Founded | USBn | Rank | Company | Platform business model | Founded | USBn |
| 1 | PetroChina | 1999 | 728 | 1 | Apple | * | 1976 | 890 |
| 2 | Exon | 1870 | 492 | 2 | Google | * | 1998 | 768 |
| 3 | GE | 1892 | 358 | 3 | Microsoft | * | 1975 | 680 |
| 4 | China Mobile | 1997 | 344 | 4 | Amazon | * | 1994 | 592 |
| 5 | ICBC | 1984 | 336 | 5 | Facebook | * | 2004 | 545 |
| 6 | Gazprom | 1989 | 332 | 6 | Tencent | * | 1998 | 526 |
| 7 | Microsoft | 1975 | 313 | 7 | Berkshire Hathaway | | 1955 | 496 |
| 8 | Shell | 1907 | 266 | 8 | Alibaba | * | 1999 | 488 |

Source: The Innovator, 2019, https://innovator.news/the-platform-economy-3c09439b56, accessed 30 November 2019

implies that first movers have a considerable advantage and are able to lock out competitor companies.

Platforms provide opportunities for smaller firms, and even individuals, to develop platform-enabled service business models (see Chap. 3). These platforms provide access to a very large potential customer base as well as being a launching point for marketing by service businesses. Existing and potential customers can very quickly be made aware of what is available, when and where, and at what price and to the extent that a snowball effect can occur in hours or days for an event or a product that is widely discussed and shared through digital platforms including social media. These platforms also allow service businesses to identify suppliers, to collaborate with one another and with clients, to develop capabilities and to learn across geographical spaces that, in the past, were much more constrained.

Facebook estimated that in 2019, about 90 million SMEs, many of which will be service businesses, used its pages—double the figure for 2015. About 30% of these SMEs have cross-border 'fans'. Likewise, in 2019, Amazon's 12 platforms (the US, the UK, Germany, France, Canada, Japan, India, Italy, Spain, Mexico, Brazil and China) hosted about 5 million third-party sellers. The likelihood that service SMEs with a presence on Facebook will export will certainly be higher than for offline businesses. This is further enhanced by the ways in which PayPal or Alipay provide platforms for cross-border financial transactions for service SMEs and their customers. A key issue with cross-border trade is the ability to move money simply across borders and between different currencies and payment systems. Specialist payment platforms have been established that provide firms with the ability to transact cross-border business, but with the payment difficulties dealt with by a specialist third-party payment provider. SMEs can also extend their search for funding using crowd-funding platforms such as Gofundme, Indiegogo and Kickstarter.

## 4.8   Technology as a Service

Technology provides service businesses with a set of tools that can support existing business models or strategic goals. But these tools can also be used to create services in their own right for use by other service and non-service businesses. As digitization has deepened and penetrated all areas of the economy and society, it has stimulated new ways of thinking about how all the objects that are digitized can be used in new and innovative ways for the benefit of businesses and customers. The starting point is that every digitized object, smartphone, smart meter, server, laptop, computer, weather sensor, biochip transponder, DNA analysis devices, environmental/food/pathogen monitoring and smart thermostat is by definition electronically connected to something else and that object in turn is connected to other objects. There is a network of objects, buildings, vehicles, aircraft, devices and many other things mediated by software and sensors. Such a network allows objects not only to collect data for transmission somewhere else but also allows for two-way flows of data between devices.

### 4.8.1   The Internet of Things

The opportunities created by integration between computer-based systems and the physical world are encapsulated in the term Internet of Things (IoT). The term was introduced in 1999 by a British entrepreneur (Ken Ashton) at Auto-ID Labs by way of reference to a global network of radio-frequency identification (RFID) connected objects. The interconnections at the heart of the IoT allow greater automation of tasks in many sectors such as transport and traffic management, health care or local government services, as well as in the operation, for example, of smart cities (using ICT to improve interactions between urban services, to improve contact between citizens and government or to better manage the costs of city management and consumption).

An example of a service business promoting and harnessing the IoT as a medium for service businesses to open up new horizons by working together in new and different ways is Iotic Labs. Based in the corridor between East London and Cambridge (UK), this group of creative engineers starts from the premise that service businesses (or individuals) are stuck in a 'linear world, connecting more and more devices to bigger and better data centres' rather than following a different path that Iotic Labs imagines as a world of distributed but connected data. Existing data systems exist for specific organizations for a particular purpose, resulting in numerous data 'silos' with little or no exchange of data with other organizations that might have an interest and who might benefit from the same source. This is an Intranet of Things, not an IoT.

The principle behind distributed data is simple to express but many questions that a typical service business might ask need to be answered before putting it into practice, such as how can things share data together?, how can all sorts of different types of data be mashed together?, would the outcome make any sense?, what about privacy and security?, does a business hide proprietary information that it does not want to be found, but wants to share with a client that it trusts?, how can things that are part of or owned by a business such as data or key documents be protected from misuse? The Iotic Labs solution is Iotic Space; things can interact within this creative space but to do so they must be present inside it so that all variety of things can be 'mashed' using Iotic's Mashapps and application programming interfaces (APIs) (sets of routines, tools and protocols for building software and applications).

Security within the Iotic Space is managed by a Registrar that retains metadata about everything and everyone that joins it. Thus, the data within the Space and what the data means are separated so that it will be possible for someone to identify a data value from a thing, such as a sensor, but this would be meaningless without knowing the kind of sensor and its location. Without access to the Registrar, the data makes no sense at all.

The IoT has not escaped the attention of large and prominent services businesses. SAP AG, which provides enterprise application software and software-related services worldwide, suggests that companies:

> Transform the way you do business with Internet of Things offerings from SAP. Our end-to-end offering for Internet of Things provides everything your business needs to create a System of Things—M2M Connectivity, cloud platform, device management, big data management, event stream processing, predictive analytics, and apps-to make IoT projects real, repeatable and scalable.

Oracle Corporation develops, manufactures, markets, hosts and supports database and middleware software, application software, cloud infrastructure, hardware systems and related services worldwide. This business model is based on the understanding that the proliferation of intelligent and connected devices has created a market for entirely new solutions based on IoT technology. Key to the IoT is effective communication between all the elements that are part of the architecture of the IoT. Oracle has developed an IoT platform that provides an integrated, secure, comprehensive platform for the entire IoT architecture across all vertical markets. A key danger with the IoT, and a business opportunity, relates to cyber protection as any product connected to the IoT may be subjected to a cyber-attack.

### 4.8.2 Big Data

Intertwined with the IoT has been the rise in the importance of big data—very large and complex data sets that are difficult to process using established methods of data processing. Big data are data streams that have increasing *volumes*, greater *variety* and *velocity*. Combined these are known as the three Vs. Volumes matter with big data and, in this case, firms and governments can access high volumes of unstructured data, from data feeds, clickstreams, apps, webpages and sensors. Velocity includes data that is streamed in real time. Variety includes data that includes text, images, video and audio, and these types of data require pre-processing. Big data is used by companies for product development, predictive maintenance, monitoring customer experiences, identification of fraud and compliance issues, machine learning and AI to monitor and enhance operational efficiency and to support innovation.

Big data is generated continuously by digital processes including sensors and social media exchanges. The resulting datasets contain such a variety of information that the application of predictive analytics (data mining, predictive modelling, machine learning) is required to compile historical and current facts that form the basis of predictions about future trends and developments. It has reached the stage where big data is an essential factor of production, alongside human capital and physical assets. The ways in which big data creates value for service businesses has implications for how they are structured, organized and managed. According to Manyika et al. (2011, pp. 4–5):

> For example, in a world in which large-scale experimentation is possible, how will corporate marketing functions and activities have to evolve? How will business processes change, and how will companies value and leverage their assets (particularly data assets)? Could a company's access to, and ability to analyze, data potentially confer more value than a brand? What existing business models are likely to be disrupted? For example, what happens to industries predicated on information asymmetry—e.g., various types of brokers—in a world of radical data transparency? How will incumbents tied to legacy business models and infrastructures compete with agile new attackers that are able to quickly process and take advantage of detailed consumer data that is rapidly becoming available, e.g., what they say in social media or what sensors report they are doing in the world? And what happens when surplus starts shifting from suppliers to customers, as they become empowered by their own access to data, e.g., comparisons of prices and quality across competitors?

Service businesses in the computer and information sectors are already gaining substantially from the application of big data, with government, finance and insurance and business and professional service sectors also benefiting from big data provided that barriers to use, such as concerns about personal data security and freedom, can be overcome. Factors such as the availability of talent, the IT intensity of service businesses, the degree to which the management and employees have a data-driven mindset and whether suitable data is available contribute to the ease with which service businesses benefit from big data (Table 4.7).

Big data overlaps with cloud computing, essentially storing and accessing data and programs via the Internet rather than from a computer's hard drive. The tangible benefits of deploying cloud services include more flexible access to technology, faster access to technology, cost savings over on-premise solutions, reductions in capital expenditure and on demand/predictable costs. There are intangible benefits including improved customer service, improved collaboration between departments, improved customer engagement, undertaking more development using an agile methodology and improved communication between departments.

Adobe and Microsoft, for example, offer monthly subscription services providing clients with access to imaging and design programmes (Adobe) or the Office suite (Microsoft) without the need to store programmes or the images or data that they generate locally on hard drives. They permit collaboration between employees within the same business or amongst those distributed across a number of businesses as well as with clients. The key consideration is that one master document is modified or updated in one place as and when the collaborating employees work on it. Software-as-a-Service (SaaS) arrangements such as Think Salesforce.com are one option. Another, Platform-as-a-Service (PaaS) that allows a service business to create its own custom applications for use by all in the company, while Infrastructure-as-a-Service (IaaS) provides rented space in the cloud from platforms provided by companies like Amazon, Microsoft, Google and Rackspace for use by other service businesses.

**Table 4.7** Service businesses and big data

| Company | Big data | Application |
|---|---|---|
| Amazon | Search and order histories | Advertising algorithms |
| American Express | Purchasing transactions | Predict customer churn and loyalty |
| BDO | Client accounts | To identify risks and fraud during the client audit process |
| Capital One | Customer demographics and spending patterns | Targeted marketing |
| General Eclectic (GE) | Data streams from machinery—gas turbines, jet engines | Predict problems and plan pre-emptive servicing |
| Miniclip | Customer data, including use and experience | Enhance user experience to increase customer retention |
| Netflix | Viewing habits and customer demographics | Informs the commissioning of original programming content as well as purchasing rights to films |
| Next Big Sound | Data from Spotify streams, iTunes sales, SoundCloud plays, Facebook likes. Wikipedia page views | Insights to predict potential consumer reactions to new music. Artists and companies access this data to inform promotion strategies |
| Starbucks | Traffic, area demographics, customer behaviour | Informs decisions to open new stores. The analytics enables Starbucks to make a fairly accurate predication regarding the likely success of a new store location |
| T-Mobile | Customer transactions and interactions data | Enhanced customer retentions |

Source: Adapted from ICAS, https://www.icas.com/thought-leadership/technology/10-companies-using-big-data, accessed 30 November 2019

Working with big data can take advantage of cloud computing but the objective is different. IBM Analytics, for example, provides service businesses with a range of analytics that enables them to target the right customers using predictive modelling (predictive customer intelligence), to identify dissatisfied customers by uncovering patterns of behaviour using social media analytics), and correlating and analysing a variety of data that enable customer service issues to be addressed more promptly (customer service analytics). Big data analytics can also be tailored to the requirements of different types of service businesses. For example, IBM offers retailers advanced sales analytics; by analysing detailed information about customers and their purchasing habits, it is possible to tailor product offers to better match individual buyers' demands. In the case of banking services, behaviour-based customer insights based on predictive models derived from big data are used to identity patterns of individuals' transactions and spending behaviour to understand their needs and propensities, to anticipate life events, and thereby allow some customization of their experience of using a bank's services. By the very nature of big data and the skills required to undertake predictive analytics, most service businesses will require the services provided by specialist providers. IBM is just one of a growing number of big data companies that include HP, Teradata, Oracle, SAP, Microsoft, Amazon Web Services and Google.

## 4.9 Technology and the Shift Towards Self-Service

The interactions between service businesses and their customers/clients occur along a continuum from total control by the provider, a balanced contribution from the provider and the customer, to almost total control by the customer. Technology and digitization are involved at any stage in this continuum, but their most obvious contribution is associated with the rise of self-service technologies (SSTs). These are interfaces that allow customers to produce services independently of direct involvement with service business employees. There are various types of SST that can be grouped as follows:

1. *Telephone and interactive voice response (IVR) systems.* These are often used by banks, car and home insurance providers, restaurants providing home delivery services, and utilities to manage and process customer orders and billing inquiries but can also be used to perform tasks including customer surveys.

2. *Interactive freestanding kiosks.* These are increasingly used in large retail stores or in shopping centres as sources of customer information about product availability and location, the appropriate replacement battery for a specified equipment item, or passport verification and for issuing airline tickets at airport check-in.

3. *Internet-based connection systems.* Pay-at-the-pump petrol stations and bank ATMs are good examples, along with Internet banking, credit card services and bill management by utilities such as electricity, water or gas services. Logistics services such as DHL or UPS, or retailers such as Amazon, use online technologies to allow customers to track the progress and likely arrival times for their packages.

4. *Video/DVD/CD-based technologies.* Companies increasingly use these to train their employees, to familiarize sales representatives with new products and to introduce new products to consumers. In addition to online courses, colleges and universities provide undergraduate, graduate and continuing education classes via video and CD formats.

### 4.9.1 Implementing Successful Self-Service Technologies

Using extensive interviews with a range of companies that adopted or were thinking of adopting SSTs, Bitner, Ostrom, and Meuter (2002; see also Meuter et al. 2005) identified six critical success factors for their implementation. First, a service business should be very clear about the strategic reasons for introducing SST. There are several questions to address,

such as whether it is being introduced to reduce costs, to develop relationships with customers, to add to customer satisfaction or to diversify a client base. It is not enough to introduce SST just because competitors have adopted this approach. Second, it is essential not to lose sight of the need for SST to be first and foremost customer friendly. Third, SST does not market itself; customers need to be educated in how to use it and what steps to take if the SST fails. This is the case even if customers already understand the benefits of using SST. Fourth, even the best-managed SST will fail; a contingency plan for service recovery is essential. Fifth, do not assume that SST, however good they are will be used by every customer every time they deal with the company. Make sure that alternative methods for undertaking transactions are always available. Finally, introducing SST is not a one-off activity; the technology environment as well as the customer environment is constantly changing and firms successful with SST delivery must be prepared to adapt and adjust their offer accordingly (Zhu et al. 2013).

### 4.9.2 Artificial Intelligence, Robotics and Technological Transformation

The relationship between innovation and radical economic change can be traced back to the origins of the industrial revolution. In 1620, Francis Bacon, the English philosopher, argued that:

> It is well to observe the force and virtue and consequences of inventions; and these are nowhere to be seen more conspicuously than in those three which were unknown to the ancients ... namely, printing, gunpowder and the magnet. For these three have changed the whole face and state of things throughout the world.

In combination, these three inventions transformed the world. The invention of printing made it possible for ideas to be preserved and transmitted across time and space. Gunpowder altered warfare, whilst the magnet led to the development of the mariner's compass that laid the foundations for navigation, and ultimately global commodity chains. Since 1620, engineers and technologists have continued to be ingenious, but with some important alterations. Three are worth highlighting here. First, the escalation in the pace of technological change. Second, the rapid pace of technology adoption, combined with the ability to shift ideas around the world in the twinkling of an eye. Third, the extent and variety of technological changes that impact all aspects of everyday living.

There are two on-going transformations that are changing 'the whole face and state of things throughout the world', in Bacon's words: artificial intelligence (AI) and robotics, and developments in the application of platforms to economic activity. These are related innovations. The three inventions identified by Bacon created employment with very limited displacement. This reflects the introduction of new inventions that created new markets (Bryson and Ronayne 2014). In contrast, the application of AI and platforms to production systems is destroying existing processes and business models and creating new business opportunities. These represent disruptive technological innovations that will continue to create new forms of labour combined with the displacement of existing firms and business models.

It is worth considering the core driver behind the application of new technology to production systems and to labour. This represents the application of capital to alter the ways in which labour is involved in the production of both goods and services. It is possible to identify a set of what can be termed timeless processes that emerged with the development of capitalism, and which continue to transform space and place (Andres and Bryson 2018). These timeless processes produce different outcomes depending on the context. The primary timeless process is perhaps the 'division of labour' (Smith 1977 [orig. 1776]), and the 'spatial division of labour' (Massey 1984) (see Chap. 2). This process refers to the disaggregation of

complex tasks into several simpler tasks that can be undertaken by different individuals or groups of individuals. This division of tasks can occur on the same site or at the same location, or tasks can be transferred to other places so that a spatial division of labour emerges that is the foundation of global value chains or global production networks.

There are three important points to make about the division of labour. First, a division of labour always precedes mechanism; tasks are disaggregated, facilitating the identification of which tasks can be mechanized or replaced with artificial intelligence and robotics, and which are more effectively undertaken by people (Bryson et al. 2017; Bryson 2018). Second, the division of labour is the primary driver behind global value chains. At a city-region scale, tasks may be allocated to one place, given the existence of concentrations of specialist labour or other forms of place-based processes or incentives that provide a specific city-region with a competitive advantage in the performance of a task. Third, the division of labour is on-going. Day-by-day decisions are made to further sub-divide tasks, and to replace people with machines or robots, and to alter the geographic distribution of tasks. In this process, jobs are restructured or reshaped; some jobs are destroyed, and new jobs emerge (Bryson 2018).

### 4.9.3 The Future Impact of Artificial Intelligence

The application of AI, including robotics and autonomous systems (RAS), to some types of labour represents the most recent reworking of the relationship between an evolving division of labour and technological innovation (Bryson and Andres 2018). RAS are combinations of physical and software systems that can perceive their environments, and reason, adapt and control their actions. Developments in RAS are making it possible to automate tasks that previously could only be undertaken by people. There is much media discussion about RAS and its impact on work, but very few studies have assessed the potential impacts RAS will have on labour markets more generally.

One difficulty is that there is no rigorous and robust technique for forecasting such impacts. Nevertheless, RAS can be seen as just another stage in the application of machines to labour that could potentially increase productivity, destroying some forms and employment, but also creating new forms of work. It might be that RAS increases unemployment, by creating jobs with higher barriers to entry based around capabilities in computer programming and mathematics or highly developed social skills. Any assessment of RAS impacts, at the moment, is based on speculation.

There have been high-profile predictions regarding the impacts of AI/RAS on economic activity and labour markets. The Frey and Osbourne (2014) study estimated that 35% of jobs that existed in the UK in 2013 had a greater than 66% chance of being automated in the coming decades. In 2016, Arntz et al. (2016) explored 2012 data and estimated that for 10% of UK jobs, it would be possible to automate 70% of their component tasks over the next decade and that another 25% of jobs could have at least 50% of their tasks automated. The most recent study by the OECD suggests that 14% of all jobs across 32 countries have a high risk of automation, and a further 32% of jobs may experience significant change (Nedelkoska and Quintini 2018).

AI places more low-skilled jobs at risk compared to previous rounds of technological displacement. The OECD analysis suggests that the risks related to AI in the labour market decline as educational attainment and skill levels rise (Nedelkoska and Quintini 2018). The difficulty with these studies is that they say nothing about new tasks and jobs that might be created through the application of RAS. This is the 'known unknown' of the implications RAS will have on future labour markets. Another key issue is that AI and RAS are also among the drivers behind the reshoring of manufacturing tasks back to developed market economies. The application of AI to manufacturing is transforming labour-intensive tasks to capital-intensive tasks (Vanchan et al. 2018).

## 4.10  Wrapping Up

There is an interesting paradox to explore. This is the tension between the role service workers play in creating and delivering service experiences through face-to-face encounters versus the substitution of service workers by technology. On the one hand, service customization and the quality of a service experience are still founded on interactions between service producers and service consumers. On the other hand, there is the emergence of service encounters in which service workers are a hidden rather than a visible part of the service experience. They are hidden as frontline service workers may have been replaced by back-stage or back-office workers and some of this substitution involves computer programmers (see Chap. 6).

There is no question that technology is playing a much more important role in service delivery and service experiences. This is challenging existing business models as well as consumer expectations, but it also provides opportunities for the development of new types of service-based business models. The drivers behind these alterations are the interactions between technologies that create streams of big data and developments in computing. Big data facilitates machine learning and continued developments in AI.

It is perhaps possible to identify three types of services. First, there are services in which face-to-face encounters between a service provider and a consumer will always remain essential. It would perhaps be possible to replace service workers by technology, but this would undermine the nature of the service experience. Second, there are services in which technology has displaced service workers. Here it is important to highlight the replacement of service workers initially by computer code and eventually by robots. The codification of money and markets is on-going, and this includes the codification of trust through the analysis of big data (Ross 2016). These two categories are perhaps the extreme ends of a continuum. The final service type is based on firms developing a segmentation approach to service delivery based on blending face-to-face delivery systems with technology. In this case, a consumer will be able to access a service either via a face-to-face encounter or through interacting with some type of interface with a set of algorithms. This third strategy is becoming dominant in financial services and retailing reflecting the on-going delivery of these services via e-commerce or face-to-face encounters.

The balance between these three different types of service delivery system will be challenged by developments in quantum computing. There have been important recent developments in quantum computing. This includes the announcement by IBM in September 2019 of the introduction of a new 53-qubit quantum cloud-based 'mainframe' computer. Quantum computing is beginning to transform research and development and, at some point in the future, will begin to develop solutions to problems that are currently impossible to solve with conventional computers. Nevertheless, there is a real danger that existing forms of data encryption will be undermined by Quantum computing. One implication is that, for some services, face-to-face encounters will become much more important as being present in a service encounter may be the only way of confirming a service client's identity.

It is worth revisiting two short essays written by John Maynard Keynes (1930a, b) in the second year of the Great Depression. In these essays, Keynes reflected on the economic impacts of technological change for our grandchildren, introducing the concept of 'technological unemployment'. His argument was that a 'temporary period of maladjustment' occurs in labour markets because of technologically driven, disruptive change. But he noted that this was a temporary phenomenon, as technology would transform production systems creating new employment opportunities. This continues to be the case; technological innovation simultaneously destroys and creates employment, firms and business models.

**Learning Outcomes**

- Technology and service businesses have long been allies.
- Services are increasingly digitized—both knowledge-intensive and manual services.
- Digitization enhances productivity.
- Internet of Things, big data, robotics and artificial intelligence are enhancing self-service deliveries.
- Service businesses must develop strategies for adopting digitization, and this should include an appreciation of the disadvantages, costs, security problems and consequences for employees.
- Online platform businesses have reconfigured capitalism.
- Digitization creates new forms of employment and business models but also destroys jobs and existing business models.

## References

Andres, L., & Bryson, J. R. (2018). Dynamics and City-Region Regeneration Economies: Shaping the Directions of a New Research Agenda. In J. R. Bryson, L. Andres, & R. Mulhall (Eds.), *Research Agenda in Regeneration Economies: Reading City-Regions*. Cheltenham: Edward Elgar.

Arntz, M., Gregory, T., & Zierahn, U. (2016). *The Risk of Automation for Jobs in OECD Countries*. Paris: OECD.

Arthur, W. B. (2009). *The Nature of Technology*. New York: Free Press.

Bacon, F. (1620). *Novum Organum Book 1* (Aphorism 129). London: Ellis & Spedding, edition: 300.

Bitner, M. J., Ostrom, A. L., & Meuter, M. L. (2002). Implementing Successful Self-Service Technologies. *Academy of Management Executive, 16*(4), 96–108.

Brynjolfsson, E., & McAfee, A. (2011). *Race against the Machine: How the Digital Revolution Is Accelerating Innovation, Driving Productivity, and Irreversibly Transforming Employment and the Economy*. Boston: Digital Frontier Press.

Bryson, J. R. (2018). Worker to Robot or Self-Employment and the Gig Economy? Divisions of Labour, Technology and the Transformation of Work. In A. Paasi, J. Harrison, & M. Jones (Eds.), *Handbook on the Geographies of Regions and Territories*. Cheltenham: Edward Elgar.

Bryson, J. R., & Andres, L. (2018). Towards a Research Agenda for City-Region Regeneration Economies: From Artificial Intelligence, the Gig Economy to Air Pollution. In J. R. Bryson, L. Andres, & R. Mulhall (Eds.), *Research Agenda in Regeneration Economies: Reading City-Regions*. Cheltenham: Edward Elgar.

Bryson, J. R., & Ronayne, M. (2014). Manufacturing Carpets and Technical Textiles: Routines, Resources, Capabilities, Adaptation, Innovation and the Evolution of the British Textile Industry. *Cambridge Journal of Regions, Society and Economy, 7*(3), 471–488.

Bryson, J. R., Clark, J., & Mulhall, R. (2017). Beyond the Post-Industrial City? The Third Industrial Revolution, Digital Manufacturing and the Transformation of Homes into Miniature Factories. In K. Nawratek (Ed.), *Urban re-Industrialization*. New York: Punctum.

Catlin, T., Scanlon, J., & Willmott, P. (2015). Realizing Your Digital Quotient. *McKinsey Quarterly*.

Dawson, A., Hirt, M., & Scanlan, J. (2016, March). The Economic Essentials of Digital Strategy. *McKinsey Quarterly*.

Duffy, C., & McEuen, M. B. (2010). The future of meetings: The case for face-to-face. *Cornell Hospitality Industry Perspectives, 1*(6), 6–13.

Fitzgerald, M., Kruschwitz, N., Bonnet, D., & Welch, M. (2014). Embracing Digital Technology: A New Strategic Imperative. *MIT Sloan Management Review, 55*(October), 1–12.

Frey, C. B., & Osborne, M. A. (2013). *The Future of Employment: How Susceptible Are Jobs to Computerisation?* Oxford: Oxford Martin Programme on the Impacts of Future Technology.

Frey, C., & Osbourne, M. A. (2014). *Agiletown: The Relentless March of Technology and London's Response*. London: Deloitte.

Hilbert, M., & López, P. (2011). The World's Technological Capacity to Store, Communicate, and Compute Information. *Science, 332*(6025), 60–65.

Keynes, J. M. (1930a). Economic Possibilities for Our Grandchildren. *The Nation and Athenaeum, 48*(2), 36–37.

Keynes, J. M. (1930b). Economic Possibilities for our Grandchildren II. *The Nation and Athenaeum, 48*(3), 96–98.

Levitt, T. (1972). Production Line Approach to Service. *Harvard Business Review, 50*(5), 41–52.

Manyika, J., Chui, M., Brown, B., Bughin, J., Dobbs, R., Roxburgh, C., & Byers, A. H. (2011). *Big Data: The Next Frontier for Innovation, Competition, and Productivity*. New York: McKinsey Global Institute.

Manyika, J., Ramaswamy, R., Khanna, S., Sarrazin, H., Pinkus, G., Guru, S., & Yaffe, A. (2015). *Digital America: A Tale of the Haves and Have-Mores*. New York: McKinsey Global Institute.

Massey, D. (1984). *Spatial Divisions of Labour: Social Structure and the Geography of Production*. London: Macmillan.

Meuter, M. L., Bitner, M. J., Ostrom, A. L., & Brown, S. W. (2005). Choosing among Alternative Service Delivery Modes: An Investigation of Customer Trial of Self-Service Technologies. *Journal of Marketing, 69*(2), 61–83.

Milner, G. (2016). *Pinpoint: How GPS Is Changing Our World*. London: Granta.

Nedelkoska, L., & Quintini, G. (2018). *Automation, Skills Use and Training*. OECD Social, Employment and Migration Working Papers No. 202. https://doi.org/10.1787/2e2f4eea-en.

Olanrewaju, T., Smaje, K., & Willmott, P. (2014). The Seven Traits of Effective Digital Enterprises. *McKinsey Insights*, 1–7.

Ross, A. (2016). *The Industries of the Future*. New York: Simon & Schuster.

Smith, A. (1977 [orig 1776]). *The Wealth of Nations*. London: Harmondsworth.

Standage, T. (2014). *The Victorian Internet: The Remarkable Story of the Telegraph and the Nineteenth Century's on-Line Pioneers*. London: Bloomsbury Publishing.

Thompson, C. (2019). *Coders: Who They Are, What They Think and How They Are Changing Our World*. London: Picador.

Vanchan, V., Mulhall, R., & Bryson, J. R. (2018). Repatriation or Reshoring of Manufacturing to the US and UK: Dynamics and Global Production Networks or from Here to there and Back Again. *Growth and Change, 49*(1), 97–121.

Zeithaml, V. A., Bitner, M. J., & Gremler, D. D. (2006). *Services Marketing: Integrating Customer Focus across the Firm*. McGraw-Hill/Irwin.

Zhu, Z., Nakatabl, C., Sivakumar, K., & Grewal, D. (2013). Fix It or Leave It? Customer Recovery from Self-Service Technology Failures. *Journal of Retailing, 89*(1), 15–29.

## Further Reading

Breidbach, C., Sunmee, C., Ellway, B., Keating, B., Kormusheva, K., Kowalkowski, C., Lim, C., & Maglio, P. (2018). Operating without Operations: How Is Technology Changing the Role of the Firm. *Journal of Service Management, 29*(5), 809–833.

Čaić, M., Odekerken-Schröder, G., & Mahr, D. (2018). Value Co-creation and Co-destruction in Elderly Care

Networks. *Journal of Service Management, 29*(2), 178–205.

Huang, M.-H., & Rust, R. T. (2018). Artificial Intelligence in Service. *Journal of Service Research, 21*(2), 155–172.

Kenney, M., & Zysman, J. (2020). The Platform Economy: Restructuring the Space of Capitalist Accumulation. *Cambridge Journal of Regions, Economy and Society.* https://doi.org/10.1093/cjres/rsaa001.

Wirtz, J., Patterson, P., Kunz, W., Gruber, T., Lu, V. N., Paluch, S., & Martins, A. (2018). Brave New World:

Service Robots in the Frontline. *Journal of Service Management, 29*(5), 907–931.

## Useful Websites

http://www.businessdictionary.com/definition/technology.html#ixzz3l9dEZbF2.

https://www.internetsociety.org/ota/.

https://ifr.org/service-robots.

# Service Operations and Productivity

## Key Themes

- How are service operations organized, and how is productivity growth achieved?
- How is value created and what types of values are created by service businesses?
- Divisions of labour and timeless theory
- Emergence of service operations management
- The services duality: production- and product-related services
- Service operations, the industrialization of services and artificial intelligence
- Service operations, back and front regions and the McDonaldization thesis
- Network learning and knowledge-intensive services
- Services, productivity, quality and value

Reading service businesses involves the development of an integrated or systemic approach that recognizes the complex interrelationships between a firm's business model or models (see Chap. 3), operational delivery, marketing and customer relationship management (see Chaps. 8 and 9), creating and managing service experiences, financial management, business strategy (see Chap. 3), process and product innovation (see Chap. 7) and internationalization (see Chap. 10). It is possible to identify a firm's core

**Electronic Supplementary Material** The online version of this chapter (https://doi.org/10.1007/978-3-030-52060-1_5) contains supplementary material, which is available to authorized users.

business functions or domains and activity systems and to explore each of these in turn, but then it is important to consider these as a complex whole (see Chap. 14). The relationship between operations and productivity highlights the interdependencies that work together to produce successful or less successful business outcomes.

At the core of any service business are two sets of processes. First, there is the business model or the firm's focus on delivering products and services to realize some type of value (see Chap. 3). It is important to note that the business model literature is a development of the strategy literature. Second, there is the operational delivery of the business model. This includes processes, practices and routines. The relationship between a service business model and operational delivery determines a firm's profitability and productivity. The primary measure of a firm's success is its profitability rather than productivity. Productivity is a measure of process or operational efficiency and can be applied to firms, organizations or nations as one measure of the relationship between the production of services and goods and the factors of production or inputs (land, labour, machinery, raw materials including components). It is a measure of the relationship between outputs and inputs and is consequently a measure of a firm's efficiency or ability to convert inputs into profits. Productivity is an analytical tool used by governments and academics with the emphasis placed on the efficient or inefficient use of resource inputs. For governments, an increase in the national standard of living reflects an improvement in productivity. This link between the national economy, living standards and productivity explains the emphasis that is placed by government on measuring and enhancing productivity.

This chapter explores service operations management focusing on the on-going application of operational innovations to the delivery of service outcomes. This is a complex process. Different innovations have been applied to firms that are producing different types of services. Innovative solutions to improve service operational performance reflect current developments in product and process innovation. This discussion of service operations is then placed in the context of the on-going debate over service productivity.

## 5.1   Emergence of Service Operations Management

Operations management emerged as an academic discipline and practice to enhance the efficiency of manufacturing production processes. Much of the early history of operations management can be traced back to the work of Frederick Winslow Taylor (1856–1915), the father of Scientific Management and of 'Taylorism'. Taylor's contribution to management practice rests on a combination of four related principles (Bryson 2000, p. 167):

1. The application of time and motion studies to understanding the everyday performance and delivery of organizational routines and practices which demystified skills by standardizing work tools and practices by dividing production processes into their simplest constituent tasks. This is a practical shop floor application of the division of labour via the identification and timing of discrete tasks that combined result in the delivery of complex production processes.
2. Once the tasks are identified and standardized, then each task should be undertaken by employees best suited to the tasks. This often

involves the development of a least cost worker solution to the task delivery process.
3. Supervisors, and an incentive system based on differential rates, ensure that the scientifically determined task is matched to the right employee.
4. The execution of the work is separated from its conception. Control, and understanding of each task, is transferred from employees to a planning department and to a supervisor.

The work of Taylor led to the establishment of consultancy firms and alternative time and motion approaches to the management of operations.

Taylorism, and the emergence of scientific management, was part of the separation of ownership from control with the professionalization of management tasks, the establishment of business schools and the emergence and growth of management consultancy. Both business schools and management consultancy firms play a critical role in creating and transferring management theory and techniques between firms and countries (Bryson 2000, p. 173) by operating as bridges between competing companies and countries.

Service operations management (SOM) is part of a much older debate on operations management. SOM emerged relatively late reflecting the dominance of manufacturing-based perspectives in business schools. Originally, operations had been considered to be an engineering rather than a business and management issue, and this further intensified the focus on manufacturing.

Initially, services were included in debates over the importance of understanding the marketing of services as intangibles (Lovelock 1991; Grönroos 2000); the debate on marketing became one of the dominant accounts of services in the business and management literature. An earlier debate had emerged in economic geography that focused on understanding the growth and location of service industries (Daniels 1982). Nevertheless, the focus of the operational management literature was predominantly on manufacturing. Thus, in a review of the service management literature, Metters and Marucheck (2007) highlighted that:

Amoako-Gyampah and Meredith (1989) noted service operations was the subject of only 6% of manuscripts in 10 journals from 1982 to 1987. Pamnirselvam, Ferguson, Ash and Siferd (1999) stated that service operations was the topic in only 3% of publications in seven OM journals from 1992 to 1997 ... Machuca, Gonzalez-Zamora, and Aguilar-Escobar (2007) surveyed 10 OM journals from 1997 to 2002 and found service operations composed 7.5% of all articles. (2007, p. 200)

In an article that reflects on the neglect of services in the operations management field, Metters noted that the management of supply chains 'has been an organizing principle for the field' (2010, p. 314). This is an important point. Here it is worth noting the substantial literature that has emerged not only on supply chain management, but also on global value chains and global production networks (see Chaps. 10 and 11). There is no question that these are important debates. It is worth noting that research on supply chains has focused on inter-firm relationships or on exploring the management of transactions that cross organizational boundaries with an emphasis on the movement of raw materials and components rather than service inputs. Service operations management includes supply chain management as it is important to understand inputs into the service delivery process. Nevertheless, supply chain management must be applied to understanding the ways in which service supply chains function. In addition, it is important to develop an intra-firm analysis of the creation and delivery of service outputs.

## 5.2   The Services Duality: Production- and Product-Related Services

The development of innovations in service operations and the management of service operations is an important aspect of all firms. Service operations flow throughout all organizations. We first must differentiate between the management of inter- and intra-firm operations. The former involves the management of relationships with other firms. This includes manufacturing firms managing service inputs provided by other firms.

This involves the identification of potential suppliers, managing the selection process and then developing the client and service provider relationship. This also includes service-to-service supply chain relationships. The latter involves the development, enhancement and management of all internal service operations. This is a complex process.

Intra-service operations management involves a complex set of processes. All manufacturing firms contain significant service functions. This is to argue for the appreciation of the existence of a 'services duality' that 'recognizes that services are entwined within production processes, but at many different stages' (Bryson and Daniels 2010, p. 92). This duality highlights the importance of production-related services or services that are intermediate inputs into a company's production process and product-related services that are directly linked to the sale of a service or a good, for example, training, product support, finance agreements including insurance (Bryson and Daniels 2010, pp. 91–93) (Fig. 5.1) (see Chap. 12). It is important to develop an overall understanding of the ways in which service tasks contribute to value creation in firms. It is worth developing the example of the legal firm that we considered in Chap. 3 (see Sect. 3.9). This firm engaged in three types of service tasks that combined account for this firm's competitiveness and productivity.

First, there are service tasks and processes that support the firm's delivery of client services. These are production-related services including accounting, human resource management, facilities management, information communication technologies (ICT) and procurement. These supporting services are critical for service delivery and the management of the law firm. Innovations in operational delivery of these services will enhance profitability. These services are not directly fee earning, but support fee-earning lawyers. Nevertheless, some firms will provide supporting services to other firms. For example, a manufacturing firm with an in-house design team will provide design services to support the firm's creation and delivery of products to customers, but the design team may also sell design services to other firms.

| | | | |
|---|---|---|---|
| –Management functions | –Management functions | –Management functions | –Management functions |
| –Information searching | –Packaging design | Trade fairs and exhibitions | –Servicing |
| –R&D | –Logistics | Consultants | –Software |
| –Engineers | –Supply chain management | –Marketing mix | –Recycling |
| –Designers | –Product development | | Updating products |
| –Testing | –Production design | | |
| | –Quality control | | |
| | –Product development | | |
| Design process > Design prototype | Production process > Product | Circulation > Packaged product | Consuming customizing > |
| –Material inputs | –Material inputs | –Packaging | –Training |
| –Finance | –Technical knowledge | –Logistics | –Provision of content |
| –Expertise | –Capital (finance and funding—revenue) | –Supply chain management | –Provision of additional services to support goods |
| –Technical inputs | –Land | –Marketing channels | –Finance packaging including leasing |
| | –Labour | –Finance | |
| | –Machines | | |
| Pre-production | During Production | Marketing/selling/distribution | Consumption |
| | **Production-related services** | | **Product-related services** |

Source: Authors' own

**Fig. 5.1**  The services duality: Production and other product-related services

Second, there are legal services that have been converted into price-sensitive commodities. This reflects a process of commoditization in which goods and services are no longer purchased by clients based on some distinctive feature, for example, branding, quality, special expertise, but are purchased based on price. Such goods and services have been transformed into simple price-sensitive commodities. There is a tension here that all firms need to manage between products and services which are sold not solely based on price compared to products and services that have been commoditized. Firms must continually resist this process of commoditization by product and process innovation. Commoditization is a result of enhanced competition in which competitors compete on price. This also includes firms that copy existing products and services. It also emerges through innovations that may transform products or services into simple commodities. The application of supply chain management, including procurement processes, can also transform intermediate inputs into price-sensitive commodities.

Legal services that are funded through legal aid, or the provision of state funding to individuals unable to pay for legal representation in criminal, housing, family, immigration and other cases, are the prime legal services that have been subjected to a process of commoditization driven by reductions in barristers' and solicitors' hourly rates for legal aid work. For some types of legal services, legal aid is no longer provided using hourly rates, but fixed rates have been imposed. For law firms, the provision of commoditized legal services requires a focus on economies of scale and on process efficiency. One impact of the long-term decline in legal aid funding has been consolidation amongst smaller firms and the acquisition of smaller firms by larger firms.

Third are high value-added legal services that are customized to meet the needs of an individual client and are sold not on price but on reputation and quality. These have very different operational delivery systems compared to commoditized legal services. These services are partly based on reputation and relationship networks developed by individual lawyers and partly based on a process of continual innovation that is intended to differentiate one lawyer or law practice from another. An innovative legal service may eventually become commoditized as competitors alter the conditions of competition for this service or as clients no longer consider these to be high value-added intermediate inputs.

The realization that the development of service work, and service dominant production processes, required a focus on exploring service operations can be traced back to articles published by Levitt (1972) and Sullivan (1982) that explored the need for research on SOM. Levitt's paper on the development of a production-line approach to services was especially important. It remains one of the most cited papers on services and was path-breaking in its identification of the application of industrial processes to service operations. It is to this focus on the industrialization of services that we now turn our attention.

## 5.3  Service Operations, the Industrialization of Services and Artificial Intelligence

### 5.3.1  Industrialization, Service Operations

Services are very different to the production and delivery of goods. For services the product is often the operational process and for many services this process is co-created, and production and consumption occur simultaneously. Thus, the argument is that services are immediate, experiential and intangible. This also means that the geography of service creation is closely related to the location of the producer. Increasingly, service production and consumption have become dislocated with developments in ICT. The location of the service provider is still an important factor in the development of a service operational delivery system. One reading of service businesses highlights their labour rather than capital intensity.

Nevertheless, innovations are increasing the capital intensity of service delivery systems and reducing or controlling labour intensity. This reflects the substitution of labour with technology and the application of technology to act as an intermediary between service producers and consumers.

Levitt's article on service industrialization begins by arguing that 'there are no such things as service industries. There are only industries whose service components are greater or less than those of other industries. Everyone is in service' (1972, pp. 41–42). This is reflected not only in the concept of a services duality (Bryson and Daniels 2010), but also in the service-dominant logic (S-D) perspective (Vargo and Lusch 2004; Vargo et al. 2010). The fundamental premise of the S-D approach is the same as Levitt's statement that 'everyone is in service', but there is an important distinction (see Chap. 2). In the S-D perspective, all exchanges are based on services. In this analysis, purchasing goods is the acquisition of physical things providing consumers with services. In this account, direct service-for-service exchange is often hidden by a complex set of intermediaries associated with exchange including goods, money and organizations. The shift from a goods-dominant logic to an S-D logic perspective is one that emphasizes a shift from a focus on tangible to intangible resources and from a focus on exchange that is dynamic rather than static. Purchasing a good is a static transaction involving the exchange of an artefact while a service involves an on-going dynamic process of co-creation.

The key argument in Levitt's paper rests on a comparison between services and manufacturing. This mirrors the service-dominant distinction between goods-dominant and service-dominant logic. To Levitt:

> Service (whether customer service or the services of service industries) is performed "out there in the field" by distant and loosely supervised people working under highly variable, and often volatile conditions. Manufacturing occurs "here in the factory" under highly centralised, carefully organized, tightly controlled, and elaborately engineered conditions. (1972, p. 42)

The argument is that services should be considered as manufacturing in the field and that operational solutions should be developed to enhance service delivery and operational efficiency. There are many examples of 'manufacturing' solutions to the delivery of services. These include e-commerce and the application of Big Data to predict and influence consumer behaviour. They include credit cards in which a single decision to issue a credit card replaces many individual decisions regarding the application of credit to individual acts of consumption (Levitt 1972, p. 46).

The primary example developed by Levitt of the application of a manufacturing in the field perspective to services is through the analysis of McDonald's and fast food. The key question set by Levitt is 'why each separate McDonald's outlet is so predictably successful and why each is so certain to attract repeat customers?' (1972, p. 44). The answer to this question is that McDonald's has transformed a people-intensive service, through the application of a manufacturing perspective, into an industrialized process. This transformation includes a system that is focused on standardization and quality and the removal of individual discretion in service delivery. This involves automation of the tasks required to deliver every order, and the development of a distinctive but standardized design that is applied to each McDonald's outlet.

The industrialization of services is an ongoing process that has been applied to service tasks that can be standardized. Service delivery can be undertaken in back offices with no face-to-face interactions with customers. The rise of back offices, including data processing centres and customer-facing call centres, is one part of the industrialization of service tasks but also the internationalization of service tasks (see Chap. 10). Remote provision of service tasks can be undertaken in the same country as the consumer or from long distances. Back offices and call centres were only one stage in the industrialization of services, and this has been followed by the application of algorithms to the delivery of service tasks by the identification of sets of rules and calculations performed by automated systems (see Chap. 4).

More recently developments in deep learning, or the neural networks approach to machine learning, are beginning to transform the industrialization of services. Deep learning is based on the application of algorithms that explore substantial amounts of data—often Big Data or a continual stream of data—to make decisions to optimize desired outcomes. The algorithm trains itself to identify patterns and correlations by identifying connections between many different data points. Deep learning is defined as 'narrow' AI as it is based on the analysis of a specific data stream to develop an optimized outcome. Narrow AI is limited to the algorithm and the data compared to AI that might eventually be able to replicate human decision-making processes. Deep learning can be applied to many different service tasks including finance to identify patterns amongst potential borrowers to minimize default rates. Another example is the application of deep learning to optimize logistic systems including identifying delivery routes. The application of deep learning to services is just beginning and will continue to transform the operational delivery systems of all services that involve significant quantities of big data that can be used to model decision-making processes.

## 5.3.2  Productivity, IT and AI

The industrialization of services, and the application of AI and ICT to the delivery of service tasks, is directly related to service industry productivity. There are two points to note here. First, technological innovation, including AI, alters the wider framework conditions that support economic activity. One consequence is that opportunities to create new services have emerged that were impossible. One example is the development of on-line streaming services including Netflix, Amazon Video, Hulu Live, Sling TV, DirecTV Now, PlayStation Vue and YouTube. Second, technological innovation enables the redesign of existing service delivery systems enhancing productivity combined with alterations in the service values co-created with customers.

According to Karmarker, all the driving factors that led to the industrialization of manufacturing tasks are now applicable to information production processes (2004, 2010). They include, on the one hand, push factors or technologic innovation including the seamless integration of communication systems with digital processing and data storage enabling end-to-end integration of information between places, companies and people. On the other hand, they include pull factors that come from the 'actions of firms both established and new, to compete more effectively and to create markets and profits' (2010, p. 424). In 2004, Karmarker identified seven strategies developed by firms to industrialize service tasks:

1. Automation often in response to technological development
2. Outsourcing
3. Offshoring and the geographic redistribution of tasks
4. Process reengineering including modularization
5. Service redesign including the standardization of services
6. Operations including shifting tasks in information processing chains
7. Self-service as an example of a specific form of task shifting

These strategies are similar to approaches developed and applied to manufacturing tasks, but self-service and task shifting are more prevalent in the delivery of services. These seven strategies are underpinned by the application of a division of labour to service tasks. Automation, outsourcing and reshoring involve dividing tasks into sub-routines and identifying which can be automated or outsourced. Modularization is based on the subdivision of tasks into discrete modules, while service redesign focuses on identifying which tasks in a service delivery chain can be standardized. Self-service alters the balance in the division of labour between producers and consumers.

Developments in the application of online platforms to services represent a very sophisticated approach to the industrialization of services

that also supports internationalization (see Chap. 10). These include automated chatbots or a form of AI which engages in a text- or voice-based discussion with customers. Chatbots try to replicate human conversational interactions and try to meet the threshold set by the Turing test. This test was developed by Alan Turing (1950) to test the ability of a machine to replicate intelligent behaviour that was equivalent to, or indistinguishable from, that of a human.

Platforms have developed approaches to 'collaborative filtering' as part of the development of a platform's choice architecture. Platforms like Amazon, YouTube and Google have millions and even billions of possible consumer choices. An effective platform will have developed a choice architecture that enables customers to search easily by using preferences. Such platforms try to shape consumer decisions by nudges. A nudge 'is any aspect of the choice architecture that alters people's behaviour in a predictable way without forbidding any options or significantly changing their economic incentives' (Thaler and Sunstein 2009, p. 6). Nudges are interventions that are inexpensive and easy to ignore. Platforms analyse customer behaviour and make recommendations to users based on the preferences of other users. Collaborative filtering is at work when a platform recommends other products and services to be considered by possible consumers. This technique alters the nature of the service delivered by a platform; each platform will provide a different set of recommendations based on that platform's assessment of a consumer's preferences compared to other consumers. It also enhances the platform's effectiveness by targeting consumers with nudges contributing to improvements in productivity; one sale may through collaborative filtering lead to additional purchases. Collaborative filtering is one example of the application of AI and deep learning to platforms that is intended to enhance consumer experiences simultaneously increasing profits and the platform's competitive position in the marketplace.

Algorithms, combined with a continual stream of live data, enable companies to apply dynamic pricing to the sale of services (Grewal et al.

2011). This type of pricing strategy is also termed surge pricing, demand pricing or time-based pricing. The live data streams of past and current demand for the supply of a product or service enable a business to alter prices in response to current demand. An algorithm is developed that alters prices in real time based on supply and demand and is sometimes informed by competitor pricing. Uber uses dynamically adjusted prices for the pricing of its services and prices reflect supply or the availability of Uber drivers and demand in real time. Airline prices alter depending on the time of day, day of the week, days left before departure, the number of seats available, the departure time and an average based on profit generation from similar flights. Dynamic pricing is also applied to the sale of electricity, entertainment and public transport. In 2019, Albert Heijn, the Dutch supermarket, began to experiment with an algorithm that provided shoppers with dynamic discounts related to a product's expiry date. These discounts increased the closer the product was to its expiry date. This is an interesting example of a business acting responsibly to minimize waste, but at the same time to increase profits.

In Singapore, an area licensing scheme (ALS) was introduced in 1975 to restrict entry into the city centre. This was based on the display of a paper license on the windscreen and enforcement officers were stationed at entry control points. This was a labour-intensive scheme with enforcement officers exposed to air pollution, noise and heat. In 1998, this manual system was replaced with an automated Electronic Road Pricing (ERP) system (Singh 2017). The ERP is a pay-as-you-use system in which motorists are charged for the use of priced roads during peak hours. The rates vary for different roads and depend on local traffic conditions. Similarly, tolls to use the San Francisco Bay Bridge vary depending on the hour and the day. During periods of peak demand, the charging structure reduces demand, but also increases revenue. This system also encourages drivers to travel during periods of reduced demand by distributing demand throughout the day. The ERP system contains hardware including computers, display screens and cables and a consumer or user interface. This reflects a system based on combining activities that are hidden to the consumer—back room activities—and front room activities.

## 5.4  Service Operations, Back and Front Regions and the McDonaldization Thesis

A service delivery chain can be divided into front and back regions. This duality comes from the work of Goffman who argued that people perform 'roles' (sister/brother, son/daughter, teacher, management consultant, computer scientist, etc.) and that these roles are created through interactions that occur between *back* and *front regions* (see Chap. 6). In most cases, an individual is only aware of what is occurring in a front region (Goffman 1984, pp. 109–140). Front regions are places where performances are given and, for services, these performances are often service experiences that are enacted in service spaces. A back region is a place that is 'relative to a given performance, where the impression fostered by the performance is knowingly contradicted as a matter of course' (Goffman 1984. p. 114). In the back region the performance may be created, illusions and impressions will be openly constructed, and props and equipment stored. The front region might be site of fantasy, theatre, fun, control and the co-creation of service experiences by consumers and producers. The back region could be a back office that is heavily industrialized, and which is required to deliver the service outputs that are experienced in front regions.

The service literature has tended to concentrate on understanding the co-creation of services in the front regions of service production systems (Bryson and Daniels 2010) at the expense perhaps of exploring back regions and the interplay between back and front regions. Facing services tend to be consumed and partially produced in front regions, but are also partially planned, designed, supported and delivered in back regions. The shift towards the industrialization of services reflects alterations in the distribution of service tasks between the front and back regions of a service delivery chain.

One account of alterations in the balance between front and back office regions was identified in 1983 by George Ritzer and developed in 1993 as the McDonaldization thesis (Ritzer 1993). This is a sociological thesis that has been largely ignored in the business and management literature. In sociology a substantial literature developed based on this thesis that focused on understanding the wider McDonaldization of economic activity and of society in general. It is worth noting that Ritzer appears to have been unaware of Levitt's 1972 account of the emergence of McDonald's production-line approach to service delivery. The McDonaldization thesis, however, is not about McDonald's or even about fast food restaurants. Instead,

> McDonald's serves here as the major example, the paradigm, of a wide-ranging process I call McDonaldization, - that is, the process by which the principles of the fast-food restaurant are coming to dominate more and more sectors of American society as well as the rest of the world. (Ritzer 2000, p. 1)

McDonaldization is an approach to service operations management that affects not only restaurants but also financial services, education, health care, retailing, travel, leisure, politics and virtually all economic sectors.

The McDonaldization thesis is a development of Max Weber's broader theory of the rationalization process. To Weber capitalism is a system based not on the maximization of profit, but on unlimited accumulation and the rationale organization of production and work (1968). Bureaucracy (1968) is used by Weber as a model for the study of rationalization and Ritzer uses the fast-food restaurant in the same way as a model for understanding McDonaldization. To Weber, capitalism has developed a distinctive form of rationality based on bureaucracy that has several structural traits. These include cooperation amongst many individuals with each undertaking a specialist function. A bureaucrat's function is distinct from family life and is impersonal. This function is undertaken according to a

set of rules and regulations which implies that a bureaucracy operates in a highly predictable manner. Weber's definition of capitalism is one based on enterprises that are focused on the unlimited accumulation of profit and that function according to a rationality that is embedded in a bureaucratic process. Ritzer's account of Weber's bureaucratic rationality identifies four basic dimensions of rationality that are also applied to McDonaldization (Ritzer 2000, pp. 23–24). These are as follows:

1. A bureaucracy is the most efficient structure for handling large numbers of tasks.
2. A bureaucracy is based on the quantification of many things. The quantification of tasks enables a bureaucracy to measure success including productivity.
3. Bureaucracies are based on well-entrenched rules and regulations that result in predictability.
4. Bureaucracies control people through the replacement of human judgement with rules, regulations, structures and the application of a division of labour which allocates a limited number of tasks to each position.

The final point builds on the division of labour; the identification of discrete tasks is the first stage in substituting people by machines and ultimately by AI and deep learning.

A similar approach is adopted by Ritzer to developing the McDonaldization thesis. Thus, four dimensions are central to this thesis that come from an analysis of McDonald's. These four dimensions can be applied to many different types of production process. These are *efficiency, calculability, predictability and control*. The first dimension, efficiency, highlights that workers employed in McDonaldized systems 'function efficiently following the steps in a predesigned process' (Ritzer 2000, p. 12). The system is designed for the efficient delivery of a service output with an emphasis on time efficiency. The second dimension emphasizes the quantitative aspects of the production system based on calculability. This includes a focus on the quantitative rather than qualitative aspects of work. Quality is built into the system as this is regulated and controlled by operational processes. The third dimension is predictability or a system that ensures that all products and services that are provided are the same irrespective of the location or the time of purchase. This predictability is not only part of the product, but also a feature of the rules and regulations that control the conditions of employment. The fourth dimension is control through the application of nonhuman technology to the service delivery system. This includes not only the application of a division of labour, but also the regulation of work and the production of products by machines. In a McDonald's restaurant decisions made by human beings have been replaced by machines including 'the french fry machine that rings and lifts the basket out of the oil when the fries are crisp, the programmed cash register that eliminates the need for the cashier to calculate prices and amounts, and perhaps at some future time, the robot capable of making hamburgers' (Ritzer 2000, p. 15).

The four dimensions of McDonaldization provide a framework for considering the design and management of McDonaldization-style service production operations. It provides an approach to exploring the interface between employees and the application of nonhuman technologies to control and regulate routines and everyday practices required to produce service tasks or sets of service tasks. The focus is on the creation of efficient systems that are highly controlled to deliver relatively standardized products and services.

There are obvious problems with this approach. Perhaps the most important is the emphasis that is based on the design of rational systems. Thus, it is important to consider that all systems experience path dependency reflecting the impacts of decisions made in the past on current and future decisions. Path dependency can prevent the continuation of a system that was initially designed around Ritzer's four dimensions. In addition, all firms suffer from information asymmetry that is reflected in bounded rationality. This bounded rationality may limit the ability of a firm to maximize system operationality. Combined path dependency and bounded ratio-

nality lead to sunk costs that make it difficult, in some cases impossible, for a firm to make dramatic alterations to its business model and operational procedures. Sunk costs are costs that have been incurred by a business that cannot be recovered. These investments constrain future investments. They also provide opportunities for new firms to develop alternative approaches to providing similar services that might out-compete existing firms that are unable to rapidly alter their business model and service operations.

## 5.5 Networking Learning and Knowledge-Intensive Services

The application of Ritzer's approach to understanding service operations highlights a tension between the production of standardized service experiences compared to highly customized experiences. This suggests that a different approach is required to understanding service operations in service delivery chains that are based on the co-creation of knowledge-intensive services. Here it is important to differentiate between knowledge-intensive services that focus on the provision of 'recipe knowledge' rather than unique solutions to particular problems (Bryson and Daniels 2015b, pp. 426–428). These recipes are learnt either formally or informally. Formal acquisition includes training provided during the acquisition of a professional qualification and informal reflects the adaptation or translation of recipes in everyday practice.

Service operations within knowledge-intensive business services (KIBS), or business-to-business (B2B) service providers, combine the application of recipes that can be imitated by competitors with the ability to provide creative solutions. The challenge for a KIBS firm involves developing effective operational procedures to deliver recipe knowledge that might have been subjected to a commoditization process versus the creation of innovative solutions (Gardner and Bryson 2020). One approach to understanding the mechanisms and processes underpinning value co-creation in KIBS is to explore four basic questions that can be applied to all production processes (Bryson and Rusten 2011, p. 18):

- What is produced?
- How is the production process organized?
- Where are the tasks required to produce the product or service located?
- Exploring alterations over time in the 'what', 'how' and 'where'.

These questions add extra dimensions to reading service businesses. This approach is similar to that adopted by Füller (2010) and Breidbach and Maglio (2016) to exploring value creation through examining three core constructs: actors (who?), resources (what?) and practices (how?).

There are two points to consider. The first involves exploring responses to commoditization or the translation of high value-added knowledge into recipe knowledge that is sold increasingly on price. One difficulty facing the Big 4 accountancy firms (PwC, Deloitte, Ernst & Young and KPMG) is that 'the reality to clients buying services from the Big 4 [is that] they all look the same' (Hollis 2015, p. 66). There are many ways of trying to overcome the pressures related to commoditization. A firm can focus on developing a highly distinctive brand but can also continually invest to develop new innovative service products that replace those that have been commoditized. Alternatively, firms can compete by investing in the development of relationships with actual and potential clients. Relationships reflect an accumulation of interactions between people. These interactions include those directly related to work and social interactions. To Hollis, 'the single biggest challenge that professional service firms face is being able to differentiate their products and services' (2015, p. 77). His solution is the development of good client relationship-handling skills that recognize the importance of two distinct categories of relationship skill:

*Relationship builders*: Professionals who link clients with the expertise inputs required.
*Challengers*: Professionals with excellent relationship-handling skills, but these relationships are used to challenge potential and actual clients.

The argument is that B2B firms need to shift from a focus on developing relationship builders to relationship challengers. It is the challengers that will develop high value-added business opportunities with higher margins. It is these challengers that will develop innovative solutions to new problems facing clients.

The second point to consider is operational procedures that enhance the ability of a KIBS provider to innovate. KIBS firms used to be conceptualized as providers of B2B service inputs that were expertise- or labour-intensive rather than capital-intensive. Establishing a KIBS firm was considered to have very low capital barriers to entry, but high relationship barriers. Thus, a consultancy firm competes on the reputation and relational networks of their primary fee earners. KIBS firms were considered to be local firms providing co-created solutions to customers. Developments in ICT have enabled 'economic actors to exchange resources, and thereby cocreate value, through virtual rather than physical interfaces' (Breidbach and Maglio 2016, p. 73) resulting in the development of technology-enabled value creation processes. There is a tension here. On the one hand, client service provider interactions are based on face-to-face (F2F) encounters that create trust and that enable a challenger within a KIBS firm to persuade clients to consider altering some dimensions of their business with the assistance of B2B inputs. On the other hand, there are developments in ICT that potentially challenge local production processes and that could undermine and replace trust-based face-to-face relationships.

This tension can be reconciled by appreciating that a technology-enabled value creation process may be invisible to a client. This might reduce the cost of service delivery through the application of a spatial division of labour and/or increasing the quality by developing a distinctive blend of expertise, information or knowledge inputs. In an analysis of six consulting firms, Breidbach and Maglio (2016) identify different roles played by the actors involved in the delivery of a project.

These included 'conductors' who operate as a single point of contact for interactions within a consultancy team and 'governors' who undertake a similar role in client companies. The key point of this paper is to differentiate between roles that are based on F2F encounters and those that involve being part of a technology-enabled value creation process. The latter includes videoconferences, telephone calls and e-mails. This is a paper that highlights the contribution ICT makes to project delivery, operations and management, but F2F encounters remains a critical part of the process, but 'although F2F remained an exception, individual actors were exposed to more F2F contact if their roles were related to the facilitation or coordination of the value co-creation process' (Breidbach and Maglio 2016, p. 80). This is a process that blends back with front office functions.

The Breidbach and Maglio approach is positioned within the marketing literature, but there is another on-going debate in operations management that makes an important contribution to understanding the application of ICT to service delivery systems. In this analysis, firms deploy different types of inter- and intra-firm network learning to create value and to manage global operations (Brady and Davies 2004; Galbraith 2014; Zhang et al. 2016). Network learning includes people-based encounters based on trust-based relationships that are used to transfer information and knowledge within and between firms, but it also includes the development of technological solutions in the form of intra-firm knowledge management systems.

Network learning facilitates the creation of knowledge by blending inputs from across a distributed firm's network to create new knowledge or to develop a distributed, but customized client-focused project team that is assembled to develop a required solution for a client. This process of network learning can be informal or be very carefully managed. The most successful firms will have an employee or team responsible for the management of the firm's network learning architecture (Love et al. 2011). Knowledge boundary spanners were identified by Brown and Duguid (1998) as playing an

important role in facilitating knowledge sharing and in developing social relationships that support network learning. Boundary spanners operate as knowledge brokers as well as translators as they identify opportunities to apply a firm's experience and expertise to develop novel client solutions. The translation role is complex as this requires understanding the client, and the ability to challenge the client, combined with understanding the KIBS firm's distributed expertise, information and knowledge base. Boundary spanning tools can be applied to support the network learning process as these include repositories, standardized forms and methods and approaches to documenting and indexing a firm's existing information and knowledge base (Hislop 2009). Network learning provides opportunities for firms to learn and this learning may lead to improvements in service quality and productivity. It is to these operational processes that we now turn our attention.

## 5.6  Services, Productivity, Quality and Value

### 5.6.1  Productivity in Services

In his economic theory of services, Baumol (1967; see also Baumol et al. 1989) distinguishes 'progressive' services (those oriented towards the application of technology in production and which can therefore achieve improved rates of output per capita) from 'non-progressive' services in which substitution of technology for labour is impossible. In relation to the latter, the nature of the production process determines that the work performed (such as a ballet or an opera) cannot be speeded up or abbreviated in the interests of improved productivity by reducing the number of dancers or performers. These types of alterations would be unacceptable to those watching or listening to the performance. There is therefore very little scope for productivity improvements of the kind possible in 'progressive 'services, where innovation, economies of scale or developments in ICT, for example, can be adopted to achieve increases in productivity. The overall implication is that over time services become more costly relative to goods. This reflects the existence of a productivity gap between goods and progressive services, on the one hand, compared to non-progressive services, on the other. If it is assumed that the demand for services is inelastic to price, but that demand will continue to increase as living standards rise then there will be a steady transfer of employment from the progressive to the non-progressive parts of the economy. The result is not only a general shift of employment from manufacturing to services but also a shift from the progressive to the non-progressive sectors within services.

The Baumol model has the attraction of simplicity but it does assume that measures of output and productivity used for progressive activities are not readily transferable to non-progressive activities. Recent advances in ICT imply that many service activities are much more open to the substitution of new technology and economies of scale, thus diminishing the credibility of the 'productivity gap' thesis that is central to Baumol's case. There is a direct link between the application of technology to the delivery of services and improvements in productivity. The challenge is that productivity is 'easy to define but difficult to measure' (Djellal and Gallouj 2008, p. 3) and this is especially the case for the measurement of productivity in services. Productivity is defined as the relationship between the output of the processes that lead to the production of a service or good and the factors of production or inputs into the production process; productivity is a measure of the rate of output per unit of input. Thus, productivity is a simple measure of the efficiency of a production process, of a firm and of a national economy. Productivity is a comparative measure based on the comparative assessment of productivity alterations.

For services, the concept of productivity and its measurement come with major challenges (Table 5.1). First, the production of a physical good produces an easily definable and measurable output, but this is not the case for all ser-

**Table 5.1** Service characteristics and their impacts on productivity

| Characteristic | Impact on productivity measurement |
|---|---|
| Value systems | Different outputs and different performances based on differences between producers and consumers and also differences in the co-creation of service experiences and consumer perceptions of these experiences. |
| Subjective outputs | The value placed on a service output varies by the quality assigned to the service by the consumer. There are great difficulties in defining service quality; every consumer will have a different perception of the service experience. It is difficult to separate service outputs from the production process. |
| Temporal effects | Lag times exist between the delivery of the service and the creation of value for clients. Thus, an undergraduate degree or a consultancy project may create impacts over an extended period. |
| Cannot be stored | Services are consumed as they are produced. The impact is an alteration in some state, but different consumers may perceive this change in state in very different ways. The perception of the producer may be very different regarding what has been delivered. The inability to store services makes it difficult to identify the relationships between production inputs and outputs. |
| Co-production of services | The co-production of services makes it difficult to identify the parameters required to measure productivity. No two haircuts or consultancy products are alike. Differences will occur between customer perceptions of the service output—some change in state. Consumers with different attitudes to a service will receive, or perceive they have received, different qualities of service. It is difficult to isolate the contribution made by consumers compared to that of service providers. Different consumers will create different values during the service co-creation process. Industrialized services try to exclude consumers from the co-production process, but the service will still be co-produced in some way. |

Source: After Djellal and Gallouj (2008, pp. 32–40)

vices. For many services it is difficult, often impossible, to define a single unit of output; each unit of output is often shared between many individual consumers. Thus, attendance at a performance is shared by many individuals. To complicate matters the quality of the experience is often related to the interactions between the audience and the performers. Second, improving productivity in the fabrication of a physical good should not have a material impact on quality. For services there is a danger that an alteration in service operations to enhance productivity will reduce the quality of the service output. This is an important point that must be considered in all operational alterations intended to enhance service productivity. Replacing an F2F service encounter with call centre provision, or with an automated system, produces a major alteration in the nature of the service that is delivered. This is to emphasize that for services the output that is delivered to the consumer is produced by a process that involves the consumer in some way. This is not the case with goods; for goods the final consumer plays a passive or invisible role in the production process. Any alteration in the service delivery process may impact on service quality. The key point to reflect on here is the relationship between productivity and service quality (Grönroos and Ojasalo 2004).

It has been argued that in some economic encounters the concept of productivity loses its validity. Thus, productivity has no meaning in understanding creative processes (Djellal and Gallouj 2010). The output of a creative process should be valued not on the relationship between inputs and outputs, but in relation to the quality of the creative experience. This is to highlight that a focus on productivity might produce a contradictory outcome by reducing the quality and value of the service output. This is to raise the important and complex issue of value and the types of values that are produced by the production and sale of goods compared to services. Purchasing and using a good provides the owner with experiences that are co-created in the interaction between the user and the good. The good also provides the consumer with symbolic value contributing to the presentation and construction

of their identity. This includes clothing, cars and housing. A service provides an experience through a process of user interaction. This is similar to the experiences delivered by goods, but the difference is that service experiences cannot be transferred and the consumption of additional units of a service will require additional monetary exchange and the co-creation of another service encounter.

The difficulty is that economics has much to say about price but nothing to say about value (Slater and Tonkiss 2001, p. 49). Value involves trust, sharing, community and is performative, disparate and conflictual (Boltanski and Esquerre 2015). Value is only partly about monetarized relationships (Mazzucato 2018). Money is a tool for calculation but also has nonpecuniary values connected to personal, social or sacred life (Zelizer 2012) and which are distinct to pecuniary values. To Zelizer these are reflected in the management and allocation of expenditure with the implication being that 'not all dollars are the same' (1997, p. 11); money is reciprocally influenced by cultural and social factors that lie outside the market (Dodd 2014, p. 288). 'Value' should not be solely equated with price or monetarization as 'value' is not an economic concept but is a social and cultural construct (Bryson et al. 2018). Understanding service encounters and productivity places too much emphasis on price and under-emphasizes the complex multitude of values that are co-created through service experiences.

### 5.6.2   Total Factor Productivity

Some of the foundations for a discussion of value and service productivity are to be found in an account of productivity and the information or knowledge economy (Djellal and Gallouj 2010). To Djellal and Gallouj the knowledge economy is associated with an increase in the cognitive content of economic activities. In such activities, knowledge is both the input and the output of the production process, but the service co-creation process is based on relationships between producers and consumers. The challenge is how to measure, on the one side, the productivity of the knowledge and, on the other side, the productivity of the social relationships. In this example, productivity might be determined by the quality of the relationship rather than the quality of the knowledge. In a knowledge economy, or a 'quality economy' (Karpik 1989), what matters is the quality of the outputs rather than an analysis of the relationship between inputs and outputs. Thus, the productivity of a medical doctor is less important compared to the outcome of the treatment. An efficient highly productive health service with poor patient outcomes is a poorly performing health service. The difficulty is in differentiating between the different processes that create value compared to productivity.

One solution to the application of productivity to the measurement of services is found in the development of a measure of *total factor productivity* (TFP). TFP is an indirect measure of technological progress and is a residual that is calculated as the difference between the rates of growth of an index of inputs compared to an index of output. In other words, TFP is used to account for effects in total output that cannot be attributable to inputs (Solow 1957; Hulten 2000). Thus, TFP is, in effect, a measure of that which economists have failed to measure. According to Abramovitz (1956) it is really 'the measure of our ignorance'.

Economic growth based on increasing labour participation and capital investment is not the only source of growth and is no longer the most important driver of economic growth. Capital investment is subject to 'diminishing returns'; the more that is applied to a production process does not imply that each additional unit of investment will create the same benefits as previous investments. More investment might mean that output per unit of capital is reduced. The missing factor in this scenario is innovation. To Krugman the issue is relatively straightforward as 'rising labor productivity … has not been simply a matter of giving labor more capital to work with; it has also been the result of improved technology. It is, in other words, the result of inspiration as well as perspiration' (Krugman 1999, p. 28). Continued economic growth depends on the development

and application of new or altered processes, systems, business models, organizational structures, the development of new products and services, and new designs. Innovation produces growth in TFP. The development of new processes may reduce costs and enhance profitability. The creation of new products and services creates new values for customers and financial returns for successful innovators.

TFP tries to measure all inputs. These inputs are tangible and also intangible; tangibles include capital while intangibles include R&D, knowledge, expertise, design, copyrights, market research, advertising, branding, organizational improvement, software development and labour quality improvements that are achieved through enhancing skills and competency. Many of these intangibles are difficult to define let alone measure. The difficulty for economists is that the TFP residual, in other words the missing factor X, appears to be one of the most important drivers of economic growth. This is a major problem as the residual consists of a complex set of interrelated intangibles. For policymakers this is a challenge as the tangible drivers of economic growth can be easily incorporated into policy, but the intangibles are difficult to address and, more importantly, require the development and application of long-term strategies. The TFP debate is a challenge for economists and, according to Krugman, 'it is therefore a source of embarrassment for economists that most of the interesting action in economic growth usually turns out to arise from changes in this mysterious residual [TFP]' (Krugman 1999, p. 29).

## 5.7   Wrapping Up

Service operations management and productivity are related processes. There are a number of critical dimensions of service operations that need to be considered and evaluated in the design and modification of service operations. These include the structure and flow of operational processes developed to co-create service outputs.

A particular problem is related to 'non-progressive' services such as a ballet or a consultancy project. For these types of services, productivity cannot be increased by speeding up production processes and delivery times; this is not the case for progressive services. An excellent example is the difference between service as convenience in the delivery of fast food (a progressive service) and the experience of dining in a Michelin starred restaurant (a non-progressive service). Fast food should be delivered as fast as possible, while the service delivery process in the Michelin starred restaurant should be a pleasure and should last long enough to ensure that consumers experience a high-value, high-quality and high-cost service experience.

Different service operational systems deliver different qualities of service outputs (cf. Chap. 8). There is a tension between attempts to increase the productivity of service production processes and service quality. This is to highlight both the difficulties of measuring service productivity and the complex nature of service outputs. The measurement of a service must be partly based on an assessment of the quality of the service experience (cf. Chap. 13). This quality might have a limited relationship to the cost of the factor inputs required to create a service. Thus, reading productivity in service businesses is an exercise in understanding the complex interrelationships between value, quality, operations and productivity. This also involves understanding the interrelationships between the co-creation of values between service consumers and producers. This interaction between service employees and customers plays a critical role in the creation of service experiences. In this book, we focus on customers in Chap. 8, but in the next chapter we explore service employees and their management.

**Learning Outcomes**

- Services can be divided into production-related and product-related services.
- Many services have become industrialized.
- Productivity is difficult to measure in services and there is an important relationship between quality, value and productivity.
- For many services it is difficult, often impossible, to define a single unit of output; each

unit of output is often shared between many individual consumers.
- IT and AI provide new possibilities for increasing productivity.
- The balance between front (office) and back (office) regions is altering as front region tasks become automated and shifted into back regions.
- Measuring service productivity requires, on the one side, understanding the productivity of the knowledge and experiences that are created and, on the other side, the productivity that is embedded in social relationships.
- Network learning facilitates the creation of knowledge by blending inputs from across a distributed firm's network to create new knowledge that may lead to process innovations impacting on productivity.

## References

Abramovitz, M. (1956). Resources and Output Trends in the U.S. since 1870. *American Economic Review, 46,* 5–23.

Amoako-Gyampah, K., & Meredith, J. R. (1989). The Operations Management Research Agenda: An Update. *Journal of Operations Management, 8*(3), 250–262.

Baumol, W. (1967). Macroeconomics of Unbalanced Growth: The Anatomy of an Urban Crisis. *American Economic Review, 57,* 415–426.

Baumol, W., Blackman, S., & Wolf, E. (1989). *Productivity and American Leadership.* Cambridge, MA: MIT Press.

Boltanski, L., & Esquerre, A. (2015). Grappling with the Economy of Enrichment. *Valuation Studies, 3*(1), 75–83.

Brady, T., & Davies, A. (2004). Building Project Capabilities: From Exploratory to Exploitative Learning. *Organization Studies, 25*(9), 1601–1621.

Breidbach, C. F., & Maglio, P. P. (2016). Technology-Enables Value Co-creation: An Empirical Analysis of Actors, Resources, and Practices. *Industrial Marketing Management, 56,* 73–85.

Brown, J. S., & Duguid, P. (1998). Organizing Knowledge. *California Management Review, 40*(3), 90–111.

Bryson, J. R. (2000). Spreading the Message: Management Consultants and the Shaping of Economic Geographies in Time and Space. In J. R. Bryson, P. W. Daniels, N. Henry, & J. Pollard (Eds.), *Knowledge Space, Economy.* London: Routledge.

Bryson, J. R., & Daniels, P. W. (2010). Service Worlds: The 'Service Duality' and the Reise of the 'Manuservice' Economy. In P. P. Maglio, C. A. Kieliszewski, & J. C. Spohrer (Eds.), *Handbook of Service Science*. New York: Springer.

Bryson, J. R., & Daniels, P. W. (2015b). Developing the Agenda for Research on Knowledge-Intensive Services: Problems and Opportunities. In J. R. Bryson & P. W. Daniels (Eds.), *Handbook of Service Business: Management, Marketing, Innovation and Internationalisation*. Cheltenham: Edward Elgar.

Bryson, J. R., & Rusten, G. (2011). *Design Economies and the Changing Work Economy: Innovation, Production and Competitiveness*. London: Routledge.

Bryson, J. R., Mulhall, R. A., Song, M., Loo, B. P. Y., Dawson, R., & Rogers, C. D. F. (2018). Alternative-Substitute Business Models and the Provision of Local Infrastructure: Alterity as a Solution to Financialization and Public-Sector Failure. *Geoforum, 95*, 25–34.

Daniels, P. (1982). *Service Industries: Growth and Location*. Cambridge: Cambridge University Press.

Djellal, F., & Gallouj, F. (2008). *Measuring and Improving Productivity in Services: Issues Strategies and Challenges*. Cheltenham: Edward Elgar.

Djellal, F., & Gallouj, F. (2010). The Innovation Gap and the Performance Gap in Service Economies: A Problem for Public Policy. In F. Gallouj & F. Djellal (Eds.), *The Handbook of Innovation and Services: A Multidisciplinary Perspective*. Cheltenham: Edward Elgar.

Dodd, N. (2014). *The Social Life of Money*. Princeton: Princeton University Press.

Füller, J. (2010). Refining Virtual Co-creation from a Consumer Perspective. *California Management Review, 52*(2), 98–122.

Galbraith, J. R. (2014). *Designing Organizations: Strategy, Structure, and Process at the Business Unit and Enterprise Levels*. London: Wiley.

Gardner, E., & Bryson, J. R. (2020). The Dark Side of the Industrialisation of Accountancy: Innovation, Commoditization, Colonization and Competitiveness. *Industry and Innovation*.

Goffman, E. (1984). *The Presentation of Self in Everyday Life*. Harmondsworth: Penguin.

Grewal, D., Ailawad, K. L., Gauri, D., Hall, K., Kopalle, P., & Robertson, J. R. (2011). Innovations in Retail Pricing and Promotions. *Journal of Retailing, 87*(1), 43–52.

Grönroos, C. (2000). *Service Management and Marketing: A Customer Relationship Management Approach*. Chichester: Wiley.

Grönroos, C., & Ojasalo, K. (2004). Service Productivity: Towards a Conceptualisation of the Transformation of Inputs into Economic Results in Services. *Journal of Business Research, 57*, 414–423.

Hislop, D. (2009). *Knowledge Management in Organizations: A Critical Introduction*. Oxford: Oxford University Press.

Hollis, S. (2015). The Role of the Big 4: Commoditisation and Accountancy. In J. R. Bryson & P. W. Daniels (Eds.), *Handbook of Service Business: Management, Marketing, Innovation and Internationalisation*. Cheltenham: Edward Elgar.

Hulten, C. R. (2000). *Total Factor Productivity: A Short Biography*. NBER Working Paper No. W7471. SSRN. Retrieved from http://ssrn.com/abstract=213430.

Karmarkar, U. (2004, June). Will You Survive the Services Revolution? *Harvard Business Review*.

Karmarkar, U. (2010). The Industrialisation of Information Services. In P. P. Maglio, C. A. Kieliszewski, & J. C. Spohrer (Eds.), *Handbook of Service Science*. New York: Springer.

Karpik, L. (1989). L'économie de la qualité. *Revue Française de Sociologie, 30*(2), 187–210.

Krugman, P. (1999). *The Return of Depression Economics*. Harmondsworth: Allen Lane.

Levitt, T. (1972). Production-Line Approach to Service. *Harvard Business Review, 50*(5), 41–52.

Love, J. H., Roper, S., & Bryson, J. R. (2011). Openness, Knowledge, Innovation and Growth in UK Business Services. *Research Policy, 40*(10), 1438–1452.

Lovelock, C. (1991). *Services Marketing*. Englewood Cliffs, NJ: Prentice-Hall.

Machuca, J. A. D., Gonzalez-Zamora, M., & Aguilar-Escobar, V. G. (2007). Service Operations Management Research. *Journal of Operations Management, 25*(3), 585–603.

Mazzucato, M. (2018). *The Value of Everything*. Harmondsworth: Allen Lane.

Metters, R. (2010). The Neglect of Service Science in the Operations Management Field. In P. P. Maglio, C. A. Kieliszewski, & J. C. Spohrer (Eds.), *Handbook of Service Science*. New York: Springer.

Metters, R., & Marucheck, A. (2007). Service Management: Academic Issues and Scholarly Reflections from Operations Management Researchers. *Decision Sciences, 38*(2), 195–214.

Pamnirselvam, G. P., Ferguson, L. A., Ash, R. C., & Siferd, S. P. (1999). Operations Management Research: An Update from the 1990s. *Journal of Operations Management, 18*(1), 95–112.

Ritzer, G. (1983). The McDonalization of Society. *Journal of American Culture, 6*, 100–107.

Ritzer, G. (1993). *The McDonaldization of Society*. Thousand Oaks, CA: Pine Forge Press.

Ritzer, G. (2000). *The McDonaldization of Society – New Century Edition*. Thousand Oaks, CA: Pine Forge Press.

Singh, M. (2017). Transportation: Mobility, Accessibility, and Connectivity. In H. C. Kiang (Ed.), *50 Years of Urban Planning in Singapore*. Singapore: World Scientific.

Slater, D., & Tonkiss, F. (2001). *Market Society*. Cambridge: Polity.

Solow, R. (1957). Technical Change and the Aggregate Production Function. *Review of Economics and Statistics, 39*(August), 312–320.

Sullivan, R. S. (1982). The Service Sector: Challenges and Imperatives for Research in Operations Management. *Journal of Operations Management, 2,* 211–214.

Thaler, R. H., & Sunstein, C. R. (2009). *Nudge: Improving Decisions about Health, Wealth, and Happiness.* London: Penguin.

Turing, A. (1950). Computing Machinery and Intelligence. *Mind, LIX* (236), 433–460.

Vargo, S. L., & Lusch, R. F. (2004). Evolving to a New Dominant Logic for Marketing. *Journal of Marketing, 68*(1), 1–17.

Vargo, S. L., Lusch, R. F., Akaka, M. A., & He, Y. (2010). The Service-Dominant Logic of Marketing: A Review and Assessment. *Review of Marketing Research, 6,* 125–167.

Weber, M. (1968). *Economy and Society.* New York: Bedminster Press.

Zeilzer, V. A. (1997). *The Social Meaning of Money.* Princeton: Princeton University Press.

Zelizer, V. A. (2012). How I Became a Relational Economic Sociologist and What Does that Mean. *Politics and Society, 40*(2), 145–174.

Zhang, Y., Gregory, M., & Neely, A. (2016). Global Engineering Services: Shedding Light on Network Capabilities. *Journal of Operations Management, 42,* 80–94.

## Further Reading

Bryson, J. R. (2018). Worker to Robot or Self-Employment and the Gig Economy? Divisions of Labour, Technology and the Transformation of Work. In A. Paasi, J. Harrison, & M. Jones (Eds.), *Handbook on the Geographies of Regions and Territories.* Cheltenham: Edward Elgar.

Chase, R. B., & Apte, U. M. (2007). A History of Research in Service Operations: What's the Big Idea? *Journal of Operations Management, 25*(2), 375–386.

Fitzsimmons, J., Fitzsimmons, M., & Bordoloi, S. (2014). *Service Management: Operations, Strategy, Information Technology.* New York: McGraw-Hill/Irwin.

Hoekman, B., & Shepherd, B. (2017). Services Productivity, Trade Policy and Manufacturing Exports. *World Economics, 40,* 499–516.

Johnston, R., Clark, G., & Shulver, M. (2012). *Service Operations Management: Improving Service Delivery.* London: Pearson.

Maroto, A., & Rubalcaba, L. (2008). Services Productivity Revisited. *The Service Industries Journal, 28*(3), 337–353.

## Useful Websites

https://www.mckinsey.com/business-functions/operations/how-we-help-clients/service-operations.

https://www.ibm.com/uk-en/services/process.

https://www.rundeck.com/self-service.

https://www.ons.gov.uk/economy/economicoutputandproductivity/publicservicesproductivity/articles/publicservicesproductivityestimateshealthcare/financialyearending2017.

https://smallbusiness.chron.com/reasons-productivity-difficult-improve-service-sector-18834.html.

https://www.oecd.org/sdd/productivity-stats/.

# Service Personnel and Their Management

**Key Themes**

- How is the management of service personnel organized?
- Service work and competencies
- Moment of truth—the service encounter
- Standardization versus flexibility
- Efficiency and productivity
- Service workers' reaction to working conditions
- Salaries, social position and labour
- Corporate culture and empowerment
- Services and the gig economy

Reading and managing service businesses involves understanding service relationships. This involves operational processes and the service employee/customer interface. At the centre of interactive service relationships are three important elements: client interactions, service workers and embodied knowledge. In this service age, the workplace is increasingly conceptualized as a stage upon which employees must execute an effective performance. Service employment is not simply the exchange of goods or services but is a complex skill in which presentation, communication and display are integral to success. The demands placed on service personnel and the challenges of managing them must be considered within

the framework that has been developed to identify the specific characteristics of service work. This was explored in the introduction to Chap. 1 and in Chap. 5 on service operations. The challenges of managing service personnel are generic and are explored across the Human Resource Management (HRM) literature (e.g. Boxall et al. 2008). This is not surprising as 70–80% of employed people are employed in services; the HRM literature to a large degree reflects the challenges faced by service workers and their management. Any reading of service businesses must appreciate the nature of service work and the challenges of managing service employees.

Nevertheless, some aspects of service work are specific reflecting the fact that service production and delivery is different from the production and delivery of goods (cf. Chap. 1). Service work has some peculiarities, or distinct characteristics, compared to, for example, manufacturing or agricultural work. Amongst these are that customer-facing service personnel may interact directly with customers often customizing services during the co-creation and delivery process. Unlike the production of physical goods, failures cannot be corrected before the 'product' is delivered and the 'product' cannot be pretested. These service 'peculiarities' are rarely emphasized in the general HRM literature, but the specific service management literature (e.g. Normann 1991; van Looy et al. 2013; Lovelock and Wirtz 2004; Fitzsimmons and Fitzsimmons 2006) focuses on

**Electronic Supplementary Material** The online version of this chapter (https://doi.org/10.1007/978-3-030-52060-1_6) contains supplementary material, which is available to authorized users.

J. R. Bryson et al., *Service Management*, https://doi.org/10.1007/978-3-030-52060-1_6

the challenges faced by service employees and their managers. It is important to understand the specific characteristics of service work and the implications for the management of service personnel.

This chapter explores the peculiar characteristics of service work focusing on employees' performance and the management of service personnel. In this chapter, we will first examine the particular characteristics of service work and the requirements for service personnel. Then we will consider service workers reactions to their working conditions. Finally, the chapter explores the management of service personnel focusing on HRM tasks that service managers must address in response to the peculiar characteristics of service work.

## 6.1    Characteristics of Service Work

### 6.1.1    Problem-Solving

Service work may involve the delivery of standardized services, often involving learnt scripts, or customized services. In many cases, the delivery of standardized service experiences includes customized elements. Providing a service involves a problem-solving activity where the outcome cannot be seen beforehand (see Chap. 1) and this is a particular characteristic of service work. The outcome includes the quality of the service experience that is co-created between producers and consumers. Service production and delivery involves a process that may alter depending on the nature of the service encounter between producers and consumers. The acquisition of a manufactured good involves a commercial transaction but the characteristics of the good do not alter during this process. Service production and delivery processes are intertwined and must be responsive to meet the needs of every consumer. This means that failure in the service delivery process is always a possibility. For manufactured goods, quality control should reduce the possibilities of failure. For services, the co-creation process adds another layer of complex-

ity that leads to potential problems. Service delivery commences during the initial encounter with the consumer. Service personnel must be more flexible and self-governing compared to manufacturing employees. Management must be prepared to accept that service workers are able to respond to each consumer and sometimes to act on their own. Service firms can attempt to standardize service work, but even then, unforeseen events will emerge in the service delivery process requiring the creation of customized solutions.

### 6.1.2    Back Office and Front Office Functions

Service work has traditionally been divided into two functional categories, back office and front office functions. In a restaurant, back office functions include cooking and logistics and the sequencing of tasks and activities whilst front office activities involve direct interactions with customers. The back office is also the location for administrative and management functions and is the place in which service encounters are planned and monitored. Back office employees often are not directly involved with customers. The front office function is the location for the final stage in the production and delivery of services, and sometimes of sales which are integrated into customer encounters. In some service encounters, sales are a back office function, for example, purchasing an airline ticket or making a hotel reservation. Back office and front office work involves different types of activities and require very different skills. Front office workers interact with customers, while back office workers and managers may not directly engage with service consumers. Nevertheless, back office employees must consider front office personnel customer interactions during the planning and monitoring of the service delivery process. Back office functions must support the co-creation of services by front office functions.

This distinction between back and front offices is also referred to as frontstage versus backstage or front versus back regions. This terminology highlights the performative nature of many service encounters and builds upon the work of the sociologist Erving Goffman (1984) on roles and regions (see Chap. 5). An ideal role prescribes the rights and duties of a social position by informing the individual of what is expected from, for example, the roles of mother, father, teacher, doctor, designer, accountant, consultant or politician. Actual role behaviour is always partially determined by the social setting as well as by the personality of the individual. In a number of seminal books, Goffman developed the concept of roles but restricted the definition to the concept of *role performance*. Undertaking a role is similar to playing a part on stage or on film. Every individual plays the role by articulating props and learnt conventions providing indicators to observers concerning the role being performed. Such role performance may remain just a performance, or it may transform the identity of an individual so that they are no longer able to distinguish between themselves and the role.

Roles are performed in *back* and *front regions*. A region is any place that is bounded by barriers to perception, for example, the division between regions in an office or shop set aside for interactions with customers and offices and rooms set aside only for employees. Services are the products of interactions that occur in back and front regions, but in most cases the consumer will only be aware of what is occurring in the front region. To Goffman the term front region refers to places where performances are given, whilst back regions are places that are 'relative to a given performance, where the impression fostered by the performance is knowingly contradicted as a matter of course' (Goffman 1984, p. 114). A waitress may project an image of quiet courtesy when serving customers in a restaurant but become loud and aggressive behind the swing doors in the back region. A shop assistant may respond to an irritating customer requesting a garment in a different size by going to the back region to search the stockroom. In the back region, the assistant does nothing but rests and eventually returns to the customer informing them that the store does not have the item in that size. In the back region, the performance may be created, illusions and

impressions will be openly constructed, and props and equipment stored.

Within the front region, two standards that govern behaviour can be identified. First, standards related to the ways in which performers engage with the audience; the forms of talk and body language that are deployed and, second, the ways in which performers comport themselves whilst viewed by an audience, but not necessarily engaged in talk with consumers. Consumers adopt roles in the front region that are learnt conventions, for example, the way a patient responds to a doctor.

### 6.1.3 Service Work in Different Service Sectors

'Service' is enacted in very different industries or economic activities and the nature of the core service work undertaken is often completely different between these industries. Service work is extremely heterogeneous. The type of service work undertaken by an accountant in an accountancy firm is very different to that provided by a cleaning assistant in a cleaning company. To create some order from this great diversity, service industries are classified into four service subsectors with each having common tasks leading to specific demands placed on the delivery of the core service work. These sectors, the nature of their tasks and their core work characteristics are explored in Table 6.1. On the one hand, many service tasks involve the provision of relatively low-value standardized services, while, on the other hand, there are services that are high value involving significant degrees of customization.

Classifying service businesses into meaningful groups is a difficult task; similar service outcomes can be delivered via very different processes (see Chap. 1, Sect. 1.1.3). Table 6.1 can be usefully compared with Table 1.2 as both provide very different approaches to classifying services. To complicate matters, all service firms and manufacturing companies are supported by service employees providing different forms of production-related services. These include accountancy, human resource management,

**Table 6.1** Service sectors, tasks and core work characteristics

| Service sector | Examples | Tasks | Core work characteristics |
|---|---|---|---|
| Professional knowledge services | Accountants Lawyers Management consultancy Education Research laboratories | Provide knowledge and solve intellectual problems for clients (such as how to behave, decide, understand, develop new technology and products) | High degree of specialized knowledge, professional norms, co-creation of advice with clients |
| Customized manual services | Craft-based Taxi companies Restaurants Small shops Rescue services | Solve practical problems and create material structures on a customized basis (for example, moving objects and people, repairing machines and selling specialist goods) | High degree of manual and technical skills, much tacit knowledge, flexibility in problem-solving with a customer focus |
| Mass-produced services | Supermarkets IT-networks including service engines Tele-services Railways Banks and financial services | Delivering standard services via customers' self-service (for example, canteens, telephone/data communication) | Delivering uniform quality (repetitive work), not front office work, engineering competencies in designing technical systems, responding to customer complaints and monitoring customer satisfaction |
| Personal services | Doctors Wellness Luxury hotels Home help or social care support for older people | Taking care of individuals' mental or physical wellbeing (for example, health care services, hairdressers, clinical psychologists) | High degree of formal and tacit knowledge involving managing social encounters, broad interaction with people, psychological empathy (customer care) |

Source: Authors' own

IT-support, security and cleaning services. Further complications arise, as these service inputs can be provided in-house, externally or in some combination.

### 6.1.4  Place Fixation

Traditionally, services had to be produced and consumed in the same place and at the same time. They could not be stored and could not be transmitted across space (see Chap. 1). A significant proportion of a service might be produced at the service provider's back office location, but at least the final moment of delivery had to occur as part of an exchange between service providers and their customers. Service personnel must be co-present with customers. The emphasis placed on co-presence in service relationships led to the creation of an HRM tradition that emphasized service employees as outgoing and who often worked away from

their employer's place of business. This includes, for example, management consultants and service engineers. This requires that service employees must be independent and be able to make decisions regarding the delivery of service processes.

Nevertheless, much service work has experienced a process of distanciation that has broken the relationship between place and service delivery. There are two processes at work here. On the one side, there is the remote delivery of services via various forms of information communication technology (ICT) including on-line platforms. On the other side, there has been a growth in self-service in which service customers are directly involved in creating services that are provided remotely. This has partly altered the fixation with place in the delivery of services, but service personnel must still adapt service delivery to meet customer needs. This includes adaptations to national and regional cultures including language localization.

### 6.1.5 Informatization

Developments in ICT have opened up possibilities for the automation of information services including insurance, financial services, audiovisual media and educational services (see Chaps. 4 and 5). These new technologically mediated services require the development of new employee competencies and management approaches. To utilize these possibilities, service firms must employ individuals with technical and software skills. ICT and automation are the basis for innovations in the development of new services and modifications to existing service business models and operational systems (cf. Chap. 7). The application of ICT to service delivery provides economies of scale but also the provision of new types of services. It also contributes to enhancing productivity. Informatization also means that service organizations may need to manage two types of corporate culture or organizational logic, a technical logic, which may be very introverted, and a service-orientated logic, which must be very extrovert. One is a back region function, whilst the other is a front region people-focused relationship based on the co-creation of services.

## 6.2 Requirements for Service Personnel

### 6.2.1 Moment of Truth

The 'moments' when and where service employees encounter customers—particularly the final moment involving the delivery of a solution to a problem—are critical for the sale of services and thus for turnover and profitability. Since the outcome of a service delivery process cannot be tested beforehand (as discussed in Chap. 1), trust plays an important role in the service encounter. Customers must trust the service personnel they encounter to deliver the type and quality of services anticipated. Third party referrals, a firm's brand or social media provide proxy measures that are used by consumers as measures of the quality of a service provider. The service encoun-

ter, which one of the early service gurus, SAS (Scandinavian Airline Systems) managing director Jan Carlzon (1989) termed the 'moment of truth', plays an important role in customer satisfaction and loyalty and in repeat transactions. This is front office work. It is important that front region service personnel have the right attitude and ability to understand customers' problems and in co-creating service solutions and experiences.

Front region service employees are required to identify the customer's problem by developing customer empathy. This involves being service minded and being willing to provide additional services to customers (Carlzon 1989). This is about thinking like customers and responding to their needs to enhance customer satisfaction. Front region service employees must have extrovert personalities and be service minded with an ability to empathize with customer. There were attempts in the 1980s to train employees in the adoption of a service-mindedness approach, but this often resulted in stereotypical behaviour, for example, stewardesses adopting a fixed smile for all passengers. This type of false or learnt behaviour might be considered by customers as superficial and maybe even appear as false. Thus, genuine service-mindedness is not easy to procure. Furthermore, front region service personnel are still expected to perform on the technical-professional dimension. The technical core of the service creation process must be effective; front region employees must combine technological expertise with a service mindset. Nevertheless, a service-minded front region employee may persuade customers to overlook some aspects of service delivery failure (Bittner et al. 1994).

Front region service employees may depersonalize their work by 'surface acting' and 'deep acting'. This approach to understanding service work was heavily informed by the work of Constantin Stanislavski, the creator of method acting (Wellington and Bryson 2001). In surface acting 'we deceive others about what we really feel, but we do not deceive ourselves' (Hochschild 1983, p. 33). In surface acting, the body not the soul is the main tool of the trade; the smile on the face of the worker is a false smile, but it is still a smile. In this account, service work is seen as a form of emotional labour. In emotional labour, a smile becomes attached to the feelings that a company wishes to project rather than being attached to its usual function—to show a personal feeling (Hochschild 1983, p. 127). Some flight attendants' distance themselves from the role they are playing by 'faking' (Taylor and Tyler 2000, p. 92). Here they smile, but do not go out of their way to hide that it is a pretend smile. In one case, a young businessman asked a flight attendant:

> Why aren't you smiling?" She put her tray back on the food cart, looked him in the eye, and said, "I'll tell you what. You smile first, then I'll smile." The businessman smiled at her. "Good," she replied. "Now freeze, and hold for fifteen hours." Then she walked away. In one stroke, the heroine not only asserted a personal right to her facial expressions but also reverses the role in the company script by placing the mask on a member of the audience. (Hochschild 1983, pp. 127–128)

Deep acting means 'deceiving oneself as much as deceiving others … we make feigning easy by making it unnecessary' (Hochschild 1983, p. 33). It is about persuading employees to be sincere 'to go well beyond the smile that's just 'painted on' (Hochschild 1983, p. 33).

### 6.2.2   Competencies

The characteristics of service work are related to special requirements regarding the competencies of service workers. These competency requirements are different for front office compared to back office personnel. The important difference here is the need for front region employees to be customer focused with well-developed social skills (Table 6.2).

Both front and back office personnel must be qualified in their professional and technical fields. The lawyer must have appropriate legal expertise, the cleaning assistant must be familiar with cleaning methods and products and the IT technician must be able to deal with hardware and software. Front region personnel must be able to deliver customer satisfaction during the moment of truth by being generally service minded and being aware of customers' problems.

The moment of truth is important for the competitiveness of service firms and should therefore be supported by the whole service organization. This is enhanced when back office personnel support front office personnel considering themselves to be in-house service suppliers. The key issue is to ensure that back office staff support the front office in meeting customer expectations.

Front region personnel encounter customers and there is always the possibility that they are able to sell additional services during these encounters (cf. Chap. 8). A sales ability is therefore an important requirement. Back office personnel do not encounter customers directly; however, they are engaged in undertaking construction and production tasks—creating services and systematizing them.

Both personnel groups are encouraged to be entrepreneurial and engage in the firm's development and to identify and recommend potential innovations (cf. Chap. 7). All employees should be encouraged to identify opportunities for enhancing the service encounter and the moment of truth. Employees should be encouraged to develop an inward- and outward-facing service mindset. The inward mindset is to encourage employees to identify opportunities to improve operational processes and to identify and solve quality and organizational problems.

Different internal support systems can ensure and enhance fulfilment of a service firm's competency requirements. These systems include formal education—procured via the formal education system; training—which is often via internal short courses or on-the-job training; corporate culture (Schein 1985)—the norms, traditions and goals of the organization and personnel recruitment—recruiting people that have the required personal characteristics.

### 6.2.3   Flexibility and Standardization

An essential requirement for much service work is that employees must be flexible in the delivery of work tasks and have a service mindset focusing on service content and service delivery. This

**Table 6.2** Competency requirements and support systems in service organizations

| Front office work | | Back office work | |
|---|---|---|---|
| Competence requirements | Support system | Competence requirements | Support system |
| Technical-professional (the service discipline) | Education and training | Technical-professional (the service discipline) | Education and training |
| External customer orientation and service-mindedness including deep and surface acting | Corporate culture and recruitment procedures | Internal customer orientation (considering the front personnel as service customers) | Corporate culture and recruitment procedures |
| Sales ability and ability to develop relationships with customers | Training and recruitment procedures | Service engineering (systematic construction and production approach) | Education |
| Intrapreneurship and engagement | Corporate culture | Intrapreneurship and engagement | Corporate culture |

Source: Authors' own

is a consequence of the focus of service work on solving customer problems. Many services are customized in some way to meet the needs of specific customers. Flexibility also involves the provision of extra or additional services. For example, a plumber might provide advice during the delivery of an existing service. This extra service may be either free or the service provider may make an additional charge. Different conventions exist in different parts of the service economy. Additional services may already be part of the service bundle that has been developed to enhance the quality of the service encounter or any additional services may result in additional time inputs by service employees. A lawyer whose fees reflect time spent may charge for additional inputs.

Much service work has been standardized with service workers expected to provide standardized services often using scripts. Call centres, for example, combine technology with scripts to provide standardized services. They follow a fixed procedure in handling service encounters. Scripts are used to control and standardize the service encounter and employees may be unable to deviate from a script (Tansik and Smith 2000). Such scripts may involve language, but also the application of machines to standardize services. McDonald's, for example, standardizes portions and food quality. The mechanization of the food delivery process is designed to ensure that the same menu selection will be similar irrespective of employee or location (see Chap. 5).

A service firm may provide both customized and standardized services. These seemingly contradictory approaches reflect approaches to market segmentation with the provision of both high-cost and low-cost service solutions. Employees providing standardized mass market services may be allowed, or even encouraged, to provide additional services for clients, but they may also be forbidden from making any alterations. Providing additional services adds time to the service encounter, and therefore generates additional costs. It must be noted that service businesses often have low profit margins (cf. Chap. 3) and additional costs may reduce these margins. Some service firms therefore develop business models based on the provision of additional services or care for customers, but these come with additional fees. If customers are not satisfied, they can seek services provided by competitors. Service firms that develop this type of business model compete on price rather than the provision of additional services. Discount airline companies, such as Ryanair and Easy Jet, and discount supermarkets, such as Lidl and Aldi, are examples of service firms that adopt this type of lean service business model. It is also important, for marketing reasons, that employees signal that no additional service will be delivered without additional payment. This is to manage customer expectations and to ensure that customers appreciate that these firms are competing on price rather than on quality and additional service values. These different types of service business—from customized to standardized—have implications for service workers. These include salary levels but also the service work experience in terms of quality and level of employee satisfaction (Table 6.3).

The provision of customized or bespoke services requires employees to participate in interactive service delivery processes in which they engage with clients to co-create distinctive service solutions. Service employees play an important role in creating and enhancing the quality of the service encounter. In this case, the personality and reputation of the service employee matters. In standardized services, the requirements are that employees follow a process and sometimes a script. The emphasis is on the delivery of a uniform standardized service with limited engagement with customers. In this case, the actual service employee plays a relatively unimportant role in the service moment. This represents deskilling and an attempt to restrict or control the role played by service employees in crafting the moment of truth.

### 6.2.4   Efficiency

The pressure for increased productivity in service businesses (cf. Chap. 5) leads to pressures on employees to work faster, smarter and to be more goal oriented. In services, it is often difficult to replace labour with machines. The application of the division of labour to manufacturing continues to identify opportunities to substitute labour with

**Table 6.3** Types of service work and impacts on employees

| Types of service work | Impacts on employees |
| --- | --- |
| Tailor made with the provision of free additional services | Interactive, flexible and customer empathy |
| Tailor made with charging for additional services | Interactive, flexible, customer empathy, sales and cost minded |
| Standardized with flexibility | Repetitive, keeping personal feelings out of transactions but with customer empathy |
| Standardized without flexibility | Repetitive, keeping personal feelings and customer engagement out of the transaction |

Source: Authors' own

machines, but this process is much more complex for services. This places additional pressures on service workers to enhance efficiency. This pressure is not evenly distributed. It is highest in the delivery of mass-produced services, particularly manual mass-produced services, where comprehensive productivity-increasing work systems have been introduced. Employees must rapidly learn to work within these systems. Manual service work, for example, in supermarkets, cleaning services, the provision of home help for older people and transportation, has become increasingly routinized, efficiency centred and low paid. Some service work has been transformed so that it has become similar to factory work. Call centre service workers have similar working conditions to factory workers.

Developments in ICT, including artificial intelligence (AI) and machine learning, are beginning to transform service processes and service work. This is especially the case within business and professional services (Chap. 4), but work and service processes have already been transformed by the application of ICT in the areas of financial services, retailing with the rise of e-commerce and in the application of platform-based solutions to the provision of services. Professional knowledge workers had not experienced the same pressures to increase productivity compared to the experiences of service workers involved in the provision of standardized manual mass-produced services, but more recently there have been pressures to increase productivity and reduce prices. This potential to enhance productivity commenced, for example, with the application of machine learning by lawyers to read documents. But this process is at a very early stage. The more ICT is applied to these services then the more there will be a shift from front region to back region service workers, but also from service workers to automated service delivery systems (see Chap. 5). One consequence is that the balance of workers within professional service firms is altering with an increase in the roles performed by ICT professionals including data analysts, computer programmers and modelers.

If technology cannot be applied to increase productivity, then service personnel must work harder and faster or there must be some type of process innovation. Job descriptions and procedures would have to alter. In catering and social care for older people work procedures, for example, are often described in detail including how many minutes every work task should take and how each task should be completed. These descriptions can also be found in knowledge-based services, for example, education services. Productivity increases can be achieved by reducing the time required to perform a task. Such initiatives may produce reactions from employees undermining their commitment to the job and reducing their motivation and this could then reduce productivity.

Service firms therefore search for smart HRM systems that can be applied to increase productivity without decreasing employee motivation and job satisfaction. Two Swedish-Finnish banks have attempted to increase productivity, but by adopting different approaches. Nordea, which has a more hierarchical management style, introduced a combination of indicators evaluating individual employee performance and work quantity combined with a pecuniary incentive scheme. Svenska Handelsbanken, which has a more empowering management style, introduced competition between bank branches. Productivity benchmarking across the branches was applied encouraging competition. This was combined with a negative sanction mechanism leading to branch rationalization and closure.

## 6.3    Reaction of Service Employees to Work Conditions

Like all employees, service employees react to their working conditions. Service workers have their own lifegoals, aspirations and interests. Trade unions have developed agreements with service firms. The unionization of some types of service work must be taken into consideration when exploring the management of service work and enterprises. Service work also creates distinctive demands from service employees and trade unions. It is worth noting that only a proportion of service work is unionized.

### 6.3.1    Different Service Employees with Different Work Attitudes

Service work is extremely heterogeneous as it includes highly paid business and professional service employees who are able to control the conditions of their employment to manual service workers (such as cleaning assistants and assistants in car service stations) involved in the delivery of highly routinized service work with low salaries. The reactions to service work vary by the conditions of employment and the degree of control that service employees have over their conditions of employment. Furthermore, there are differences between countries in terms of trade union traditions and institutional structures involved in regulating service work and workers.

Rules formulated in national and local agreements must be taken into consideration when service work and delivery is planned, and this is especially the case for manual service workers and employees involved in providing routine knowledge services. Agreements with trade unions may focus on the conditions of work emphasizing salaries, social welfare including pensions and working time, but it may also include training and education. Employees have an interest in remaining qualified for the demands placed on them by the labour market. Thus, service employees' reactions to the challenges they experience in the labour market often involves seeking additional training. Many manual service workers, particular part-time and short-time employees, are not interested in enhancing their competencies by training as they consider that their experience of work is unpleasant, of low prestige and is only provisional or temporary. Here it is worth noting that low paid service workers often must undertake two or three different service jobs to earn enough to support themselves.

## 6.3.2  Work Cultures

Service employees establish, as all work groups do, their own work cultures and routines (Alvesson 2002), which may, or may not, fit with the culture developed and projected by the service company's management. Often there is a fit, which may benefit both employees and the service firm. Nevertheless, sometimes there is a limited fit, or the service business might want, or is forced by market pressures, to change its business model and operational processes; the corporate culture might alter dramatically with employees having to adjust to a new culture and routines. Established conventions in a firm or an industry can alter. This can be observed in aviation with the emergence of discount airlines such as Ryanair, Easyjet and Air Berlin and the transformation of flight work into a form of much more routinized labour with reduced employee prestige, lower salaries and an on-going reduction in additional services provided at no additional cost. The established airlines such as British Airways, American Airlines and Air France were forced to copy many aspects of the new low-cost airline model, but aircraft employees in these airlines tried to maintain their existing more prestigious or even 'aristocratic' cultures. The former airline business model encouraged airline employees to be considered as providing prestigious services as part of a relatively low pressure, high service and high-salaried occupation.

Employees in manual service companies may also develop a counterculture to the company's official corporate culture. In this counterculture, they emphasize that the company is exploiting workers, and this results in employees working to contract. In this situation, employees will not provide additional or special services, but focus on the development of a common internal social community amongst employees. Such countercultures have been observed in transport companies, cleaning companies and restaurants. Countercultures have weakened over the late decades as the old trade union culture and political opposition to firm owners and managers has altered, but countercultures may still be found, particularly in larger manual service companies.

Service employees' attitudes to their work reflects their general values and general societal values. A society consists of different social groups or cohorts and service employees therefore reflect different general value systems. Within knowledge and professional service work, career lifestyles have led employees to being very focused on engaging with their work and in contributing to developing the overall performance of their employer. This reflects the prestige and salaries associated with these occupations. It is noteworthy that this leads to long working hours and difficulties in managing any type of work life balance. In these types of occupations, emotional work represents or becomes a form of deep acting. At the other end of the scale, within manual routine service jobs, employees have to a high degree learnt to be more efficient and customer orientated. However, their life values are often not connected to undertaking manual service routine work and the work does not fit with their life expectations. Employee identification with their work roles in these types of service encounters thus becomes a form of surface acting or an external role that is played to manage the tension between the employee's identity and their place in the labour market.

## 6.3.3  Reactions to Unpleasant Work Situations

Service encounters can be pressured and unpleasant experiences for all types of service employees. Customers do not always behave pleasantly towards front region personnel—whether in manual mass market services or the provision of advanced knowledge-intensive services. Employees sometimes experience extremely demanding customers who adopt a negative attitude towards the service encounter and the service worker. This type of negative customer reaction is often directed towards front region employees, and sometimes it becomes very personal. Front region employees must adopt a professional approach rather than taking this type of experience personally. Many service firms train employees in dealing with demanding and difficult customers, but it can nevertheless be a stressful employee experience. This situation often emerges in call centres, telephone sales departments and the provision of public social services; in the latter clients might in extreme situations become physically violent. Nevertheless, all service employees, with customer contact, may experience such situations. Some service firms have an agreed policy of not pleasing all customers and, in some situations, service personnel can turn away extremely unpleasant customers. It may be more beneficial for a firm to reduce employee pressures and stress by refusing to transact business with some potential customers.

Service employees may also be very engaged in managing service encounters, but the work engagement may reach a point where their work experiences have a negative influence on their family life. An example was a small Danish bank (Lån and Spar) which in the 1990s successfully engaged all types of employees in organizational learning and entrepreneurial activities (Sundbo 1999). Employees had to combine this additional activity with their usual daily work tasks. After some time, entrepreneurial activities began to decrease because employees became too stressed with the additional workload and developed problems with their work life balance and with their families.

Hochschild has shown that much face-to-face interactive service work (flight attendants, debt collectors, waitresses, secretaries, fast food operations) involves having to present the 'right', managerially prescribed, emotional appearance or mask to the customer or client, and that this involves real labour. In these occupations, workers are faced with the dilemma of how to identify with their work role without it becoming part of their identity. Some of these roles come with 'service uniforms', frequently 'the acrylic A-line dress' that render people 'invisible'. Carol Midgley, a British Journalist, went undercover working as a hospital cleaner and found that in a cleaner's uniform she had become so invisible that:

> after my first day I tried to flag down a taxi, still wearing the uniform, and stood astonished as cab after cab, their yellow "For Hire" lights shining,

sailed past, refusing to acknowledge me. (Midgley 2001, p. 9)

Employees are trying to control not simply what people say and do at work, but also how they feel and view themselves. In deep acting the disjunction between displayed emotions and private feeling is severe and potentially psychologically damaging. The danger is that deep acting becomes part of the worker's personality and is used beyond the workplace. If this occurs than the new 'emotional proletariat' (Macdonald and Sirianni 1996) might find it difficult to 'interpret and take appropriate action in response to bodily signals' (Shilling 1993, p. 119). Hochschild also provides a small comparative case study of male debt collectors. This shows that emotional labour is not just performed by women. The point about this case study is that the display of aggression required by debt collectors may also spill over into personal relationships with wives and children. Emotional work may damage the emotions of the workers, but it is also physically damaging. Shilling (1993, p. 120) suggests that the face-work required in the form of frequent smiling leaves permanent marks—lines and wrinkles that devalue particularly women in the eyes of their employers and of society.

### 6.3.4   Low Prestige and Manual Routine Service Work

Manual services are services involving the physical movement of people and things. These occupations include, for example, transportation, trade, canteens and restaurants. A particular problem for manual service firms is that much manual routine service work has low prestige. In fact, in some instances, the prestige associated with this type of work is so low that it is often considered that unemployment is more prestigious. Manual service firms, such as cleaning companies, have high labour turnover rates. Such firms must continually recruit and train new employees, and once trained many leave the firm and the sector. For example, ISS, the global cleaning company's greatest challenge in developing the company is employee recruitment and retention (Sundbo 1996).

## 6.4   Management of Service Work

This section explores managerial approaches that have been developed in response to the special characteristics of service work. Service management concerns how managers in service businesses, or those managing service functions in other businesses including the public sector, handle the challenges associated with service work. By management, we primarily mean middle and line managers that have direct responsibility for managing service employees. However, senior managers also have overall responsibility for the firm's general HRM approach, salary systems, corporate culture and in supporting middle managers with HRM responsibilities.

### 6.4.1   Salaries and Labour Force's Social Position

Salaries and related benefits can be used to influence employee behaviours in all occupations including services. Salaries may be negotiated individually between a service worker and their employer or be agreed across a firm or heavily unionized sector A key issue is the relationship between skills, expertise and the perceived or actual value of a service role. However, two particularities of service work must be emphasized.

On the one hand, there is expertise-intensive service work based on the reputations of individual workers, for example, management consultants, tax consultants, corporate lawyers and computer programmers. These occupations tend to be well-paid and employees are able to control their conditions of work. The balance of power in any salary negotiation tends to be towards the professional with an established reputation rather than with their employer. This alters the traditional superior-subordinate relationship. Employees in professional knowledge service works are amongst the highest salaried occupa-

tions. These occupations are able to establish their own businesses by spinning out from existing firms and client companies. There are relatively low barriers to new firm formation as new firms form around founders' existing reputations and client networks.

On the other hand, for more generic service roles there is no direct relationship between workers' reputations and their ability to negotiate or influence their conditions of employment. This represents a tension between service employees who must engage in collective bargaining compared to those who are able to negotiate individually. There is significant social polarization here with most service workers being disadvantaged; there is only a minority of well-paid service workers. This 'service particularity' is found at the other end of the social scale: operational jobs in manual services are often the lowest paid in a society. This raises the question of 'how low salaries can be if manual service firms want to attract employees?' In some countries, these salaries are below the subsistence level. In other countries, such as the Scandinavian countries, this is not the case. These countries have developed social security systems that implies that for many people the premium, or additional income, from taking a low-income job in manual services, in some cases, may be very small. For many manual service employees there is a low economic incentive for them to retain their service jobs and this is especially the case if they can obtain another income source. On the one hand, this forces manual service firms to increase salaries, but, on the other hand, the firms must cope with severe market and price-based competition. This is especially the case as the entry barriers for establishing new manual service firms are low. Thus, many manual service firms experience extremely high labour turnover, but are unable to increase salaries and are also unable to accumulate capital to invest in innovation and new technology (Sundbo 1996). Such firms have major difficulties when there is near full employment in a local labour market. It is only during times of high unemployment that these firms can attempt to reduce salaries to enable investment in capital-intensive solutions. Alternatively, these firms must try to reposition the status of these occupations to attract new entrants. Part of this is about altering the expertise intensity of these roles as this would attract more qualified individuals. The nature of the services would have to alter in such a way that their perceived value to customers would increase leading to higher prices that would support increased salaries. It is only through innovation, or altering the status of manual service work, that companies will be able to breakout from the challenge of attracting and retaining employees compared with being able to invest in capital-intensive solutions that would replace labour with machines and even robots. One company that has attempted to increase the prestige of the lowest manual service jobs is McDonald's. In their restaurants they have defined specific work positions, given them formal titles and tried to increase the professional status of these occupations.

Some manual service firms have developed a responsible business approach to managing their companies. This is part of a corporate social responsibility agenda that focuses on inclusivity in the recruitment process. Such firms seek to employ people that have difficulties entering the labour market (for example, alcoholics, chronically ill people, immigrants and so forth). This approach is one way of developing an alternative solution to recruitment difficulties, but it also provides a company with additional values that may contribute to enhancing the firm's competitiveness. An example is the small Danish service company, Magaflex, which employs people who have difficulties finding employment as part of a public subsidy program. Megaflex delivers services to the public sector including providing gardening services for older people. Megaflex has developed expertise in recruiting and training more vulnerable individuals. Work teams are organized in employee-centric self-governing teams. For example, if a worker does not show up for work a team member will drive to their home and collect them. This firm generates revenue through combining service delivery with the creation of a set of social values. The public sector gains as individuals are employed and some acquire permanent position in the labour market.

Social entrepreneurship (Fayolle and Matlay 2010) very often involves developing solutions to social problems by providing services that are organized and managed by entrepreneurs who are trying to create financial, societal and environmental values—a triple bottom line of values. This highlights that service businesses may also be responsible businesses as they balance profitability with developing and managing wider societal values. Managing low-margin service businesses, that are associated with low paid employment, involves managing the tensions between recruitment, working conditions and investing in technological solutions. This highlights the interdependencies between work and technological innovation that is central to the division of labour and the substitution of labour with technology. We now turn our attention to exploring this tension.

**Case: ISS and the Manual Service Squeeze**

ISS is a global manual business-to-business (B-to-B) service company primarily providing cleaning, but also catering, environmental services, facility management building services and industrial services such as cleaning factories and disinfecting machines involved in the production of food. The company has about 600,000 employees.

ISS faces the same main problem as many manual service companies: their services are not of strategic importance to their customers but are just considered to be irritating additional costs. Cleaning is not of great importance except for a few client industries (such as hotels and the food industry). This means that services become standardized based on price-based competition as many firms can provide similar services to the same quality. Price-based competition leads to low profit margins, which makes it difficult to accumulate capital for investment in development and innovation. Furthermore, customers are not interested in purchasing more advanced services involving basic functions such as cleaning. ISS also suffers from a high employee turnover rate. In some countries, on average, employees stay in their jobs for less than a year. It takes some time to train new employees to undertake tasks leading to a low rate of return (ROI) on the investment in recruitment and training. Employees generally are poorly motivated and are not particularly service-minded because the jobs are perceived to be of poor quality; most employees have no alternative.

To break out from the 'squeeze' between recruitment and limited investment, or to try to modify it, ISS in the 1960s and 1970s standardized service work, introduced fixed work procedures including time steering and control systems and strengthened the employee hierarchy. This did not solve the squeeze, but instead it created a negative attitude across the firm's labour force making it even more difficult to recruit and retain cleaning personnel. Then, in the 1980s and 1990s, the company changed its service and personnel policy. Services now became more customized, HRM motivation oriented and employees were encouraged to sell new services to customers. This led to more satisfied employees, a decrease in labour turnover, but this still did not solve the fundamental squeeze. ISS then introduced modularized services—a combination of standardization and control with customization and empowerment of front region personnel. This has modified the squeeze and ISS has continued to grow, but not increased their profit margin significantly.

ISS attempts to take care of its employees and tries to be a responsible business. The company is socially responsible in employing immigrants and individuals who have a marginal position in the labour market. This is not because these are the only potential applicants for this type of work but reflects an inclusive approach to recruitment. ISS also negotiates with unions and does not try to reduce wages to the very minimum.

ISS has also learnt to identify the more stable and cleaning-minded individuals as part of their personnel recruitment process. In many countries, the ideal employee is a woman between 35 and 55. This cohort often perceives cleaning to be a natural task and is often service minded. ISS often promotes individuals from this cohort to middle manager positions in the company because they are good at identifying potential recruits who would fit into existing cleaning teams.

## 6.4.2   Core Skills and Education

Procuring a labour force with the right competencies and maintaining and renewing these competencies are core HRM functions in service businesses. These competencies are the core skills required to undertake the necessary service tasks ranging from advanced advisory services such as management consultancy and accountancy to manual services including cleaning and repairs. Required competencies include service-mindedness and flexibility as these play an important role in customer satisfaction.

Formal qualifications are provided by the public education system. When this does not function effectively then service businesses may experience major difficulties hindering growth and development. The key issue here is any mismatch between the supply of skilled labour and demand. A Danish study, undertaken in 2015, of 35 successful service firms from all industries identified that the greatest barrier to growth was related to hard-to-fill vacancies and difficulties in recruiting labour with the right competencies. The required competencies included professional ones (labour force with the education and experiences to undertake the required service tasks), service-mindedness and customer relationship management, but also the ability and willingness to work outside normal working hours. Much service work, particularly manual service work, must be delivered during the night, on Sundays and holiday periods.

Service-mindedness skills may be included in programmes delivered by the public sector, but this is unusual. Service businesses must rely on recruiting individuals with these skills that either have been acquired through experience of service work, or by training or reflect their personality types. Such training can also be purchased from public or private sector vocational institutions. Often these skills are acquired informally by learning on-the-job or by experiential learning; this may be efficient but is outside management control.

### 6.4.3 Work Organization

The organization of work activities is the most important management task. This is extraordinarily challenging for much service work given that services are traditionally tailor made and co-created with consumers. Furthermore, work motivation is always important for employees' performance but is particularly important for service front region office personnel, who are continually engaged with customers. One challenge faced by service firms is how they can cope with these conditions. Some service firms choose to standardize, or at least modularize services, whilst others focus on the provision of bespoke services. If the service is standardized, then management must develop fixed procedures, but often these must permit frontline personnel to be flexible in meeting special customer requirements and to solve problems that may emerge during customer interactions. However, this depends on the firm's business model. Some service firms, typically discount retail and hotel chains, emphasize that service workers should not provide additional services. The emphasis here is on keeping costs low, but the business model is based on the provision of low-cost price-sensitive services. Service firms providing customized, or tailor made, services, must still control costs and must develop strategies ensuring that additional services are paid for either directly or indirectly by customers. When a service firm provides standardized services, it is important that employees follow the rules, particularly when there is a script.

Quality control is an important management task. This includes controlling failures, managing complaints and employee procedures. Many service firms, particularly manual ones, have control inspectors that from time-to-time monitor employees' work including talking to customers. The issue is to balance control with employee motivation ensuring that frontline employees signal a positive attitude during customer encounters.

If services are customized, then management still must provide guidance for the tasks undertaken by employees. Service personnel must be instructed in work procedures and in the custom-ization of services. These procedures are not fixed as is the case for the provision of standardized services. Management must rely on service personnel to be flexible and to solve problems as they occur. Frontline managers are extremely important here as they observe how tasks are performed. In customized services, firms must ensure that the organization of work is based on motivating and empowering frontline employees.

### 6.4.4 Motivation, Empowerment and Corporate Culture

Whatever the service concept or business model, employee motivation is always important in creating enhanced employee performance, particularly for frontline personnel. Good employee performance implies motivated employees who are customer oriented, service minded and flexible and can make decisions themselves. Management is able to encourage this type of attitude via corporate culture including values, empowerment, trust and developing a flattened hierarchy.

Corporate culture influences working values, and even sometimes their general life values. Corporate culture includes behavioural norms and values that are shared by all, or at least most, employees and managers. It includes how other people—colleagues or customers—should be treated, and attitudes to general societal issues. Corporate culture is also important for creating a positive social climate within a company ensuring that employees consider that they are working for a firm that is interesting, socially safe (i.e. they have good relationships with colleagues and management) and they are not overtly controlled. Such a corporate culture increases employees' motivation. A corporate culture can be supported by physical artefacts including restaurants, sporting facilities and even uniforms. A corporate culture sometimes develops itself as employees create a shared work culture, but management may influence this and can create cultural elements and resources (Schein 1985). This is achieved by senior and middle managers clearly communicating specific values across the whole organization—and acting on these themselves.

IKEA provides mass produced furniture that customers assemble themselves. IKEA has a strong corporate culture that works across countries. It is based on the founder's, Ingvar Kamrad, business principles that emphasize helping customers (to choose furniture and providing advice on assembly), enthusiasm, cost-consciousness and empowerment. There is a limited or flattened hierarchy with employees encouraged to have common coffee breaks. IKEA also has a policy of recruiting immigrants and others that may have difficulties in obtaining a permanent position in the labour market.

To motivate employees to provide customer focused and flexible services then it is important that they are empowered. Management should trust employees—that they can plan their own work, can make decisions and are interested in co-creating service experiences with customers. Well-paid knowledge-intensive business and professional service workers, including lawyers and engineers (in service functions) and researchers, can be empowered, but it is also the case for low-paid manual service workers including cleaning and shop assistants. Middle managers should also be empowered. Empowering may be an important means for motivating employees, but in providing customized services it is an essential part of the service creation process as services are altered to meet the needs of individual customers. Only empowered employees can solve customers' problems and develop solutions that might involve working with other employees. The key personnel management challenges facing service firms include recruitment, motivation and empowerment (Table 6.4).

Managers must support frontline personnel to enhance motivation and empowerment. Nevertheless, if back office personnel are not also motivated and empowered then this will undermine performance and competitiveness. This aspect is perhaps most difficult for professional knowledge-intensive service firms where empowerment of the more subordinated back office personnel (accountants, administrators, cleaning assistants, etc.) is often forgotten because there is

**Table 6.4** Personnel management challenges within service businesses

| Issue | Challenge |
|---|---|
| Managing customers | The customer is often co-present during the service encounter and service employees must be able to read the moods and attitudes of individual customers. |
| Servicescape | The servicescape, or the place in which the service is co-created, is part of the service delivery process and must be designed to create the right atmosphere. |
| Delivery of services in real time | Many services are co-created in real time and the service encounter needs to be carefully managed involving managing capacity and developing a supportive culture. |
| Co-ordination | The challenge of developing an integrated approach involving marketing, recruitment, people management and resource management. |
| The relationship between operational decisions and business outcomes. | Success may depend on satisfying and retaining existing customers, entering new markets, attracting new customers and balancing delivery costs versus the quality of the service experience with profitability. All these are interrelated and altering one variable impacts on the others. |
| Enhancing and improving operations | This involves improving processes and service products and ensuring that a firm's culture is supportive of service delivery and change. |
| Managing the delivery of an outcome and an experience | With service delivery there is often no clear distinction between outcomes and the nature of the experience. A restaurant customer purchases both the meal, the servicescape and the quality of the service. Service workers must simultaneously manage outcomes and experiences. |
| Customization | The same service will attract different customers with different expectations. Service employees must be clearly able to communicate the service concept to different customers in such a way that they support the creation of different outcomes and experiences. |

(continued)

**Table 6.4** (continued)

| Issue | Challenge |
|---|---|
| Distinguishing between different types of customers | The customer might be the service user, the purchaser/procurer, or the funder. These roles could be undertaken by different people, for example, with the procurement of business services, or by the same individual. Each role comes with different expectations and service workers must be able to identify and manage these expectations. |
| Recruitment | Identifying and selecting individuals with the required skill sets. This varies by role and service type. |
| Training | An on-going challenge is to ensure that all employees are able to craft service delivery processes and identify opportunities for innovation. |

Source: Authors' own

so much focus on professional frontline employees.

The organization of service work, according to this prescriptive framework, should not be via a traditional hierarchical top-down system. Management's primary task is service delivery, and this does not involve steering and controlling frontline personnel because the latter is the most important element during the 'moment of truth'. Instead, management should ensure that frontline personnel are supported throughout the whole organizational hierarchy.

Motivation and empowerment may seem to be most obvious for the delivery of customized services, but even in standardized services these are important. Research has shown that in most standardized services (e.g. Netbank services, supermarkets, local transport) customers expect service workers to be able to solve problems as they arise.

Motivation and empowerment are not the only tasks involved in the management of service businesses. As in other work, it is important to monitor and control operational processes and customer satisfaction. Dealing with problems and failures can be undertaken in a supportive and positive manner maintaining employee moti-

vation. Service standardization and employee motivation can go hand-in-hand and this is the case for companies such as McDonald's. In Denmark, McDonald's has been identified, over many years, as the best company to work for and this is a company which is hierarchical and in which working practices are highly standardized. In this case, managers try to develop a supportive company culture motivating employees and also encouraging them to develop practical solutions to problems as they emerge.

### 6.4.5 Negotiation Frameworks: Extended Barter

Service firms and their managers need to have developed a formal framework for executing their HRM strategy. A service business must develop a general approach to service management that includes a suitable salary framework and which specifies working times and conditions. These agreements are essential for service production and the delivery of service tasks to customers.

In some service firms, professions and even in some countries, these agreements are negotiated individually whilst in other firms, industries and countries they are made collectively with trade unions and with possibilities for local adaptation to meet local circumstances. In parts of Asia and the US the focus is on individual agreements whilst in Europe the tradition is more orientated towards negotiations with trade unions. International service corporations from non-unionized parts of the world sometimes experience conflict with unions when they begin to provide services in a unionized part of the world. McDonald's when it began to develop a network of fast food restaurants across Europe decided to negotiate with trade unions. Ryanair, a European service company, which employs many Asians and other non-Europeans, adopted a more confrontational approach to try to avoid trade union agreements. This has exposed Ryanair to negative media commentary, but this company competes on price with low margins.

HRM is not only about formal agreements and salaries. Increasingly employees demand other benefits from their employers, and these other benefits are often more important than salaries. This is especially the case for well-paid knowledge-intensive service work rather than manual routine service work. These other benefits include professional and personal development, motivation and a pleasant working environment, flexibility in time management and interesting work. These 'softer' working conditions are negotiated partly with senior management, but mostly with middle level managers, who are more directly involved in recruiting and incentivizing employees. Such agreements, which have been described as a form of extended barter (Bevort et al. 1995), are particularly important for services because of the importance of enhancing frontline personnel's satisfaction, motivation and behaviour. Strikes may be more serious for service businesses compared to manufacturing as they immediately impact on customer relationships.

The Scandinavian airline company SAS was famous in the 1980s for introducing a personnel policy which attempted to increase employee satisfaction by emphasizing extended bartering (Carlzon 1989). SAS was a successful airline company and a frontrunner at that time and this policy was effective. The SAS case also highlights the impacts of organizational inertia on company performance. When the airline market altered from 2000 towards more price-based competition then all airline companies had to alter their salary structures and working conditions. SAS experienced major problems in this transition because of the working conditions introduced in the 1980s and which were protected by strong trade unions. In 2012, SAS tried to implement further cost-cutting measures. Eventually, agreement was reached to increase workloads, to reduce salaries between 12% and 20% and pension benefits. In 2017, SAS formed a new airline, Scandinavian Airlines, Ireland, that would operate from Heathrow and Malaga Airports and staffed with crews based outside Scandinavia. This would reduce service delivery costs. Companies may develop responsible employee friendly policies, but these must be balanced against wider structural changes within an industrial sector that might alter market structures.

Business and professional service firms are engaged in two types of competition. First, they compete for clients and this involves client retention and acquiring new clients. Second, they compete for talented fee-earning as well as support staff. The ability to attract, develop and retain staff is the single biggest determinant of a business and professional service (BPS) firm's competitive success. Attraction involves persuading the best graduates to work in a BPS sector and for a particular firm. Human resource systems in most smaller BPS firms are underdeveloped. Most BPS firms are small and medium-sized enterprises (SMEs) and many do not operate staff appraisal and development systems. A relatively recent development is for BPS firms to substitute higher paid workers with partly trained lower paid paraprofessionals. Some BPS sectors, including accountancy and law, have discovered that important project tasks can be undertaken by semi-trained employees and especially employees that may never obtain a full professional qualification.

Retaining well connected fee earning professionals is of central concern for highly successful BPS firms. The issue is the ways in which BPS firms can dissipate the risks associated with embodied expertise and reputations. The key question that must be addressed by BPS firms is: what strategies can be developed to reduce the risks associated with staff loss and related subsequent client loss? The difficulty is that professional employees can be headhunted by rival companies, they can retire, or they can leave to establish their own firms. This means that BPS firms are constantly exposed to risks that are difficult to control and that revolve around the most important element within their business models—expert labour and personal relationships between fee-earning professionals and client employees.

Strategies designed to retain fee-earning staff can be constructed around positive and negative incentives. Positive strategies include salary levels and the provision of a range of benefits that might include leisure facilities. Negative strategies are part of the contractual agreement that is negotiated between the firm and the employee. These strategies can include a specified period of gardening leave during which a former member of staff is unable to work and restrictive covenants against soliciting, canvassing, dealing with or accepting instructions from clients with whom the former employee has dealt with during their employment. Another strategy revolves around a system of staggered bonus payments or financial incentives; this is the golden handcuffs strategy. Golden handcuffs are a system of employee financial incentives that are designed to discourage an employee from seeking alternative employment. Examples of golden handcuffs include employee stock options that can only be acquired over a number of years and contractual obligations to repay bonuses if an employee resigns. In such a system, an employee is awarded a bonus at the end of a financial year that is paid in stages throughout the following year and resignation means that an employee loses the bonus payments that have been awarded, but not paid.

## 6.4.6 Recruitment

Recruitment of service personnel is a core service business management task. For service businesses, this is a complex task as applicants must be assessed on the basis of their formal qualifications, but also on their service-mindedness, independence and ability to interact with customers. It can be difficult to assess these softer people-centric skills from a written application or during a short interview.

The recruitment of professionals to knowledge-intensive service firms is often based on the applicants' academic merits combined with their social and professional networks. The latter is taken as a guarantee of their ability to engage with clients. On the one hand, the academic background of a recruit without an established reputation is often taken as a proxy measure of their abilities to work in the sector. On the other hand, established professionals are identified based on their extant client network. A key issue is to recruit individuals who fit with a firm's and sector's business culture. For some firms, recruitment processes have changed with applicants being ranked without reference to their names, photographs or academic backgrounds. This is to try to develop a more inclusive approach as part of a responsible business strategy that is trying to recruit individuals on their ability based on merit rather than gender or background.

## 6.4.7 Organizational Learning

Service organizations should learn from all instances involving positive or negative incidents and the service delivery process. All service businesses should practice organizational learning (Senge 1990). Innovation and development within service firms depends on organizational learning and this is often experiential learning. This is, however, difficult, especially in customized services because employees develop relationships with individual customers, and they may be unwilling to share their experiences. The shift towards employment in BPS occupations represents a shift towards expertise-based production systems in which elements of a production system rely on inputs that are difficult to control and manage. What has occurred is a shift in which control or power in the employment relationship is transferred from the employer to 'expert' employees. The competitiveness of many BPS firms is founded upon three interrelated factors: expertise that is embodied in fee-earning staff, the individual reputations of fee-earning staff and the contact networks of fee-earning staff. By itself expertise is not enough; highly successful BPS professionals are identified or perhaps defined by their ability to commercialize their expertise.

The best managed service businesses will develop systems for inter-organizational learning. This may be difficult because much learning involves tacit knowledge (Nonaka and Takeuchi 1995) developed by individual employees (see Chap. 5). A social neighbour learning system can be developed where individuals share and discuss new service experiences.

Some service firms attempt to formalize tacit knowledge. Consultancy firms such as Deloitte and PWC have established IT-based knowledge management systems where consultants document and describe project experiences and how client problems have been solved. This opens up possibilities for this learning to inform the development of solutions for clients located in other countries. But there are major challenges here. Consultants do not often search this type of database on the understanding that client problems require special solutions. There are also problems in finding possible project cases reflecting the difficulty of indexing and linking former projects with the needs of current clients.

## 6.5    Services and the Gig Economy: Employees, the Self-Employed and Workers

A new term—the 'gig economy'—emerged in the US as part of an old process that is central to the operation of capitalist economies. The gig economy reflects the on-going adaptation of work and workers to digitalization and developments in ICT including smartphones. The application of technological and process innovations is central to the operation of capitalism as new ways of creating use and exchange values are developed and applied to the economy (see Chaps. 4 and 5). These new ways may lead to completely new business models, products and services transforming lives, but may just replace existing processes and technologies while enhancing productivity. The gig economy is particularly widespread in the service sector and represents a shift towards part-time, impermanent employment, freelance work, self-employment and precarious employment. The gig economy is transforming the nature of work, but only for some workers by providing alternative employment opportunities.

It is important to be careful with the language that is used to describe or classify involvement in

the gig-style labour market. For example, the 2016 UK court case concerning Uber taxi drivers transformed 'self-employed' drivers into 'workers' with benefits and the court case revolved around employment status, employment rights and responsibilities. This was a debate about 'employees' versus 'self-employed contractors'. Under UK law, there are three types of employment relationship: 'employees', 'self-employed' and 'workers'. The majority of people are 'employees' under a contract of employment and entitled to minimum employment rights with an obligation by law for the employer to deduct Income Tax and National Insurance contributions. A 'self-employed' individual does not have a contract of employment, but will be contracted to provide services or some form of work for a certain period of time for a fee. The self-employed pay their own tax and National Insurance and do not have employment rights. 'Workers' represent any individual who works for an employer, under a contract of employment or any other contract, where someone undertakes to provide work or services. 'Workers' are mostly casual workers, temporary workers and some freelancers and have rights to the National Minimum Wage, rest breaks, paid holidays and some other benefits. These three categories give different types of protection in the labour market.

During the 1970s, the crisis in mass production led to the emergence of more flexible ways of organizing production based, in part, on the replacement of full-time employees with part-time or temporary workers. This led to the emergence of a group of advantaged full-time employees with benefits and a disadvantaged and more precarious group. Thus, from the 1970s many economies such as the US witnessed a steady growth of 'contingent' labour, that is, involuntary part-time jobs, a process that has heralded the birth of the 'working poor'. During the 1980s and 1990s, the on-going development of the global economy further exposed employees to overseas competition leading to a transfer of employment to lower cost locations. This was part of the offshoring of economic activity that initially involved only manufacturing work. During this century, this led to the 'second global shift' in which 20% of service work located in developed market economies potentially could be offshored to countries like India and the Philippines (see Chap. 10).

The current threat to work and workers involves not offshoring but digitalization and ultimately the substitution of labour by software and artificial intelligence. The gig economy can be considered as a stage in a longer term process that has displaced full-time employees and increased the number of employees in precarious jobs. This does not mean disadvantaged, but 'differently advantaged' as it involves an alteration in the ways in which some individuals are able to control and co-ordinate when and where they work. The gig economy could mean emphasizing the growth in temporary positions with companies contracting with workers for short-term engagements. It could also mean stressing the decoupling or dislocation of work from location through the application of digital technologies. In this latter case, the office or the shop becomes mobile and is relocated to the home, pocket, car or motorbike. This is perhaps a return to home working and the role that this played during the early years of the Industrial Revolution.

The gig economy is also part of the so-called 'sharing economy' or collaborative consumption in which consumers rent or borrow goods rather than purchase them outright. This is transforming physical goods into services in which there is no transfer of legal title. Individuals have the opportunity to convert assets they own for their use values into assets that provide them with exchange values. The onset of pervasive computing via smartphones means that assets that are not fully utilized can be monetized; the technology enables peer-to-peer temporary linkages to occur facilitating monetary exchange. Participants in this part of the gig economy must be advantaged as they must own or control assets that have the potential to be monetized. This part of the gig economy is very visible as it includes eBay, car-sharing services and Airbnb.

The key questions are what does the gig economy mean for employment, education and politics? First, the gig economy is creating new business and employment opportunities that are different from older forms we are used to. The winners in the gig economy will be well-educated, flexible and with specialized skills and/ or assets that provide them with an advantage. This does not mean that all work will be transformed by the gig economy as existing forms of production and work organization will continue alongside gig-enabled work. Entrepreneurs will benefit as the new technologies reduce the barriers to establishing new businesses. For many entrepreneurs, the gig economy enables them to establish 'born global firms'; firms that from the moment of start-up are international businesses.

The losers are those without the expertise or assets to benefit from this part of the economy. Nevertheless, there are other benefits from the application of 'gigs' to the economy. The UK court case concerning Uber taxi drivers complicated matters as it transformed self-employed drivers into 'workers' with benefits. Uber's taxi drivers work under similar conditions to most taxi drivers—low pay and limited benefits—but Uber provides an alternative opportunity for individuals who want to control how much they work and when they work.

This is similar to other gig companies using business models based around on-demand workers. Task Rabbit, for example, provides a same-day service platform that instantly connects someone with a need for a skilled 'tasker' to help with odd-jobs and errands. Workers have low pay and limited rights and protection and peoples' motivations for working for such companies remain unclear. They could be precarious workers, they could prefer the ability to determine the extent of their involvement with work, or this might be a survival strategy.

Second, one of the most interesting aspects of the gig economy is the relatively rapid development of new business models combined with the application of digitalization to existing forms of work. This involves an increase in the acceleration of process or operational innovations linked to the creation of new products and services. On-going innovation continues to transform local labour markets, meaning forecasting future skill needs is difficult and perhaps impossible, but it implies that excellence in a country's educational system is a mandatory requirement to maintain and enhance national competitiveness and to ensure better long-term outcomes for every citizen.

The gig economy is part of a much longer term process that can be traced back to the beginning of industrial capitalism in which new process and product innovations transform labour markets. The application of computing and digitalization to work can be traced back over the past three decades. For the future, the only known is that product and process innovations will continue to radically alter the nature of work and worker and that the only survival strategy is based around education. Education still matters but matters more as the economy is transformed through the development of gig-style business models. It is important not to over-emphasize this shift as labour markets will still consist of a balance between employees, workers and the self-employed and some work will be knowledge-based, some more focused on people-based skills and some will be undertaken by robots.

## 6.6     Wrapping Up

Service personnel occupy many different positions in companies. Some occupy back office and others front office positions. The latter requires the recruitment of employees who are able to handle customer relationships, and this is in addition to any technical competencies. Frontline service personnel must also possess service-minded competencies including being empathic towards customers and be willing to provide additional services. The management's task is to support frontline personnel; all layers in the organizational hierarchy should support frontline personnel.

Service personnel are also exposed to productivity increases, rationalization and other pressures that can destroy working conditions and the quality of the work experience. Employees may react to these changes and this might affect productivity and service quality. Therefore, an appropriate work culture and human resource

management approach is critical for the management of successful service firms. It is important to remember that at the heart of a service business are service-minded employees.

Manual service work (e.g. cleaning, catering, social work) experience a double burden linked to recruitment, profit margins and an inability to invest in capital-intensive innovations that would replace labour with machines. These types of service companies have difficulties in attracting and retaining competent employees. Therefore, this contributes to difficulties in increasing productivity and service quality leading to difficulties in competing on quality and in increasing profit margins. This results in low profit margins, which restricts investment in development and innovation. One solution is to develop services by adding more advanced service elements and making service delivery more professional and thus more valuable for customers. The problem is that service employees must then increase their competencies, and this requires better educated employees. Low value service work needs to acquire greater prestige, and this would increase the perceived and actual value of the services making them more attractive for potential employees. This would increase profit margins and also reduce labour turnover. Alternatively, robotics must be applied to deliver service tasks, and this would both enhance productivity and profitability.

Service businesses involve complex interactions between service employees and their customers. These interactions may involve the provision of customized service experiences or standardized services. Central to these interactions are services processes. Innovation in service processes is very different compared to research and development in manufacturing and the next chapter focuses on exploring these differences.

**Learning Outcomes**

- Service work is heterogeneous ranging from highly educated and salaried professionals providing knowledge-intensive services to low-paid unskilled manual service work.

Some service work is undertaken in back offices, or backstage, and some is performed in front offices, or frontstage. Technological innovation is altering the balance between frontstage and backstage service workers.

- Some service deliveries are standardized, others are customized (tailor made to meet the requirements of individual customer) and some are modularized. These different forms lead to different requirements for service employees.
- Frontline personnel must be customer oriented, service minded and flexible.
- Service management must create a strong corporate culture, motivate and empower employees and reduce the hierarchical pyramid.
- Efficiency management is necessary, but this is a difficult task because it easily clashes with empowerment, working culture values and employee motivation.
- Service personnel react to working conditions by negotiating both individually and via unionized collective bargaining.
- Service worker recruitment is difficult because this involves recruiting individuals with personal competencies including service-mindedness, flexibility and independence. These softer skills are harder to identify in a conventional interview.
- Organizational learning is important for enhancing the quality of service encounters but is challenging for customized services.
- The gig economy is altering service employment leading to an increase in part-time and temporary work creating conflicts between service firms and unions

# References

Alvesson, M. (2002). *Understanding Organizational Culture*. London: Sage.

Bevort, F., Pedersen, J. S., & Sundbo, J. (1995). Denmark. In I. Brunstein (Ed.), *Human Resource Management in Western Europe*. Berlin: de Gruyter.

Boxall, P., Purcell, J., & Wright, P. (Eds.). (2008). *The Oxford Handbook of Human Resource Management*. Oxford: Oxford University Press.

Bittner, M. J., Booms, B. H., & Mohr, L. A. (1994). Critical Service Encounters: The Employee's View. *Journal of Marketing, 58*(October), 95–106.

Carlzon, J. (1989). *Moments of Truth*. Cambridge, MA: Harper.

Fitzsimmons, J., & Fitzsimmons, M. (2006). *Service Management*. New York: McGraw-Hill.

Fayolle, A., & Matlay, H. (2010). *Handbook of Research on Social Entrepreneurship*. Cheltenham: Edward Elgar.

Goffman, E. (1984). *The Presentation of Self in Everyday Life*. Harmondsworth: Penguin.

Hochschild, A. R. (1983). *The Managed Heart*. London: University of California Press.

Lovelock, C., & Wirtz, J. (2004). *Services Marketing: People, Technology, Strategy*. New Jersey: Pearson.

Macdonald, C. L., & Sirianni, C. (1996). *Working in the Service Economy*. Philadelphia: Temple University Press.

Midgley, C. (2001, February 7). Undercover Cleaner: Life on the NHS Front Line. *The Times*, 9.

Nonaka, I., & Takeuchi, H. (1995). *The Knowledge-Creating Company*. Oxford: Oxford University Press.

Normann, R. (1991). *Service Management*. London: Wiley.

Schein, E. (1985). *Organizational Culture and Leadership*. San Francisco: Jossey-Bass.

Senge, P. (1990). *The Fifth Discipline. The Art and Practice of the Learning Organization*. London: Century Business.

Shilling, C. (1993). *The Body and Social Theory*. London: Sage.

Sundbo, J. (1996). Development of the Service System in a Manual Service Firm. A Case Study of the Danish ISS. In T. Swartz, D. Bowen, & S. Brown (Eds.), *Advances in Services Marketing and Management* (Vol. 5). Greenwich, CT: JAI Press.

Sundbo, J. (1999). Empowerment of Employees in Small and Medium-Sized Servicer Firms. *Employee Relations, 21*(1–2), 105–127.

Tansik, D., & Smith, W. (2000). Scripting the Service Encounter. In J. Fitzsimmons & M. Fitzsimmons (Eds.), *New Service Development*. Thousand Oaks: Sage.

Taylor, S., & Tyler, M. (2000). Emotional Labour and Sexual Difference in the Airline Industry. *Work, Employment and Society, 14*(1), 77–95.

van Looy, B., van Dierdonck, R., & Gemmel, P. (Eds.). (2013). *Services Management. An Integrated Approach*. Harlow: Prentice-Hall.

Wellington, C. A., & Bryson, J. R. (2001). At Face Value? Image Consultancy, Emotional Labour and Professional Work. *Sociology, 35*(4), 933–946.

## Further Reading

Bowen, D. E., & Schneider, B. (2014). A Service Climate Synthesis and Future Research Agenda. *Journal of Service Research, 17*(1), 5–22.

Bratton, J., & Gold, J. (2012). *Human Resource Management, Theory and Practice*. Basingstoke: Palgrave.

## Useful Websites

ISS: http://www.issworld.com/en.

IKEA: http://www.ikea.com/ms/en_GB/this-is-ikea/index.html.

McDonald's: http://www.mcdonalds.com/us/en/careers.html.

The gig economy: https://www.investopedia.com/terms/g/gig-economy.asp.

# Process and Product Innovation in Service Businesses

7

**Key Themes**

- How do service firms innovate new services and processes?
- What is service innovation?
- What are the drivers of service innovation?
- Practice-based approaches to service innovation
- Structured approaches to service innovation
- Entrepreneurship and institutional entrepreneurship
- Intellectual property rights in service businesses
- Balancing innovation and strategic reflexivity

Reading and managing service businesses is an exercise in understanding dynamics and evolution as firms and service subsectors innovate and respond to innovations that arise in other industrial sectors. Innovation not only engages with and responds to technological innovation (see Chap. 4) but also may involve the creation of new business models (see Chap. 3) and new forms of work (see Chap. 6). Innovation thus is a cross-cutting business process.

Innovation—the realization of new ideas into business practice—is a concept that is applied by researchers and practitioners to understand change processes in service businesses and society. Service businesses innovate

by developing new services or improving existing ones to compete in the marketplace and to develop service solutions that meet societal needs. They do so partly because they need to solve specific problems for customers in new ways, and partly because they need to adapt to other actors' innovations in the economic ecosystem of which they are a part. The actions of companies and their employees, customers, suppliers, financial institutions, governments and other stakeholders are closely intertwined, and service businesses need to co-develop products and services. Pressures to innovate can emerge from changes in market structures, such as a greater emphasis being placed on experiences, sustainability, the circular economy, digitalization and responsible business. Service companies are part of a broader process of on-going technological and institutional development that constantly changes the conditions for doing business. Innovation can mean something that is new to the world or is new to a firm. Innovation can be hidden from view; new ways of delivering services may be developed that are not apparent to final consumers. In this case, the process but not the service might have been altered.

Most service companies do not, however, engage in innovation as a separate activity. Separate technical development research departments are relatively uncommon. Innovation is not regarded as a special task or function within service companies. This does not mean that service

**Electronic Supplementary Material** The online version of this chapter (https://doi.org/10.1007/978-3-030-52060-1_7) contains supplementary material, which is available to authorized users.

J. R. Bryson et al., *Service Management*, https://doi.org/10.1007/978-3-030-52060-1_7

businesses do not innovate. Owners, management or employees can generate new ideas regarding company operations, how products and services are sold, and which new products and services can be developed. Ideas are implemented 'under the radar' but do result in changes in business practices and service outcomes. In services, experimenting with incremental small-step changes is an important development model (Sundbo 1997), for example when a receptionist in a hotel addresses a guest in a different and more customer-centric way. Incremental innovations accumulate over time and can transform a business.

Larger and more financially robust service companies can play a more strategic and leading role in development and innovation within a service sector. For example, a retailer such as Tesco plays a dominant role in how and what products can be developed and sold and in designing service processes in mass-market retailing. Companies that play a leading role in sector innovation are found throughout the economic system and these benefit both customers and suppliers by supporting the creation of a sector development trajectory that reduces uncertainty (Jacobides et al. 2018). Therefore, other companies' services and products converge on a leading company's development trajectory. Another example is Apple's iPhone and its platform, which involves many different standards including the development and distribution of apps and hardware. The disadvantage of such a system, if it becomes too closed, is that it is very difficult to introduce new developmental features. Such a closed innovation system produces path dependency preventing some types of innovation from occurring.

A retailer must take responsibility, for example, for the whole value chain ensuring product quality and avoiding fake or fraudulent products. This was the case in 2013 with the horse meat scandal in the UK. Retailers like Tesco reacted promptly when it became apparent that some of its beef contained undeclared horse meat. It turned out to be very difficult and complicated to identify the origins of this horse meat in the supply chain. Nevertheless, retailers were the key actors overseeing these value chains and had to take responsibility for these products to maintain their reputations and customer trust. This is an extreme example, but it highlights how service firms play important roles in setting and enforcing product standards and thereby also standards and trajectories for potential new innovations. Adding horse meat to beef products was not an acceptable innovation.

The next section explores the definition and characteristics of service innovation and how it occurs. Next, we distinguish between a technological view, a service view and an integrated view of service innovation and the consequences for drivers of service innovation. Then we explore the implications of a practice-based view of service innovation, comparing this approach to structured forms of service innovation. Finally, three aspects of service innovation are explored: entrepreneurship, intellectual property rights (IPR) and process innovation. We conclude with a model of balanced innovation management.

## 7.1   What Is Service Innovation?

A definition of innovation originally suggested by Joseph Schumpeter (1883–1950) (1969 [1934]), the acclaimed 'father' of modern innovation theory, continues to have major impacts on how we understand and apply the concept of innovation in research and practice. In this account an innovation process involves identifying and developing 'new combinations' of society's productive means consisting of several elements:

1. The introduction of a new good.
2. The introduction of a new method of production.
3. The opening of a new market.
4. The conquest of a new source of supply.
5. Developing a new organization. (Schumpeter 1969 [1934], p. 66)

Following on from Schumpeter, innovation research distinguishes between invention and innovation. Invention is the first occurrence of an idea for a new product or process, while innovation is the first attempt to apply it in practice (Fagerberg 2005, p. 4). Similarly, in research on service companies, Sundbo defined innovation as follows: 'I will use 'innovation' to describe the effort to develop an element that has already been invented, so that it has a practical commercial use, and to gain the acceptance of this element' (Sundbo 1998, p. 12). This means that innovation is not about invention or developing new ideas, but more about selecting, realizing and transforming invention into practical use.

Schumpeter did not include 'small steps', 'continuous adjustments' or 'incremental innovation' in his concept of development and innovation. Nevertheless, this omission is not very helpful for service innovation, which is often incremental with many small adjustments based on rapid experimentation and the introduction of new ideas into everyday practice. Innovation must, however, be distinguished, from minor changes that are classified as being more akin to learning. To count as innovation, there must be a step-change or a 'jump' in behaviour (Sundbo 1997) that is perhaps best described as a discontinuity. Such step-changes can emerge as a consequence of an accumulation of small incremental adjustments with each changing the ways in which a problem is defined and solved. Even the combustion engine was not the outcome of a rapid radical innovation but was based on many small incremental changes in services and technology over many years. It was a radical innovation in the sense that it had far-reaching impacts on transportation, and on the ways in which we live and work in urban, suburban and rural areas.

As a process, the relationship between invention and innovation can extend over many years. For example, the innovations that combined to produce the first helicopter stretched over several hundred years starting with Leonardo da Vinci (Fagerberg 2005). Fagerberg explains how long 'time-lags' can exist between an invention and its realization in practice. In services, there are many instances of retro-innovation, where traditional and old ideas within, for example, food are rediscovered and given a new form in connection with the development of a new type of service. For example, Wedum (2019) has revealed how traditional Norwegian cheese was reinvented as a process of 'retrovation' and incorporated into the creation of a New Nordic Cuisine. Many service innovations are characterized by relatively small time-lags between invention and realization; new ideas can be easily and rapidly tested in relation to user groups through a process of 'rapid application' (Toivonen and Tuominen 2009).

There are different types of service innovation (Sundbo 1997): product innovation, a new service; process innovation, a new service delivery system; market innovation, a new behaviour in the market (e.g. addressing new customer segments); organizational innovation, for example, introducing self-governing groups; and business model innovation, for example, delivering knowledge services via the Internet for free, but financed by advertising revenue (see Chap. 3 on multi-sided business models). Service innovations can be behavioural, for example, training employees to be service minded and to provide extra services to customers, or technological, for example, introducing vacuum cleaning robots or Internet banking. The product, the production and the delivery processes are interconnected in services and this means that service innovations are normally integrated including, for example, both product and process innovations and often linked to market, organizational and business model innovations.

In traditional service theory and literature, technological innovations are often overlooked as the academic debate focused on understanding behavioural change in service encounters. Recent developments in IT networks, including the Internet and smartphone eco-systems, highlight that technological innovations play an increasing role in facilitating service innovation. It is impossible to isolate service innovation from product innovation; new products and new technologies open opportunities for the creation of new services and for innovations in service processes.

It is important to explore the interrelationships between service, product and technological innovation. The introduction of the World Wide Web, including secure electronic payment systems, transformed retailing and financial services. This has included innovations not only in logistics and supply chain management, but also in the design of websites. Potential customers can compare goods on retailers' websites and can order and pay for them using an international payment system. Several technological innovations lie behind the introduction of e-commerce and combined this has resulted in disruptive radical innovation that has transformed retailing. The US-based retail company Amazon is built on these innovations. It sells goods all over the world; it started by selling books but now sells all kinds of goods. This company has grown from nothing over 25 years. Recently, Amazon has been identified as the world's most valuable company compared to companies like General Motors, US Steel, Apple and Microsoft. Amazon includes the development of a new retail business model that introduced a new combination of warehousing, a Web-based platform and a complex set of logistics and supply chain algorithms (see Chap. 11). Amazon is an excellent example of a company that can only be understood by applying an integrated approach to understanding the interplay between many different business activity systems.

Another example of a radical and disruptive service innovation is Ryanair, the Irish-based airline. This started as part of a wave of low-price airlines using a new business model. Ryanair developed this new disruptive business model ignoring the established airline business model based on high-value business and first-class customers. These high-value business passengers were attracted by the provision of extraordinary peripheral services including free champagne and extremely service-minded flight attendants. The new business model targeted another market segment—travellers requiring extremely low prices. Low prices are possible because the airplanes are almost always full, and flights only occur during 'rush hours' when many passengers want to travel and only to popular destinations. Passengers often need to transfer to reach less popular destinations. Low-price airlines tend to fly to airports located away from city centres as they target airports with low landing fees.

Administration costs are kept to a minimum. The primary service provided is transportation and the low-cost airlines do not focus on the provision of additional services or additional services are not included in ticket prices. This business model innovation has completely transformed commercial aviation.

There is an important question to consider. Should service innovation be considered as part of a debate on responsible business? Low-cost airlines have increased the number of flights, including flights as part of weekend holiday packages. This has contributed to enhanced pollution and is a key element in debates over climate change. The introduction of e-commerce has created new jobs but destroyed existing jobs in conventional high street retailing. It has also contributed to an escalation in deliveries between local distribution centres and homes contributing to air pollution. Thus, a new service-based business model may both disrupt existing forms of provision and be associated with perverse consequences.

## 7.2  What Drives Innovation in Service Businesses?

Research on service innovation has explored different research perspectives on service innovation including discussions that focus on definitions, drivers and the evolution of service innovation (Gallouj and Savona 2009; Tether 2005). Gallouj and Savona (2009), for example, distinguish between three perspectives on service innovation (assimilation, differentiation and integration), whilst Gallouj (2010) and Djellal et al. (2013) identify four perspectives (assimilation, differentiation, inversion and integration). Each perspective has something to say about the drivers behind service innovation including what managers involved in service innovation need to look for as key aspects within the service innovation process. An overview is provided below (see also Table 7.1). We will now consider each perspective in turn.

In the *assimilation* perspective, service innovation is considered to be driven by, and adapted

**Table 7.1**  Perspectives on service innovation processes

|  | Assimilation perspective | Differentiation perspective | Inversion perspective | Integration perspective |
|---|---|---|---|---|
| Driver of service innovation | Adoption of new technology drives innovation in services | Employees and managers drive small and large innovations in services | Service innovations drive innovations in all sectors | Innovations in services and technology are driven by multiple actors across sectors |
| Key sector | High tech, manufacturing | Service | Service | Cross-sectoral |

Source: After Gallouj (2010)

to, technological innovation. Pavitt (1984), drawing upon a large set of empirical material, identified a service innovation pattern. This pattern is the usual way in which innovation in services is undertaken and to Pavitt this is based on a 'supplier dominated' approach in which service innovation is driven and dominated by technological innovation by manufacturing companies supplying new technology to service businesses. Service innovation is triggered by the introduction of new technology, which a service company then adapts to its specific situation and needs.

A 'reverse product life cycle' was proposed by Barras (1986, 1990) to explain the process by which new technology was integrated into services and its relationship to service innovation. This model suggests that service innovation starts with the adoption of new technology. This leads to process improvements, for example, in the storing and processing of data by financial institutions. As a service company learns to apply ICT to store data, then this can lead to more radical process changes, for example, the introduction of new ways to monitor financial transactions. From such process changes, new services can emerge including new types of savings and investment accounts or new types of home banking. There are three stages to the reverse product life cycle: incremental process innovations, radical process innovations and product innovations. The assimilation perspective is still relevant because of the growing role played by information technology and digital transformations that affect many service companies. Digital transformations have encouraged or forced companies, including service companies, to integrate digital technology into their operational systems, to adjust or reshape their value propositions to

include digital content (Berman 2012) (see Chaps. 3 and 4).

In the *differentiation* perspective, the starting point is based on the assumption that service companies have special characteristics that are reflected in the service innovation process. The four service characteristics that are often identified are: intangibility, heterogeneity, inseparability and perishability (Zeithaml et al. 1985) (see Chap. 1). Thus, services often have intangible aspects that are difficult to formalize or codify; they are also not entirely the same (homogenous) across employees and customers. Production and consumption often occur at the same time and in the same place through a process of co-production. Finally, this implies that services are difficult to store. Such service characteristics are less dominant for particular types of services and have greater or lesser impacts on service innovation and production. An example of a service where these characteristics are supposedly dominant is care services. However, a service like Netflix is homogeneous, storable and separable; in this case, the four service characteristics do not play the same dominant role in service innovation and in service delivery processes. Particularly important is the fact that services often have intangible aspects and that employees interact with service clients during service delivery. It is during this 'moment of truth" (Normann 1983) that the quality of a service is determined.

Service companies, especially smaller service businesses or public service providers, can be characterized as having limited resources devoted to innovation. It is unusual for such firms to have their own research and development (R&D) departments and there are limited opportunities to purchase external research or innovation inputs. The concept of *bricolage*, or do-it-yourself problem solving (Fuglsang 2010; Witell et al. 2017), has been developed to understand how innovation can emerge in such resource-constrained environments. Employees, managers or owners solve problems on the spot using available resources. In service firms, bricolage activities can be invisible or hidden in service relationships. Sometimes they are deliberately kept under the radar especially if they express some form of resistance to management's decisions. In other cases, bricolage activities can be elevated to become part of strategic decision-making processes enabling a company to remain in control by using existing resources to support innovation contributing to the continued survival of the firm.

Employee-driven innovation in service businesses sometimes creates tensions between management's need for linearization of decision-making processes and employees' activities and initiatives that emerge with irregular frequency from practice. In services, employees' work activities are sometimes only loosely coupled to management's strategic initiatives and employees have some autonomy, whether by design or not, to experiment with their work. Such experiment is a form of bricolage that results in continual incremental innovation.

The *inversion* perspective (Djellal et al. 2013; Gallouj 2010) represents a shift in the balance of power between manufacturing and service companies. Certain types of business services, for example, knowledge-intensive business services (KIBS), can drive innovation processes not only in their own companies, but also in other companies, including manufacturing and high-tech companies. Developments in apps enhance smartphone functionality and may encourage alterations in the next generation of smartphones. Similarly, local and national governments responsible for the provision of public services and public sector procurement can be the driving force for innovation processes in private companies. The outsourcing of public services to private companies and public/private infrastructure partnerships can drive innovation in private high-tech companies. A new area that has not yet received enough attention is the creation of networks between public services, private services, manufacturing companies and civil organizations or non-governmental organizations (NGOs). There are many areas in which NGOs have special knowledge of problems and opportunities that can lead to meaningful innovations to which other actors can contribute. One example is emergency aid, including products and services, and another is the provision of social or welfare services. The inversion perspective highlights the importance of interactions and collaborations across sectors as important drivers of innovation. Here it is important to appreciate that productivity enhancements in one sector might be driven by service innovations elsewhere in the economy (see Chap. 5). Comparative productivity differentials between companies and between countries may reflect problems in the interactions between different subsectors within an economy.

The *integration* perspective attempts to develop models for understanding innovation by drawing upon insights from service innovation research that are also applicable to manufacturing and public services. This perspective assumes that all sectors produce service, in the singular, or services, in the plural. Even a car can be considered to be a service as it provides the service of transportation. The implication of this perspective is that organizations develop their businesses according to the overall 'rationales' or 'logics' that are selected and this might reflect a more service- or manufacturing-orientated approach.

One attempt to construct an integrative perspective on service innovation is found in the Gallouj and Weinstein's (1997) model. This is known as the service characteristics-based approach or the Lancastrian model (see also Gallouj and Savona 2009) (Fig. 7.1). Each product or service is deconstructed into a number or 'vector' of final service characteristics, competencies and technical characteristics. The characteristics of a service co-evolve with competencies to produce and make use of them together with material/technological characteristics. Radical innovation is about changing all these characteristics at the same time, while

**Fig. 7.1** A characteristic-based model of products and services: innovation involves changing one or several of the characteristics. (Source: Developed from Gallouj and Weinstein 1997)

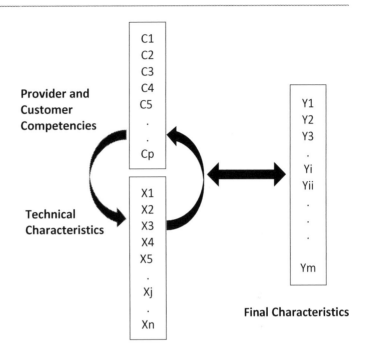

incremental innovation involves changing some of them.

Windrum and García-Goñi (2008) have developed a more complex characteristics-based vector model for understanding public sector innovation. They include vectors of competencies and preferences of users, service providers and policy makers; together these add up to the final service characteristics. This model contributes to enhancing understanding of the necessary preconditions required for service innovations to occur. Many elements must be in place before a service innovation can become a reality including alterations in user preferences and skills. This explains, for example, why it is so difficult to transform a healthcare system that is focused on patients and treatments to a healthcare system focused on prevention and rehabilitation. It is difficult because this type of transition involves simultaneously changing the competencies and preferences of healthcare professionals and patients. In other words, alignment across policy makers, service providers and users becomes an important driving force as well as a condition for innovation. Failure to align is a barrier to service innovation.

## 7.3    Practice-Based Understanding of Service Innovation

Most models of service innovation that have been developed have focused on the identification of formal organizational processes. Practice-based approaches offer an alternative perspective where practice is at the centre of the service innovation model. Practice incorporates everyday routines and behavioural patterns consisting of a number of interrelated elements: bodily and mental activities, material elements, background understandings and emotional learning (Reckwitz 2002). It has also been suggested that practice consists of three elements: image, skill and material (Pantzar and Shove 2010). Innovation involves integrating such elements to form practice.

A practice-based approach to service innovation contributes to exploring how human social practices generate consumer demand for specific services—for example, transportation—as a consequence of alterations in behavioural patterns involving the movement of people between places. It can also enhance understanding of how actors cope with, and innovate, using limited resources in the context of where they work and live. Service innovation, based on this perspective, is about designing practice including designing and integrating images (emotional commitments), materiality and skills to form innovative services. A practice-based approach involves more than designing a technological or behavioural component of a service and integrating this into new value propositions. It must also focus on the development of the competencies required to perform new or revised practices including the design of material conditions and emotional commitments.

This approach to service innovation, where demand patterns are linked to service design, has practical relevance in relation to the development of solutions to major societal challenges (Cass and Shove 2017). For example, if individuals are required to reduce their $CO_2$ emissions, then meaningful social and professional practices must be designed that will enable a reduction in energy consumption in the context of where people live and work and how they travel.

A practice-based approach to service innovation must therefore address elements that are part of consumers' everyday social practices. This provides a broad space for service innovation, but there are also limitations. If, for example, the purpose is to reduce tourism's $CO_2$ footprint then this would require the development of tourism services with a reduced $CO_2$ footprint (hiking, cycling, environmental or eco-friendly tourism). Nevertheless, tourists' competences and perceptions about tourism would also have to be altered. Promoting the enjoyment of nature as a tourism objective is acceptable as long as it does not require transportation by sea or air. This implies that this type of innovation in the creation of tourism services would require a strategy that would also alter consumer perceptions of their experiences and expectations.

Major tourist destinations such as Barcelona, Mallorca, Venice or the Galapagos Islands are experiencing *overtourism* or the process by which too many tourists are attracted to a particular destination. Overtourism is defined subjectively by local residents, business owners and tourists, but there are objective measures including holiday rentals and second homes displacing local residents from the housing market. Overtourism has a negative impact on the quality of the natural and cultural environment and on the tourist experience. To develop a solution to overtourism requires the design of new tourist practices. Mallorca has, through significant political effort, tried to reposition itself as a tourist destination that emphasizes culture and nature rather than sun, sea and sand.

Health care is another example of the application of a practice-based approach to service innovation. In many countries, the design of health services has shifted from a focus on treatment to prevention and rehabilitation. This shift is driven by the on-going escalation in the costs of health care provision. Research and technological development continues to create new but expensive medical treatments. Instead, by designing and encouraging the adoption of new social practices centred on where people live and work, it is possible to significantly reduce hospitalizations involving chronic diseases including chronic obstructive pulmonary disease (COPD) or Type 2 Diabetes. To design new prevention and rehabilitation practices that are meaningful to people requires the development of non-health interventions by policy makers and innovators. Innovation in health care provision, focused on prevention and rehabilitation, requires the adoption and development of a whole life approach that includes interventions that are indirectly related to health. Such interventions include policies designed to encourage behavioural alterations to increase physical fitness and the adoption of healthier lifestyles.

A practice-based approach to service innovation also includes a focus on the application of limited resources to develop and alter practices. Nudges can be used to direct changes and align people's intentions and behaviours in a constrained environment, such as nudging tourists towards more sustainable behaviour or patients towards taking care of their own health. Bricolage activities play an important role in service innovation as service companies and/or civil actors involved in service development often have access to limited resources. Innovation does not always have to be the result of planned and strategic capital-intensive initiatives but can arise from activities initiated by local actors and employees in service firms who are interested in creating new resilient practices.

## 7.4   User-Based Innovation in Services

Service innovation is often user- or customer based, and, in some cases, innovations are driven by end-users that find new ways of defining and solving problems that are then later capitalized or commercialized by firms. The success of an innovation depends on how it is accepted by consumers. If the point of departure taken by firms are customers and their needs, interests and ideas, then the probability of success will be greater. Service firms have the advantage of meeting customers in service encounters (see Chap. 8) and this means that a service firm has the opportunity to engage with customers identifying their preferences. Such user-centric innovation processes are applied by successful service companies (Sundbo and Toivonen 2011). Users can be informants in the innovation process, but they can also be involved in the process of testing services or they may be active participants in the innovation process. Often service firms work with user communities to refine and further develop an innovation after it has been launched. Failure can be corrected, and the new services can be adapted to user needs. IT-based service innovations involve a continual process of service creation as computer programmes are modified to enhance user experiences including developments in smartphones and other Internet connected devices.

Employees may play a role in user-based innovation (Sundbo et al. 2015) (see Chap. 6). Employees continually co-create service experiences with customers and during this process gain insight into customer preferences and expectations leading to service innovation. Employees can also develop user-based innovation via bricolage and through the everyday practice of service delivery and co-creation.

## 7.5   Structured Forms of Service Innovation and Strategic Reflexivity

Managers are interested in structuring service innovation and linking innovative initiatives, by employees and others, to business. This implies that the innovation process is divided into stages that include: an awareness and planning phase, an idea generation phase, assessment and selection of ideas, design of prototypes, testing, validation and final development and marketing (see e.g. Alam and Perry 2002). Employees, managers and users can be involved in different stages. Employees that are not R&D personnel can participate from the beginning, especially with service innovation. Users typically have a role to play in the final stages when a new service is being tested. In practice, this type of service innovation process is rarely linear. It will include feedback loops including on-going criticism, processes that start over, recasting and even rejection of ideas and abandonment of entire innovation proposals. Therefore, it is important that a structured innovation process is integrated with practice- and experience-based approaches. It is often through the combination of structured and practice-based approaches that important innovations occur (cf. e.g. Jensen et al. 2007).

Innovation research has identified patterns of innovation by economic sector in the service, manufacturing and public sectors, and this includes a supplier-dominant pattern within service innovation based on technological adoption. An innovation pattern is a widely spread innovation practice. This is an important starting point for understanding the organization of innovation processes. Other patterns include R&D-based innovation, strategy-driven innovation or employee-driven reflexive processes of innovation. Yet there has been a growing recognition that service innovations arise through combinations of different approaches. On the one hand, managers must create an innovation climate that is internal to their business supporting employees' intrapreneurship and bricolage activities. On the other hand, innovation must also be structured in relation to a company's strategy and interpretations of what is going on in the market and the environment. This dialectic between structured, strategic processes and employee inputs has been termed 'strategic reflexivity' (Fuglsang and Sundbo 2005). Strategic reflexivity is thought to be particularly relevant to service innovation because of the duality in the innovation process that combines management strategy with employee initiatives.

There have been attempts to identify specific patterns of innovation in public services. It might be expected that the political system plays a special role in public service innovation (Fuglslang and Sundbo 2016). Nevertheless, many innovation capabilities are the same for public and private services including design and R&D, customer/client interaction, ICT adaptation and collaboration with external actors. Indeed, public sector innovation is influenced by the political system through rules, regulations, public-private partnerships and public-private innovation networks. Thus, it appears that 'strategic reflexivity', where strategies, and structured innovation processes, are reflected upon from different angles through feedback processes, is important for innovation in private and public services (see Fig. 7.2).

## 7.6    Entrepreneurship and Service Innovation

Entrepreneurship is as important within services as it is within manufacturing. Service entrepreneurs emerge in the same way as manufacturing entrepreneurs. Entrepreneurship can be understood as the establishment of new businesses. From this perspective, entrepreneurship is often more common within services than within manufacturing as many types of service businesses have low barriers to entry compared with manufacturing. Most business start-ups emerge within retail, consultancy and IT-based services. Whether entrepreneurship must be based on innovation is, however, unclear. Most retail and consultancy new business start-ups are not innovative but are just based on the repetition of existing concepts and often involve the application of

recipe knowledge. IT-based services are different as they may involve disruptive innovation. This is perhaps the area with the highest number of innovative start-ups, and which have the potential to grow rapidly. IT-based service business models have the potential to reach many customers extremely rapidly. This is part of the on-going speed-up in capitalism's velocity that is linked to technological development (see Chap. 4). Thus, it took the telephone 75 years to obtain 50 million subscribers, television 13 years, the Internet 4 years, Facebook 2 years, YouTube 10 months and Angry Birds 35 days.

Service entrepreneurs have a less complicated establishment phase compared to manufacturing and software entrepreneurs. The development of a new service product is much faster compared to the R&D required for a new technological-based innovation. There are normally no patent procedures required and the service delivery production apparatus is often much simpler and is less capital intensive. Subsequently, service entrepreneurs soon experience more severe problems than many manufacturing entrepreneurs. Entering a service market is much easier but this also implies that there is intense competition. Service innovations are also much easier to copy with competitors able to copy service processes and products. It is generally more difficult for service entrepreneurs to procure external investment capital because investors have difficulty in assessing and calculating product (service) and company value. In expertise-dominated service firms, the primary value of the business may be based around the founder's reputation and contact network.

The analysis of entrepreneurship patterns in developed market economies highlights the dominant role played by service firms. Across China, South Africa, the United Kingdom and the United States, for example, there are more service sector start-ups established than in any other sector, and market expansion or growth expectations are much greater (Table 7.2). This pattern is similar in many other countries.

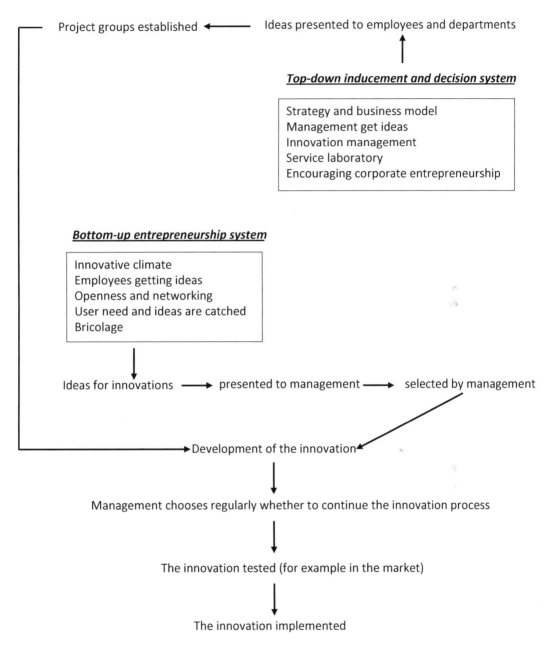

**Fig. 7.2** Balanced innovation management system in service firms. (Source: Authors' own)

## 7.7   Institutional Entrepreneurship and Service Innovation

Service innovation is related to politically and socially determined goals and frameworks. Political decisions, and other institutional struc-

tures, enable and constrain the service innovation process. Institutional entrepreneurs (Battilana et al. 2009; Wallin and Fuglsang 2017) are actors that seek to change institutional structures by creating new types of services that are meant to change hitherto dominant patterns of innovation. For example, by launching new digital platforms,

**Table 7.2** Sector distribution of new entrepreneurial activity (2019) (Percentage of Total early-stage Entrepreneurial Activity)

|  | China | South Africa | United Kingdom | United States |
|---|---|---|---|---|
| Agriculture | 1.7 | 4.2 | 0.2 | 3.5 |
| Mining | 1.0 | 4.9 | 8.8 | 6.7 |
| Manufacturing | 6.8 | 13.1 | 7.6 | 10.5 |
| Transportation | 2.7 | 4.7 | 0.2 | 24.6 |
| Wholesale/retail | 55.0 | 46.1 | 20.4 | 24.6 |
| Information communications technology | 2.9 | 2.9 | 4.9 | 5.4 |
| Finance | 1.5 | 1.7 | 3.9 | 11.0 |
| Professional services | 2.3 | 1.2 | 19.7 | 11.5 |
| Administrative services | 4.4 | 3.9 | 7.0 | 4.0 |
| Health, education, government and social services | 20.3 | 16.2 | 23.1 | 15.4 |
| Personal/consumer services | 1.4 | 1.3 | 4.2 | 2.6 |

Source: Adapted from Global Entrepreneurship Research Association (2020) page 210

service businesses have contributed to changes in the institutional provision of health care, and by promoting new visions of local food, service businesses have contributed to building new structures of food production and delivery. This type of disruptive service innovation involves strategies to justify and legitimize new initiatives. An example is the new Nordic cuisine based on using local and seasonal ingredients in restaurants. Institutional entrepreneurs were able to create a divergent vision and then mobilize actors in support of this new vision for Nordic cuisine. This vision of a new Nordic cuisine was promoted publicly by, amongst others, the Danish chef Klaus Meyer as conflicting with previous food traditions. Nevertheless, this new cuisine was justified and legitimized as something that could be justified on the grounds of better health, experiences, creativity and the utilization of local resources.

One aspect of service innovation concerns the ability of actors to justify their actions in a broader societal context. In line with theories of justification, entrepreneurs draw on general arguments that have wider public relevance to justify their innovations enabling actions and service adoption (Boltanski and Thévenot 2006; Thévenot 2001; Fuglsang and Nordli 2018). General arguments include the proposition that innovation leads to enhanced efficiency or that they result in greater environmental and health benefits. All economic actors and businesses can draw on such arguments that provide the basis for critical discourse. Thus, justifying and legitimiz-

ing innovation entails conflicts about existing values that may be difficult to resolve. Service businesses are involved in this process of legitimization, both as business service firms that deliver and inform debates and as service companies that develop new and 'better' services within a wider institutional framework.

## 7.8  Intellectual Property Rights and Appropriability

What role do intellectual property rights (IPR) play in service businesses? In technological innovation, patents and other forms of property protection are extremely important, especially in areas where it is relatively easy to take out patents and where patents are the norm for the protection of intellectual property. Patents restrict imitation and are critical for innovations that require considerable revenue and capital investment. A patent is intended to protect the return on the financial investment. Yet, patents do not always provide sufficient protection; it is possible for other companies to innovate 'around' a patent using slightly different technologies and approaches. For example, the iPhone with the use of icons and a touchscreen that was promoted by Apple has been reinvented by other companies that have been innovating around Apple's concepts and patents. Many technologies can be made in slightly different ways thereby escaping the protection of a patent. In other areas, notably in the pharmaceutical industry, IPR regimes play a major role and are difficult to avoid through the development of an alternative solution.

The social value of the patent system is that it incentivizes innovation. Patent protection further ensures that the knowledge included in a patent becomes publicly available. The disadvantage is that a company gains a monopoly on a technology or service often resulting in higher consumer prices to access the service(s) and this might impede diffusion to consumers with more restricted purchasing power.

Innovation within the service sector is often strategically driven, fast and based around employees' experiences and knowledge. As a result, it is sometimes difficult to apply patents. For example, it may be challenging, if not impossible, for a restaurant to patent its menu or the distinctive service experience it provides to customers. Further, fashion in relation to food is constantly changing and this implies that it makes limited sense to take out a patent in this area. In addition, single, off the shelf innovations can be difficult to distinguish and describe. Rather, it is the overall concept, which is the innovation, for example, Nordic food, and how this is implemented by single service businesses continuously changes.

The complexity of service innovation means that it is difficult to patent and protect. A winter sports destination in Norway wanted to develop services targeted at the summer season. This would extend or stretch this venue's season. They decided to introduce downhill biking. This innovation emerged from a complex interplay between local cycling enthusiasts, managers, security services and health services, volunteers and landowners. The challenge was to try to make this destination attractive both for elite cyclists and their families. By organizing large sporting events, including world cups and world championships, this destination developed its own place-based brand as part of an appropriability strategy that is intended to curb attempts by competitors to copy this approach (Fuglsang and Nordli 2018).

Copyrights (especially in communications and the media) and trademarks may also be used by service businesses to protect innovations and to restrict copying by competitors. In food ser-

vices, retailing, insurance and transport, for example, trademarks are used (such as Coca Cola, McDonald's, Levi's, AXA, American Airlines, 85 °C Bakery Café, Jollibee, Tim Hortons Cafe and Bake Shop). A brand is a form of guarantee of a certain quality or price or combination of price and quality (see also Chap. 9). Other important strategies in services include first-to-market and the complexity of innovations that can be embedded in very complex organizational structures or creative environments making them difficult to copy. Examples of the latter type include the organizational structure of McDonald's or the creativity environment of the Danish world-famous restaurant, Noma.

Intellectual property rights (IPR)—patents, trademarks, design rights or copyrights—involve the acquisition of legal rights to own and earn rents—profits—from an invention or innovation. These legal rights depend on national and international law and the ways in which such laws are implemented in practice. The risks of imitation and the effective use of IPR regimes are higher in some countries than in others (Pilat 2001). A study based on a comprehensive survey of service firms using the Eurostat Community Innovation Survey (CIS4; Battisti et al. 2015) identified that companies that develop services that are 'new in the world' make greater use of IPR compared to companies that develop services that are only new to themselves. IPR (patents, copyrights), therefore, seems to be used more by 'leading innovators' in services or those companies that develop radical innovations. Radical service innovators more often protect their internally driven innovations and thus have a closed innovation process whereas service companies that can be described as 'followers' are less likely to protect their internal innovation processes and are more likely to use external sourcing—that is, open innovation.

The application of patents and copyrights by service businesses should not be ignored. Nevertheless, there is a large group of service companies that do not engage in R&D or make use of IPR. They manage to innovate through strategic, complex innovations that often include imitation and adaptation of existing innovations to local markets.

## 7.9 Productivity and Process Innovation

Process innovations may increase productivity leading to a possible reduction in price or an increase in profitability (see Chap. 5) enhancing a service firm's competitive advantage (Pilat 2001). As the service product and the production and delivery processes are connected, process innovations can also lead to better services for customers. Process innovations can increase the quality of a service ensuring more satisfied and loyal customers (see Chap. 8). Process innovations may be considered to be as important as product innovations within services. Organizational innovations are often connected with process innovations; service production and delivery are connected and generally labour intensive. Process innovation in services very often involves changes in employees' working procedures, but also often includes the introduction of new technology. Digital technology is a main driver of process innovation in services as in other sectors (see Chaps. 3, 4 and 11). Digitalization and the Internet of Things can rationalize service delivery processes. Sensors embedded in oil or gas boilers, industrial pumps and engines enable them to be monitored from afar and for adjustments to be made by a service company (see Chap. 12). Digital technology can also rationalize administrative procedures including accountancy, human resource management, procurement and invoicing. This reduces administration costs facilitating a reduction in prices or enhanced profitability. Technological innovations in other sectors are also the basis for innovation in services. For example, cleaning companies have adopted new eco-friendly chemicals and cleaning machines simplifying work processes and increasing the speed of service delivery.

An example of a process innovation is the distribution of postal packets. Logistics and distribution companies such as FedEx and DHL have introduced new procedures that are based on optimizing the logistics for the delivery of packets. This involves the selection of the optimal routes for packages including how a package is collected, the route selected to the connection hub and how receivers obtain final delivery (see Chap. 11). IT programs have been developed as part of an optimization process, including tracking systems, enabling customers to track packages as they travel through the logistics system. This enhances service quality. These tracking systems make it possible to identify process failures in real time and to develop solutions. These logistics companies have been extremely successful in the development and application of process optimization innovations and have outcompeted many more conventional providers of postal services.

Another example of an IT-based process innovation is in the security service industry. Security guards can visit customer's properties or can monitor them remotely using sensors and cameras. The application of sensors and cameras that are monitored over the Web has reduced service delivery costs and increased effectiveness. IT-based process innovations can be found across a range of service industries. Lawyers are using machine learning to read documents to search for those pages that need to be read by the lawyer. Millions of documents can be searched extremely rapidly. Architects used to sit and draw plans by hand, but software is now used to create digital drawings and virtual three-dimensional (3D) visualization models. This has transformed the design of buildings as customers can now imagine the spaces before they are built.

Nevertheless, process innovations do not always result in significant cost savings. The challenge is that technology can be expensive and moreover often a service business and its employees do not have the capabilities to apply new technologies to existing service processes. The development of new organizational procedures may create turbulence within the organization leading to inefficiencies and problems with service delivery. There is often a tension between service innovation and productivity in services. Businesses that focus on productivity enhancement often find it difficult to profit from innovation (Aspara et al. 2018). The danger is that productivity improvements reduce service quality or result in price-based competition. The application of technological solutions to service processes can be easily copied by competitors. Service businesses must combine a focus on service innovation that results in alterations that are inimitable, or difficult to copy, with innovations intended to enhance productivity.

## 7.10   Managing Innovation in Services: The Balancing Challenge

Innovation in service businesses involves iterative processes involving many different stakeholders. They are connected through value chains; yet each actor is often able to act in creative and autonomous ways. A coffee supplier to a restaurant has a weaker supply chain relationship compared to a parts supplier to an automotive manufacturer but can independently develop the service. Internal and external R&D activities, professionals, managers, customers, competitors and the public sector will also develop services, or parts of services, relatively independently of one another in what are often described as loosely coupled innovation systems (Sundbo and Gallouj 2000).

This means that innovations in service companies are connected to each other in complex ways. Interdependent innovations do not always happen simultaneously. The components of a service may be changed from one day to the next, from one customer to another, one employee to another and one company to another. Nevertheless, some elements must be repeated synchronically over time to form innovations enabling revenue generation and service coordination (Sundbo 1997; Toivonen and Tuominen 2009). This paradox of multiplicity alongside uniformity can be challenging for managers of service innovation. On the one hand, this facilitates better integration of services with the value creation process for each customer making use of the individual experiences of employees. On the other hand, too many parallel developments can create coordination problems preventing service innovation and growth. Selective approaches to innovation are required to coordinate services, ensure quality, reduce costs and make services tradable. But too much emphasis on streamlining services to upscale service innovation also comes with risks. The knowledge gained from employee-customer interactions becomes more restricted, leading to a less robust business and fewer ideas to support further innovation. Therefore, service innovation managers must try to achieve and maintain a difficult balance between multiplicity and uniformity of innovations. This is to balance standardization with customization. Different types of service experience require a different type of balance. On the one hand, are extremely standardized services in which no alteration is permitted, for example, in call centres that deploy regimented scripts. On the other hand, are services that are completely customized to meet individual needs.

Innovation management in services often does not usually involve the management of an R&D department. Very few service companies have an R&D department. Large retailers have units that specialize in data analytics targeted at identifying innovations and alterations that are intended to influence consumer behaviour. They will also develop and test new store concepts.

Innovation management in services is generally about ensuring that innovation and entrepreneurship activities occur across the organization. It becomes part of HRM activities (see Chap. 6). Some service firms, particularly large organizations, have an innovation department with an innovation manager whose task it is to collect ideas for further innovations from employees and managers, to induce innovation in the organization, to oversee innovation projects that have been identified by management and to ensure that innovations support organizational strategy and the firm's business model (Love et al. 2011). Innovation management entails communication and strategy (Sundbo 1997). Innovation in services is generally focussed on open innovation (Chesbrough 2011) where the firm is open to ideas from customers and even competitors. Many 'new' service products and processes that are introduced by service firms imitate competitors.

The typically loosely coupled and open innovation system that exists in service organizations has several advantages. It catches ideas from employees, it is suitable for user- or customer-based innovations, it is flexible and practice-based and innovation processes can occur rapidly. There are also disadvantages. One is that it predominantly leads to incremental innovation and very rarely to radical change. Another is that this system can have difficulties in adopting new technology from the outside. It can also lead to diffuse innovation processes with no common goal and resources can be wasted by employees and managers as they engage in idea creation. This openness also implies that competitors can copy ideas and gain first-mover advantage.

A typical innovation management process, at least in larger service firms, is a balanced one (Fig. 7.2). Management encourages employee- and customer-based innovation and induces entrepreneurial behaviour across the firm. Management may restrict innovation activities to avoid too much waste of resources (time) and to try to ensure that innovations support the organization's strategy and business model. Management also selects which ideas should be further developed and considered for implementation. Top-down and bottom-up innovation processes are balanced by management, either by the managing director or a designated innovation manager.

Some large service companies develop top-down systems and systematize the innovation process to try to avoid these disadvantages—without abandoning the advantages of having an open and flexible process. More standardized services tend to come with a more systematic innovation and development process. IBM, the IT and software service company, has established a department that organizes innovation competitions amongst employees and customers; everybody can participate in an open innovation process. Even service innovation laboratories have been established in the service sector. The German technology agency, the Fraunhofer Institute, has created a service laboratory based around a specially designed room in which service innovations, servicescapes and service experiences can be projected on to screens. A complete hotel lobby can, for example, be cre-ated by projecting pictures and videos. Service firms can then experiment with how employees and customers react to different room layouts or new or modified employee behavioural routines. The Nordic insurance company, Tryg, has created a service innovation room—a service innovation laboratory—equipped with chairs, pillows and removable walls. Employees and consumers are invited to work in this service laboratory on the development of new ideas and to experiment with the design of new service journeys (see Chap. 13).

## 7.11  Wrapping Up

Innovation management in service companies is thus an act of balancing customization with standardization. Systems can be developed within service organizations to assist managers in balancing top-down decision systems with bottom-up entrepreneurial systems. There are two critical points to note here. First, service innovation is more complex than R&D activity as it involves creating and managing the interface between service providers and service consumers—between people. People play a central role in this process. Sometimes the relationship between producers and consumers is mediated by technology and increasingly the service provider has been replaced with technology (see Chaps. 4 and 5). Second, services are extremely heterogeneous. It is important not to overstate this heterogeneity compared to manufacturing; manufacturing is also very heterogeneous. Often service innovation is directly related to innovations in manufactured goods.

Within a service business there are at least three types of service innovation. There are process and product innovations creating new or modified service experiences that are a service firm's primary revenue source. Moreover, there are service innovations in the administrative processes supporting the delivery of service experiences. These are three very different innovation systems that form a very complex innovation environment. The complexity of service innovation systems can be highlighted by returning to the example of the law firm that we explored in Chap. 3 (Sect. 3.9) and Chap. 5 (Sect. 5.2). A law practice, for example, has within it two types of customer-focussed innovation system. On the one side, are legal services that are subsidized by the state in the form of legal aid. Innovation is applied to the creation of these legal services that is focused on stripping out costs and on productivity improvements. These are low-value service encounters. On the other side, there is the provision of extremely high-value and customized legal services. Here the focus is on developing new legal solutions to meet the needs of a specific customer. In addition, a law firm must innovate in the administrative processes that support the delivery of its services to clients including how to approach and interact with clients, how to organize client encounters and how to maintain client relationships over time. A legal practice contains three different but interconnected innovation spaces or innovation challenge areas.

All this complexity within the service sector requires leadership to encourage and facilitate service innovation. This is a critical point. The average small- to medium-sized service enterprise does not have the resources to employ a full-time innovation manager. Nevertheless, all service businesses must designate someone with responsibility for encouraging, identifying and leading intra- and inter-firm innovation projects. Service innovation often involves the co-creation of innovation with customers. This includes alterations to the service experience and to service processes. These play an important role in service innovation processes and it is to these that we now turn our attention.

**Learning Outcomes**
- Service firms innovate to enhance their competitive position.
- Innovation is both practice-based and structured.
- Innovation is both customized and standardized.
- Innovation in services is a complex multidimensional process involving customers and suppliers.
- Service innovation can be managed but requires leadership.

## References

Alam, I., & Perry, C. (2002). A Customer-Oriented New Service Development Process. *Journal of Services Marketing, 16*(6), 515–534.

Aspara, J., Klein, J. F., & Luo, X. (2018). The Dilemma of Service Productivity and Service Innovation: An Empirical Exploration in Financial Services. *Journal of Service Research, 21*(2), 249–262.

Barras, R. (1986). Towards a Theory of Innovation in Services. *Research Policy, 15*(4), 161–173.

Barras, R. (1990). Interactive Innovation in Financial and Business Services: The Vanguard of the Service Revolution. *Research Policy, 19*(3), 215–237.

Battilana, J., Leca, B., & Boxenbaum, E. (2009). How Actors Change Institutions: Towards a Theory of Institutional Entrepreneurship. *Academy of Management Annals, 3*, 65–107.

Battisti, G., Gallego, J., Rubalcaba, L., & Windrum, P. (2015). Open Innovation in Services: Knowledge Sources, Intellectual Property Rights and Internationalization. *Economics of Innovation and New Technology, 24*(3), 223–247.

Berman, S. J. (2012). Digital Transformation: Opportunities to Create New Business Models. *Strategy & Leadership, 40*(1), 16–24.

Boltanski, L., & Thévenot, L. (2006). *On Justification: Economies of Worth*. Princeton, NJ: Princeton University Press.

Cass, N., & Shove, E. (2017). *Changing Energy Demand. Concepts, Metaphors and Implications for Policy*. Lancaster: Lancaster University.

Chesbrough, H. (2011). Open services innovation. Rethinking your business to grow and compete in a new era. San Francisco, CA: Jossey-Bass.

Djellal, F., Gallouj, F., & Miles, I. (2013). Two Decades of Research on Innovation in Services: Which Place for Public Services? *Structural Change and Economic Dynamics, 27*(1), 98–117.

Fagerberg, J. (2005). Innovation: A Guide to the Literature. In J. Fagerberg, D. C. Mowery, & R. R. Nelson (Eds.), *The Oxford Handbook of Innovation*. Oxford: Oxford University Press.

Fuglsang, L. (2010). Bricolage and Invisible Innovation in Public Service Innovation. *Journal of Innovation Economics, 25*(1), 67–87.

Fuglsang, L., & Nordli, A. (2018). On Service Innovation as an Interactive Process: A Case Study of the Engagement with Innovation of a Tourism Service. *Social Sciences, 7*(12), 258.

Fuglsang, L., & Sundbo, J. (2005). The Organizational Innovation System: Three Modes. *Journal of Change Management, 5*(3), 329–344.

Fuglsang, L., & Sundbo, J. (2016). Innovation in Public Service Systems. In M. Toivonen (Ed.), *Service Innovation: Novel Ways of Creating Value in Actor Systems*. Tokyo: Springer.

Gallouj, F. (2010). Services Innovation: Assimilation, Differentiation, Inversion and Integration. In

B. Hossein (Ed.), *The Handbook of Technology Management*. Hoboken, NJ: Wiley.

Gallouj, F., & Savona, M. (2009). Innovation in Services: A Review of the Debate and a Research Agenda. *Journal of Evolutionary Economics, 19*(2), 173–196.

Gallouj, F., & Weinstein, O. (1997). Innovation in Services. *Research Policy, 26*(4–5), 537–556.

Global Entrepreneurship Research Association. (2020). *Global Entrepreneurship Monitor 2019–2020*. London: Global Entrepreneurship Research Association.

Jacobides, M. G., Cennamo, C., & Gawer, A. (2018). Towards a Theory of Ecosystems. *Strategic Management Journal, 39*(8), 2255–2276.

Jensen, M. B., Johnson, B., Lorenz, E., & Lundvall, B. Å. (2007). Forms of Knowledge and Modes of Innovation. *Research Policy, 36*(5), 680–693.

Love, J. H., Roper, S., & Bryson, J. R. (2011). Openness, Knowledge, Innovation and Growth in UK Business Services. *Research Policy, 40*(10), 1438–1452.

Normann, R. (1983). *Service Management*. New York: Wiley.

Pantzar, M. and Shove, E. (2010), 'Understanding innovation in practice: a discussion of the production and re-production of Nordic walking', *Technology Analysis & Strategic Management, 22*(4), 447–461. https://doi.org/10.1080/09537321003714402

Pavitt, K. (1984). Sectoral Patterns of Technical Change: Towards a Taxonomy and a Theory. *Research Policy, 13*(6), 343–373.

Pilat, D. (2001). Innovation and Productivity in Services: State of the Art. In OECD (Ed.), *Innovation and Productivity in Services*. Paris: OECD.

Reckwitz, A. (2002). Toward a Theory of Social Practices: A Development in Culturalist Theorizing. *European Journal of Social Theory, 5*(2), 243–263.

Schumpeter, J. A. (1969 [1934]). *The Theory of Economic Development. An Inquiry into Profits, Capital, Credit, Interest and the Business Cycle*. Oxford: Oxford University Press.

Sundbo, J. (1997). Management of Innovation in Services. *Service Industries Journal, 17*(3), 432–455.

Sundbo, J. (1998). *The Organisation of Innovation in Services*. Frederiksberg: Roskilde University Press.

Sundbo, J., & Gallouj, F. (2000). Innovation As Loosely Coupled System I Services. In J. S. Metcalfe & I. Miles (Eds.), *Innovation Systems in the Service Economy, Measurement and Case Study Analysis*. London: Kluwer.

Sundbo, J., Sundbo, D. and Henten, A. (2015). 'Service encounters as bases for innovation', *Service Industries Journal*, 35(5), 255–274.

Sundbo, J. and Toivonen, M. (2011). User-Based Innovation in Services, Cheltenham: Edward Elgar, pp. 1–21.

Tether, B. S. (2005). Do Services Innovate (Differently)? Insights from the European Innobarometer Survey. *Industry and Innovation, 12*(2), 153–184.

Thévenot, L. (2001). Pragmatic Regimes Governing the Engagement with the World. In T. R. Schatzki, K. D. Knorr-Cetina, & E. v. Savigny (Eds.), *The Practice Turn in Contemporary Theory*. London: Routledge.

Toivonen, M., & Tuominen, T. (2009). Emergence of Innovations in Services. *Service Industries Journal, 29*(5), 887–902.

Wallin, A., & Fuglsang, L. (2017). Service Innovations Breaking Institutionalized Rules of Health Care. *Journal of Service Management, 28*(5), 972–997.

Wedum, G. (2019). *Retrovasjon: Innovasjon med utspring i tradisjon i matbransjen*. PhD thesis, Inland Norway University od Applied Science, Lillehammer.

Windrum, P., & García-Goñi, M. (2008). A Neo-Schumpeterian Model of Health Services Innovation. *Research Policy, 37*(4), 649–672.

Witell, L., Gebauer, H., Jaakkola, E., Hammedi, W., Patricio, L., & Perks, H. (2017). A Bricolage Perspective on Service Innovation. *Journal of Business Research, 79*, 290–298.

Zeithaml, V. A., Parasuraman, A., & Berry, L. L. (1985). Problems and Strategies in Services Marketing. *Journal of Marketing, 49*(2), 33–46.

## Further Reading

Cooper, R. G., & Edgett, S. J. (1999). *Product Development for the Service Sector*. Massachusetts: Perseus Books.

Gallouj, F., & Djellal, D. (Eds.). (2010). *The Handbook of Innovation and Services*. Cheltenham: Edward Elgar.

Hipp, C. (2008). Service Peculiarities and the Specific Role of Technology in Service Innovation Management. *International Journal of Services Technology and Management, 9*(2), 154–173.

Miles, I., & Metcalf, S. (Eds.). (2000). *Innovation Systems in the Service Economy*. London: Kluwer.

Rubalcaba, L., Michel, S., Sundbo, J., Brown, S., & Reynoso, J. (2012). Shaping, Organizing and Rethinking Service Innovation: A Multidimensional Framework. *Journal of Service Management, 23*(5), 696–715.

Tidd, J., & Hull, F. (Eds.). (2003). *Service Innovation*. London: World Scientific Publications.

## Useful Websites

Ryanair: https://corporate.ryanair.com/about-us/history-of-ryanair/.

Amazon: https://www.aboutamazon.com/?utm_source=gateway&utm_medium=footer.

DHL: https://www.logistics.dhl/dk-en/home.html.

IT and Communication Technology Development: http://blog.interactiveschools.com/blog/50-million-users-how-long-does-it-take-tech-to-reach-this-milestone.

# Customer First: Understanding Customers

**8**

## Key Themes

- What role do customers play in service businesses?
- How is value created and what types of values are created by service businesses?
- The customer interface and co-creation
- Customer value
- Service quality
- Tailor made and standardized services
- Service experiences
- Customer loyalty
- Complaints management
- Outsourcing and service offshoring

Customers play a critical role in all businesses, but for services, and the scientific understanding of service businesses, customers are especially important. Traditionally, it was assumed that all services were produced during the moment of consumption and could not be stored (Grönroos 1990). Traditional services are tailor-made meeting the needs of individual customers; customers are part of the production and delivery process participating in the co-creation of service experiences or service encounters. This does not necessarily imply that customers are directly engaged in service production unless the service experience has been constructed using a self-service

**Electronic Supplementary Material** The online version of this chapter (https://doi.org/10.1007/978-3-030-52060-1_8) contains supplementary material, which is available to authorized users.

approach. The delivery of a service is about solving customer problems or needs; the customer must define the problem and make decisions regarding possible solutions. Customer involvement in service production and delivery plays a central role in marketing services and in the discipline of service science, and this is even the case for the provision of standardized service solutions. This is to emphasize the importance of the service encounter (Czepiel et al. 1985) (see Chap. 6) whereby service providers and customers negotiate which services should be delivered and how they should be delivered. Reading and managing a service business involves understanding the interrelationships between customers, marketing and service operations.

The service encounter, or the interactions between service providers and customers, is the basis for the development of a special service marketing approach in which service firms try to ensure that customers appreciate the qualities of the delivered service and of the service firm. The aim is to create satisfied customers who are more likely to make repeat purchases and to develop some form of attachment with the service provider and its employees. The key challenge is: 'how can a service firm create customer satisfaction?' leading to repeat purchase. This challenge is explored in this chapter before examining the service marketing approach in Chap. 9.

In this chapter, the service encounter is considered from the perspective of customers including a focus on: 'what creates customer

J. R. Bryson et al., *Service Management*, https://doi.org/10.1007/978-3-030-52060-1_8

satisfaction?' and 'what do customers want, and why?' To explore these questions requires a discussion and review of customer lifestyles, preferences or values. Service firms have two types of customers: business-to-business (B2B) and business-to-consumers (B2C). Each type is very different, and these differences are reflected in the service encounter and in the marketing of services.

## 8.1  The Customer Interface, Co-creation and Standardization

It had been assumed that all services were delivered during the moment of production involving direct interactions between service providers and their customers and this highlighted the importance of the customer interface (Czepiel et al. 1985, Coye 2004) during the moment of truth (see Chap. 6). The traditional view assumed that, during the co-creation or co-production of a service (Payne et al. 2008), customers would be able to shape the services that they required. This shaping would occur within the parameters set by the service provider's operational systems. This was advantageous for service firms because it enhanced customer satisfaction. Service co-creation is a fundamental principle for service businesses and plays a central role in the service-dominant-logic (S-D) approach (see Chap. 2). The argument is that the S-D approach applies to all firms including manufacturing companies (Vargo and Lusch 2008).

The assumption in the S-D perspective is that customers know what they require, but this is not always the case. Often the customers only know what they really would have wanted after the service has been delivered and consumed. The customer interface, and co-creation process, provides the service supplier with opportunities to create and enhance customer satisfaction. This is not always guaranteed. Service firms need to continually monitor and evaluate customer satisfaction. This is a complex process involving the perceived quality of the service solution combined with perceptions regarding the quality of the service

encounter and the relationships between service employees and customers.

Furthermore, the traditional view is not easily applied to the production of more standardized services or those provided by online platforms. In this case, service providers must decide which problems the service will be able to solve and how solutions will be delivered. The customer is then able to decide whether they will purchase the service. The decision to purchase a standardized service is similar to that involved in purchasing a material good. Standardization has the potential to transform services into commodities purchased on price rather than quality and this is reflected in the emphasis placed on cost reduction in the service delivery process (Sundbo 2002), and this includes service quality. Customers have some expectations regarding the services that will be provided. Planning a holiday, for example, may involve a decision to stay at a local, family-owned picturesque hotel. This option comes with benefits, but also some possible negatives. There are many alternative options available in the hotel and hospitality industry ranging from local hotels, chains and Airbnb. The decision to select a hotel chain compared to a family-run hotel reflects a distinction between perhaps a bespoke boutique hotel compared to a more standardized service experience. Thus, hotels managed by Novotel or Marriott provide similar qualities of accommodation, related services and service standards. This reflects the emphasis placed by Ritzer (2000) (see Chap. 5, Sect. 5.4) on *efficiency, calculability, predictability* and *control* in the provision of standardized services. In other words, customers know what to expect; these are safe known and reliable service providers and the chain's branding acts as a proxy measure of service quality. Many business travellers prefer to stay in chain hotels. These have known facilities with rooms having similar layouts. In addition, special deals can be negotiated between a business with many frequent business travellers and a hotel chain resulting in significant savings. For the business traveller, the key issue is a service experience that is as frictionless as possible. Standardization and predictability of service quality and of the service experience can, in some situations, be more highly valued than an individualized service.

The interactions between service providers and customers include three steps or stages (Tsiotsou and Wirtz 2015) (Fig. 8.1). Operational solutions to each stage must be developed by all service businesses.

Many services are delivered without any form of direct personal encounter between customers and frontline employees. All types of self-service and knowledge services are provided via Internet-based platforms and are available without service employees being directly involved in the customer interface. Customers are engaged in a process of co-creation but with the material facilities developed and provided by a service firm—for example, self-service payment tills in supermarkets, Internet banking or e-commerce. This co-creation process is between the material system, the software and the hardware, and the cus-

tomer. This approach shifts the delivery of the critical moment of truth, the service encounter, from frontline employees to the material systems and to the company's back region. In many instances, there are very few employees, occasionally none, who are engaged directly with customers. In these types of service relationships, a key challenge for customers may be the availability of limited and restricted choices provided by online systems. Thus, does a supermarket or Internet banking platform provide sufficient possibilities for customers to customize the service experience?

The shift from services delivered through face-to-face encounters to standardized self-service and the influence this has on customer satisfaction has been explored in a number of studies (Sundbo 2002; Fuglsang and Sundbo 2006). On the one hand, this shift removes the possibility for frontline employees to be service

---

**Pre-purchase stage**

The *customer* searches for information, becomes or is aware of the service provider
The customer decides to buy

The *service provider* must be visible and attractive (e.g.via web sites)

**Service purchase (encounter) stage**

The *customer* requests a certain service. The customer experiences service delivery

The *service provider* must have a plan for the delivery and how the provision process can add value for the customer

**Post-purchase (encounter) stage**

The *customer* evaluates the delivered service and the delivery process. The customer decides whether to buy from this service firm again

The *service provider* must learn about customer satisfaction

**Fig. 8.1**  The three stages in service purchase transactions. (Source: Authors' own)

minded and to focus on providing services to a single customer limiting the ability to sell additional services by developing a direct relationship between service employee and customer. Nevertheless, algorithms embedded in platforms use big data to predict combinations of services that customers combine within service bundles and the platform is then able to suggest additional choices to consumers. On the other hand, this shift removes the possibilities for frontline employees to deliver poor or unsatisfactory service experiences. Self-service systems can ensure a certain standard of service is provided that is predictable and highly regulated by the service business. Many self-service systems, for example, online platforms, provide customers with many options to combine individual service modules into a service bundle, for example, a hotel, flight and local travel bundle (Sundbo 1994). Furthermore, price is important but may not always be offset by the quality of the service delivery process as is claimed in many service marketing theories (Grönroos 1990).

Sometimes customers do not want to be involved in co-creating a service. They just want a solution to their problem with limited trouble and effort on their part. They want the service firm to select and implement a solution even though it might still want to try to involve customers in a co-creation process by offering additional optional service modules (see Chap. 9). Nevertheless, a service business must ensure that attempts to persuade customers to purchase additional services do not undermine a customer's overall perceptions of service quality reducing repeat business.

## 8.2    B2B Interactions

Service businesses want customers to be interested in considering purchasing their services. This requires that potential customers are aware of these services as well as the existence of service providers. General marketing (see Chap. 9) is as necessary for selling services as it is for selling goods. Nevertheless, service businesses experience particular challenges and possibilities

because of the nature of the service delivery process and of the service product. As a service is mostly immaterial and cannot be stored, then customers are unable to directly experience a service before purchase. A physical good, for example, cars, smartphones and washing machines, can be examined before purchase.

A service should provide a solution to a problem being experienced by a customer. This is a complex process and is more complex compared to transactions involving physical goods. On the one hand, in services that are customized during face-to-face encounters with front region service employees then customers are directly involved in shaping the service delivery process, the service solution and the quality of the service experience. All these characteristics have led to service firms, and service science, focusing on customer lifestyles and related problems that require service solutions. During this type of service co-creation process information and ideas may be exchanged between customers and service employees that may lead to process and service innovations (cf. Chap. 7) benefitting both providers and consumers. On the other hand, there are standardized services in which customization options are included, but as standard options. Learning is automated as big data is captured and analysed leading to incremental and sometimes radical innovation.

Service businesses are not only interested in obtaining information about their customers to develop existing and new services and to enhance the service delivery process. They are also interested in understanding how customers evaluate service quality. This customer assessment or service appraisal process is important as it influences pricing and customer willingness to enter into repeat transactions. Satisfied customers are critical for service businesses. A key point is that a satisfied customer may lead to third-party referrals. A physical good is often seen by a purchaser's friends and family, but the intangibility of services makes this type of informal observation extremely difficult. Thus, service consumers must talk about the quality of their service encounters with friends, family and acquaintances and this type of third-party referral plays an important role in service marketing.

Customer care is a core parameter for the competitiveness of service businesses. As a general rule, service businesses must be more preoccupied with obtaining information about customer interactions compared with technological developments or the rationalization of the service production process. There are different ways of obtaining this information—directly during the face-to-face encounter or indirectly by capturing streams of big data obtained from transactions. These are not mutually exclusive as data can be captured during face-to-face encounters. The challenge for services businesses reliant on face-to-face encounters is how to capture information and to convert this into knowledge. In retailing, the analysis of close-circuit television (CCTV) can be used to explore service encounters combined with big data captured from smartphones. Some large retail chains have installed trackers within their stores that are able to follow the digital pings emitted by smartphones as the phones try to identify local wi-fi networks. These pings are tracked identifying the number of customers in a store, but more importantly their movement around the store. This includes an analysis of how long they spend in a section. These big data streams are then analysed informing decisions regarding store design and layout. Monitoring and enhancing customer care must be a central consideration for all service businesses and is the basis for the service-oriented marketing approach that is explored in Chap. 9.

## 8.3   Customer Values and Value-in-Use

### 8.3.1   Customer Value

The co-creation of a service creates different forms of value. From the perspective of the service business, value is defined in economic terms including turnover and profit. But, for some service businesses value must also include employee perception of the quality of the work experience. This is important for retaining and recruiting skilled employees. The meaning of value for customers is more difficult to identify, measure and define. It can be measured in economic terms such as the price of the service, but what about quality, the nature of the experience and the quality of the relationship between customers and service providers. Use values also include the ability of a service to provide a solution to customers' problems. This value is difficult to measure as there are many different parameters involved:

(a) How important is the problem for the customer?
(b) How much are they willing to pay for a solution?
(c) Did the customer recognize and appreciate the quality of the solution?
(d) Was the service delivery process satisfactory?
(e) Were there delivery problems that reduced the value of the solution provided?

Many people have experienced a plumber or a carpenter who arrives to fix a problem but does not clean up when the work is completed or does not provide the expected or required solution, for example, the pipework might be visible and unsightly. One difficulty is in identifying service providers and persuading them to provide an appropriate service. For customers, negative experiences undermine the values created during service encounters. The problem has been solved but not in the way anticipated by the customer. All this means that next time the customer will try to identify another service provider.

In some instance, goods retain their exchange values, and, in some cases, these exchange values increase over time. This reflects the balance between supply and demand and the desirability and nature of the good. Some goods are consumed immediately or rapidly, and they are similar to services in that their exchange values evaporate at the moment of final consumption. This is the case for all services—once used or consumed their exchange values are destroyed and the service cannot be sold on to another possible consumer. A service can never be a long-term financial investment, but instead services involve the creation of *value-in-use* (Edvardsson et al. 2011; Heinonen and Strandvik 2009). This is a complex process. An investment in educational services enhances the consumer's capabilities and this enhancement cannot be sold on to others. Nevertheless, the change that is undergone by the consumer, through the application of the service, might result in a long-term economic return on the investment. It is important to distinguish between exchange values that evaporate at the moment of consumption and indirect and induced values that come from the service encounter. For some services, value-in-use evaporates rapidly and even immediately, for other services value-in-use rapidly become no more than a memory of an experience while some services create long-lasting forms of value-in-use.

A significant problem, especially for service firms, is how to observe and understand value-in-use for customers. Fundamentally the service must solve the customer's problem; if it does not, it has no value. An economic exchange might have occurred, but no value-in-use created. Value-in-use reflects customer perceptions of the quality of the service solution and the relationship to actual and perceived customer needs and expectations. This is a subjective process that varies between customers. The same service will create different perceived and actual value-in-use for different customers. The challenge for service providers is in being aware of the types of value-in-use that may be created for individual customers with distinct characteristics. Some of these values-in-use may not be recognized by a customer and this will reflect on their perception of service quality. Customers may be aware of the value of solving a specific problem and what they are willing to pay for a solution. Nevertheless, they may have limited understanding of the service delivery, or co-creation process, until service delivery is completed. Thus, any appraisal of value-in-use can only be undertaken once the service has been delivered. The challenge is that the next customer may assess value-in-use using very different parameters. Here it is worth noting that the assessment of a good's use values also varies between customers.

The general values and life experiences of customers—for example, whether they are employed or retired and are wealthy or poor—also influence their assessment of the value-in-use of a specific service. Service firms develop a customer segmentation approach (see Chap. 9) to develop suitable frameworks for understanding different customer segments' perceptions and experiences of value-in-use. In addition, employees involved in a service firm's encounter with customers can influence the latter's assessment of the value of the service. As service employees often encounter customers directly, they shape service delivery providing additional customer services. These may be provided at no additional cost but are included in a service bundle to enhance perceptions of value-in-use. This is the 'moment of truth' explored in Chap. 6. Service firms work closely with frontline employees to encourage and train them to deliver services that are as customized and personalized as much as possible and which add to the value-in-use experienced and perceived by the customer (see also Chap. 9).

Value-in-use has become more complicated as additional consumer expectations emerge which influence perceptions of value. The shift towards consumers adopting ethical, social and political values alters the types of services provided by service businesses, but also customer expectations and perceptions of value-in-use. This shift is reflected in the enhanced importance of corporate social responsibility and the expectations that businesses will act responsibly. Some customers will search for firms that explicitly embrace their values and this is playing an increasingly more important role in influencing consumer behaviour. This relationship between consumer values and behaviour may, for some consumers, be more important than price or even service quality. Consumers will make decisions that are the outcome of a series of trade-offs between exchange and service-in-use values combined with their belief systems.

It is difficult for a service business to understand differentiated customer value frameworks and the ways in which they influence consumer decision-making processes. Often service business managers and employees will draw upon their own personal experiences to specify the values-in-use which they consider a service will create for a specific customer. There are also measurement instruments that have been developed to try to measure value-in-use for different customer segments (see Chap. 13).

### 8.3.2 Value Proposition

Services are sold based not only on their objective functionality (solving a problem in a specific technical way), but also on their value-in-use, which is a broader phenomenon. A service provider cannot know beforehand which wider framework a customer is going to apply to evaluate value-in-use and cannot predict how a customer will, in the end, assess the whole service delivery process. The implication is that service providers cannot deliver a clearly specified level of value-in-use. Value-in-use varies by customer. A provider delivers a service process that they believe provides a certain value-in-use for customers, but they cannot know whether the customer will ascribe the same value to the service. The service provider can only deliver a service that will hopefully provide the customer with the intended value-in-use. The actual and perceived value-in-use is related to the value propositions developed and provided by service firms (Skålen et al. 2015) (see Chap. 3). Only once the customer has consumed the service is it possible to observe if the proposed value was identified and accepted by the consumer or whether the consumer ascribed a different value-in-use to the service.

From a marketing perspective, the most important activity involves assessing the value of the service to the customer rather than its functionality or whether it solves the customer's problem. This marketing approach has been disputed (Sundbo 2002). It can be interpreted as meaning that service firms may sell services that clients do not really need as long as these services are delivered in a way that fits with customers' general value frameworks. This is partially correct. Nevertheless, it is unrealistic to assume that a ser-

vice could be sold that only satisfies general values held by customers without any requirement to solve a problem.

## 8.4 Creating Good Service Experiences

Service theories highlight the importance of creating good customer experiences (Payne et al. 2009). This is in line with the creation of value-in-use for customers. A service experience involves many different dimensions:

1. How customers remember and perceive service delivery?
2. Did the service provide an appropriate solution?
3. How was the solution provided?
4. Was the co-creation process effective?
5. Was the service delivered on time?
6. Did frontline employees adopt a flexible approach?
7. Did frontline employees adopt a service mindset?
8. The willingness of frontline employees to provide additional services.
9. The qualities of supporting infrastructure, including websites.
10. The qualities of the servicescape or the environment in which the service encounter occurred.

The service experience plays an important role in encouraging repeat purchases as well as customer acceptance of high prices or any proposed increase in prices. Therefore, service firms must work on creating good service experiences for customers. This can be facilitated by training frontline employees, by asking customers about their experiences, by developing the service and identifying additional services that could be included in the service bundle.

For digitized services, the experience is constructed around the design of the website. This includes digitized content, but also links to other services. Websites must be supported by chatbots and helplines and be facilitated by predictive algorithms which identify opportunities to offer additional services. No website is perfect; customers will balance weaker elements of the site against functions that enhance service quality.

An experience is elusive and is often tacit and intangible. It may be an emotional reaction that is difficult to describe and evaluate. Alternatively, an experience occurs when some undefined and difficult-to-measure alterations occur in the mind and/or body without any direct material alteration. An experience is a state of being or a change in a state of being. A change occurs when we watch a movie, view a painting or participate in a music festival. Experiences of this kind are 'expressive' as they engender feelings and atmospheres that are enjoyable or hedonic. They can be part of a service experience and might compensate for failures in other service elements, including failure to provide a complete solution to a customer's problem. The outcome of a service experience may be unpredictable—for some the outcome might be contentment or happiness and for other people a moment of sadness and reflection. There has been considerable discussion regarding the ability of 'expressive' elements to compensate for failures in core service delivery.

Service experiences have been characterized as instrumental because customers are predominantly interested in whether the service solves their problem (Sundbo 2015). Any hedonic or other experiences are of secondary importance and cannot in the long run compensate for failures in the delivery of a services primary purpose. In the 1980s, airline companies, particularly SAS (Scandinavian Airlines), began to market themselves as business airlines (cf. Carlzon 1989). Fares were increased and in return passengers received free champagne, a selection of meals, and flight attendants were trained to be very service-minded. It was considered that this would compensate for flight delays, crowded cabins or the absence of business class lounges at airports. In the long run, these hedonic experiences did not compensate for system wide delays. This was later seen as an opportunity for new market entrants, initially Ryanair, to completely reshape and disrupt the aviation market based on the premise that the only good experience that would attract passengers would be extremely low prices. Such has been the success of low-cost airlines that they now account for the largest market share; other airlines, often national carriers, have in the meantime reduced their hedonic service elements as they struggle to compete on price with budget airlines. Traditional competition parameters, including low prices, can therefore still outcompete the provision of additional services intended to enhance the service experience. It is important for all services businesses to regularly evaluate and alter service processes to enhance the quality of customer experiences.

Frame analysis is an important concept for conceptualizing service experiences (Goffman 1974). Framing is a sociological concept describing the ways in which individuals experience events and control or regulate behaviour to meet the demands of a particular situation. Front regions frame interactions between service producers and consumers; individuals identify the role they are playing and its associated frame modifying language and behaviours to meet the expectations of the situation. A good example of this process is the ways in which a management consultant acquires understanding of a client's expertise and begins to modify their language to meet the client's knowledge. A knowledgeable client will be treated differently to one who is less aware of the technical aspects of the problem. Service experiences occur through blending tasks that are undertaken in front and back regions and encounters with customers are explicitly and implicitly framed.

To develop this further these concepts must be explored by drawing upon examples of the relationship between service experiences and framing. Wulff (1998a) provides an account of ballet drawing upon a detailed ethnography of the Royal Ballet (London) and Ballet Frankfurt (Frankfurt-am-Main). She is concerned with the framing of dance performances and especially with repairing frames, or rectifying mistakes. The secret of a ballet performance is to provide the audience with a perfect frame; a performance in which the audience forgets that this is a socially created performance. But this frame is constantly broken as technical errors break the spell reminding the audience that this is only a performance. Entrances are missed, wigs fly off and costumes come undone (Wulff 1998b). The location of the viewer plays an important role in the service experience; back stage, on-stage and front stage all provide different types of experience. In the case of live theatrical performances, the viewer's knowledge of theatrical conventions, coupled with their location within the auditorium, is often one of the deciding factors in what they see and experience. Arnold Haskell, the English ballet critic, noted that four people watching the same ballet production may see different things: 'an enchantment to the person in seat No. 1, a mystery to the person in seat No. 2, a display of technical fireworks to seat No. 3, a thoroughly satisfying and connected whole to seat No. 4' (Haskell 1950: 17). Similarly, Caryl Brahms, another English ballet critic, wrote a well-known account of British ballet under the title 'A Seat at the Ballet' (1952). The point of this title is that Brahms always sat in seat A77, in the stalls-circle at the Royal Opera House Covent Garden, and her account is of her experiences from that seat and no other.

**Case: IKEA—An Experience Landscape**

The world's largest furniture retail chain is the Swedish company IKEA which owns and manages 276 stores in 25 countries. By 2019 there were 313 IKEA stores in 38 countries, but 37 were owned and run by franchisees IKEA has developed a business model, and related set of operational processes, that emphasizes the importance of creating high-quality service experiences and in the creation and application of a service mindset. All their stores have been designed as experience landscapes in which customers may experience the firm's products in room settings. Visitors to an IKEA store can recline in chairs, bounce on beds and experience the company's products in settings designed to reflect everyday living. Many visitors do not come to purchase specific items, but to experience the architecture and the atmosphere. IKEA stores offer inexpensive meals

emphasizing children's food. Families visit IKEA on a Saturday, or during the evening, to dine and to experience the furniture and soft furnishings within the context of a designed environment intended to encourage visitors to interact with the company's products. IKEA's products are flat packed. Highly industrialized furniture, and related goods, are purchased using an operational process based on the principle of self-service; customers must find the products they want to purchase and transport them to the nearest sale's point or order at a sale's point and then collect the items from one of the collection points. This is a highly standardized service system intended to attract customers by enhancing the service experience of selecting and purchasing relatively inexpensive furniture.

IKEA's business model has evolved to provide additional services. IKEA can assist in helping customers identify companies that will move larger items from the store to customers' homes. The company's website has been developed to support the service experience; customers can play with placing and arranging furniture in a virtual world environment experimenting with different layouts and combinations of the company's products. IKEA's business philosophy is to provide customers with experiences rather than just selling furniture. In this business model, the assumption is that sales will follow on from experiences and that more sales will result compared to a business model that ignores the experience and focuses on trying to sell furniture. For IKEA, the stores have become destinations in which service experiences occur that might lead to customers' purchasing products.

These service experiences, and additional services, are combined with social, ethical and political values. IKEA takes standpoints on key ethical issues. They have a policy of employing immigrants and more vulnerable people. One aim is to create a working culture amongst employees based on creating service-oriented experiences (see Edvardsson and Enquist 2010).

## 8.5    Customer Loyalty

Customer loyalty is related to satisfied customers who perceive that a service experience, combined with the service solution, has provided them with high value-in-use (Grönroos 1990). These are customers who will engage in repeat purchases of similar or related services from the same firm because they have perceived that they have obtained a satisfactory experience. For service firms, customer loyalty provides captive customers who are willing to continue to consume. Satisfied customers will tolerate and accept price rises as their relationship with the firm discourages service substitution by alternative service providers. Customer loyalty may result in some form of emotional attachment to the company and/or its service experiences.

Customers are sometimes loyal by habit or laziness as they may be unwilling to spend the time or resources in identifying an alternative provider. There are problems here with information asymmetry and difficulties in assessing the qualities of unknown service providers. Households should regularly compare the services provided by their banks, energy suppliers and Internet or mobile telephony providers. This process should include an assessment of current service provision against needs including price, reliability of service, customer support, contract flexibility and transparency of charges. The problem is that too many customers fail to engage in price and service comparisons. Path dependency occurs based on decision-making processes that occurred in the past and that may no longer reflect the actual needs of the household. Service businesses may make it difficult for customers to switch between suppliers. Nevertheless, governments have intervened to try to encourage customers to switch providers including the seven-day guarantee switching service for current accounts in the UK. In addition, platforms that act as intermediaries between consumers and service providers have emerged providing a price and service comparison service. These include uSwitch (UK) that specializes in scanning the market assisting customers in switching energy suppliers or Internet providers.

Loyalty programmes are another way to improve customer loyalty by providing additional or free services, information and cultural experiences. Some bank branches include cafés and host 'meet the author' evenings. The branch then becomes the location for service experiences providing opportunities for the bank to engage with existing and potential customers. Airline companies introduced bonus systems designed to provide customers with points for every journey; supermarkets provide loyalty cards offering priority notification of special offers and in store services including coffee and a free newspaper with purchases above a specified threshold. Point-based loyalty programmes offer points which can be exchanged for free flights, meals or additional services. These programmes provide a company with two benefits. First, there is the ability to collect data from customers that can be analysed and used to enhance service experiences and to inform innovation. Second, such programmes may contribute to creating customer loyalty as travellers may only book with one airline to ensure that they maximize the benefits from the bonus scheme. This may result in perverse consequences including travellers not selecting the most direct routes resulting in additional travel miles and environmental pollution. Customer loyalty will not prevent customer switching in response to service failure or a dramatic escalation in prices. It may be that other companies reduce prices and a threshold will be reached resulting in customers' switching affiliations to alternative providers.

Another way of encouraging customer loyalty is by selling services as subscriptions. Customers pay a fixed fee per month and can then access services whenever they are required. It may be more expensive for customers compared to purchasing services as and when they are required, but with a subscription costs are known beforehand, customers are familiar with how the service functions, and the service is always available. The value proposition developed by the service firm is accepted by customers, but consumer use of the service might decline overtime. Maybe consumers never or infrequently use the service. This is the case with monthly gym subscriptions;

many users sign up planning to make regular visits to the gym, but rapidly these visits become more infrequent. It is important that consumers trust the service provider and that the service provider continues to provide the values-in-use expected by consumers. If a mismatch between value-in-use provided and expected develops, then customers may switch to alternative service providers. Such a switch may reflect alterations in consumer expectations, for example, a new requirement to engage in responsible or more ethical consumption.

Subscription packages have been developed and applied to access satellite TV channels, rescue services and software services. They might be provided using a freemium service business model in which a basic service is provided free to consumers, but with restrictions and advertising whilst additional features, including no advertising, are offered via a paid subscription revenue model (see Chap. 3, Sect. 3.3). Subscription-based services are spreading rapidly to other fields, including house repair, consumer advice, cloud storage for computer data, computer software packages which were previously sold as standalone services, on-demand video services (Amazon Prime or Netflix) and online fitness classes. Peloton, for example, the American provider of exercise equipment and related services, is based on a business model in which customers purchase an exercise bike that allows users to stream spinning classes from the company's fitness studio for a monthly subscription.

Platform-based service firms, and services that are sold online via websites, have new challenges in creating customer loyalty. Personal contact with customers is limited or non-existent, and the Internet makes it easy to compare prices and conditions offered by competing providers. Larger platforms benefit from networking effects that prevent customers from leaving and also restrict new platforms from gaining market share. Online comparison websites, such as Trustpilot and PriceRunner, make it much easier for customers to compare different service providers. These comparison sites, combined with social media, are a serious challenge for service firms as they try to develop and maintain customer loyalty.

## 8.6 B2B Customers: Outsourcing and Sparring

Services provided to business are called business and professional services (BPS) or producer services. To some degree they have the same characteristics and are subject to the same conditions as consumer services. They also have different characteristics. Customers are not single individuals or households, but larger organizations with many layers of management, many employees and often more formal, contractual relationships with service providers. The volume of services being provided by business service providers is much larger, for example, maintenance and cleaning of several office buildings or undertaking an annual audit. These are still service relationships that are strongly influenced by reputations and relationships between individual service providers and representatives of client companies. Nevertheless, the procurement decision must meet the client's strategy and business policy.

BPS firms have a double significance: they create wealth in their own right, but they also enhance wealth creation in client companies. This means that the activities of BPS firms contribute to two types of gross value added (GVA). First, GVA produced directly by their own activities and, second, indirect GVA that is produced by client firms that can be attributed to the activities of BPS firms. It is very difficult to measure the impact BPS firms have on the competitiveness and profitability of client companies, but in some cases enhancement to GVA occurs. One difficulty is identifying a direct simple linear relationship between the activities of a BPS firm in a client firm and impact. Time complicates the assessment and measurement of such impacts as a BPS project might produce an impact over a long period.

## 8.6.1  Outsourcing

In common with households or individuals, business customers are also interested in obtaining quality services which are appropriately priced. Firms and public institutions may decide to produce services in-house or to outsource them to other service providers (Rubalcaba-Bermejo 1999). A manufacturing firm or a consultancy service firm may, for example, outsource catering and cleaning as well as the administration and development of IT systems. A national government, or a municipality, may outsource road maintenance or the management of railways. Both knowledge-based and manual services may be outsourced, but they also may be offshored. Outsourcing reflects the transfer of tasks that were previously undertaken in-house to an external provider whist offshoring describes either the transfer by a business of a task to a facility owned or managed by the company and located in a foreign country or a task that is outsourced and also offshored. The former represents offshoring without outsourcing and the latter is outsourcing combined with offshoring.

Tasks that have been offshored include IT systems and customer helplines or call centres and sometimes these services are offshored, for example, to suppliers in India, Vietnam or the Philippines (Table 8.1). Advanced call routing and networking technologies enable companies to implement a 'follow-the-sun' geographical policy. Companies can link two or more facilities together with each open from between 8 to 12 hours per day. When one centre closes, tasks are routed to other facilities located elsewhere in the world. India or Pakistan are suitable locations as they are four to five hours ahead of Western Europe and 10–13 hours ahead of North America. The majority of Indian and Pakistani call centres operate during the evenings to deal with enquires from America and Europe. Successful offshoring of customer-facing services requires the development of an appropriate level of service quality that is acceptable to customers. The key issues revolve around language and accents (Bryson 2007). Call centres provide a form of virtual face-to-face (voice-to-voice) interaction with customers

**Table 8.1**  Service jobs that have been sent offshore

*Customer-facing: Constant contact between producer and consumer*
- Call centres
- Customer services
- Out of hours claims (call centre)
- Back office administration
- Back office processing
- E-commerce
- Credit control
- Internet services
- Internet claims
- IT helpdesk
- Rail timetable enquiries

*Back-office: Business process outsourcing*
- Business services
- Accountancy services
- Finance and accounting processes
- Legal services
- Finance
- Engineering services
- Human resource management
- IT provision
- Business systems
- Graphics and architectural services
- Document production
- Underwriting
- Technical lists
- Freelance writers
- Marketing services
- Graphic design
- Equity research
- Airline ticketing and related services
- Business analysts
- Legal secretaries
- Software development
- Computer programming
- Information technology support
- Security services
- Cybersecurity
- R&D
- Design
- City analysts
- Technicians
- Legal secretarial services
- Transcription services (voice and shorthand)
- E-commerce including ordering, warehousing and distribution
- Data management
- Data storage

Source: Authors' own

being able to engage in a dialogue with call centre workers. Training courses have been developed to provide call centre operatives with the requisite skills in people management, including dealing with angry and irate customers, and for offshored call centre employee accent neutralization. There have been major problems with the offshoring of these types of services. Service reshoring has occurred by firms concerned with customer retention related to perceived or actual problems with service quality. For service offshoring, the challenges concern cost versus the advantages that are associated with local provision, for example, local accents, knowledge, shared everyday experiences between consumers and service providers and lived experiences of local cultures. In addition, some companies that have offshored services have experienced data theft including customer addresses.

The outsourcing of service functions by clients and the creation of new types of service occupations represents an extension of the division of labour and this may become a spatial division of labour. There are many types of outsourcing. First, a company providing business services can provide these from outside the client's premises. This includes, for example, entering into a contract with a specialist business travel agent that will arrange all employees' business travel. Second, outsourced services can be provided by blending provision from outside the client's premises with provision onsite. This includes all types of business and professional services, including management and design consultancy. Third, a client can outsource services to a company who will employ staff who will work at the client's sites. This includes providing cleaning, catering, security services and facilities management.

Beyers and Lindahl (1996) provide a useful review of the major forces contributing to the outsourcing, or externalization, of business and professional services. They divide their account into cost-driven and non-cost-driven explanations. They found that cost-driven externalization was not a major factor behind the growth of producer service firms. The most important driver was a growth in demand for specialized technical expertise combined with a myriad of non-cost- and cost-driven factors. Nevertheless, manual services that are outsourced tend to be purchased on the basis of price combined with quality including reliability (Rubalcaba-Bermejo 1999).

**Table 8.2** Advantages and disadvantages of outsourcing service functions

| Advantages | Disadvantages |
|---|---|
| • Cheaper<br>• More competent and efficient<br>• No concerns over the management of service functions<br>• The service provider engages in on-going innovation<br>• Quality assessment is explicit and formalized<br>• The outsourced service provider is responsible for any service delivery problems with the exception of problems related to exchanges between the client and service provider | • The outsourcing firm/institution no longer has specialist expertise in this area and there is a reduction in internal capability to assess service quality<br>• The outsourcing firm/institution no longer has any ability to undertake these service tasks and becomes overtly reliant on an external provider<br>• It may be difficult to handle customer and employee dissatisfaction with the provider of the outsourced service<br>• Objections from internal personnel, particularly when the outsourcing decision is made<br>• Difficult to change a contract once delivery is underway |

Source: Authors' own

Specialized providers of producer services are more efficient and can share training and other costs across many clients providing them with cost advantages over in-house provision. Nevertheless, not all firms will outsource all or some services. There are considerations apart from cost that must be considered (Table 8.2).

Business customers must ensure that the contracted service is delivered to the expected quality. This first requires that the commissioning firm's requirements are clearly specified. This is not always the case and difficulties begin to emerge with operational processes. In all cases, a written contract will have been negotiated and signed, but this may not clearly specify some aspects of service delivery. Second, controls must be in place to check that the negotiated service is delivered to specification. This often involves quantitative measurements (see Chap. 13). For example, a cleaning contract might specify that office floors should be cleaned weekly and the client then monitors this arrangement. Service providers will develop and apply their own systems to monitor contract delivery and this will include providing customers with regular updates regarding performance and quality. Outsourcing contracts are released via invitations to tender and a beauty parade is held in which shortlisted firms are assessed and interviewed.

There is another stage related to the monitoring and assessment of outsourced services. The outsourcing firm will have employees whose work is directly affected by the outsourced service provider's activities. The client's customers may also be impacted by this outsourcing contract. Thus, customers using an outsourced call centre function will be unaware that the services they are trying to access are not provided directly by the company they are trying to transact business with. It is important that companies that have outsourced services monitor quality and the impacts of the contract on their business by engaging with their employees and customers to assess service quality. Employees and customers may assess the quality of such outsourced services using criteria that had not been specified in the contract. When this occurs, the service and related experience should be reviewed and any mission creep between in-house and external customers' expectations identified, explored and reconciled.

## 8.6.2  Sparring

Managers in companies, public institutions and other organizations engage with knowledge-intensive business service firms as sparring partners. They deliver ad hoc analyses and suggestions for solutions to organizational, technological, market and other problems experienced by clients. Sometimes consultants act as permanent sparring partners for managers. Large international consultancy, accounting and legal firms including Accenture, PWC, Deloitte, Arthur Andersen, Baker and McKenzie, Clifford Chance and McKenzie are retained as sparring partners to work with the senior managers of large client corporations. They have extensive experience of solving problems in international corporations across all industry sectors. They can transform knowledge and they often catalyse innovation in client firms drawing on their international knowledge of ideas, technologies and innovation methods (Ehret and Wirtz 2015). Such knowledge-intensive business service firms exert enormous influence on business development in all industries (Hollis 2015) and it is quite usual for consultants from McKinsey, for example, to move directly into CEO roles in large service or manufacturing corporations and vice versa.

Small local firms and institutions rarely have the resources to be able to engage with the larger consultancy companies. Instead, they rely on small local providers of knowledge-intensive services, typically local lawyers, accountants, consultancy firms or banks. The encounters between these service firms and their clients are based upon person-to-person business relationships and membership of local social and business networks.

It is essential that providers of external business services understand their clients, their value propositions and business models. This is especially the case for consultancy firms contracted to undertake a sparring role since it is not always clear what services they should provide. Clients can identify problems, but a problem identified by a client might be related to other issues that need to be resolved across a company. Even if a problem is specified, the client might have underestimated or misidentified the real or fundamental issues. In these instances, the consultant's task is to identify the fundamental problem. This requires that the consultant develops a broad understanding of the client company. This includes all operational and management processes rather than a focus on a specific area such as IT systems or a particular HRM problem. Large consultancy firms must develop a balance between the provision of standardized or commoditized advice and bespoke or customized advice (Hollis 2015). The latter provides clients with a specific solution that requires mutual personal trust, regular interactions, including social contacts, and sometimes a fit with personalities. More standardized advice draws upon a consultancy firm's large pool of experiences and knowledge derived from other projects and clients. All these experiences can inform the development of standardized solutions that appear to be customized to meet the needs of an individual client. Management consultants do not deliver a pre-defined product, but rather they customize standard solutions to meet the needs of a client or develop a unique solution. The consultancy relationship is founded on trust usually formed through experience of working with individual consultants, or indirectly by assuming that a firm's brand is a proxy measure of quality and trust. This must translate into the creation of additional value for clients in the form of appropriate solutions. Business consultants should possess empathy, be adaptable, be able to develop and maintain social relationships, be able to read business cultures, and all these softer skills are in addition to professional competencies and specialist expertise.

## 8.7 Service Quality

Service businesses must focus on co-creation, customer values and service experiences and these are the basis for the concept of service quality. Service companies and academics have tried to understand service quality and to develop methods that would enhance quality.

Quality and quality assurance are a core business process within manufacturing where it means zero product failures. Such failures can be identified using technical inspections and product testing. Product failure can be designed out of the production process and out of the product. It is, however, very different for services because there is no material product that can be observed and

tested. Instead, quality is more subjective depending on customer values and their experiences and perceptions of service delivery. Service quality has developed as a specific subdiscipline (Brown et al. 1991) and several methods have been developed to measure and assess service quality (see Chap. 13).

Service quality is very dependent on the assessment criteria adopted by customers. These vary greatly, not only from individual to individual, but also from one situation to another. Grönroos (1990) has developed a model to explain how customers evaluate service quality by balancing expected quality against service delivery (Fig. 8.2).

Service quality may involve the delivery of a good service or may be related to low expectations held by consumers. Service providers may focus on the delivery of very good services or create low expectations and then perform better than expected. There is also a cost issue. To provide an outstanding service with an excellent service delivery process may be very expensive and the price will reflect the relationship between cost and delivery. Competitors may deliver cheaper services (and perhaps with reduced service quality) and thereby win market share. A service business has to decide on the level of service quality it wants to provide and then communicate this level to the market to determine customer expectations. It is better to create low expectations and then to exceed them rather than to adopt the opposite position based on creating high expectations with poor service delivery. Within this framework, service businesses should control service delivery processes ensuring that they are always as planned. Failures in service delivery processes result in a reduction in customer experiences of service quality.

$$\text{Service quality experienced} = \frac{\text{The service delivered (including the delivery process)}}{\text{Expected service quality}}$$

**Fig. 8.2** Service quality defined. (Source: After Grönroos 1990)

## 8.8    Complaints Management

The best service quality control systems will still experience moments of failure. Customers may develop high expectations that conflict with the quality indicators that are being projected by a service business. Customers then complain that the services do not meet their expectations. Such complaints may be considered as problems for service businesses, but it is important that such matters are taken seriously and always addressed. These failures may be in service delivery and it is not only important to listen to customers but to provide compensation. This is still necessary even if there has been no failure and the failure is due to unrealistic customer expectations. In this case, adding additional services to a service bundle enhances customer satisfaction as well as the firm's reputation.

Service businesses, particularly large companies, often establish dedicated complaints management teams and complaints departments. These can be used to compile data on systematic delivery failures and to identify improvements and innovations in service products and delivery systems. The analysis of complaints might identify customers with unfulfilled needs that might lead to the development of new services.

## 8.9    Wrapping Up

The 'customer is the king/queen' or 'the customer comes first' are expressions that are important for all service businesses. Satisfied customers become loyal customers who are willing to pay relatively high prices for service quality. Value-in-use for service customers is created in the service encounter. Customers' assessment of the delivered service depends on their beforehand expectations. How the service firm communicates its service quality levels to customers is extremely important because this determines or influences customers' pre-impression of the service. The highest service quality is not necessarily the ideal service quality. Price is also important; service firms that clearly signal that

they are providing low levels of service quality, but at low prices, may also be successful.

Private and public sector enterprises often outsource internal service functions to specialized independent service firms (e.g. HRM administration, accounting, catering, security, transportation). It is important for providers of outsourced services to satisfy all customers: the buyer (maybe a departmental manager), the funder (senior management in the client firm) and users (employees in the client firm). Knowledge-intensive business service firms, including consultants, accountants and lawyers, often act as sparring partners for clients This is a challenging role and it is essential that the service provider understands the client's situation and business model to deliver a satisfying sparring service experience.

**Learning Outcomes**

- The service encounter plays the central role in the construction of all service experiences.
- Value-in-use needs to be explored in all service transactions, but this value varies between individual consumers and is difficult to measure and evaluate.
- Value-in-use is complicated as additional consumer expectations emerge which influence perceptions of value.
- Actual and perceived value-in-use is related to the value propositions developed and provided by service firms. The quality of a service experience is determined by the service provider and customers' expectations.
- In-house services may be externalized or outsourced to specialized service firms.
- Outsourcing may involve offshoring and the application of a spatial division of labour to services.

## References

Beyers, W. B., & Lindahl, D. P. (1996). Explaining the Demand for Producer Services. *Papers in Regional Science, 75,* 351–374.

Brahms, C. (1952). *A Seat at the Ballet*. London: Evans Brothers.

Brown, S., Gummesson, E., Edvardsson, B., & Gustavsson, B.-O. (Eds.). (1991). *Service Quality*. Lexington: Lexington Books.

Bryson, J. R. (2007). The 'Second' Global Shift: The Offshoring or Global Sourcing of Corporate Services and the Rise of Distanciated Emotional Labour. *Geografiska Annaler. Series B, Human Geography, 89*, 31–43.

Carlzon, J. (1989). *Moments of Truth*. Cambridge, MA: Harper.

Coye, R. W. (2004). Managing Customer Expectations in the Service Encounter. *International Journal of Service Industry Management, 15*(1), 54–71.

Czepiel, J., Solomon, A., & Surprenant, C. (Eds.). (1985). *The Service Encounter*. Lexington: Lexington Books.

Edvardssson, B. and Enquist, B. (2010). 'The IKEA Saga' - How Service Culture Drives Service Strategy. *Service Industries Journal, 22*(4), 153–186.

Edvardsson, B., Tronvoll, B., & Gruber, T. (2011). Expanding Understanding of Service Exchange and Value Co-Creation: A Social Construction Approach. *Journal of the Academy of Marketing Science, 39*(2), 327–339.

Ehret, M., & Wirtz, J. (2015). Creating and Capturing Value in the Service Economy: The Crucial Role of Business Services in Driving Innovation and Growth. In J. Bryson & P. Daniels (Eds.), *Handbook of Service Business*. Cheltenham: Edward Elgar.

Fuglsang, L., & Sundbo, J. (2006). Flow and Consumers in E-Based Self-Services: New Provider-Consumer Relations. *Service Industries Journal, 26*(4), 361–379.

Goffman, E. (1974). *Frame Analysis*. New York: Harper and Row.

Grönroos, C. (1990). *Service Management and Marketing*. Lexington: Lexington Books.

Haskell, A. (1950). *Going to the Ballet*. London: Phoenix House.

Heinonen, K., & Strandvik, T. (2009). Monitoring Value-in-Use of e-Service. *Journal of Service Marketing, 20*(1), 33–51.

Hollis, S. (2015). The Role of the Big 4: Commoditisation and Accountancy. In J. R. Bryson & P. Daniels (Eds.), *Handbook of Service Business*. Cheltenham: Edward Elgar.

Payne, A. F., Storbacka, K., & Frow, P. (2008). Managing the Co-creation of Value. *Journal of the Academy of Marketing Science, 36*(1), 83–96.

Payne, A., Storbacka, K., Frow, P., & Knox, S. (2009). Co-creating Brands: Diagnosing and Designing the Relationship Experience. *Journal of Business Research, 62*(3), 379–389.

Ritzer, G. (2000). *The McDonaldization of Society – New Century Edition*. Thousand Oaks, CA: Pine Forge Press.

Rubalcaba-Bermejo, L. (1999). *Business Services in European Industry*. Bruxelles: European Communities.

Skålen, P., Gummerus, J., Koskull, C., & Magnusson, P. (2015). Exploring Value Propositions and Service Innovation: A Service-Dominant Logic Study. *Journal of the Academy of Marketing Science, 43*(2), 137–158.

Sundbo, J. (1994). Modulization of Service Production. *Scandinavian Journal of Management, 10*(3), 245–266.

Sundbo, J. (2002). The Service Economy: Standardisation or Customization? *Service Industries Journal, 22*(4), 93–116.

Sundbo, J. (2015). Service and Experience. In J. Bryson & P. Daniels (Eds.), *Handbook of Service Business*. Cheltenham: Edward Elgar.

Tsiotsou, R., & Wirtz, J. (2015). The Three-Stage Model of Service Consumption. In J. Bryson & P. Daniels (Eds.), *Handbook of Service Business*. Cheltenham: Edward Elgar.

Vargo, S., & Lusch, R. (2008). Service Dominant Logic: Continuing the Evolution. *Journal of the Academy of Marketing Science, 36*(1), 1–10.

Wulff, H. (1998a). *Ballet across Borders: Career and Culture in the World of Dancers*. Oxford: Berg.

Wulff, H. (1998b). Perspectives towards Ballet Performance: Exploring, Repairing and Maintaining Frames. In F. Hughes-Freeland (Ed.), *Ritual, Performance, Media* (ASA Monograph 35) (pp. 104–120). London: Routledge.

## Further Reading

Edvardsson, B., Thomasson, B., & Øvretveit, J. (1994). *Quality of Service*. London: McGraw-Hill.

Grönroos, C. (2011). Value Co-creation in Service Logic: A Critical Analysis. *Marketing Theory, 11*(3), 279–301.

Helkkula, A. (2010). Characterising the Concept of Service Experience. *Journal of Service Management, 22*(3), 367–389.

van Looy, B., van Dierdonck, R., & Gemmel, P. (2013). *Services Management. An Integrated Approach*. Harlow: Prentice-Hall, Chapters 9 and 10.

Prahalad, C. K., & Ramaswamy, V. (2004). *The Future of Competition: Co-Creating Unique Value with Customers*. Boston: Harvard Business School Press.

Vargo, S., & Lusch, R. (Eds.). (2006). *The Service-Dominant Logic of Marketing*. New York: Sharpe.

## Useful Websites

IKEA: http://www.ikea.com/ms/en_GB/this-is-ikea/index.html.

SAS: https://www.sasgroup.net/en/category/about-sas/.

PriceWaterhouse-Coopers: https://www.pwc.com/.

# Marketing Services

**Key Themes**

- How do service firms sell/market their services to customers?
- Marketing strategy and tools
- Hedonic and sensorial marketing
- E-marketing and big data
- Branding and reputation
- Service marketing
- Customer relationship marketing
- Mass customization
- Service subscription business models
- The public sector as a customer

Marketing is fundamental for selling everything, including services. All businesses must develop strategies for reading markets, competitors and actual and potential customers and for selling products and services. Marketing is one of the most prominent and researched activities within service businesses and many marketing perspectives, models and theories have been developed. All are relevant for service firms, but a specific field of service marketing has emerged (e.g. Lovelock and Wirtz 2011) based on exploring the customer interactions that typically accompany service provision. All chapters in this book have highlighted that many services cannot be stored, but must be consumed during the moment of pro-

duction. The implication is that relationships between customers and service suppliers are at the centre of service businesses (see Chap. 8). The dominant perspective in service marketing is based on understanding customer relationships in service encounters and this has also influenced and changed the ways in which some goods are marketed.

This chapter explores marketing theories and models and how they have been applied to services. In Chap. 8, service sales and marketing were explored from a micro perspective focusing on employees' personal relationships with customers and how these have been transformed with the onset of e-based service businesses including online platforms. In this chapter, the focus is on the more macro level including how service firms develop market share through the application of marketing models and theories. It is worth noting that marketing academics were amongst the first scholars to discover service businesses and to begin to explore business processes within service firms.

**Electronic Supplementary Material** The online version of this chapter (https://doi.org/10.1007/978-3-030-52060-1_9) contains supplementary material, which is available to authorized users.

## 9.1   Marketing: Market Analysis, Segmentation and Advertising

### 9.1.1   Modern Marketing Is More Than Just Advertising

Modern marketing is not only about selling more goods or services or about selling at the lowest price (Kotler and Keller 2016). Marketing is fundamentally an economic, functional and social exchange between two parties, the provider or seller, and the customer or buyer. The buyer wants to fulfil a certain function; it may be a car for transportation or a legal service that can solve a problem. Providers must create value for buyers but must also fulfil certain social demands: being trustworthy, delivering good products or service quality—at least related to price, and perhaps to deliver the service in a special way or by making it more memorable through the curation of a service experience. Buyers may ascribe social values to the moment of consumption and may act from political or ethical considerations that may be more important than price; customers may be willing to pay higher prices for products or services that fulfil specific ethical, political or health requirements. The firms' reputation may also influence the purchasing decision as consumers often develop attachments to specific companies or their employees.

Furthermore, marketing is not just about advertising. Before advertising, the firm must first consider what, when and where to market. Analysing market opportunities and market demands is important. Very few firms sell to individual customers, from all social groups, located in all countries; perhaps Coca Cola, Apple and Microsoft are amongst those firms that sell in most national economies. The firm must consider market segments and be aware of which segment is occupied by existing customers and which segments could possibly be a source of new customers. The latter is much more difficult requiring much more marketing than taking care of an existing segment where customers will often purchase goods or services by habit or routine.

There are many instruments available to firms and professional marketing companies for analysing which segments a firm sells to, customer expectations in these market segments, and which consumers or firms could potentially be new customers. The firm may have data about its existing customer base that may be analysed to reveal whether it is primarily selling to a special segment or to the whole market. Several sociological methods are used to procure knowledge about actual or potential market segments. The most common marketing method are quantitative surveys asking customers about their experiences and degree of satisfaction with specified products or services or exploring general consumer preferences and lifestyles. Most of us will have been contacted by a market research company requesting information about our consumer preferences and purchasing behaviours. Qualitative research methods including focus groups, interviews and observation are also used to explore consumer behaviour. Even future consumer demands can be investigated by developing future scenarios using a Delphi approach. The Delphi method is a forecasting process based on multiple rounds of questionnaires sent to members of an expert panel (Hollesen 2015). Exploring possible futures may alter a firm's business model and this has been the case for the Ford Motor Company, and it is to this case that we now turn our attention.

**Case: Ford Motor Company—Changing the Company's Business Model**
The Ford Motor Company was established by Henry Ford and incorporated on 16 June 1903. This company was established to manufacture and sell cars—the famous Ford Model T. In recent years, Ford has analysed developments in markets and societies and predicted that the future of the automotive industry will not involve selling cars, but in providing transportation services. The implication is that customers will be offered transportation services involving moving them between A and B. This might involve regular movements involving commuting between home and work or more ad hoc movements. Transport services can be provided by

selling vehicles to customers, by Ford providing a form of taxi service involving its vehicles and drivers, or autonomous vehicles, transporting people and goods, or by customers leasing vehicles or participating in a carpool. Ford is altering its business model and marketing from being a car provider to becoming a transportation service provider with a focus on satisfying customers' individual transportation needs. At the same time, this shift in emphasis enabled Ford to engage with on-going societal challenges including climate change and air pollution. Ford also must focus on creating safe, reliable and enjoyable service experiences.

This alteration in Ford's business model has emerged from identifying and exploring future scenarios. Ford, along with many other large companies, understands that disruptive business models and technologies will emerge that have the potential to destroy the company. To avoid, influence or adapt to such disruptions, companies must try to predict future technological developments and societal changes. They apply methods developed to identify and explore different futures and try to identify how these different futures will impact on consumer behaviour. Companies then engage and contribute to much broader societal debates on change, including technological developments and climate change, and highlight that they are acting responsibly.

Market analysis and marketing requires a different approach for business-to-consumer services (B2C) that involves selling to individual customers compared to selling business-to-business services (B2B) that are sold to other firms. In B2C service encounters customers tend to be more anonymous and numerous whilst in B2B relationships service providers can explore futures with established clients during the sales process.

A firm should not only analyse its customers, but also its competitors (Hollesen 2015). Competitors may develop more innovative ways of reading the future or identifying new market segments. A company can assemble information about customers via employees' general knowledge of the industry and can learn about competitors not only by exploring their products and

services, but also by recruiting employees who used to work for competitor companies. Companies can explore competitors' annual reports, financial accounts, commercials and press coverage. Companies may also measure customers' assessment of competitors' services through customer surveys (see Chap. 13) or via syndicated research undertaken by market research firms. Sometimes a firm's employees may even become customers of competitors to investigate the services and goods that are available and the qualities and characteristics of service encounters and service experiences.

It is important to price services before a marketing campaign commences (Hollesen 2015). Pricing is not just a matter of cost of delivery including any actual or potential productivity gains (see Chap. 5), but also concerns the value-in-use provided by a service to specific market segments and the relationship between value and what customers are willing to pay (see Chaps. 3 and 8).

### 9.1.2   Marketing Campaigns and Strategies

Marketing campaigns require careful planning. There are a number of key questions that must be considered by all service businesses including:

(a) What does the firm want to sell and to whom?
(b) Is it necessary to advertise or to make other types of public promotion?
(c) Who are the actual or potential customers and how can they be reached?

Marketing is expensive, so it must be planned and targeted. Sometimes firms allocate a budget to the marketing division and the marketing team and then develop a plan to spend the allocated sum. Marketing campaigns should be planned in relationship to expenditure versus anticipated returns and the budget set to maximize the returns on the investment.

First, firms must decide on whether there is a need to launch new products or services and whether there is a need to embark on a marketing campaign. Firms must consider the product or service life cycle (Kotler and Keller 2016): a new product or service requires marketing to raise customer awareness while a service that is already successfully established in the market often sells itself and there will be no need to invest in advertising. A service or product might have reached a stage of maturity and further investment might be required to enhance the service or product in some way. Such enhancement might require a marketing campaign to ensure that an adequate return is made on the investment. This requires a different form of marketing campaign with more emphasis given to price, brand, reputation and additional services. The key point is to provide some way of differentiating the product/service from similar offerings available from competitors.

Marketing of new services is particularly important to raise customer awareness and expectations of the new service. Planning the marketing campaign for a new service or product starts with the development of a strategy (see Chap. 3) including an assessment of market behaviour and market competition (Porter 2004). A strategy must deal with three factors: (1) the firm's competencies and resources, (2) customers and the market, and (3) competitors. Many models have been developed to support strategy formulation. Often companies start by developing a simple SWOT analysis based on the analysis of four themes: the firm's strengths (competencies, resources), weaknesses (vis-à-vis competitors),

market opportunities (e.g. trends in customer preferences) and threats (e.g. competitors introduce new, innovative services, alterations in market trends) (Table 9.1).

Once the company completes a strategic analysis, then the firm must decide about future possible customer segments and must then consider developing solutions to the four 'Ps' within traditional approaches to marketing (Kotler and Keller 2016). In 1953, Neil Borden developed the concept of the *marketing mix* (MM) based on the identification of 12 interrelated factors that defined the relationships between firms, customers and competitors. These were grouped by McCarthy into '4Ps'—Product, Price, Place and Promotion (1960). The MM approach is the predominant framework that informs the development of marketing strategies. The '4Ps' played an important role in understanding the marketing of goods, but problems emerged in its application to services. The differences between goods and services complicated matters. These differences included problems of quality control as standardization was difficult, and services could not be transferred between people, patented or inventoried. Booms and Bitner (1981) extended the MM approach beyond the '4Ps' to include an additional '3Ps'. This new *service marketing mix* (SMM) approach, or the '7Ps', included Process, People and Physical Evidence. It is worth noting that for services, changes are required in the application of the original '4Ps'. For services, People are especially important. In 2006, Zeithaml et al. added another 'P'—Productivity and Quality.

Marketing is not just about advertising but includes wider communications and broader interactions. B2C marketing involves developing strategies designed to convince people to purchase certain services or products. It is about consumer psychology: the consumer needs to be aware of the product. That is where advertising then comes in; advertisements and commercials can rarely sell a service, but they can create awareness. The next step is that consumers should be interested in purchasing the service. This requires the creation or perception of a need—either a need that is already known by the

**Table 9.1** The SWOT strategy framework

| Strengths | Opportunities |
|---|---|
| Based on own core resources and competencies | Future opportunities in the marketplace, based on the analysis of market developments, consumer behaviour and societal trends |
| Weaknesses | Threats |
| Lack of competencies and resources required to utilize opportunities in relation to the behaviour, competencies and resources of competitors | Better utilization of the opportunities and new, unforeseen, market trends and competitor behaviour |

Source: Authors' own

consumer or a need, or a value-in-use, that will be created by advertising. This also concerns how valuable the value-in-use provided by the service will be for the customer related to price. Finally, should the consumer act or decide to purchase the service, then they will explore if other similar services are available, and if so, whether these are of better quality (including the delivery process), provide more value-in-use or are cheaper. This is the important point; potential consumers do not decide their purchases in a vacuum as they will ask friends, family and acquaintances for advice or consult online customer reviews. Opinion leaders, or influencers, play an important role in informing and shaping consumer behaviour. Vloggers and social media influencers have become important sources of 'free' consumer advice and represent another type of multi-sided business model (see Chap. 3). Purchasing a service is particularly complex because services cannot be viewed or handled beforehand as is the case with physical goods (see Chap. 8). Service firms must develop relationships with consumers—including third-party referrals, or develop brands, that potential customers use as proxy measures to evaluate a firm's ability to deliver a service.

Modern marketing books often proclaim that power within markets has been transformed and that now markets are customer-led and that the customer is now king/queen (Gummesson 2000). Such proclamations may be just buzzwords or clichés that are commonly used across the marketing discipline. However, there is a scientific basis for stating that political and ethical issues have become more important for consumers and that these issues influence consumer behaviour. They may choose not to purchase from a service provider that does not meet their political and ethical demands. For example, we have seen customers abandon banks that have been involved in political scandals, for example the so-called Panama-paper case of 2015 that revealed that many international banks had been involved in large-scale tax evasion. Increasingly, service businesses must demonstrate that they have ethical values and that they act responsibly.

B2B services are marketed in other ways. Business service firms often have direct personal contacts with potential customers and these relationships are used to market new services and increase the sales of existing services. Some service industries do not advertise at all, or very rarely. They rely on reputational capital; knowledge about their services is often diffused via person-to-person interactions or third-party referrals and, in some cases, the convention is that there are services that should never be advertised as marketing would reflect badly on the firm or on a profession. It is therefore rare for large providers of business and professional services (BPS) to advertise; for such firms, advertising is based on social relationships and existing client relationships combined with the projection of an international brand for the provision of professional expertise.

### 9.1.3 Advertising

The means to create awareness of a service—advertising—are many. These include using mass media such as magazines, newspapers, television and online platforms; individualized marketing where selected individuals are targeted with messages adapted to their assumed interests and needs; and using direct mail including letters, email or telephone calls to selected individuals or firms. It is important that the commissioning service firm specifies which market segments an advertising campaign should reach and selects the channel/s that most effectively targets the selected segment and is most effective at convincing that market segment to purchase the service.

McDonald's, which is a global provider of highly standardized fast food services primarily intended for children, young people and families, targets its advertising in all countries towards this market segment. In addition, McDonald's is careful to tailor its television commercials, for example, to take account of national cultures. Thus, the launch of new restaurants uses videos that are placed, for example, on YouTube and that focus on local music, stories and fantasy that appeal particularly to McDonald's target customer segment.

Much research has been dedicated to investigating which types of advertising are most effective in which customer segment. As new advertising channels have emerged, the placing of advertisements has changed. Printed media, such as newspapers and magazines, lost market share initially to television that, in turn, has experienced a shift to Internet and social media advertising. Telephone sales have also increased in some service industries include selling energy, servicing of solar panels, mobile phones, insurance and pension services.

## 9.2    Hedonic and Sensorial Marketing

Traditional marketing is now being challenged. Recent theory and research have revealed that consumers not only search for information that helps them rationalize purchasing decisions, but they also seek experiences, with respect both to the attention they give to advertising and their consumption of products or services. Hirschman and Holbrook (1982) were amongst the first to identify this shift in consumer behaviour. Customers not only seek to acquire goods or services that provide rational solutions to their practical needs or problems, but they are also seekers of sensorial experiences. Buying and consuming should also have a joyful or emotional element appealing to all senses whilst marketing services should have a hedonic element based on sensory experiences. This interpretation of services was first introduced in the early 1990s as part of an analysis that highlighted that service consumption also included the consumption of hedonic experiences (Hirschman and Holbrook 1982).

The focus of research on this aspect of marketing has been directed towards understanding how consumers can obtain hedonic experiences during the purchase and consumption process (Caru and Cova 2003) (see also Chap. 8). Research has investigated how consumers may be immersed in the consumption of a service (Hansen and Mossberg 2013). Immersion is a feeling of being absorbed by a phenomenon, for example, a movie. Consumers can be immersed in, for example, tourism involving travelling to another country where tourists experience the everyday lives of inhabitants. Immersion can occur in financial services and the buying and selling of stocks and shares as individuals develop emotional attachments to companies or investment analysts. Visiting a gastronomic restaurant or a gastropub is another example of a typical hedonic-sensorial and immersive form of service consumption.

The identification of the importance of hedonic consumption meant that this had to be incorporated into marketing campaigns. The hedonic and experiential aspects of a service can be emphasized in advertisements. For example, travel companies can highlight some of the elements of a service bundle that contribute to hedonic experiences including local travel, food, music and wildlife. A socially immersive interaction with a financial advisor can also occur, even though they are primarily there to sell investment products on behalf of the bank. Not all services are suitable for hedonic and sensorial marketing; it is difficult for legal or cleaning services to use hedonic elements. Nevertheless, some cleaning firms have attempted to introduce hedonic-sensorial elements including leaving a bunch of flowers when they have cleaned a house.

The latest development is to include hedonic elements in the marketing campaign itself. Sensorial marketing (Lindstrom 2010) is a new discipline that experiments with how consumers can have hedonic experiences and be immersed in the marketing process. Potential consumers are invited to events where they can see, smell or hear something that can be associated with the service. Mobile telephone companies have launched new services by inviting people to beach parties and food service providers invite people to taster events and are represented at all types of festivals. Even TV and Internet marketing can be hedonic; new services are presented with music or videos that appeal to the senses.

Experience as an integral part of consuming has also given rise to another new marketing sub-discipline, experience marketing (Schmitt 1999).

This emphasizes the experiences that customers can obtain when they consume services, and this is highlighted in marketing activities. Some variants of experience marketing even claim that marketing should include place-based experiences, for example, at music festivals or at scenic locations. Scent marketing, also known as aroma marketing, olfactory marketing or ambient scent marketing, has also emerged as an important element within retailing and hospitality services. Companies specialize in the design and supply of scents designed to attract and encourage consumption. Scent marketing influences how long customers remain in a building. It is used by companies trying to develop a deeper connection with customers compared to visual stimulation. Scents will trigger customer memories including emotions.

While the emergence of hedonic marketing is fully acknowledged, more conservative market theorists argue that hedonic elements are often exaggerated. Sensorial marketing can easily become negative when consumers consider that the hedonic elements are superimposed on to the commercial aspects of the transaction. The danger is that customers assume that the hedonic elements will not be replicated when they purchase and consume the service.

## 9.3 E-marketing and Big Data

### 9.3.1 E-marketing

Services are increasingly marketed and provided using an e-commerce approach via the Internet, smartphones and other IT media. This is often called e-marketing and is different from traditional marketing (cf. Chap. 4). Both individual and business customers use e-commerce. The Internet and all other information and communications technology (ICT) network channels are still used for traditional advertising, but these channels now also offer new possibilities for interactive hedonic-experiential advertising. However, ICT networks have transformed sales procedures as customers have become much more active in seeking information and services.

Service firms must create web pages and other social media platforms, for example, within Facebook, Twitter or smartphone operating systems, that pop up automatically when customers are searching and are also convincing. The 'window' of opportunity is very small; customers often only remain on a website for a few seconds, especially if they do not find it attractive. Pop-up advertising is based on algorithms using big data to identify patterns of consumer behaviour. Data includes the websites that have been clicked by users and terms entered into search engines.

E-marketing has made it much easier and cheaper to advertise and sell services but the competition for customer awareness, attention and potential purchasers has intensified. In addition, the barriers to entry have been lowered by the rise of e-marketing so that there is much more scope for new competitors to emerge. National service markets have become more international since it is much easier to market services internationally using IT networks, and sometimes even to provide service internationally, for example, financial services. Consumers can even contact each other for mutual help, thereby bypassing the need to use traditional service firms. As a result, new services have emerged that capitalize on this shift; Facebook and Airbnb, for example, now offer new platform services that specifically support consumers' mutual help and interactions.

Individualized marketing can be more refined using IT distribution channels. It is easier and cheaper to reach individuals and firms; data programs can segment the audience and individualize messages. Service businesses that manage to create appealing and interesting web or Facebook sites find it easier to lead customers from the awareness stage to an actual purchase. There are many pitfalls; consumers can easily leave a web page or delete an email and because e-marketing is so pervasive it is increasingly subject to national and international regulation.

E-marketing by service businesses requires agility and interactions with customers, even individuals. It must project values and ethical principles and provide experiences. There is also scope for service businesses to build customer loyalty (see Chap. 8) and involve customers in innovation processes (Chap. 7) via interactive communications on ICT network media. Some service firms, typically those providing software services, succeed in establishing user communities where customers promote the firm and its services and often help with feedback and innovations that improve the reliability and capabilities of software products.

### 9.3.2 Big Data

Sales and delivery of services via IT networks create large caches of data about customers and market segments. 'Big data' has become a new and important marketing tool (Chap. 4). Service firms can themselves collect data about sales and customers. They can see who and how many customers have ordered a service, what customers are interested in the firm's website and services and, conversely, customers can seek for additional information. Visitors to a service firm's web pages, app or other platforms can be asked to provide personal information such as age, gender and address. For large IT platform service companies, including Google and Airbnb, customer data is a business in itself; they can sell it on to other companies who use it for marketing purposes (see Chap. 3).

The analysis of big data requires significant technical and analytical capacity and capabilities. In general, only large service firms have the resources required to conduct big data analytics. The focus on big data is relatively new and not all firms have yet developed the analytical capability and are not fully aware of the scope of big data and how they can use it for new, more sophisticated marketing initiatives. Small firms rarely have the resources for in-house big data analysis and may be at a competitive disadvantage as they might have to rely on specialist providers of business data analytic services.

There are also risks accompanying the use of big data. Customers, consumer organizations and media are critical of the ways that Facebook, Google, Amazon, amongst others, mine consumer data that is then sold on to other firms to be used for marketing purposes. This challenges the assumption that personal data about individual consumers is private and confidential and should be retained securely by the IT platform and other service firms that have collected it and, if appropriate, deleted after a designated period. Service firms that use big data inappropriately will attract increasingly negative consumer reactions and risk much greater political regulation. National governments and transnational entities such as the European Commission are under pressure to protect consumers from, often unknowingly, sharing their personal and private information with big data users such as Facebook for use in ways that they cannot control. There is no question that big data has come to be a permanent part of marketing, but its use will be increasingly regulated.

## 9.4 Branding and Reputation

### 9.4.1 Reputation and Brands in Services

Service firms must constantly strive to retain consumer awareness as well as convincing potential customers that they should purchase services from a service provider. Consumers always have difficulties selecting which products or services they should purchase, especially services because of their immaterial nature—they cannot be seen and tested beforehand as is the case for goods (Lovelock and Wirtz 2011). Thus, customers must trust that service businesses can deliver the expected services and, furthermore, in a way that provides customers with satisfactory service experiences (cf. Chap. 8). The consumer is able to evaluate their earlier experiences with a service business. Feedback from other consumers about their experiences may inform purchasing decisions or the service may be selected on the basis that it is available from a generally well-known service provider. The latter arises from a firm's reputation for delivering good service quality, providing inexpensive services, providing one clear service package or whatever the wishes and needs of the consumer might be.

Reputation is important for service businesses. It reflects the attributes, good or bad, of the interactions between service providers and consumers. Service firms can influence their reputations by presenting a company story that is more powerful and convincing than the stories their clients construct based on their individual experiences. A service firm must create awareness of its services as rapidly as possible. Developing a brand identity is one way of achieving this. A brand is a symbol, word, sign, image or even smell that customers associate with a service or a service firm and is intended as a form of differentiation from competitors. Many large banks, or software services such as Google, Facebook or Twitter, use distinctive logos or name styles and all their communications and marketing campaigns incorporate these signs to reinforce their global brand identity.

Services are traditionally dependent on the service encounter (cf. Chaps. 2 and 8). This creates a challenge for service firms as all employees should be service minded (cf. Chap. 6) and be trained in handling reputational damage associated with single service failures. A brand can create more trust and confidence in a service than individual consumer experiences with a service firm's earlier service deliveries (de Chernatony and McDonald 2002). Single service deliveries can vary. Such individual variations in service deliveries can, to some degree, be eliminated by the provider developing, projecting and managing a brand, for example, Zara, BNP or ISS. When dealing with well-recognized brands, customers, whether individuals or businesses, tend to mix their actual service experiences with the reputation of the brand. If the brand is generally valued as positive, the customer will often forgive service failures. If the brand is generally valued negatively, the customer will not be so forgiving.

## 9.4.2 Branding of Services and Service Firms

The word 'brand' comes from the Old English word *biernan* meaning 'to burn'. A brand meant that something was burnt with hot iron for marking or cauterizing. Branding literally meant marking something indelibly with fire as proof of ownership. During the nineteenth century, the term 'brand' was used to describe a return address, or a trademark burnt on products, for example, casks of wine. The concept of a brand became a social construction of possession and it was this meaning that was enshrined in American law in 1905 when Congress passed trademark legislation. In this legislation, brands legally became a name, term or design intended to clearly identify and differentiate a seller's products from those of a competitor. The original meaning of a brand as a mark burnt to identify ownership of animals and even slaves has been transformed into a process by which consumers, both individuals and companies, brand themselves with what are often designer names and logos—Ralph Lauren's RL, Gucci's Gs, Tommy Hilfiger's Tommy, Chanel's Cs and IBM's Watson. For individual consumers, displaying brands on their bodies and in their homes represents a form of inclusion, but it is also a form of exclusivity and social exclusion.

Brands signal a certain service quality contributing to shaping customers' expectations (Chap. 8). This signalling of quality does not need to emphasize high quality, but can also signal inexpensive and more utility service experiences. Singapore Airlines attempts to brand itself as a luxury airline, while Ryanair's brand is based on affordability rather than service quality. Ryanair focuses on providing transportation services rather than including additional services into the service bundle at no additional cost. Additional services are available, but for additional charges.

Brands are signals of values. These may be ethical values such as treating employees fairly, functional values such as high levels of craftsmanship, ideological values such as only selling organic food or political values such as climate friendliness. Such corporate social responsibility (CSR) has become an increasingly important business parameter.

Single products or services can be a branded in their own right, for example, TGV trains and Eurest, which is the personnel canteen division of the Compass Group. A firm can be the brand, for example, Netflix and Deloitte. Branding a single service can help to assure more sales whilst branding the service firm can improve sales and has the advantage of brand equity or the phenomenon whereby it is easier to launch a new service when the firm's brand is already well known. Customers seeking to buy a new service will often tend towards a purchase from a well-known and reputable brand ahead of unknown providers.

Branding leads towards standardization of services (see Chap. 8). The service must be the same every time if branding is to have any meaning. Non-standardized, even B2B service firms may have a brand; the large consultancy and accountancy corporations such as PWC or McKinsey are widely recognized global brands. They have a reputation for providing individualized services.

A brand must be managed. Negative publicity can rapidly destroy a brand's reputation. When the financial service company Lehman Brothers experienced financial trouble in 2008, negative press coverage rapidly altered the firm's reputation from being a well-managed, traditional and low-risk financial provider to being almost a criminal enterprise. That made restructuring this firm difficult as customers lost trust and confidence in the company. In November 2019, Peloton, the American producer of exercise bikes and service bundles, released a new commercial for Christmas entitled 'The Gift that Gives Back'. In this commercial, a wife is given a Peloton exercise bike and subscription by her husband for Christmas. She begins recording a video diary of her daily use of the bike and notes that she had not realized how much she had been changed in her use of this gift. This commercial was viewed almost 2 million times on YouTube and was criticized as being dystopian and being a male fantasy. This negative publicity led to nearly a £1.1bn ($1.5bn) reduction in this company's value. Nevertheless, the share price will recover, and perhaps more exercise bikes and subscriptions will be sold by the company.

Some examples of brands and service reputations are shown in Table 9.2. Service reputation refers to whether customers' perception is that the service firm provides good or bad service

**Table 9.2**  Brands and service reputation

| *Good brands with 'good' service reputations* |
| --- |
| The department store Fortnum and Mason, London, is a globally recognized brand that is perceived as having a reputation for extremely high levels of service. Fortnum and Mason will do almost anything for their customers including procuring goods that they do not have in stock and employees are very competent and knowledgeable. But the goods are expensive. |
| Large companies often employ McKinsey, which has an extremely good international brand, as a provider of management consultancy services. It devises individual, highly competent solutions for clients. McKinsey combines customization with standardization, but this firm is an authority on business systems and processes with an established reputation. The quality of the McKinsey brand is used by clients to legitimize their decisions to employ this firm. |
| *Good brands with 'poor' service reputations* |
| Discount supermarkets have developed as well-known brands. Their core competitiveness parameter is constructed around low prices combined with low profit margins. Generally, customers often relate lower prices with poor service. Thus, the discount supermarket stores are designed as functional shopping environments with goods on simple shelving and often presented in cardboard boxes. Part of the discount supermarket effect is in maintaining low prices in a cost-effective and very functional environment and with very limited additional services provided. |
| Local firms often use local providers of management consultancy services. They may have a good local brand; the managers or owners of the client firm may, for example, know the lawyers from attending the local golf club or through membership of the Chamber of Commerce. The perception might be that such firms are unable to provide the quality or breadth of advice compared to larger consultancy firms. Nevertheless, local clients know the consultants and their fees reflect the ability of local firms to pay for these services. |

Source: Authors' own

quality. Service quality is a relative concept (Chap. 8); for example, does the service provider exceed the expected service quality independently of how high or low the expectations are? Both good and poor brands can lead to significant sales; it very much depends on the price and at which market segment the service is targeted combined with the actual and perceived value-in-use of the service.

### 9.4.3   The Function of Brands for Consumers

Today's post-modern society has been characterized as individualistic at the expense of collective stories and identification phenomena including social class, religion and membership of a profession (Giddens 1991). People therefore seek identity and meaning in their lives. Identification with a brand can provide such an identity. The service, or service provider, that you use project's messages—signs—about your identity that can be read by others.

The theory of the identity-loose post-modern society is perhaps not true. People establish values, collectively with other people. For example, lobbying to prevent climate change, to adopt healthier lifestyles or against data mining of personal data. Such ideologies lead to individuals acquiring common values and the formation of group identities or affiliations. A brand enables individuals to find and promote alternative values. Consumers may select service providers whose brand corresponds with their own values. A brand may contribute to helping consumers strengthen their values.

Brands create loyal customers who identify themselves with the brand. Users of the Apple ecosystem consider that their choice signals a set of values, including lifestyles, that are different to users of the Microsoft ecosystem—maybe more youthful, designer, fashionable, desirable and 'the thing to have'. Service firm must decide which values they want to be identified with. It cannot signal all the values in its brand. It must select a market segment and create a brand story that appeals to that segment's values.

Do brands function as a legitimizing quality stamp for the clients of business and professional services (BPS) firms? If a company selects an accountant or an advertising agency with a strong international brand, for example, Arthur Andersen or the advertising agency Ogilvy, then the brand is assumed to be a proxy measure of quality. This proxy might be intended for financial analysts, investors, business journalists and regulators rather than the client's management team. Thus, the client is projecting an identity of being the type of company that works with high-profile international providers of expertise.

It may be that smaller, less well-known service firms might provide better services, but smaller firms would be unknown to analysts and investors. For larger BPS firms, a brand reflects the incremental accumulation of many individual employee reputations and the successful completion of many projects. The firm's brand is one element in the client decision-making process. Nevertheless, the decision to employ a BPS firm with a well-known brand may still rest on third-party referrals and established relationships.

## 9.5   Service and Customer Relationship Marketing

### 9.5.1   Service Marketing

The service encounter is the basis for the development of personal marketing approaches that are targeted at customers by front-facing personnel. Traditional marketing approaches—market strategies, segmentation, advertising, branding and so forth—remain important for service businesses. Service encounters cannot directly procure new customers, but existing and former customers may provide third-party referrals to potential consumers and this process plays an important role in the marketing of services. Successful service encounters, with direct person-to-person interactions, can lead to the sale of more services to satisfied customers and will create customer loyalty (see Chap. 8). Service marketing is now recognized as a specific discipline (e.g. Lovelock and Wirtz 2011) and is accepted as being different from traditional marketing, which is focused on selling material goods. Service firms must understand the service marketing literature as this is customer focused and based on the principles that were explored in Chap. 8.

The service marketing approach has evolved into a subdiscipline within marketing: customer relationship marketing (CRM) (e.g. Gummesson 2000; Hollesen 2015). The on-going servitization of manufacturing companies has meant that

CRM has become a mainstream approach in the marketing literature.

### 9.5.2  Customer Relationship Marketing (CRM)

CRM is based on an extension of the service encounter. Markets are not anonymous meeting places for the supply and demand of goods and services but consist of a conglomerate of actor networks. Service firms are embedded in these actor networks and must interact and create relationships with other networks apart from focusing on networks linked to the sale of their services. These wider networks include corporate social responsibility or ethical and political discussions regarding local economic development, labour force inclusion and personal health. The aim is for service firms to become locally embedded and this process enhances the firm's local reputation and may ultimately influence customer purchasing decisions.

Gummesson (2000) suggests that the traditional 4Ps in marketing (Product, Price, Place, Promotion) should be replaced with 30 Rs (Relationships). These relationships include special market relationships (e.g. the relationship with the customer's customers, non-commercial relationships, green-based relationships), mega relationships (e.g. mega customers—municipalities, multinational organizations), mass media relationships and nano relationships (e.g. internal customer relationships—departments and employees in the service firm should be aware of one another's customers, relationships with external providers of marketing services, relationships with owners and investors).

### 9.5.3  E-marketing as CRM

Person-to-person encounters are largely absent when services are provided via online platforms and websites. Customers interact with a 'machine'—for example, a website or a mobile phone service. CRM may still apply, but it requires that interactions are possible between the website or mobile phone service system or other digital platforms and customers; the service encounter must be individualized or customized in some way. Online banking is an example; research has highlighted that it is important that customers are able to communicate with employees if they need to query a bank statement or request assistance with an application for a personal loan. Many service firms are reluctant to undertake this type of activity as this adds additional costs and complexity. Waiting in a phone queue to interact with an advisor or service employee is a common experience. The waiting time might be a planned part of the service encounter designed to discourage customers from contacting the firm by phone. This would be poor CRM that might result in a loss of earnings as customers decide to go to alternative providers.

E-marketing on IT networks may be as efficient as person-to-person CRM, but in its current form it needs further refinement. In China, WeChat (see Chap. 3, Sect. 3.8) has developed into an integrated lifestyle app with multiple opportunities to cross-sell services and to apply big data analytics to target consumers. The size of WeChat's user base, and the integrated nature of its big data streams, provides this platform with unusual opportunities to identify and model consumer preferences.

## 9.6  Mass Customization

Services were traditionally considered to be customized to meet the requirements of individual customers. The service encounter is behind the creation and management of many successful firms and led to the development of the Service-Dominant-Logic approach (Vargo and Lusch 2006) (see Chap. 8) and to CRM. Service businesses often highlight that their business is based around the quality of the service experience and the ability to customize this to meet the needs of individual customers. Customized services are quite expensive to produce and deliver. Price competition plays an important role in the service economy and there is a general tendency towards

standardization and the mass production of services. This is especially the case for the production and delivery of IT-based services.
Standardized services come with economies of
scale and scope and their qualities and values-in-
use are more predictable (see the discussion on
service quality in Chap. 8).

Service firms face a dilemma: should they
produce customized services or mass produce
more standardized services? For smaller service
firms, standardization is often not an option compared to larger service firms. A solution to this
dilemma is that a service business can provide
customized, but standardized services or, in other
words, can adopt a business model and operational
approach based on mass customization (Pine
1993).

Mass customization involves the development
of a segmentation approach to the provision of
standardized services. They can be individualized, or customized and targeted at specific customer segments using a flexible specialization
approach—a standardized service is adapted to
meet the needs of individual customers.
Telecommunication companies provide standardized mobile phone contracts that are contained in service bundles. This service bundle can
be adapted to meet the needs of each customer.
For example, a customer may decide to include
mobile roaming in other countries as part of their
service bundle.

Service businesses may adopt a mass customization approach for the provision of customized
service bundles. These bundles are developed by
selecting from a set of possible options that can
be included. This provides the advantages of customization with standardization and enables a
service business to compete on price. It also has
important implications for operational design and
productivity (see Chap. 5). Segmented marketing
may be used to target specific markets or individual market segments and even direct marketing to single consumers using a mass customized
marketing approach. IT networks have made
mass customized production and delivery of services and mass customized marketing much simpler and less expensive.

This combination of customization combined
with the mass production and delivery of services
has been characterized as an approach based on
modularization (Sundbo 1994). Service businesses must develop a set of standardized service
modules that can be produced and delivered inexpensively and effectively. Each service module
may be combined in many different ways into
service bundles that are designed during service
encounters with customers. This highlights the
necessity of developing an integrated approach to
service co-creation and marketing—marketing
decisions impact on decisions regarding service
operations and vice versa.

## 9.7   Service Subscription

Some service businesses have developed
subscription-based business models (George and
Wakefield 2018). Customers pay a fixed monthly
or annual fee and have the right to access or use
the service as required and as specified in a contract. This has been a long-established service
delivery principle in sectors including insurance,
telephony, security and rescue services. This
principle has been applied to other service sectors including food deliveries, car services, house
and garden services and computer software.

A subscription system might seem to be
expensive and difficult to cost for a service business. Nevertheless, profits might be greater compared to selling individual services because
customers may not make frequent use of the service. Over time, service businesses can read the
market and set subscription rates at levels protecting margins but also to attract and retain customers. In addition, service firms collect
subscription fees in advance and are able to invest
in the development of new products, in process
innovation or in financial investments. The latter
represents a form of financialization (see Chap.
3).

For the consumer, a subscription may be more
expensive than purchasing single services.
Nevertheless, the costs are known, and they can
access the service when required avoiding delays.
Subscription-based business modules provide

opportunities for service businesses to develop longer-term relationships with customers. They can provide additional services at no extra cost and can increase service quality as the number of subscriptions increase. This approach provides opportunities to enhance customer loyalty and is a marketing tool in its own right.

Falck, the international rescue company, operates via subscriptions. Customers subscribe to different service packages: personal care, which includes transportation to hospital in case of illness, provision of first aid equipment in the home and health care services; car servicing, which includes assistance in response to car accidents and problems related to vehicles. Falck also provides fire and rescue services. Customers are private individuals or public and private sector organizations who have entered into a service contract. Peloton, the American exercise bike company, offers a £39 monthly subscription (Dec 2019) providing owners of a Peloton bike with access to unlimited Peloton online classes, 20+ online classes daily, instructed curated training programmes and live workout metrics. A Peloton subscription brings the gym into the home but as part of an online social community of users of Peloton equipment and services.

## 9.8   The Public Sector as Customer

Public sector entities—municipalities, government administrations and so on—purchase many services and are major customers. The list of services that are procured is very long including accountancy, management consultancy, transportation, health care services, cleaning, catering and data analytics. This outsourcing of public services to private service firms is widespread. The public sector behaves as any other business customer engaged in B2B service provision. Nevertheless, there are distinctive features, and these are reflected in the ways in which services are marketed to the public sector.

Sales of services to the public sector may be ad hoc such as the provision of one-off legal advice but usually the public sector procures ser-

vice packages, for example, a two-year contract for cleaning schools or an auditing contract. For such contracts, public sector organizations issue calls for tender for which several service firms may apply. These calls specify conditions relating to the quality and delivery of a service, but also the expected and required environmental and social credentials of the service provider. This type of procurement process must meet a set of rules regarding public procurement ensuring that public funds are used in an accountable manner. The cheapest bid will often be selected, but the reputation of the service firms will be considered. Public bodies must balance risk of service failure against cost as any service failure would perhaps have greater consequences compared to a B2B contract with a private sector business. The process of selecting service providers must be transparent. Occasionally, legal action occurs over discrepancies in the contracting process. Scrutiny of public service procurement is much more open compared to private sector organizations; citizens and opposition parties may challenge the selection of a service contractor in public discussions. Once the selection process concludes, a contract is awarded that will include key performance indicators that will be closely monitored. Public sector contracts will be subjected to on-going political discussions and media debate.

Marketing services to the public sector is different compared to marketing services to the private sector. Advertising is of limited importance since most public service outsourcing relies on responding to calls to tender. The decision is based on price, risk and the ability to deliver services. CRM activities intended to cultivate relationships with public sector officials are important in raising awareness of service providers and their abilities to meet the values-in-use specified in the tender document. However, CRM must be used with care as a service business must ensure that it does not try to engender any form of bias or undue influence in the procurement process. This could be considered as fraudulent behaviour and could lead to a contract being terminated and the service provider being barred from participating in any future tendering rounds.

The best marketing approach is to issue a response that meets the terms of the tender and that the company has the assets, resources and expertise to deliver the specified services. A key issue is price. Many service firms have encountered difficulties with pricing responses to public sector tenders. To win, some firms compete on price, but then are unable to provide the required services to the agreed quality. This sometimes leads to an early or forced termination of a contract. The firm's reputation would be damaged and there are instances where a firm has failed. In Denmark, the provision of meals, for older more vulnerable people living in a municipality, was outsourced. Relatives criticized the quality of the food and the delivery process and this became a matter for public debate. Members of the opposition political party began to use this contract to criticize the current administration. This contract, and the service provider, became heavily politicized with recommendations for the provision of additional services. The existing contract holder claimed that they were providing the services as agreed and to specification but decided to break the contract with the municipality. This break might have damaged the service provider's reputation, but on-going political debate and media discussion would have been even more damaging.

## 9.9   Wrapping Up

Service businesses, just like all businesses, must engage in marketing activities. Traditional marketing such as advertising, branding and customized mass marketing are important tools for service firms. Services have particular characteristics in that they are consumed at the moment of production (Chap. 8). This provides service firms with opportunities to sell services and to develop and project reputations in person-to-person encounters and this has led to the development of customer relationship marketing (CRM). CRM has become a dominant marketing theory and marketing approach in service companies. The

personal encounter is the basis for introducing hedonic and sensorial elements into marketing.

Service companies apply special approaches in their attempts to create loyal customers and to increase income and profit. This includes mass customization and subscriptions. CRM is currently challenged by the application of the Internet, smartphones and other IT networks to support innovations in e-commerce and e-services. In e-services and e-commerce no person-to-person encounters are required, and this prevents consumer loyalty and additional sales from occurring in face-to-face service encounters. Special forms of e-marketing have emerged focusing on maintaining customer loyalty and on brand development (see Chap. 4).

Manufacturing firms have transformed themselves into service firms with the development of product service systems. This creates opportunities to develop longer-term relationships with customers by the application of CRM and other service marketing tools and approaches. This diffusion of service marketing to manufacturing is part of the servitization of manufacturing and it is this topic that we explore in Chap. 12. Marketing services plays an increasingly important role across all businesses including international business. For services, internationalization provides very different challenges compared to manufacturing companies and it is this topic that we explore in the next chapter.

**Learning Outcomes**

- Marketing is fundamental for selling everything, including services
- Modern marketing is more than just advertising
- Hedonic and sensorial marketing and e-marketing are new trends and are important for service businesses
- Brands play an important role in purchasing decisions, but so do third-party referrals
- Customer relationship marketing is especially important for service businesses but is also

applicable     for     some     manufacturing companies

- Mass customization and service subscriptions are means that service firms use in their attempts to create loyal and satisfied customers.

## References

Booms, B. H., & Bitner, M. J. (1981). Marketing Strategies and Organization Structures for Service Firms. In J. H. Donnelly & W. R. George (Eds.), *Marketing of Services*. Chicago: American Marketing Association.

Borden, N. H. (1964). The Concept of the Marketing Mix. *Journal of Advertising Research, 4*(2), 2–7.

Caru, A., & Cova, B. (2003). Revisiting Consumption Experience: A More Humble but Complete View of the Concept. *Marketing Theory, 3*(2), 267–286.

de Chernatony, L., & McDonald, M. (2002). *Creating Powerful Brands in Consumer, Service and Industrial Markets*. Oxford: Butterworth-Heinemann.

George, M., & Wakefield, K. L. (2018). Modeling the Consumer Journey for Membership Services. *Journal of Services Marketing, 32*(2), 113–125.

Giddens, A. (1991). *Modernity and Self-Identity*. Cambridge: Polity.

Gummesson, E. (2000). *Total Relationship Marketing*. Oxford: Butterworth-Heinemann.

Hansen, A. H., & Mossberg, L. (2013). Consumer Immersion: A Key to Extraordinary Experiences. In J. Sundbo & F. Sørensen (Eds.), *Handbook on the Experience Economy*. Cheltenham: Edward Elgar.

Hirschman, E., & Holbrook, M. (1982). Hedonic Consumption: Emerging Concepts, Methods and Propositions. *Journal of Marketing, 46*(3), 92–101.

Hollesen, S. (2015). *Marketing Management*. Harlow: Pearson.

Kotler, P., & Keller, K. L. (2016). *Marketing Management*. Harlow: Pearson.

Lindstrom, P. (2010). *Brand Sense*. New York: Free Press.

Lovelock, C., & Wirtz, J. (2011). *Services Marketing*. Boston: Prentice Hall.

McCarthy, E. J. (1960). *Basic Marketing: A Managerial Approach*. Homewood, IL: Irwin.

Pine, B. J. (1993). *Mass Customization*. Boston: Harvard Business School Press.

Porter, M. (2004). *Competitive Strategy*. New York: Simon and Schuster.

Schmitt, B. (1999). *Experiential Marketing: How to Get Companies to Sense, Feel, Think, Act and Relate to Your Company and Brands*. New York: Free Press.

Sundbo, J. (1994). Modulization of Service Production. *Scandinavian Journal of Management, 10*(3), 245–266.

Vargo, S., & Lusch, R. (Eds.). (2006). *The Service-Dominant Logic of Marketing*. New York: Sharpe.

Zeithaml, V. A., Bitner, M. J., & Gremler, D. D. (2006). *Services Marketing: Integrating Customer Focus across the Firm*. New York: McGraw-Hill/Irwin.

## Further Reading

Greenberg, A. (2002). *Customer Relationship Marketing. Electronic Customer Care in the New Economy*. Berlin: Springer.

Grönroos, C. (2016). *Service Management and Marketing*. London: Wiley.

Munter, A. (2002). *Customer Relationship Marketing*. Berlin: Springer.

Mossberg, L. (2007). A Marketing Approach to the Tourist. *Scandinavian Journal of Hospitality and Tourism, 7*(1), 59–74.

Loken, B., Ahluwalia, R., & Houston, M. J. (Eds.). (2015). *Brands and Brand Management. Contemporary Research Perspectives*. New York: Psychology Press.

## Useful Websites

Ford Motor Company: https://hbr.org/2018/05/how-ford-is-thinking-about-the-future; https://media.ford.com/content/fordmedia/fna/us/en/news/2017/10/fords-future-evolving-to-become-most-trusted-mobility-company.html.

McDonalds: https://profitworks.ca/blog/marketing-strategy/541-how-mcdonalds-became-the-leader-fast-food-industry-marketing-strategy.html.

https://www.pri.org/stories/2013-07-09/10-amazing-mcdonalds-commercials-explain-world.

Falck: https://www.falck.com/en/.

# Internationalizing Service Businesses

**10**

**Key Themes**

- How do service businesses internationalize?
- Localized services that cannot be directly exported
- Trading services
- Types of cross-border provision of services including soft and hard services and the four modes of service internationalization
- Services are heterogeneous and this means that different service sub-sectors require very different business models and internationalization strategies
- Globalization, the division of labour and global value chains
- International business theory and emerging markets
- Outsourcing and offshoring
- The platform economy, the cloud and service internationalization
- Born-global service firms
- Regulating and liberalizing service trade

Until the 1990s academics and policymakers classified service businesses as local establishments providing locally produced or co-created service solutions. Service businesses are still predominantly small, local firms, but the internationalization of services has become an important

aspect of the evolving global economy. Most of the literature on service internationalization, export strategies, foreign direct investment (FDI) and international marketing has focused predominantly on manufacturing (Daniels 1993; Bryson and Daniels. 2015). Much of this literature has highlighted the importance of size, age, ownership and sales on understanding the internationalization of manufacturing activities. Nevertheless, the internationalization of services is very different to that of manufacturing. The characteristics of a service business, including size and age, do not explain why some service firms engage in international business and others remain local businesses (Javalgi et al. 1998). Research on the internationalization of service businesses is still relatively underdeveloped. It is still possible to argue that international business theory, including research on Global Value Chains (GVC), Global Production Networks (GPN) (Coe and Yeung 2015) and the eclectic paradigm or OLI (Dunning 2000), has not yet adequately developed a conceptual framework for understanding the internationalization of services.

Innovations in logistics (see Chap. 11) and financial services have been at the centre of internationalization. One of these service innovations was the establishment of the Society for Worldwide Interbank Communications (SWIFT). SWIFT emerged as a European project to try to prevent an American bank monopolizing the market for the exchange of financial information. An American bank had introduced a proprietary

**Electronic Supplementary Material** The online version of this chapter (https://doi.org/10.1007/978-3-030-52060-1_10) contains supplementary material, which is available to authorized users.

system and was trying to force this on the global financial system. In response, SWIFT was established in Brussels in 1975 as a global cooperative between 270 banks in 15 countries. Today, the SWIFT network enables over 11,000 financial institutions, in more than 200 countries, to send and receive information about financial transactions in a secure, standardized and reliable environment. On average, over 32 million messages are sent via SWIFT daily.

Reading service businesses involves understanding the contributions that they make to internationalization. Services businesses play two roles in the on-going development of global economic activity. First, they are internationalizing in their own right by FDI, mergers and acquisitions (M&A) and by developing approaches to service delivery to meet the needs of clients in many different locations. This reflects different forms of direct internationalization in which services are locally produced and consumed or exported or indirect internationalization in which services are embedded and exported within physical goods and within other services (see Chap. 12). Second, service businesses provide the supporting service infrastructure to support trade and FDI in goods, raw materials and in the provision of other services (see Chap. 1). On the one hand, they play a critical role in the movement of goods, people, information and knowledge flows and most importantly money. This role includes the provision of financial and logistics services that are critical supporting services that underpin the development of the international economy and of the on-going fragmentation of GVC/GPN (see Chap. 11). On the other hand, a growing proportion of trade in services is embedded in material goods. This includes the provision of digital content including software, legal services but also financial packages designed to support consumption (see Chap. 12). The role services play in supporting the internationalization of other economic activities represents a form of indirect internationalization in which services contribute to countries' or regions' wider framework conditions. This is an important point. The internationalization of a national economy is partly related to the presence of concentrations of business and

professional service (BPS) firms. Services are at the centre of the evolving global economy or, as we argued in Chap. 1, act as a lubricant or a critical catalyst; without services, there would be no international trade or any type of internationalization.

This chapter explores the internationalization of services focusing on direct internationalization via FDI, exports and the movement of service providers and consumers. The contribution services make to indirect internationalization through their encapsulation in manufactured goods is explored in Chap. 12.

## 10.1   Localized Services

Services can be divided between those that can be traded over distances and those that can only be provided locally. The latter are localized services that cannot be exported. Localized services have to be produced and consumed in the place and at the time of their production. Providers of such services must be located close to demand as the nature of the service output prevents consumption and production from being undertaken in different places. Thus, dining out, attending a concert or cinema, cleaning services, cosmetic and beauty services and medical interventions must be consumed where they are produced. Such services cannot be stored. Localized services can be delivered in other countries through FDI, strategic partnerships with local providers or by the temporary or permanent migration of service providers or consumers.

Four factors have been identified to explain why some services must be locally produced and consumed. First, some services are considered to be intangible as they include the creation of experiences, performances, interpretations, knowledge-intensive expertise and symbolic, experiential and tacit knowledge. The provision of intangibles, often culturally inflected language-based interactions, is particularly challenging over distances. Second, many services are delivered through a co-creation process with consumers. This reflects some of the classic definitions of services. Thus, to Gershuny, 'at the moment of acquisition by the consumer. A good is a thing whereas a service is a state or activity or sensation' (1978, p. 56). This definition highlights a close synergistic relationship between service producers and consumers. Third, some services are perishable. Unlike manufactured goods, they cannot be stored to cope with variations in demand and supply. Demand for services might be predictable and well-known in domestic markets, but completely unpredictable in foreign markets. Cultural norms, including lifestyle differences, make it much harder to predict and manage variations in demand and supply. Fourth, the provision of service is considered to be too heterogeneous. By this it was assumed that the demand and supply of service provision varied from location to location, from service employee to service employee and from moment to moment (Winsted and Patterson 1998; Javalgi and Martin 2007). This heterogeneity includes services that are based on the production and consumption of experiences via dyadic encounters but also services that have been industrialized. A dyad describes the interaction between two people, the smallest possible social group. Unpredictable variations in service delivery would undermine the consumer's service experience. This is especially the case for service delivery systems that are heavily reliant on face-to-face encounters between service providers and customers. The development of an international service business would intensify these problems. Differences in employee and consumer cultures, including expectations, and in the ways in which people engage in dyadic encounters complicate the internationalization of services.

The impacts of these four characteristics on service internationalization are further complicated by sector-specific processes. These characteristics require the development of appropriate operational and management strategies by service providers. Nevertheless, service internationalization occurs, and firms have developed appropriate strategies that have transformed local service firms into international businesses. It is these processes of internationalization that are explored in this chapter.

## 10.2 Trading Services

There is an important distinction to be made between the internationalization of service businesses and international trade in services. These two processes are connected. On the one hand, there is a developing academic debate on the internationalization of services that can be traced back to the early work of Clairemonte and Cavanagh (1984) on services and transnational corporations. This article began to explore some of the international business dimensions of the emergence of service businesses. The literature on GVC and GPN (Yeung 2018, p. 102) has focused predominantly on the internationalization or globalization of manufacturing production. This is unfortunate as this approach has ignored the emergence and growth of international service businesses (Enderwick 1989), but also the complex interdependencies that exist between manufacturing and services (see Chap. 12). There is no question that the literature on international business and strategy needs to increasingly focus on understanding the differences that the provision of services makes to firms that are engaging in international transactions.

On the other hand, there is a well-developed literature on the emergence of service trade. This takes two forms. First, during the 1990s academic research began to identify that business and professional services were not just locally produced and consumed, but that intra- and inter-regional trade was an increasingly important aspect of their business operations. This realization led to the appreciation of the role BPS firms played in contributing to regional exports. Second, during the 1980s academic and policy research began to identify and explore trade and the internationalization of services (Krommenacker 1984; Feketekuty 1988).

Services were ignored until the 1980s in policy debates on trade and in international trade negotiations. There are many reasons for this neglect including the preoccupation with manufacturing firms, jobs, exports and FDI. Part of this preoccupation can be traced back to the identification of a positive correlation between the share of employment in manufacturing and income per capita across countries. This relationship encouraged policymakers to define developed economies as industrialized economies. In these accounts, 'manufacturing ... was "good", that is, associated with higher living standards. A related notion is that manufacturing jobs are "good jobs" whereas service jobs are low-skill, low-paying, "burger-flipper" jobs' (Jensen 2011, p. 12). The perception that manufacturing jobs are better than service jobs influenced policy and media debates. There is an added complication in that the comparative neglect of services is also explained by problems with data availability that also reflects the heterogeneity and complexity of the service sector.

Identifying and measuring service transactions is extremely challenging, and this is especially the case with the emergence of platform-based businesses. This difficulty is reflected in the on-going debate regarding the taxation of American technology companies including Facebook, Amazon, Apple, Netflix and Google (now owned by Alphabet). These firms are collectively known as the FAANGs and, in some accounts, as the 'Faang-tastic five' (Fletcher 2018). For governments it has become difficult to identify the relationship between the location of a transaction and where and how this should be taxed. Amazon UK, for example, accounts for UK sales and profits through a company based in Luxembourg.

The emergence of companies providing services using online platforms is an excellent example of the ways in which technological innovation is altering the ways in which services are provided (see Chap. 4). This represents a form of disruptive innovation that has transformed operational delivery of some services (see Chap. 3). It must be noted, however, that a platform-based business requires local investment. This includes the localization of the platform into a foreign language, including local payment systems, and the provision of related and supporting infrastructure, for example, service centres, warehousing and logistics.

## 10.3  Soft Versus Hard Services and Cross-Border Service Delivery

There are many different types of services—from complex high-value-added services based on the co-creation of knowledge to one-to-one face-to-face encounters in retailing or tourism. Services are heterogeneous, but so too are manufactured goods—from the fabrication of cars to chocolate, or from satellites to magnetic resonance imaging scanners. In some accounts, service businesses that have internationalized are classified into two types (Erramilli 1990). On the one hand, there are *hard services* in which service providers do not have to be co-located with consumers. This separation can involve the application of information and telecommunication technologies (ICTs) to the service delivery process. Hard services include the provision of architectural design, educational services, music and financial products. On the other hand, there are *soft services* in which service co-creation occurs at the same time and in the same place. These are services that include not only face-to-face delivery systems, but also the application of local services to material goods. Such services require a significant local presence or local representation. Soft services include restaurants, hotels and health care. There is some research that argues that there are very few significant differences between the foreign market entry modes of hard services and manufacturing (Ekeledo and Sivakumar 1998).

This simple classification between hard and soft services is an interesting approach to understanding service internationalization, but this is too much of a simplification. In addition, process and technological innovations have challenged this approach. Higher education services can be provided from afar using a distant-learning approach that is supported by an online interactive teaching platform. Alternatively, a provider can engage in FDI and establish a campus in another country and recruit local employees. There is another way to provide higher education. A provider of higher education services can enter into a strategic partnership with a local provider. In the latter case, the local host provider will undertake day-to-day administration related to service delivery including the provision of teaching space, library facilities and hospitality services. In this case, however, teaching is provided by flying faculty who are full-time employees of the home university. Programmes are structured to enable effective, but intensive local delivery. There are two points to make here. First, some universities use all three modes of educational provision. In this case, these types of educational services are both hard and soft. The University of Birmingham, UK, is an excellent example. It has a campus based in Dubai that is staffed by both local staff and flying faculty. This is a hybrid mode of service provision. In addition, it delivers programmes via distance learning and has a strategic partnership with the Singapore Institute of Management (SIM). SIM provides local administrative support and the space required to host teaching programmes, but the teaching is provided by flying faculty. Second, these different forms of service provision will come with different types of service experience. The University of Birmingham Dubai campus provides a complete Birmingham experience in a building that projects the brand of the university. While, in Singapore, the relationship between the student and the University of Birmingham is with the programme, the academics, or flying faculty, and not with the building or campus. The building or campus projects SIM's identity rather than that of the University of Birmingham.

The internationalization of service businesses is a complex process. For manufacturing, internationalization involves trade, FDI, outsourcing production to third parties located in another country and strategic alliances. These different approaches to internationalization also apply to services. The special characteristics of services create alternative ways for them to internationalize. Like manufacturing, the internationalization of services is driven by two motivations. On the one hand, service businesses may adopt a resource or asset seeking approach. In these cases, firms will develop

international operations to access some benefits that are available from offshoring. This includes accessing highly skilled staff or low-skilled labour inputs. An excellent example is the establishment of a call or data-processing centre in another country that is intended to reduce the cost of service provision to the home market. In this case, a firm is trying to blend the advantages that come from these different locations to increase the efficiency of service delivery. This is part of a process of cost arbitrage in which companies are attracted by lower labour and other costs combined with the advantages of closer proximity to new and existing customers in or near to the countries where they have established an offshored service facility.

On the other hand, service businesses may follow a market-based approach. In this instance, the primary rationale behind the development of international business is a search to enter new markets and to provide services in a different geographic setting. These two approaches are not mutually exclusive. Thus, a call centre may be established to assist clients in the firm's home market but will also service clients located in other places. Both approaches may be driven by the same business objective—risk reduction, contingency planning and impacts on profitability, including cost reductions or additional sources of revenue. In this scenario, a service business develops a dispersed client base to provide some protection from national recessionary cycles or as one response against future global pandemics. Alternatively, operational delivery is dispersed across different locations to enhance continuity of provision. Both strategies would impact on profitability and these impacts might be positive as well as altering the balance between operational delivery and risk.

The internationalization of service business has many drivers. Internationalization could be intended to reduce costs, to provide services to a foreign market, to develop 24-hour 7 days a week provision, to reduce exposure to country risks or to access skilled labour.

## 10.4 The Four Modes of Service Internationalization

Many classifications have been developed for grouping different methods of cross-border service delivery (Sampson and Snape 1985; UNCTAD 1983; Vandermerwe and Chadwick 1989; Edvardsson et al. 1993; Roberts 1998; Ball et al. 2008). The most influential classification of modes of cross-border service delivery is that detailed in Article I of the *General Agreement on Trade in Services* (GATS) which identifies four modes of cross-border service supply (United Nations 2002, p. 1) (Table 10.1).

Three of these modes are concerned primarily with service transactions between residents and non-residents. Mode 1 involves the provision of services that require no direct contact with customers, but procedures must be developed to overcome cultural barriers that exist between countries. This includes remote delivery via online platforms, but also offshored call centres. Recently, there has been a particular interest in Mode 3, whereby enterprises supply services

internationally through the activities of foreign affiliates (Bryson et al. 2004). For services, this 'method of serving foreign markets is particularly important because it is often the only method that permits the close and continuing contact between service providers and their customers necessary to compete effectively with indigenous firms' (UN 2002, 54). This type of service FDI represents *captive* offshoring or offshoring without outsourcing. Trade in services must address cultural differences between countries that restricts the ability of service providers to export standardized services. Modes 3 and 4 enable service providers to localize services to take into consideration local cultures and client expectations. Modes 1, 3 and 4 involve what is commonly termed 'service offshoring' or more correctly 'service global sourcing'.

Mode 3 accounts for the majority of service internationalization given the importance of local service delivery through the establishment of a commercial presence. Mode 1 is next in order of importance and much of this is accounted for by the provision of digital content including services that are enabled through ICT. This is followed by the movement of consumers (Mode 2), and, in particular, all types of tourists, including those seeking leisure-, educational- or medical-related services.

Different countries are more involved with different modes of service internationalization. Thus, for South Asian countries Modes 1 and 4 are particularly important. For India, the export of information technology (IT) and information technology enabled services (ITES), including call centres and data processing centres, is especially important. ITES provided from India reflect the application of IT to deliver impersonal or non-facing services to consumers over long distances. In addition, for South Asian countries, Mode 4 is important and this involves the movement of natural persons across borders to provide services to consumers. This can take two forms. First, there is a small number of skilled temporary migrants providing highly skilled service inputs. Second, there is a much larger flow of migrants involved in the provision of less-skilled intensive services, for example, domestic worker,

**Table 10.1** Four modes of cross-border service supply

| Mode | Type | Characteristic |
|---|---|---|
| Mode 1 | *Cross-border supply* | Occurs when suppliers of services in one country supply services to consumers in another country without either supplier or consumer moving into the territory of the other. |
| Mode 2 | *Consumption abroad* | The process by which a consumer resident in one country moves to another country to obtain a service. |
| Mode 3 | *Commercial presence* | Occurs when enterprises in an economy supply services internationally through the activities of foreign affiliates. |
| Mode 4 | *Presence of natural persons* | The process by which an individual moves temporarily to the consumer's country to provide a service, whether on his or her own behalf or on behalf of his or her employer. |

Source: Authors' own

cleaning services and construction. This latter type could be classified as temporary migration, or a form of indirect service internationalization, based on migrants seeking employment in other countries.

Services are heterogeneous and this means that different service sub-sectors require very different business models and internationalization strategies. Even within the same firm different approaches to internationalization will have developed that include exports, FDI and employee or consumer movements. Within a service sub-sector individual firms will adopt different internationalization strategies, and these will reflect factors including firm size and the experience and ambitions of the senior management team. In an interesting analysis Roberts (2015) identifies some of the service-sub-sector differences in common mechanisms for cross-border delivery. This highlights important differences between consumer services that require a physical presence, for example, hotels and restaurants and business and professional services that can be delivered through strategic partnerships, the development of informal networks, FDI and also provider and consumer movements (Table 10.2).

For advanced business and professional services internationalization can include FDI, M&A and the development of strategic partnerships. In a study of design consultancy firms, Abecassis-Moedas et al. (2012) explore 11 firms which had significant international activities ranging from 10 to 75% of revenue. Only two firms had established a foreign office to be close to clients. This reflects a fixed capital investment. The other firms based their international client activities on investments in human and organizational capital. Three types of internationalization strategy were identified. First is a group of firms that are classified as star-based design creative knowledge-intensive business services (KIBS) which do not require foreign offices. The competitive advantage of these firms is based on the reputation and individual creativity of a star designer. International transactions occur through either exports or third parties. The second group of design consultancies were process-based creative KIBS that have developed a formalized design

process based on exports. Third, there were a group of glocality-based creative KIBS which adopt a hybrid approach to internationalization based on investments in physical and organizational capital. These firms develop direct relationships with clients located in foreign countries through the establishment of local offices and applying creative processes developed in their home location.

In the hotel industry the different entry modes adopted by a firm are based on the degree of control required over the foreign operation (Contractor and Kundu 1998). There are four control aspects that need to be considered:

(a) Daily operations
(b) The building and the physical asset
(c) Organizational routines and the tacit elements of the business model
(d) Codified assets including the brand and reservation system

The responsibility for controlling these different elements depends on the internationalization mode adopted by a firm. There are three alternative strategies. First, direct investment or FDI in which the international hotel chain has complete control over all four control aspects. Second, direct investment but with some shared control. Exclusive control may be only about the codified assets with control over other aspects shared with a local partner. Third, forms that do not involve capital investment and these include franchising and management contracts. In the case of a franchise, the international chain does not manage the local hotel as the local owner controls daily operations and the physical asset (Pla-Barber et al. 2011).

## 10.5   Emerging Markets and the Theory of Multinational Enterprises

Firms based in emerging markets, the BRIC and VISTA countries of Brazil, Russia, India, China, Vietnam, Indonesia, South Africa, Turkey and Argentina, as well as Mexico and Thailand, have developed into transnational firms that are competing with firms from developed market econo-

**Table 10.2** Typical forms of services internationalization by sector and mode

| Service sector | Modes | Typical form of internationalization |
|---|---|---|
| Retailing | Mode 1: Cross-border supply Mode 2: Consumption aboard Mode 3: Commercial presence | Franchising, mergers and acquisitions, FDI, movement of consumers for retail consumption. Development of localized e-commerce platforms with related infrastructure. |
| Hotels & restaurants | Mode 3: Commercial presence | FDI, mergers and acquisitions, management contracts, franchising and hotel consortia, platforms and the sharing economy |
| Telecommunications | Mode 3: Commercial presence | FDI, mergers and acquisitions |
| Transport services | Mode 3: Commercial presence | FDI in the form of mergers and acquisitions as well as strategic alliances |
| Media & entertainment industries | Mode 1: Cross-border supply Mode 3: Commercial presence | Trade and FDI, in the form of mergers and acquisitions |
| Education | Mode 1: Cross-border supply Mode 2: Consumption aboard Mode 3: Commercial presence Mode 4: Presence of natural persons | Trade occurs through the movement of students and teachers as well as through correspondence courses and increasingly through the Internet. Franchising, joint ventures and wholly owned campuses are increasingly common in higher education |
| Utilities including water, gas & electricity | Mode 3: Commercial presence | FDI through mergers and acquisitions |
| Healthcare | Mode 2: Consumption aboard Mode 3: Commercial presence Mode 4: Presence of natural persons | Movement of patients, e.g. healthcare tourism but also a growing number of cross-border mergers and acquisitions |

(continued)

**Table 10.2**  (continued)

| Service sector | Modes | Typical form of internationalization |
|---|---|---|
| Business services | Mode 1: Cross-border supply Mode 2: Consumption aboard Mode 3: Commercial presence Mode 4: Presence of natural persons | Establishment of a presence through greenfield sites, mergers and acquisitions and the development of networks of national providers as well as trade through the movement of clients and staff |

Source: Adapted from Roberts 2015: 263

mies. The existing theory that has been developed to explain the emergence of international business has been based on the analysis of predominantly manufacturing firms located in developed market economies. This theory comes with a number of assumptions reflecting the processes and patterns of internationalization adopted or developed by firms located in developed market economies. There are problems in applying this theory to understanding the emergence of international firms in emerging economies.

The eclectic paradigm is the approach that most scholars of international business apply to understanding internationalization. This approach was developed by John Dunning based on the identification of ownership advantages (O), location advantages (L) and internalization advantages (I) held by firms (Dunning 1988, 2001; Dunning and Lundan 2008). The emphasis is on understanding the internationalization of multinational enterprises by FDI compared to firms that engage in exports, product licensing or franchising. The primary assumption is that firms will engage in FDI when they possess ownership, locational and internalization advantages.

The first condition is that a firm must have ownership-specific advantages, or firm-specific advantages (FSAs) that can be applied to a foreign location. Some of these advantages should ideally be inimitable including intellectual property rights, registered designs, brands, reputation and social networks (Dunning 1988). By themselves, ownership-specific advantages are insufficient to explain a firm's decision to engage in FDI.

The first condition must also be combined with the second condition which is the existence of locational advantages which encourage a firm to locate production there compared to an alternative location. Locational advantages, or country-specific advantages (CSAs), include a country's endowment of national resources, labour, market size, tariff and non-tariff barriers, institutions, regulations and investment incentives and disincentives. There must be some CSAs that a firm can only acquire through direct investment.

The third condition assumes that a firm may have well-developed FSAs and the target country possesses attractive CSAs, but a firm might still only negotiate licensing agreements or establish a franchise network. Thus, the argument is that another factor must be combined with FSAs and CSAs that explains why a firm would undertake FDI. Here it is important to be aware of the added costs and difficulties related to FDI including cultural, political, language and communication difficulties. The third condition is that a multinational firm must be more efficient than other firms through using their own employees to realize the value of FSAs and CSAs compared to selling or renting its FSAs to independent foreign firms. Dunning labels this an 'internationalization advantage' that emerges from market imperfections.

The OLI model differentiates between O advantages or FSAs that are firm specific and L or CSAs advantages that are country specific. To

Hennart (2012, p. 170) 'while FSAs are proprietary to firms, CSAs are properties of a given country (its natural resources, market size, labor costs, etc.)'. This is an important distinction. The assumption is that CSAs are 'specific to a particular location … but available to all firms' (Dunning and Lundan 2008, p. 96). This is very much an assumption as an American company will have unequal access to CSAs based in China compared to Chinese firms and a Chinese firm operating in America will have unequal access to American CSAs.

It is important to note three points about the OLI. First, this theory is the dominant approach used by scholars of international business to explain internationalization. The theory has been used as the foundations to develop an on-going and complex conceptual debate on international business. This is very different to the GVC or GPN debate. The OLI debate is focused on understanding why international firms emerge and why firms undertake investments in foreign countries. Both the GVC and GPN focus not on understanding the emergence of international business but on the governance, management and dynamics of global value chains or production networks (Coe and Yeung 2015; Vanchan et al. 2018; Yeung and Coe 2015; Bryson et al. 2020). These are thus very different approaches; they are complementary rather than alternative accounts of internationalization.

Second, the focus of research on the OLI and on GVC/GPN has been dominated by studies of manufacturing rather than service firms. Thus, both approaches are not that well suited as explanations for the emergence or governance of some types of cross-border service delivery. It can perhaps explain the emergence of service FDI but needs to focus more on the special characteristics of services including the co-creation and localization of service experiences in different cultural settings.

Third, the OLI is very much a theory developed to explore the internationalization of firms based in developed rather than emerging market economies (Dunning 2006). The emphasis placed on a firm having a combination of strengths in FSAs, CSAs and internal advantages is perhaps

more of a reflection of the emergence of international business from locations within developed market economies rather than from within emerging economies.

In 2012, Hennart developed a modification to the OLI on the understanding that the existing model:

> is not suited to explain the emergence of EMMs [Emerging Market Multinational] because of its dichotomy between firm-specific advantages (FSAs), which are supposed to allow firms to invest abroad, and country specific advantages or CSAs, which are properties of the target country and which determine from which location the FSA-exploiting firm will serve the target country. (Hennart 2012, p. 183)

The difficulty is the assumption in the OLI that CSAs are accessible to all firms—local and foreign—on the same terms. This is not the case and Hennart argues that these CSAs, or complementary local resources, can rarely be sold. These are place-based or country-based intangibles that are reflected in the relationships between a firm and its home location. Thus, local firms will have a better understanding than foreign firms of local consumers, local officials and politicians and local circumstances. He notes that a firm like Lenovo began as a distributor and that in this role developed a proprietary distribution network that was unavailable to foreign competitors. In this account, EMMs enjoy privileged access to CSAs including better access to local decision-makers.

The OLI assumes that transnational firms emerge based on positions of strength across all dimensions of the OLI. Nevertheless, many firms located in emerging market economies have comparatively weak firm-specific advantages compared to competitors from developed market economies but have access to distinct local CSAs in their home country. A firm does not require strong FSAs to internationalize, but instead must be able to take 'title to the profits that arise from bundling its own inputs with those of local owners in a host market, in other words when it makes these local owners its employees' (Hennart 2012, p. 184). Firms located in emerging economies are able to enter foreign markets by acquiring FSAs created by foreign firms through M&A and strategic partnerships. They are able to bundle the benefits that come from their location in an emerging economy and the CSAs that come from this location with the acquisition and/or control of complementary firm-specific advantages.

This process of bundling advantages, including FSAs, to engage in international business is a well-known aspect of internationalization. Here it is important to make two points. First, firms in emerging markets have a history of using international expansion as a springboard to acquire strategic resources (Luo and Tung 2007). An excellent example is Lenovo's acquisition of IBM's laptop division. This enables these firms to acquire FSAs that they would perhaps have difficulty in creating given the existence of extant firms in the marketplace. Second, one of the problems with international business theory, and the on-going development of the OLI, is fragmentation of theory development by country, sector and academic discipline. This is unfortunate. Thus, Hennart's argument can be perhaps equally applied to some firms in locations in developed market economies. Thus, some of these 'advantaged' firms are relatively disadvantaged in terms of their FSAs but are able to use CSAs to develop bundles of complementary resources through M&A and the development of strategic partnerships.

The difficulty is that international business theory has a poor understanding of geography. The assumption is that all places within a country will have similar access to CSAs. This assumption is reflected in the terminology used in the international business literature. The focus of the OLI is on multinational firms or firms that have many different activities located in many different countries. An alternative term is transnational firms or firms that have activities in locations in many different nations and there are some interactions between these facilities or activities. Both these terms reflect a national focus or a nation-to-nation approach to understanding international business. This is unfortunate as international firms develop relationship between places—towns, cities, localities—within national economies. Each of these places provides a firm with differential access to that country's country-

specific advantages. Given this difficulty, international business is better described using the term translocal firm. A translocal firm develops and explores business opportunities in many different places. Different places within the same national economy will provide the firm with different forms of advantage and disadvantage. This is to highlight the importance of intra-country place-based differentials.

## 10.6 Outsourcing, Offshoring and Captive Offshoring: Service Business and the Internationalization of Intrafirm Transactions

One of the primary decisions made by a firm involves strategic and operational decisions regarding tasks involved in the production of goods and services. This includes three key decisions—who will undertake the task, where will the task be undertaken and how will it be undertaken. A key issue is the decision to undertake a task in-house or to outsource it to another firm. Outsourcing involves the purchasing of intermediate inputs from other firms. This may become offshore outsourcing when the tasks are undertaken by another company abroad (see Chap. 8). This represents a traditional offshore outsourcing model that may be driven by cost differentials. Alternatively, a company may offshore a task to another country, but the task remains within the firm. In this instance, offshoring does not have to involve outsourcing. This type of outsourcing is known as a captive-site model as a firm creates its own foreign subsidiary to provide tasks within a service GVC. The foreign subsidiary includes employees from the firm's home and host location. Captive offshoring provides a firm with the financial benefits of offshoring but avoids problems related to control, quality and security that can be associated with outsourcing. A captive approach can be combined with outsourced service providers to develop a blended approach to service or task delivery.

The different types of outsourcing and offshoring models are associated with different

**Table 10.3** Factors contributing to the offshoring of services activities

| Service Demand/ service supply | Supplied from one or many sites | Supplier not fixed in space |
|---|---|---|
| Consumed from one or a many sites | *Local consumption or offshoring:* Either local provision for services that require face-to-face interaction or standardized services can be provided by cross-border trade facilitated by ICT | *Foreign trade:* Services provided by the movement of the provider to the client either directly or through internal or external third-party networks. This may be a form of offshoring |
| Consumer not fixed in space | *Specialist suppliers with mobile consumers:* Consumers travel to service providers—for example, capital-intensive services including public services (health and education); high street retailing and specialist business services providers where the client visits the provider | *Service supplier and provider are mobile:* A rare form, perhaps the best examples are educational services and the management of trade exhibitions and conferences, but even here third-party fixed capital investment determines the location of the activity |

Source: Authors' own

challenges and benefits (Table 10.3). Outsourcing a task to a third party implies that the task can be codified and standardized. The providers must undertake the task to meet the requirements of the contract including service quality. Captive offshoring requires a firm to develop and manage FDI in another jurisdiction. This includes identifying sites, negotiating with policymakers and politicians, obtaining the required business licences and then hiring, training and managing people. These two alternative approaches reflect a distinction that must be made between coordinating and controlling the procurement of tasks from abroad via contractual relationships with third-party firms versus direct ownership and control. Both types of internationalization will take time. Offshore outsourcing requires the identification and development of a relationship with third-party providers whilst captive offshoring requires substantial management time combined with capital investment.

There is an alternative strategy. This is the collaborative or partnership model in which a firm employs an external service provider to assist in the establishment of an offshore service centre. There are three types of collaborative model that combine features of the captive approach with the offshore outsourcing model. These are as follows:

1. *Build-operate-transfer* (BOT) model. A third party is employed to develop and initially operate the offshore centre, but eventually the ownership and management of the centre is transferred to the client firm.
2. *Assisted captive model.* A third party assists the company with the development of a foreign service centre, but the centre is developed and managed by the client firm.
3. *Joint venture.* A service centre is created as a joint venture between a firm and a third-party provider.

These different approaches reflect the needs of a particular firm including timing, speed, experience and the types of task involved. A key issue is scale or the size of the task that a firm wants to offshore. A provider of outsourced services will have the fixed-cost infrastructure to deliver tasks efficiently. In this case, entering into a contractual relationship with a business process offshoring provider would reduce costs. Captive offshoring should only occur when a firm requires a critical mass of tasks that more than offsets the costs of establishing and managing an offshore captive centre. The management of a GVC is a dynamic process (Bryson et al. 2020). A firm will eventually alter the geography of tasks. This might involve ending a contract with a third-party provider of business process offshoring or closing a captive centre. Closing a captive centre will result in closure costs, including redundancy payments, and writing off some of the initial capital investment.

The difference between outsourcing that is offshored versus captive offshoring is about different types of risk (Bryson et al. 2020).

Identifying the right provider of business process offshore services is difficult and significant management time will be required to ensure service quality is maintained. Captive offshoring comes with increased risks related to project development and initiation while outsourcing offshoring exposes a firm to risks related to a third-party undertaking tasks. These risks include service quality, but also data security issues.

Companies engaging in service offshoring benefit from the application of technology to access time-zone advantages. This enables service tasks to be delivered 24 hours a day without incurring overtime costs. Tasks can be transferred between time zones using a follow-the-sun approach. At the same time, a captive centre can provide services back to the firm's home market but can also provide services to clients located in the foreign country. This reflects a blended strategy in which a firm seeks to combine the benefits of a resource or asset-based approach with a market-based strategy. This type of approach balances cost and profit versus risk and is one approach that needs to be adopted to enhance resilience as one response to post-Covid-19 planning (Bryson et al. 2020).

Service outsourcing and offshoring comes with additional costs that need to be included in the outsourcing offshoring decision. These costs reflect the additional costs of performing business tasks in a foreign country. The firm must invest time and effort in understanding how to work with foreign firms, officials, governments and a different legal system. There will also be the costs of managing operations from afar including communication costs. These additional costs can be considered as either the fixed costs of offshoring or a combination of capital and on-going revenue costs or alternatively 'as a "leakage" in the profit flow of the offshored business' (Kikuchi and Long 2010). This concept of leakage needs to be treated with care. Offshoring should be treated as both a cost and revenue creating activity. As a cost, the types of service tasks that are offshored may not be directly related to revenue creation, for example, dealing with customer complaints and enquiries or supporting services that are not in themselves revenue gener-

ating. Nevertheless, all firms must explore the tensions between the additional costs of outsourcing and offshoring versus revenue generation related to risk.

The geographical distance in a service offshoring relationship can be explored by considering transport costs and non-transport costs. Transport costs include communication costs and any travel required between the two locations. Non-transport costs include cultural and linguistic differences, informational and communication barriers and tariff and non-tariff barriers. Some non-transport costs include expenditure on developing and maintaining social and business networks. The strength of these networks might reduce the overall cost by reducing information and cultural barriers (Kandilov and Grennes 2012).

Global sourcing does not have to entail the supply of services from a great distance, but may involve 'near-shoring' or the relocation or provision of services over a short distance and often from a location on the same continental landmass (Bryson 2007). The development of service offshoring reflects an escalation in the complexity of service production systems. Services can now be supplied onshore, near-shore and offshore and in any combination:

- Backyard/Onshore/Home nation—provides advantages of cultural understanding and nearness to the market.
- Offshore/Far Nation—cost advantages, but cultural problems that can undermine client customer relationships.
- Near-shore/Near Nation—capture cost advantages but retain close geographic relationship and greater cultural awareness of the target customer market.

Presented in this manner these may appear as simple alternatives but in many instances firms have developed 'blended delivery systems' that capitalize on the place-based advantages of coupling or blending activities located in a variety of different locations: home—near—far. Blended delivery systems are being introduced extremely rapidly by American, British and Indian service providers. An example to explore is Sutherland Global Services, a private company.

Sutherland Global Services, an American provider of business process outsourcing (BPO), was established in 1986 in New York to provide onshore services to American clients (Bryson 2007). For 14 years this company only provided onshore services, but in 2000 it established a nearshore facility in Canada and in 2002 an offshore facility in India. The company has implemented a blended delivery system enabling it to combine different country competitive advantages based on cost, access to labour, language skills and markets. During 2006, Sutherland established a facility in Mexico to provide services to Spanish-speaking clients. Similarly, Infosys, one of the largest Indian providers of BPO, opened its first overseas office in 1987 and since then has developed a blended delivery system with facilities located in key markets including England (Table 10.4).

A blended shore offshoring strategy provides a firm with multiple advantages including:

1. Comparative advantage—leverage the advantages of multiple locations
2. Geographic time and especially 24/7 service provision
3. Reduction of exposure to country risk
4. Development of new markets/enhanced market exposure
5. Able to dynamically route calls to the next available agent/centre
6. Able to balance needs over time

The nature of the blend evolves to meet the needs of the firm. This evolution may be in response to process and product innovation, but also a strategy intended to enhance a firm's ability to extend the geographic reach of its services.

Not all services are implicated in offshoring or the internationalization of services, for a variety of reasons related to the nature of the service production/consumption process. Services that require face-to-face contact, knowledge of local market conditions, have a high information or knowledge content, high barriers to entry and are resistant to standardization will be unlikely to be relocated offshore. In many instances, services

**Table 10.4** The evolving geographies of two offshoring providers: Infosys (India) and Sutherland Global Services (New York)

|      | Infosys (India) | Sutherland Global Services (US) |
|------|-----------------|----------------------------------|
| 1981 | Established India | |
| 1986 | | Established in Rochester New York, as a provider of Business Process Outsourcing (BPO). Founder—former Xerox Corp. executive |
| 1987 | First international office (US) | |
| 1995 | Development centres targeted at export market established across India | |
| 1996 | First European Office, Milton Keynes, UK | |
| 1997 | Office established, Toronto, Canada | |
| 1999 | Offices established in Germany, Sweden, Belgium and Australia. Two developments opened in the US | |
| 2000 | Offices established in France, Hong Kong. Global Development centres established in Canada, UK and US (3) | Offshore operations commerce: Sault Ste. Marie, Canada (1100 agents) |
| 2001 | Offices opened in UEA and Argentina. Development centre established in Japan | |
| 2002 | Offices opened in Netherlands, Singapore and Switzerland | Facilities opened in Chennai and Bombay (India) (no. of employees doubled to more than 3000 in six months). |
| 2003 | Subsidiaries established (Infosys China and Infosys Australia). Acquisition of Expert Information Services, Australia | |
| 2004 | Annual Revenue of $1 billion | |

(continued)

**Table 10.4**  (continued)

| | Infosys (India) | Sutherland Global Services (US) |
|---|---|---|
| 2005 | Expansion in China planned, additional 6000 employees over next 5 years. New centres at Shanghai and Hanghzhou | Two new operation centres established in India New Canadian Centre. Philippines facility opened (Manila) London subsidiary established |
| 2006 | Hyderabad expansion involving 550 acres and to create 25,000 software jobs over ten years | Facility opened in Kerala, India (expects to hire 3000) Searching for sites in Mexico/Central America/Caribbean for clients with Spanish-speaking customers |
| 2009 | Acquisition of McCamish Systems, US. First development centre in Brazil. First office in New Zealand | |
| 2010 | | Opens centre in Alexandria, Egypt |
| 2011 | Recruited 1200 US employees | Facility in General Santos City, Philippines, 200 employees |
| 2012 | Office established in Milwaukee, US as the firm's 18 office in the US | Investment of $50 m in the Philippines, 8000 people in a world-class Integrated Technology and BPO Campus. BPO centre in Louisiana—600 employees |
| 2013 | New branch office in Sydney, Australia. New Centre in the Netherlands | Acquisition of BPO arm of Apollo Health Street Ltd. New BPO centre, Pereira, Colombia |
| 2014 | Hiring 2100 in the US Expands partnership with Microsoft and announces partnership with Huawei to provide Cloud, Big Data and Communication Solutions | Expansion in Bulgaria |

(continued)

**Table 10.4**  (continued)

| | Infosys (India) | Sutherland Global Services (US) |
|---|---|---|
| 2016 | | Chesapeake, VA, US, expansion of Insurance Centre, 200 additional employees. New centre in Las Vegas, 2000 employees |
| 2018 | Expanding in Indianapolis, US, additional 3000 jobs | Add 750 jobs to the centre in Alexandria, Egypt |

Source: Authors' own

that can be relocated will be supplied to consumers by blending onshore and offshore delivery systems to maximize the benefits that accrue from each of these delivery models. Every company will have to develop its own blend of onshore/nearshore/offshore activity. In some cases, retaining everything onshore may become a marketing advantage associated with quality rather than the cost of service provision. The issue really concerns cost versus the advantages, or alternative non-cost-based advantages, that are associated with local provision; for example, local accents, knowledge, place-based advantages including shared everyday experiences of consumers and service providers and a detailed lived experience of local cultures (Bryson et al. 2020). Offshoring services have been facilitated by developments in ICT including intra-firm knowledge management platforms. These developments in ICT, including the emergence of a platform economy, are transforming service internationalization and it is to this that we now turn our attention.

## 10.7   The Platform Economy, the Cloud and Service Internationalization

A digital economy has emerged and continues to evolve based on the development of digitally enabled business models (see Chaps. 3 and 4). Companies like Airbnb, Alibaba, Amazon, Etsy, Facebook, Google, Salesforce, Uber, DiDi and

WeChat have created online structures providing a range of services. Digital platforms enable three forms of trade (Lund and Manyika 2016). First, a platform may facilitate pure digital exchanges, for example, the export of software and managed services including the provision of digital storage in the cloud. Second, digital platforms increase the effectiveness and efficiency of the physical flow of goods and this includes logistics platforms facilitating the cross-border movement of goods. Third, digital platforms promote transnational production, exchange and consumption including platforms that are used to coordinate global supply chains.

The development and application of platforms to economic activity has increased the speed of development of the global economy; platforms have led to an acceleration in globalization (Kenney and Zysman 2016, 2020). Compared to physical manufacturing and the international expansion of the import and export of goods, digital platforms have been proliferating globally with limited resistance, regulation and control because of disparate governmental policies and regulations (Cunningham and Craig 2016). The global reach of platforms is far in excess of anything achieved by firms selling goods; Netflix has over 80 million subscribers in 190 countries, while Facebook has 1.7 billion users or more than half of the global adult population (Cunningham and Craig 2016).

Cloud computing is the delivery of on-demand digitally enabled services including the provision of applications, storage and processing power over the Internet and on a pay-as-you-go basis or via a time-limited contract. The American National Institute of Standards and Technology defined cloud computing as:

> a model for enabling ubiquitous, convenient, on-demand network access to a shared pool of configurable computing resources (e.g., networks, servers, storage, applications, and services) that can be rapidly provisioned and released with minimal management effort or service provider interaction. In addition, the NIST definition introduces the supporting concepts of three cloud service models, five essential characteristics, and four types of cloud deployments. In total, the NIST Cloud Computing Definition is composed of 14 interrelated terms and their associated definitions. (Simmon 2018, p. 2)

These five essential characteristics are: on-demand self-service, broad network access, resource pooling, rapid elasticity and measured service. Cloud-based services can be provided privately, publicly, by a community or by some hybrid of private, public and community.

Consumers, including companies, no longer need to own computing infrastructure, including data centres, but can pay for infrastructure access from a cloud service provider. Cloud computing provides the essential infrastructure for the provision of digitally enabled services. This includes consumer services like Gmail and using the cloud to automatically back up photographs taken with a smartphone. It also includes services that enable firms to host all data in the cloud and to run all applications via a cloud-based interface. Netflix's video streaming service, for example, is a cloud-based computing service.

Three types of cloud computing service business models have emerged. First are *Infrastructure-as-a-Service* (IaaS) business models in which consumers access computing infrastructure for a fee. This type of business model enables firms to develop new services, but without the requirement to invest in data centres or in the skills required to run computing infrastructure. Second is a *Platform-as-a-Service* (PaaS) business model in which a cloud-based provider enables access for a fee to digital storage, networking and services as well as the tools and software to build and manage applications. Third are *Software-as-a-Service* (SaaS) business models or the delivery of applications-as-a-service. In this case, consumers access software that is held in the cloud to undertake different types of activity. The type of hardware, and the operating systems used to provide this software, is unimportant for the consumer and the key aspect is the ability to access required software-enabled services.

For cloud computing the location from which the service is provided, including the location of the hardware, is largely irrelevant for the consumer. Thus, cloud computing transforms how digital content is provided and how computing is undertaken, and it is much less about the geography of where this content is held and the location of the data centres. Nevertheless, for the cloud geography does matter in many different ways, but it has a very different role to play compared to the other ways of providing services. Three points need to be considered. First, there is the location of the service in relation to climate zones. A data centre produces a lot of heat as it consumes much energy. The geography of data centres partly reflects not only the location of the cables that link data centres with the Internet, but also the ability to reduce the need for air conditioning by locating data centres in cooler environments. Data centres owned by, for example, Amazon, Facebook, Google, Apple and Microsoft are major energy consumers and heat generators. In 2019, the state of Virginia, USA, was the location for over 100 large data centres and is known as 'data centre alley'. Virginia plays an important role in the global geography of data centres. Data centre providers are experimenting with innovations intended to reduce the carbon footprint of their centres. This includes Microsoft's decision to locate a centre that is submerged in the North Sea and Facebook's investment in a data centre located on the edge of the Arctic Circle in Finland.

Second, consumers accessing services provided from a data centre located far away experience a latency problem, or a delay in data transfer, following the instruction to initiate a transfer. To avoid this problem, cloud-based services must be provided relatively locally.

Third, the actual geographic location of data has become a geopolitical problem revolving around debates and concerns with data sovereignty. This is a major concern for the European Commission and for European firms and increasingly for the US government. The key issue is based on where data is processed, stored and its safety. Thus, the European Commission is concerned that European data hosted on servers located in an American-based data centre could be accessed by the US government. The large providers of cloud-based services have been developing regional networks of data centres to ensure that data can be hosted regionally rather than within a different national jurisdiction. Cybersecurity is an important factor behind where data is hosted globally. Thus, to reduce and control data security risks it is important for companies and governments to consider the location of the data centres which host their data.

## 10.8 Born-Global Service Firms

The literature on international business placed considerable emphasis on international business as an incremental approach. In this analysis, a local business had to develop successful processes and goods locally before internationalizing (Johanson and Vahlne 1977). In other words, it had to develop firm-specific advantages. Nevertheless, there are many different approaches to developing an international business and this includes the emergence of International New Ventures (INV) or 'born-global firms'. There is no agreed definition of born-global firms but these are firms that follow a born-global pathway which typically includes commencing international operations from inception (Oviatt and McDougall 1994), planning products/goods, structures, systems and finances on a global basis (Luostarinen and Gabrielsson 2006), integrating resources in multiple countries to create outputs (Harveston et al. 2000) and developing different goods and operations and global marketing strategies (Gabrielsson et al. 2008). Born-global firms rapidly become international businesses (Rennie 1993).

The emergence of born-global firms can be explained by five interrelated factors. First are facilitating factors including developments in the Internet, but also on-going globalization. Both encourage entrepreneurs to think globally or internationally rather than locally. Second, there are sector-specific factors with some sub-sectors increasingly operating internationally rather than locally. Government intervention might also be encouraging the development of a global rather than local attitude to business. Third, there are entrepreneurship-specific factors including the experience of doing business in other countries and entrepreneurs who have a global rather than local or national mindset. Fourth, there are firm-specific factors including resources, capabilities and the ownership of inimitable resources. Fifth are network-specific aspects including the social networks of the founders.

The emergence of born-global firms has been explored by Gabrielsson and Gabrielsson (2013) through the development of a conceptual framework that argues that a born-global firm goes through four phases:

1. Introductory phase
2. Commercialization and foreign entries phase
3. Rapid growth and foreign expansion phase
4. Rationalization and foreign maturity phase

They applied this approach to explore the emergence of companies providing software services. IBS Software Service Ltd. (IBS) is a leading provider of new-generation IT solutions that was founded in 1997. IBS products manage mission-critical operations for major airlines, airports, oil and gas companies, seaports and tour operators worldwide. The company operates from 12 business centres in North America, Europe, Asia-Pacific, Middle East and Africa. The firm's introductory phase (1997–1999) commenced with operations in Trivandrum, India in 1997. The initial product involved maintaining, repairing and overhauling software. In 1997, the company began operating in Europe and in 1998 began providing software services in the Middle East. In 1999, IBS experienced a cash flow problem and had to seek external funding. The commercialization and foreign entries phase (2000–2002) included the firm's first joint venture partnership and also the establishment of operations in the US and Australia. At the end of this phase, the company diversified into providing logistics services for the oil and gas industry. The rapid growth and foreign expansion phase (2003–2008) included the firm's first global acquisition in 2003 and the development of a fight management solution targeted at the operational needs of scheduled and charter airlines. These products were used globally by 12 airlines operating in Europe, Asia-Pacific, North America, Middle East and Africa. In 2008, IBS became a Microsoft gold certified partner. The rationalization and foreign maturity phase (2009–) involved IBS focusing on network expansion and innova-

tion. This included new strategic alliances. The company has grown extremely rapidly and employs over 2000 in its 12 business centres.

## 10.9   General Agreement on Trade in Services (GATS)

International trade involves the movement of goods, services and people across national borders. This involves interrelationships between different national jurisdictions. After World War II the coordination of government policies was embodied in a number of international institutions, including the World Trade Organization (WTO), International Monetary Fund (IMF) and the World Bank. These institutions have promoted and encouraged globalization. The emphasis has been on removing or reducing tariff and non-tariff barriers that inhibit trade in goods and raw materials. In 1947 the General Agreement on Tariffs and Trade (GATT) was established as an international agreement intended to reduce barriers to trade and to maximize the benefits that come from the free flow of goods. This became part of the WTO in 1995.

The WTO was formed as an outcome of the Uruguay GATT round of negotiations (1986–1993). The Uruguay round was the eighth round of multilateral trade negotiations (MTNs) conducted under the framework of the GATT, and included 123 countries as contracting parties. This round led to the creation of the WTO. The various rounds of GATT negotiations have made an important contribution to liberalizing trade in manufactured goods since 1947. By the 1980s, countries with advantages in service delivery, like the US, were trying to persuade the WTO, and its members, to include services in the GATT process (Roberts 2015). One important outcome of the GATT Uruguay round of negotiations was the establishment of the General Agreement in Trade in Services (GATS) which was implemented in January 1995. GATS cover all services with two exceptions: (1) services provided in the exercise of governmental authority and (2) the air transport sector including air traffic rights and all services directly related to the exercise of traffic rights.

The inclusion of services into the GATT, with the creation of GATS, highlighted the difficulties of including services in trade negotiations. For goods it is a comparatively simple task to track the movement of physical goods as they cross national boundaries. This is much harder for services and especially for services that are provided remotely using the Internet. New technologies have allowed the consumption of some services to be decoupled from the location of providers. This makes it difficult to tax these types of decoupled services. In addition, the intangibility of services makes it difficult to specify in a trade agreement what is provided and to what standards. For services, non-tariff barriers operate to reduce international trade and these include regulations regarding the right to practice and the requirement for local accreditations including professional qualifications.

The Organisation for Economic Cooperation and Development (OECD 2001, p. 23) provides an interesting example of non-tariff barriers and the ways in which they reduce or inhibit trade in architectural services in one unnamed country. In this country, a commercial presence is required in the country for the cross-border supply (Mode 1) of architectural services. In terms of Mode 3 the amount of foreign investment must be over a minimum threshold and there are restrictions on the value of some contracts and also on compulsory sub-contracting. The temporary relocation of executives, senior managers or specialists (Mode 3) is limited to three years. This can be extended but also limited to 90 days depending on their function. Other measures in place include annual licences that may be expensive to obtain with a time-consuming application process. All this illustrates some of the complexities of trying to liberalize the cross-border supply of services.

## 10.10   Wrapping Up

The service sector is a large and growing contributor to international trade and to internationalization. The cross-border provision of services varies by service sub-sector and product. The intangible nature of many services makes it difficult to include services in trade negotiations. A key problem is in agreeing what is being traded and in deciding on appropriate standards.

There are many similarities between trade in some services and trade in manufactured goods. These similarities include those services that can be exported or delivered via FDI. Nevertheless, there are important differences, and these are centred around the intangibility of service products. Some services must be co-created by an interaction between a co-located service provider and a consumer. These services can be traded across borders via FDI or the temporary relocation of either the service provider or consumer. The relationship between value and risk in the configuration of a firm's international business activities has become an important issue given the impacts of Covid-19 on the organization of global value chains.

A key issue to explore is the interaction between technological innovation and the development of new service products and processes. The Internet, combined with the cloud, has enabled new service processes, operations and business models to develop that use online platforms to deliver services. This is reconfiguring capitalism by developing new services, but also disrupting existing forms of provision (see Chap. 4). This is an ongoing process. The Internet has also facilitated the development of born-global firms. There is an acceleration in product and service innovation occurring as firms explore the application of existing technological innovations to conventional products.

**Learning Outcomes**

- There is an important distinction to be made between localized services and services which can be traded.
- There are four modes of service internationalization: cross-border supply, consumption

abroad, commercial presence, presence of natural persons.

- Different service sub-sectors internationalize using different combinations of modes.
- A key issue for service businesses is the decision to undertake a task in-house or to outsource it to another firm.
- Service firms have developed 'blended delivery systems' that capitalize on the place-based advantages of coupling or blending activities located in a variety of different locations: home—near—far.
- The development and application of platforms to economic activity has increased the speed of development of the global economy; platforms have led to an acceleration in globalization.
- There are many different approaches to developing an international business and this includes 'born-global firms'.
- The intangibility of services makes it difficult to specify in trade agreements what is provided and to what standards.

## References

Abecassis-Moedas, C., Mahmoud-Jouine, S. B., Dell'Era, C., Manceau, D., & Verganti, R. (2012). Key Resources and Internationalization Modes of Creative Knowledge-Intensive Business Services: The Case of Design Consultancies. *Creativity and Innovation Management, 21*(3), 315–331.

Ball, D. A., Lindsay, V. J., & Rose, E. L. (2008). Rethinking the Paradigm of Service Internationalization: Less Resource-Intensive Market Entry Modes for Information-Intensive Soft Services. *Management International Review, 48*(4), 413–431.

Bryson, J. R. (2007). The 'Second' Global Shift: The Offshoring or Global Sourcing of Corporate *Services and the Rise of Distanciated Emotional Labour. Geografiska Annaler, 89B*, 31–43.

Bryson, J. R. & Warf, B. (2004). *Service Worlds: People, Organisations, Technologies*. London: Routledge.

Bryson, J. R. & Vanchan, V. (2020). Covid-19 and Alternative Conceptualisations of Value and Risk in GPN Research. *Tijdschrift voor economische en sociale geografie*, in press. 111(3), 530–542.

Clairemonte, E., & Cavanagh, J. (1984). Transnational Corporations and Services: The Final Frontier. *Trade and Development, 5*(4), 215–273.

Coe, N. M., & Yeung, H. W.-C. (2015). *Global Production Networks: Theorizing Economic Development in an Interconnected World*. Oxford: Oxford University Press.

Contractor, F., & Kundu, S. (1998). Modal Choice in a World of Alliances: Analysing Organizational Forms in International Hotel Sector. *Journal of International Business Studies, 16*(3), 325–357.

Cunningham, S., & Craig, D. (2016). Online Entertainment: A New Wave of Media Globalization? *International Journal of Communication, 10*, 5409–5425.

Daniels, P. W. (1993). *Service Industries in the World Economy*. Oxford: Blackwell.

Dunning, J. (1988). The Theory of International Production. *The International Trade Journal, 3*(1), 21–66.

Dunning, J. (2000). The Eclectic Paradigm as an Envelope for Economic and Business Theories of MNE Activity. *International Business Review, 9*(1), 163–190.

Dunning, J. (2006). Comment on Dragon Multinationals: New Players in 21st Century Globalization. *Asia Pacific Journal of Management, 23*(2), 139–141.

Dunning, J., & Lundan, S. (2008). *Multinational Enterprises and the Global Economy*. Cheltenham: Edward Elgar.

Edvardsson, B., Edvinsson, L., & Nystrom, H. (1993). Internationalisation in Service Companies. *Service Industries Journal, 13*(1), 80–97.

Ekeledo, I., & Sivakumar, K. (1998). Foreign Market Entry Mode Choice of Service Firms: A Contingency Perspective. *Journal of the Academy of Marketing Science, 26*(4), 274–292.

Enderwick, P. (Ed.). (1989). *Multinational Service Firms*. London: Routledge.

Erramilli, M. K. (1990). Entry Mode Choice in Service Industries. *International Marketing Review, 7*(5), 50–62.

Feketekuty, G. (1988). *International Trade in Services: An Overview and Blueprint for Negotiations*. Cambridge, MA: Ballinger.

Fletcher, N. (2018, 29 June). Faang-tastic Five: Can US Tech Giants Continue Their Stellar Rise? *The Guardian*. Retrieved September 14, 2018, from https://www.theguardian.com/business/2018/jun/29/faanga-us-tech-giants-facebook-amazon-apple-netflix-google.

Gabrielsson, P., & Gabrielsson, M. (2013). A Dynamic Model of Growth Phases and Survival in International Business-to-Business New Ventures: The Moderating Effect of Decision-Making Logic. *Industrial Marketing Management, 42*(8), 1357–1373.

Gabrielsson, M., Kirpalani, V. H. M., Dimitratos, P., Solberg, A., & Zucchella, A. (2008). Born Globals: Propositions to Help Advance the Theory. *International Business Review, 17*(4), 385–401.

Gershuny, J. (1978). *After Industrial Society? The Emerging Self-Service Economy*. London: Macmillan.

Harveston, P. D., Kedia, B. L., & Davis, P. S. (2000). Internationalization of Born Global and Gradual Globalizing Firms: The Impact of the Manager. *Advances in Competitive Research, 8*(1), 92–99.

Hennart, J.-F. (2012). Emerging Market Multinationals and the Theory of the Multinational Enterprise. *Global Strategy Journal, 2*(3), 168–187.

Javalgi, R. G., & Martin, C. L. (2007). Internationalisation of Services: Identifying the Building-Block for Future Research. *Journal of Services Marketing, 21*(6), 391–397.

Javalgi, R. G., Lawson, D., Gross, A. C., & White, D. S. (1998). Firm Characteristics and Export Propensity: A Comparison of Manufacturing and Manufacturing-Based Service Providers. *International Business Review, 7*(5), 521–534.

Jensen, J. B. (2011). *Global Trade in Services: Fear, Facts and Offshoring.* Washington, DC: Peterson Institute for International Economics.

Johanson, J., & Vahlne, J. E. (1977). The Internationalization Process of the Firm – A Model of Knowledge Development and Increasing Foreign Market Commitment. *Journal of International Business Studies, 8*(1), 23–32.

Kandilov, I. T., & Grennes, T. (2012). The Determinants of Service Offshoring: Does Distance Matter? *Japan and the World Economy, 24*(1), 36–43.

Kenney, M., & Zysman, J. (2016). The Rise of the Platform Economy. *Issues in Science and Technology, 32*(3), 61–69.

Kenney, M., & Zysman, J. (2020). The Platform Economy: Restructuring the Space of Capitalist Accumulation. *Cambridge Journal of Regions, Economy and Society.* https://doi.org/10.1093/cjres/rsaa001.

Kikuchi, T., & Long, N. V. (2010). A Simple Model of Service Offshoring with Time Zone Differences. *North American Journal of Economic and Finance, 21*(3), 217–227.

Krommenacker, R. J. (1984). *World-Traded Services: The Challenge for the Eighties.* Norwood, MA: Artech House.

Lund, S., & Manyika, J. (2016). *How Digital Trade Is Transforming Globalisation.* International Centre for Trade and Sustainable Development (ICTSD) (Geneva, Switzerland). Retrieved May 19, 2019, from http://www20.iadb.org/intal/catalogo/PE/2016/16176.pdf.

Luo, Y., & Tung, R. (2007). International Expansion of Emerging Market Enterprises: A Springboard Perspective. *Journal of International Business Studies, 38*(4), 481–498.

Luostarinen, R., & Gabrielsson, M. (2006). Globalization and Marketing Strategies of Born Globals in SMOPECs. *Thunderbird International Business Review, 48*(6), 773–801.

OECD. (2001). *Trade in Services: Negotiating Issues and Approaches.* Paris: OECD Report.

Oviatt, B. M., & McDougall, P. P. (1994). Toward a Theory of International New Ventures. *Journal of International Business Studies, 25*(1), 45–64.

Pla-Barber, J., León-Darder, F., & Villaer, C. (2011). The Internationalisation of Soft-Services: Entry Modes and Main Determinants in the Spanish Hotel Industry. *Service Business, 5*(2), 139–154.

Rennie, M. W. (1993). Born Global. *The McKinsey Quarterly, 4*, 43–52.

Roberts, J. (1998). *Multinational Business Service Firms: The Development of Multinational Organisational Structures in the UK Business Services Sector.* Aldershot: Ashgate.

Roberts, J. (2015). Globalization of Services. In J. R. Bryson & P. W. Daniels (Eds.), *Handbook of Service Business: Management, Marketing, Innovation and Internationalisation.* Cheltenham: Edward Elgar.

Sampson, G. P., & Snape, R. H. (1985). Identifying the Issues in Trade in Services. *The World Economy, 8*(2), 171–181.

Simmon, E. (2018). *Evaluation of Cloud Computing Services Based on NIST SP 800–145* (National Institute of Standards and Technology (NIST) Special Publication 500–322). Washington: U.S. Department of Commerce.

UNCTAD. (1983). *Production and Trade in Services, Policies and their Underlying Factors Bearing upon International Service Transactions* (TD/B/941). New York: United Nations.

United Nations. (2002). *Manual on Statistics on International Trade in Services.* New York: United Nations.

Vanchan, V. R. Mulhall & J.R. Bryson (2018). Repatriation or Reshoring to the US and UK; Dynamics and Global Production Networks or from Here to There and Back Again. *Growth and Change* 49, pp. 97–121.

Vandermerwe, S., & Chadwick, M. (1989). The Internationalization of Services. *Service Industry Journal, 9*(1), 79–93.

Winsted, K. F., & Patterson, P. G. (1998). Internationalisation of Service: The Service Exporting Decision. *Journal of Services Marketing, 12*(4), 294–311.

Yeung, G. (2018). Global Production Networks and Regeneration Economies. In J. R. Bryson, L. Andres, & R. Mulhall (Eds.), *A Research Agenda for Regeneration Economies: Reading City-Regions.* Cheltenham: Edward Elgar.

Yeung, H.-W., & Coe, N. (2015). Toward a Dynamic Theory of Global Production Networks. *Economic Geography, 91*(1), 29–58.

## Further Reading

Baldwin, R. (2019). *The Globotics Upheaval: Globalisaition, Robotics, and the Future of Work*. London: Weidenfeld & Nicholson.

Bryson, J. R., & Daniels, P. W. (Eds.). (2015). *Handbook of Service Business: Management, Marketing, Innovation and Internationalisation*. Cheltenham: Edward Elgar.

Milberg, W., & Winkler, D. (2013). *Outsourcing Economics: Global Value Chains in Capitalist Development*. Cambridge: Cambridge University Press.

## Useful Websites

https://www.oecd.org/trade/topics/services-trade/.

https://www.wto.org/english/thewto_e/whatis_e/tif_e/agrm6_e.htm.

https://www.bea.gov/data/intl-trade-investment/international-trade-goods-and-services.

https://data.worldbank.org/indicator/BG.GSR.NFSV.GD.ZS.

# Supply Chains and Logistics Services

11

**Key Themes**

- What role do service businesses play in global supply chains?
- Supply chain management
- Logistics
- Radio frequency identification (RFID) and supply chain management
- IT and logistics
- Value chains
- Just-in-time and lean

No market economy can operate without a complex and extensive service economy that supports flows of people, money, raw materials, components, customers and completed products and service delivery systems. Thus, no business functions in a vacuum as it must be integrated into a set of inter-organizational relationships facilitating innovation, development, manufacturing and the co-creation of services. A key element within this network of inter-organizational relationships is logistics, or the industry that has been developed to transport and manage inputs that flow between places and across space. All firms need to bring together a set of inputs that vary by type of business and also must focus on organizing and distributing flows of inputs and outputs in a timely and cost-effective fashion. This includes

**Electronic Supplementary Material** The online version of this chapter (https://doi.org/10.1007/978-3-030-52060-1_11) contains supplementary material, which is available to authorized users.

just-in-time supply systems, but also operational models that involve delivering services remotely through platform-based systems. This includes on-line platforms, for example, Zoom and Skype, that played an important role during lockdown introduced in response to the Covid-19 pandemic. Raw materials and semi-manufactured articles must be brought to the next step in the manufacturing process and finished goods must be brought to retailers and then to final consumers. Information, including big data, knowledge and money must flow to support all types of transactions.

In 2005, Adam Minter, a journalist, visited Yantian, a district of Shenzhen, and the location of the Yantian International Container Terminals or YITC. This was China's second largest port and the fourth largest in the world. YITC exports most of the goods manufactured in the Pearl River Delta, otherwise known as the Workshop of the World. YITC is a deep-water port with 16 berths for ships and covers 373 ha. During Minter's visit, he was informed that $147 billion in goods had moved through this port over the last 12 months involving more than 13 million containers. Only 10% of these containers held imported goods and 90% carried exportable goods. This 90/10 split reflects the trade imbalance between China and the rest of the world. YITC, like all major ports, plays an important role in international logistics.

There is another side to YITC, and this involves the return of empty containers from their

J. R. Bryson et al., *Service Management*, https://doi.org/10.1007/978-3-030-52060-1_11

destinations back to China. Containers can be shipped empty, but this involves cost rather than profit. The alternative is for shipping companies to discount shipping rates for containers returning to China. Minter noted that 'In early summer 2012, for example, the price of shipping a 40,000-pound container from Los Angeles to Yantian was a paltry $600. Going from Yantian to Los Angeles, however, could cost four times as much' (2013, p. 86). High-volume relatively low value goods are transported in these containers from the US to China. In 2013, this good was scrap metal—copper, aluminium, lead, zinc and electronics for recycling.

YITC is one element in the network of international infrastructure that forms an essential part of the international supply chains that link Guangdong province with the rest of the world. This type of infrastructure highlights the complexity of the infrastructure networks that lie behind logistics and supply chains.

This chapter explores an important service function and related industry. In Chap. 12, the focus is on the servitization of manufacturing or the role that production- and product-related services play in manufacturing industries. It is important to appreciate that the on-going development of product-orientated global value chains (GVC), or global production networks (GPN) is facilitated and enabled by innovations in the provision of logistics services. Thus, logistics services are one of the catalysts behind internationalization. Reading service business involves understanding the ways in which logistics services and supply chain management support outsourcing, offshoring and inter- and intra-firm movements of all types. This includes the services that support flows of raw materials, components, completed goods, people, expertise and information and finance that are the focus of this chapter.

## 11.1  Development of Logistics Services

The development of the industrial revolution is associated with innovations in agriculture, manufacturing production systems, finance and logis-

tics. Logistics played a critical role in facilitating trade and travel. During the nineteenth century, the United Kingdom's 'market economy become more sophisticated and complex, and more and more resources had to be invested in those activities that reduced transaction costs in the economy' (Mokyr 2009, p. 250). This reduction in transaction costs was extremely complex and transformed national economies through infrastructure investment. In Mokyr's analysis of Britain and the industrial revolution he argued that:

> Of the many "revolutions" that were supposed to have taken place in Britain between 1700 and 1850, the transportation revolution occupies a pivotal role, in that it affected all other sectors in subtle but pervasive ways, and was itself subject to the institutional and technological advances that changed the British economy. (Mokyr 2009, p. 202)

Transport facilitates innovation across national economies but is also continually subjected to innovation. There are three key innovations that need to be highlighted.

First, there was an increase in the knowledge or the expertise intensity of firms. The origins of this shift towards knowledge-led production systems can be traced back to the early origins of capitalism. This led to a growth in professional service occupations involved in developing and providing knowledge inputs to firms. It led to a renaissance in universities with the establishment of new universities intended to provide skilled labour, but also research that would contribute to local and national economic growth. Between 1700 and 1850 the market for information of all kinds expanded dramatically. Part of this expansion included an increase in the number of specialists involved in information and knowledge distribution including teachers, lawyers and journalists and growth in economic activities that relied on accessing and translating information into knowledge, for example, merchants, speculators, financial analysts, insurance companies and merchant banks. Many of these specialists contributed to internationalization by providing the information, knowledge and expertise required to support the development of international value chains facilitated by developments in logistics and affiliated infrastructure (financial services including insurance). During the nineteenth century, there was significant investment in the discipline of geography and also in cartography. Maps were needed for military and commercial purposes including transportation; geographers played a key role in identifying commercial opportunities based around natural resources.

Second, communications played a central role in capitalism's on-going evolution. In England, major investments in the country's road network can be traced back to the period AD43–AD81 with the construction of roads, bridges, fords, a river transport network and regular posting stations by the Romans. The Romans brought with them 'the art of letter writing, an efficient postal system and the skills required for building paved roads' (Beale 2005, p. 14). Developments in infrastructure preceded the creation of a national and then international postal service. For England, plans for a national postal service were developed in 1620 and in 1635 a royal proclamation was issued to establish a national postal service centred on London. Initially all letters were sent to London and then sent on to the final address. Prior to 1635, letter carrying was restricted to the monarchy, the Church, the towns, carriers, merchants and the nobility and gentry. From 1635, innovations included the introduction of local sorting offices and roads linking all towns to the main transport routes. From 1635, developments in the English postal service 'assisted the development of trade and industry and brought great social benefits to the country' (Beale 2005, p. 271).

Third, moving ideas, people, materials, completed goods and delivering services required major innovations and investment in communications and transportation networks. These networks became the backbone of the shift towards an international economy. Britain during the eighteenth century had a well-developed transportation system that included coastal shipping and privately constructed roads and canals. To Mokyr:

There is little doubt that this transport system helped in technological progress, not just in making the mobility of people and ideas cheaper and faster, but because more integrated markets multiplied the gains from innovation and because protecting more technologically backward "niches" would become increasingly difficult. (Mokyr 2009, p. 154)

Infrastructure facilitated the integration of local markets into the national and increasingly international economy. Complex infrastructure networks emerged for the transmission of ideas, money, people and goods and included machines for processing information. The shift away from local economies to economies that are multi-scalar involving complex local, regional, national and international interrelationships is closely associated with developments in six inter related infrastructure networks: telegraph cables, broadcasting transmitters, telephone networks, satellites and global positioning systems, the Web and mobile telephony (Billing and Bryson 2019). The end result was that the globe became wrapped in millions of underground, over ground and beneath the sea, copper and fibre optic cables.

Transportation and communication infrastructure of all types contributes disproportionally to national economies and to internationalization. One reading of their impacts is the role they have played in time space compression or time space distantiation (Harvey 1990). This concept refers to technological and process innovations that alter the dimensions of time and space. Improvements in transportation systems reduce the time required to travel between places with the Internet enabling individuals to be simultaneously co-present in many locations. To Massey, technological innovation has resulted in an ongoing process involving 'speeding up' and 'spreading out' (1994). These processes facilitate internationalization, but they are also an outcome of internationalization with many complex feedback loops.

Logistics services rely on a complex array of interwoven transportation and communication networks. Each network reflects the activities of a set of companies, institutions and regulators involved in the delivery of transport-enabled services involving the movement of something from one location to another. These infrastructure networks involve ports, airports, river transport, maritime transport, air freight systems, roads and communication networks, including satellites that track flows of people, parts and goods and teleconferencing platforms. It also includes specialist logistics providers as well as warehouse operators. On-going developments in e-commerce continue to reshape the geography of retailing. Part of this reshaping shifts retailing from high streets to extremely large warehouses located in central locations and adjacent to key transportation routes. The application of just-in-time systems to manufacturing has altered supply chain logistics; a continual stream of lorries has replaced warehouses co-located with manufacturing plants.

This chapter focuses on exploring logistics services, the management and organization of supply chains and internationalization. These processes operate within GVC or GPN facilitating flows between places. Without these services it would be impossible for firms to develop and manage distributed or fragmented production systems. It is this infrastructure, and related services, that has made it possible for companies to develop GVCs/GPNs. Any disruptions to the infrastructure that supports logistics services, or to logistics processes, has major consequences.

**Case: KFC and Supply Chain Failure**

On 16 February 2018, Kentucky Fried Chicken or KFC, the American fast food restaurant chain that specializes in fried chicken, experienced a major logistics and supply chain failure resulting in the closure of over three quarters of its restaurants across the UK. The closure of these restaurants was the result of a single point-of-failure in the restaurant's supply chain combined with a failure in contingency planning. This became a major media crisis for the firm resulting in reputational damage, but the event also impacted on the company's profitability. This logistics and supply chain failure can be traced back to a decision made by KFC to replace its then current logistics partner.

On 14 February, DHL took over from the former logistics contract holder, Bidvest. One of the reasons behind this failure was the geography of warehouse provision. DHL operated from a single warehouse located in Rugby while Bidvest had supported the delivery of the KFC contract from six warehouses. At around 01.40 on 14 February 2018, a collision involving several vehicles occurred between junctions two and three of the M6 motorway. The motorway between these junctions was closed by the police. A second accident then occurred at junction 1 involving a collision between two lorries. These three motorway junctions were critical for DHL's Rugby warehouse. Its lorries were unable to move, and this initial problem led to the failure to deliver to KFC's UK restaurant network. It is common for logistics providers to operate from a single warehouse located in the 'golden triangle', the area between Milton Keynes, Rugby and Daventry. It is possible to deliver overnight from this area to most parts of the UK.

The supply problem began to impact on KFC operations on 16 February. The company began to close restaurants. By 18 February, 604 of the company's 870 restaurants were closed across the UK. KFC restaurants located in Ireland, north and south, were unaffected as they had a different logistics system in place. This high-profile supply chain failure was complex. DHL was using a new warehouse with a new IT system. The road problems, the single site, the new warehouse, automation and supply chain management software combined with demand contributed to this supply chain failure.

There is another side to this failure. KFC's UK supply chain includes over 500 farmers. This enables the firm to use fresh chicken. This supply chain failure led to a significant increase in waste with entire lorries of chicken having to be written off. Supply chain failure enhances waste and also undermines a company's reputation. There is a responsible business aspect to this. Replacing one logistics provider with another to reduce costs perhaps makes business sense. But was this a responsible business decision? The answer would perhaps have been 'yes', if no customer had noticed this alteration in KFC's logistics partner.

The KFC supply chain failure highlights the contribution that logistics and supply chain management make to business. It also emphasizes the importance of supply chain contingency planning. It is important to appreciate that competition between businesses is based on the effective functioning of all inter- and intra-company operations. A company like KFC competes on its brand, marketing, price, quality of food, a distinctive food offer, the nature of the service experience, staff recruitment and training, health and hygiene, but also on the effective co-ordination of logistics and the company's supply chain. The KFC incident highlights that a supply chain involves collaborations between many different companies, equipment, information management systems, processes, staff and a country's national infrastructure system and often international infrastructure—ports and airports. The co-ordination of company networks, and the interface with infrastructure networks, plays a central role in all economic transactions.

## 11.2 Supply Chain Management and Logistics: Definitions

Processes that involve the flow of goods and materials within production value chains are called supply chain (Hugos 2011). Wholesalers are, for example, part of a supply chain; a wholesaler represents one node within a supply chain for storing many components and goods produced by many firms. The organization and handling of a supply chain involves a process of supply chain management (Hugos 2011). This is a very complex service activity (Lusch 2011) undertaken by all types of companies—agricultural, mining and manufacturing—as well as specialist providers of logistics services.

As an example, consider the requirements of a small one-person business such as a roadside burger stall. To provide this service a suitably equipped, perhaps specially adapted, towable stall must be assembled. It may be possible to purchase one 'off the peg' but it is more likely that the necessary equipment will need to be procured from different suppliers before configura-

tion and assembly, either by the stall's owner or by a specialist fabricator. Then the raw materials required to produce goods must be acquired including meats, sauces, salad, peppers, vegan sausage rolls and so on as well as cooking oils. These inputs are purchased from various suppliers and require delivery either to the home of the stall owner or directly to the burger stall. Grease proof wrapping, plastic or paper plates, cups, knives and forks will be among the disposable and recyclable items that customers will expect to be available when purchasing from this stall. Potential customers will need to know about the existence of the burger stall; roadside signs will need to be commissioned and an Internet presence arranged. These are just some of the requirements that the owner of a burger stall must manage to create and deliver burgers into the hands of customers. This is a very simple example, but clearly what is required is the efficient coordination of each step or component in the burger stall's supply chain that ultimately ensures that the stall can provide goods to consumers. This is what logistics is all about. Now imagine, that the burger stall is a large factory owned by Boeing or Airbus that produces commercial airliners. There is a major escalation in the number of components in the supply chain. It is critical that every component is available in the factory when it is required. Any supply interruptions may prevent completion and delivery of an aircraft to a client resulting in major costs.

Logistics is the process of handling and managing supply chains, including designing supply chains, ensuring that the flow of parts within a supply chain is efficient, reducing costs, increasing the perceived customer quality of the supply chain handling process, procuring, storing and transporting goods and raw materials. Effective and efficient logistics enhances the efficiency of production processes. Transportation within logistics systems is a major consumer of fossil fuels and a major polluter. A key challenge is to remove fossil fuels from supply chains and to reduce carbon emissions.

Logistics refers to all processes involved in storing, moving and transporting a good or delivering a service to end-users or to the transfer of the upstream components of a supply chain to a service firm. According to the Council of Logistics Management (1998), logistics is defined as:

> the process of planning, implementing, and controlling the efficient, effective flow and storage of goods, services, and related information from point of origin to point of consumption for the purpose of conforming to customer requirements.

This definition includes inbound, outbound, internal and external movements, and the return of materials for environmental purposes. While all service businesses will need to engage with supply chain management and logistics management, some will themselves be suppliers of logistics services. Thus, a Vice President of United Parcels Service (UPS) customer relations described their role as one that concerns 'implementing efficiencies across a business's entire supply chain that help them achieve their strategic goals' (UPS 2016). Let us return to our simple example of the roadside burger stall.

A burger stall relies heavily on backward and forward linkages that combined form a supply chain. Backward linkages are defined as channels through which information, components, money and completed goods flow between a company and suppliers of intermediate inputs into the supply chain. This includes all the facilities and processes necessary for the procurement of raw materials (knowledge, information, office supplies) and the production of the service (equipment, office space, human resources). Forward linkages include investments in distribution networks that are intended to connect producers and/ or suppliers with consumers. This includes mechanisms for delivery (transport, broadband, warehousing and banking services) to customers or transactions with creditors.

Supply chains transport goods from the first raw material (e.g. metal or agricultural products) to places, factories, warehouses, offices, that transform materials into goods (factories) and then completed goods are transported to wholesalers, retailers and to final consumers. The consumer might be a final or end-consumer or might be an intermediate consumer with an input being incorporated into another production process.

The chain metaphor highlights that logistics operations move things between nodes or places, and these represent different links in a chain. Every link is important.

A supply chain is not a liner process. The chain metaphor is confusing as it simplifies a non-linear process into one that appears to be linear. Supply chains are non-linear; many inputs from many different locations come together at key production points in a supply chain. Companies must develop supply chain contingency plans. Such a plan would include the same part being supplied by different companies. It is important that a supply chain is not overtly dependent on one primary supplier; any disruption to that supplier's ability to provide intermediate inputs will result in an interruption of a company's production process. Covid-19 has highlighted the importance of risk management within supply chains. An analysis of SARS and its impacts on supply chains noted that 'supply-chain management and corporate strategy require a fundamental rethink to balance the pursuit of efficiency with increased responsiveness and flexibility' (Tan and Enderwick 2006, p. 515). This includes diversification in sourcing and corporate strategy, a shift from linear to contingent-based planning and scenario-informed planning.

Supply chains not only transport goods, but also ensure that the right goods reach their destinations at the right time. Depending on the size of the service business it may be necessary to use supply chain management to oversee the interface between internal and external operations of the various components of a supply chain. This is to ensure efficient performance combined with cost control. This is even more obvious when it comes to large service firms that are heavily dependent on supply chains such as supermarkets and airline companies. These firms are unable to transact business without large, complex but efficient supply chains, which are able to handle substantial amounts of goods delivered at an exact time and to a specific place. Such service companies may specialize in providing food or transportation services to customers, but they are also companies that must specialize in the management of complex supply chains and logistics.

Logistics is not only about handling goods in and out of lorries and containers. Handling and transportation must be planned and managed. IT systems are a core means to do that, particularly in large logistics systems. The logistics functions must be staffed, and the goods stored in the right places. All is assigned to an economic law of cost efficiency and price competition, but with Covid-19 the emphasis must be on cost control combined with risk management. Significant amounts of money can be wasted or made just by making minor adjustments to a large logistics system.

## 11.3   Radio Frequency Identification, Logistics and the Management of Supply Chains

Manufacturers and retailers have introduced radio frequency identification (RFID) to track components and goods as they move through a supply chain. A RFID tag uses electromagnetic fields to automatically track and identify objects. The tags contain stored information. There are two types. A passive tag collects energy from an adjacent RFID reader's radio waves, while an active tag contains a local power source. Passive tags must be located close to a RFID reader and active tags may be located much further away. Unlike barcodes, a RFID tag does not need to be within the line of sight of the reader. RFID tags are used in supply chains across different industries. That are used to track, for example, components that are part of automotive production lines and are also used to track pets and livestock. The application of RFIDs to a supply chain enables further streamlining of the supply chain and inventory optimization. Each item in a supply chain can be identified and tracked increasing enhanced inventory control and visibility. This enables the identification of items that are in the wrong location or have been stolen.

Logistics subsectors include transport at land, sea and in the air, and these transport forms may be interchangeable. It may be a matter of practical conditions, customer requirements for delivery times and conditions and price whether a good is sent by lorry, ship or aeroplane—or maybe even by bicycle or drone. Transportation providers, postal services and wholesalers are all part of the logistics industry and part of supply chains, but retailers and also cafes, restaurants and hotels are also part of supply chains. Information technology (IT) logistics planning systems are an important element in the management of logistics businesses. Some service firms specialize in the planning and management of logistics services rather than the direct provision of transportation services.

Logistics have risen in strategic importance (Potter and Mason 2015); from handling simple manual work tasks to the management of advanced IT and tracking systems. Supply chain management has become increasingly important for companies' profits, production line planning and customer relationships; often it is logistics service firms' employees that engage directly with customers representing the company. Logistics services have become a core part of the networked economy; often they are 'the spider in the center of the network', and therefore, play a central and often dominant role.

Amazon, which is the world's most valuable company, is an example of a logistics company that started as a modest supplier of books, but which has developed into a business that dominates a large part of all commerce on the Internet. Amazon is a set of warehouses linked to a supply and logistics management system that is intended to enhance the movement of goods and services from suppliers to consumers. At the centre of this business model are logistics and the organization of efficient and automated warehouses or Amazon's fulfilment centres. Amazon has built a very distinctive distribution network. Central to this is Amazon's logistics division based in Seattle and the company's supply-chain algorithm team. This team is:

> Amazon's secret weapon, devising mathematical answers to questions such as where and when to stock particular products within Amazon's distribution network and how to most efficiently combine various items in a customer's order in a single box. (Stone 2013, p. 164)

Amazon renamed its warehouses as fulfilment centres (FC) as their primary task was to fulfil customer orders. The challenge is that the exact combination of goods purchased by a customer might never be repeated. Algorithms have been developed that seamlessly match demand to the most appropriate fulfilment centre through a process that levels out backlogs to remove supply chain blockages.

Over time, Amazon's fulfilment process has been transformed from:

> a network of haphazardly constructed facilities into something that could more accurately be considered a system of polynomial equations. A customer might place an order for a half a dozen products, and the company's software would quickly examine factors like the address of the customer, the location of the merchandise in the FCs, and the cutoff times for shipping at the various facilities around the country. Then it would take all those variables and calculate both the fastest and the least expensive way to ship the items. (Stone 2013, pp. 184–185)

Amazon's logistics management systems are a core element of this on-line platform's competitiveness. A key issue is a focus on 'speeding up' and 'spreading out' Amazon's supply chain. The company refined its supply chain to reduce the cutoff time for next-day deliveries to within 45 min before the last truck leaves a FC. It also has continued to extend the company's reach, or to colonize, adjacent retail sectors. Amazon is an extremely complex company. It has developed its own branded goods including fashion brands and continues to disrupt existing retail-orientated supply chains.

Pack or package delivery to households has always been a problem. It is expensive to manage and transport packages to many households. This type of supply chain involving the last mile or kilometre to the customer is time consuming involving capital equipment and employees. The task has traditionally been undertaken by state-owned postal services; many have been privatized and converted into providers of logistics services. Package deliveries have increased substantially with the substitution of high street retailing with e-commerce. Amazon's business model is based on the efficient and low-cost

delivery of packages to households. The growth in e-commerce has been the basis for new logistics service providers including in Germany, DHL, and in America, UPS. Their business models are based on the operation and management of fast and safe package delivery systems. They use IT systems, bar codes and global positioning satellites (GPS) to identify and track package and to plan delivery routes. Additional services have been developed enabling consumers to track packages within the supply chain. These logistics firms have grown rapidly to become large translocal or transnational corporations.

## 11.4  Functions and Logistics Services

### 11.4.1  Supply Chain Management

Supply chain management incorporates several functions including managing supply and demand, logistics, purchasing, the service design interface, selling/sales system interface and defining business boundaries and relationships (Simchi-Levi et al. 2008; Hugos 2011).The latter is at the core of the design of all supply chain management initiatives; which aspect(s) of a service should be produced in-house, and which should rely on third party suppliers. This is sometimes referred to as outsourcing (cf. Chap. 8) and such decisions are made in the context of the importance of retaining proprietary knowledge relating to a service, information about the reliability and quality of third-party suppliers and the costs associated with using third-party suppliers relative to in-house provision. Logistics includes storing raw materials and goods between the time of production and transportation to retailers or customers.

A supply chain is often known as a *value chain* (Porter 1998; Sundbo 2011). The term *value chain* is predominantly used within service research as the term links customers with value creation—the service aspects of a value chain—that is emphasized in service theory (Lusch 2011, see also Chap. 2). The term supply chain is more associated with the management of logistics related to the movement of goods between producers and consumers (Tortorella et al. 2017). In this chapter, the two terms are used synonymously.

Demand management, for example, is about ensuring that all stages in a supply chain to an end user of a service acquire the required inputs in the correct quantities, in the correct sequence and at the right time conforming to end-user expectations. Purchasing management is concerned with the supply side around activities such as stationery, IT services, printing, and advertising. The selling role within a supply chain ensures that service end-users are aware of availability, how it can meet the needs of clients, how to select it, how to buy and pay for it, and what is available by way of after-sale support and upgrades, where appropriate.

### 11.4.2   Food: A Critical Supply Chain

Everyday living involves purchasing and consuming food and drink. These decisions link every consumer to a complex and evolving network of supply chains. Provision of food is an example of a supply chain that may seem simple from a traditional point of view, but which has developed into a set of extremely complex processes linking consumers with farmers. A traditional food supply chain can be exemplified by the production of pork. This involves several distinct stages based around rearing animals and their incorporation into a production process that has within it a supply chain. During the late nineteenth century, Chicago's meat-packing operations were one of the initial inspirations for the application of mass-production processes to the automotive industry, by Henry Ford. These disassembly lines led to the development of assembly lines that relied on the management of complex

supply chains. Our meat example involves the following stages (Fig. 11.1).

This very simple linear supply chain has become increasingly complex. This complexity has been driven by enhanced global competition combined with the application of new technology. Meat supply chains have become less of a local industry and now involve the management of international supply chains. This complexity is illustrated in Fig. 11.2.

Farmers are no longer responsible for the complete process of rearing pigs. Part of this process has been transferred to other countries with lower rents and labour costs. Part of the slaughtering process has moved to other countries for the same reasons. Pork meat is not delivered directly from slaughterhouses to retail shops but is processed in factories and delivered to a supermarket chain's central warehouse from which it is distributed to individual supermarkets. Factory processing has been introduced into this supply chain as consumers no longer want to handle large pieces of meat but want to purchase pre-sliced chops or complete dishes. Supermarket chains have central purchasing and storage systems that are used to manage the distribution of food to supermarkets. More firms are involved in this logistics process and this requires strict guidelines and monitoring of food handling, for example, hygiene, cooling and the management of a food product's total time within a supply chain process. This has created a market for the formation of specialist logistics service firms that provide a total supply process or third-party logistics (see next section). Alternatively, fourth party logistics service firms have been established which specialize in selling knowledge about the management of logistics processes. Such an approach to total logistics requires the application of sophisticated information technology including algorithms and RFID sensors

**Fig. 11.1**   Typical stages in a food supply chain. (Source: Authors' own)

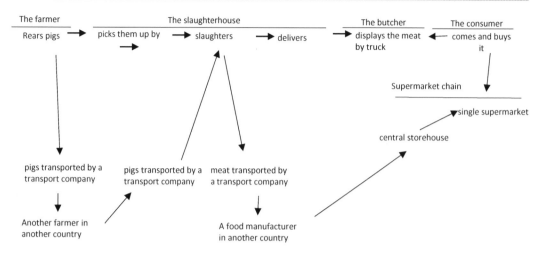

**Fig. 11.2** Complex supply chains: food as an example. (Source: Authors' own)

that can be tracked via GPS. Satellites and GPS have begun to play an extremely important role in the management of international supply chains (Billing and Bryson 2019). The core competency of logistics management service firms is thus centred on IT rather than transportation.

A total supply chain solution must be developed for the management of a supply chain. Food products must always be stored appropriately, for example. Meat or complete dishes must meet the supermarket's specification and they must be delivered on time. Furthermore, health and environmental considerations require that the primary producer of the meat, the farmer and the slaughterhouse must be identified and, in many cases, even by the final consumer. All this must be achieved by supply chain logistics systems that are able to compete on price by providing inexpensive but high-quality goods. All this requires logistics services involving one or more service firms, or internal logistics management by a manufacturing firm or retailer. Logistics is a core element of production processes and may be a primary source of good/product differentiation. This is to argue that a company's goods/products, production processes and logistics operations all contribute to enhancing competitiveness through differentiation (see the analysis of Zara in Chap. 14 section 14.4).

## 11.5  Types of Logistics

### 11.5.1 Inbound Logistics

Inbound logistics, or backward linkages in a supply chain, involves procuring inputs that are incorporated into production and service processes. These are intermediate inputs into production systems. A service business creates value through, for example, converting expertise, or knowledge, into 'products/goods' and this requires that inputs are delivered on time. The procurement of any inputs on time, at the point of use, and at minimum cost is the primary aim of inbound logistics. This includes transportation during procurement activities and, if appropriate, the storage, handling and overall management of an inventory of inputs. For many service businesses, these requirements will be less complex than is the case for manufacturing businesses but sourcing, order placement, transportation, receiving and storage must still be undertaken with a view to keeping down system costs.

### 11.5.2 Outbound Logistics

Outbound logistics, or forward linkages in a supply chain, are tasks involving the delivery of goods and services to customers. This usually includes items that possess more value, following the conversion of inputs, in line with the actual or anticipated needs of customers or clients. For some services this involves the assembly of inputs to produce service experiences. Shipment sizes, modes of transport to be used, or delivery time expectations will differ from those related to inbound logistics. Inbound logistics frequently involves the movement of larger quantities of inputs or of a continual stream of inputs in supply chains that have been developed around a just-in-time approach. Outbound logistics involves the delivery of low volumes to a single customer. This involves low quantities, but at frequent intervals. Outbound logistics must be managed to optimize systems, keep costs under close control but with the added requirement of ensuring maximum customer satisfaction. This is where companies like Amazon and Zara, the fast fashion clothing retailer, compete by integrating smart supply chain management logistic systems into their business models (see Chap. 14).

The maritime industry is an example of the application of IT to increase efficiency of outbound logistics. Prior to the development of container-based transportation systems, goods were transported by lorries to harbours and ships were then loaded by dock workers. When a ship arrived at ports, goods were then unloaded using labour intensive processes. Goods were manually loaded on to lorries and transported to customers. This labour-intensive supply process could take weeks and the labour was heavily unionized. The introduction of containers transformed logistics (see Chap. 3). Containerization is a system of intermodal freight transport using intermodal containers, or shipping containers, fabricated to standardized dimensions. Containers are handled using a completely mechanized system using cranes and special forklift trucks. In a container logistics system, goods are loaded into containers by the sender. The containers are transported by lorries to a port where an automatic system loads them on to a container ship. Loading is a rapid system based on algorithms intended to enhance the efficiency of the loading and unloading process. The turnaround time between arrival and departure decreased and this increased the effective use of merchant vessels. Containers are placed within the ship in the order in which they will be unloaded. Containerization led to major redundancies in the logistics system. Transportation became less labour intensive and much more capital intensive.

Containerization has made a major contribution to internationalization. It is much faster to move raw materials and completed goods along supply chains. This has contributed to the ongoing fragmentation of supply chains. Containers are continuously tracked and monitored. Technological innovation has transformed logistics through the application of innovations that commenced with the introduction of the container and continued with innovations enabled by GPS and with experiments in autonomous ships. Containerization has been the basis for the creation of large international shipping companies including the Danish company Mærsk and the Swiss-based Mediterranean Shipping Company. These large logistics providers have developed into total logistics service companies providing complete solutions to the management of supply chains. They invest in lorries, containers, harbours, warehouses and complex IT systems. IT systems include platforms to track containers and inventory and algorithms intended to increase the efficiency of company operations including maximizing asset utilization.

### 11.5.3 Reverse Logistics

Reverse logistics involves the return of goods to a producer including goods for reuse or recycling and for repair or repurposing. Any logistics process that occurs after a good or service has been delivered to a customer involves reverse logistics. The increase in e-commerce is associated with customers increasingly returning goods. They have the legal rights to do so and logistics services must deal with this situation effectively.

Reverse logistics is also required in circumstances where providers, seeking to maintain or expand market share, make claims about a service or a good over a period that are not fulfilled. Such warranties have a basis in law and require suppliers to facilitate systems for customers to return items for replacement, repair, or possibly a refund at companies' expense. Again, the logistics for managing these arrangements are designed not only to be efficient but also as cost effective as possible. The rapid rise of Internet retailing has reinforced the importance of reverse logistics since deliveries can be mislaid en route, goods damaged in transit, delivered to the wrong address or incorrectly assigned to customers. Likewise, a defective service or good invariably triggers a recall, especially if there are safety risks, quality standards or expiry dates involved, by suppliers who are anxious to protect their market image or brand loyalty for a service or good.

### 11.5.4   Third-Party Logistics (3PL)

Businesses that offer one or an array of logistics-related services to other firms are often described as third-party logistics (3PL) providers (Skjøtt-Larsen 2000). They enable businesses to outsource some or all their logistics needs. These are specialist providers of outsourced logistics services. Here it is worth noting that logistics is capital intensive and is a specialist activity. For smaller firms, outsourcing to a specialist logistics provider enables them to benefit from economies of scale and scope including, for example, part loads that are shared with other companies. Some examples include: distribution management and public/contract warehousing (e.g. provided by companies such as Exel, Caterpillar Logistics), freight (or transportation) management (Fedex Supply Chain, UPS, DHL Supply Chain and Global Forwarding, Ryder Supply Chain Solutions), financial-based 3PL (GE Information Services) and information-based 3PL. The latter is a recent addition that supports Internet-based, business-to-business and electronic markets/transactions (FreightQuote, uShip). 3PL incorporates a wide range of logistics services whose utility for service businesses varies depending on, for example, whether they are in retailing or in, say, investment management.

Hertz and Alfredsson (2003) (see also Langley et al. 2008) group 3PL providers into four categories:

- *Standard 3PL providers*: The most basic form performing activities such as pick and pack, warehousing and distribution (business). This is often not the primary activity of these firms.
- *Service developers*: Offer clients advanced value-added services such as tracking and tracing, cross-docking, specialist packaging or a bespoke security system. These providers are IT oriented and are most suited to clients exploring approaches to better incorporate IT into their logistics processes.
- *Customer adapters*: The provider is invited to take complete control of clients' logistics activities (Grawe et al. 2012). The objective is to improve efficiency and cost-effectiveness of existing services rather than the provision of new services.
- *Customer developers*: The provider not only controls the existing logistics operations of clients but will also embed itself to identify and implement new customers and ways of developing and introducing supporting logistics (Soinio et al. 2012). In this case, the customer developer plays an increasingly strategic role in customers' activities and in identifying new ways of applying logistics solutions to capture additional value for customers.

### 11.5.5   Fourth-Party Logistics (4PL)

Developments in 3PL have led to the emergence of 4PL logistics solutions involving the integration of resources to build and run total supply chain solutions sold as a total service to clients outsourcing their logistics and supply chain management requirements (Yao 2011). 4PL is a new concept in supply chain outsourcing. It reflects on-going rapid advances in technology over the last 20 years and is therefore a further refinement of the 3PL approach.

The application of 3PL by businesses to enhance the application of logistics and supply chain management has focused on managing larger inventories, increased the speed of transportation solutions or the provision of on-site service engineers but as part of a business environment that incorporates new activities such as e-procurement, complete supply visibility, virtual inventory management and the adoption of appropriate integrating technology. 4PL providers, therefore, integrate supply chains comprising the assembly and management of their own resources, capabilities and technologies with those of their clients delivering comprehensive supply chain solutions. This may include leveraging the competencies of other 3PL providers and business process managers to deliver a supply chain in which the 4PL providers are the centralized hub. 4PL providers will have many clients ensuring that their capital investment benefits from economies of scale. Clients benefit from accessing specialist expertise, but also the extended geographic reach that can be developed by specialist 4PL providers. Here it is important to remember that logistics and supply chain management is at the heart of all GVC or GPN. Thus, the governance of the relationships between logistics and supply chain management service providers and their clients plays a critical role in client competitiveness. This is the case for every firm; all firms must manage inter- and intra-company flows combined with flows of goods to end consumers.

## 11.6 Outsourcing to 4PL Service Companies

The advantages of outsourcing logistics to a specialized 4PL service company is seen in the case of Corus (now part of Tata Steel) in the UK. Their logistics operations were organized locally with no coordination resulting in inefficiencies and problems with supply chain coordination. Corus outsourced all inbound and outbound logistics to the Transport Development Group (TDG), a 4PL provider. This increased the delivery-on-time and reduced transport costs (Potter and Mason 2015).

### 11.6.1 Outsourcing Logistics

Businesses can develop an internal solution to logistics supply and delivery, or they can outsource this function to specialized logistics service providers (see Chap. 8 on outsourcing).

Whether a business operates from a single location or from multiple locations it will need to consider logistics requirements at some stage in its development. Most of the issues to be considered will arise from whether to outsource logistics to 3PL or 4PL providers and these may only arise when, service businesses become much larger. Size means that it may no longer be cost-efficient to use management time within the business on procurement, inventory control, shipping and storage on an ad hoc basis. A business must either develop an in-house logistics division or outsource to a specialist provider.

Some of the advantages of applying a 4PL solution include:

1. Access to state-of-the-art technology and software.
2. Application of technology to the best possible effect.
3. Facilities and space appropriate to the tasks that are outsourced.
4. Access to resources and levels of flexibility to fulfil client requirements at different times and at different locations.
5. Capability to manage the expectations of several clients simultaneously.

### 11.6.2 Investment

Supply chain management involves decisions regarding capital investment in logistics operations, compared to investments in a company's core operational activities. This type of investment decision includes the opportunity costs between investing in production operations compared to investing in logistics. Outsourcing is one solution, but the decision must reflect the needs of each business. But there are also disadvantages in outsourcing logistics and supply chain management. These include:

1. Loss of control over logistics operations, especially in relation to quality control or the nuances of trading with customers of the service business that have well-understood, but variable, expectations.

2. Failure by 3PL providers to meet expectations perhaps resulting in reputational damage for service and manufacturing businesses.
3. Operational problems arising from poor communications between the parties.
4. 3PL failure.
5. Conflicts between the strategic objectives of the service or manufacturing business and those of the 3PL provider.
6. Use of a 3PL provider with limited or no knowledge of the services or goods provided by the client.
7. Reduced ability to gather and analyse data about customers that will help with targeted marketing, continuous improvement programmes, or cost optimization.

The downsides from commissioning 4PL providers are much the same as those for 3PL providers although the financial consequences for the affected service or manufacturing businesses may be much more damaging. This is because the advantages of using 4PL providers are potentially more comprehensive impacting on all operational functions including: enhanced product/good quality, product/good availability and improved customer service—all facilitated by the application of leading technology that generates revenue growth; operational efficiencies, process enhancements and procurements, complete outsourcing of supply chain functions rather than just selected components that will create overall cost reductions for service or manufacturing businesses; reductions in fixed capital investment following on from capital asset transfer and enhanced asset utilization.

The outsourcing decision must include a company's internal logistics. For a retail company this includes internal accounting of goods, stock and management of when individual shops, for example, supermarkets, should receive deliveries. For large retail chains this is based on information flowing between each retail outlet and the logistics and supply chain management function. Often this includes information from RFID tags and bar codes. Deciding to outsource logistics and supply chain management partly depends on a company's previous history of managing these

activities. A company may not be able to afford to invest in the provision of internal logistics infrastructure. A question to consider is whether an external logistics services company can handle that part of a supply chain which requires knowledge about the client company's internal procedures and routines. Will a retail company outsource internal logistics or does this expose the retailer to risks associated with failure of the logistics provider to meet the company's needs? An internal logistics facility might be able to provide a more customized service with fewer faults. Outsourcing that involves the closure of an internal logistics division, or its transfer to a third-party provider, might mean that the company no longer has the capabilities or capacity to understand its own internal logistics requirement.

Effective decision-making about supply chain logistics requires close attention to value chain analysis including considering where value creation occurs, profitability linked to logistics and supply chain management and the creation and co-creation of customer value.

## 11.7 Value Chain Analyses

A value chain is a chain of value-added activities; products/goods pass through the activities in a chain, gaining value at each stage (Sundbo 2011). Value chain analysis provides strategic focus in understanding a company's operations and strategy. Adding value to products/goods as they pass through a chain of activities has been emphasized by Michael Porter (1998). Value chain analysis was introduced to analyse market situations and to create marketing strategies, but it also involves exploring the organization and management of a company's supply chains (Huemer 2012). A supply chain can be conceptualized as a value chain where each step adds value to a good or task or destroys value. Both specialized logistics service firms and other businesses benefit from value chain analysis as this will identify potential and actual problems that enhance costs and reduce value. Value chain analysis contributes to assessing costs that might be reduced or impacted by a change in one of the chain's processes.

Comparative value chain analysis enables a company to identify and explore competitor value chains identifying tasks, processes, operations and linkages within its own value chain that require improvement.

A value chain analysis involves exploring a supply chain's operational activities. These include:

- Incoming supplies, materials, incoming shipping
- Storing and handling
- Outgoing shipping and logistics
- Customer service—includes tracking, coordinating, scheduling and reverse logistics
- Marketing, sales and customer satisfaction

The analysis should also include exploring related business activities including:

- Accounting and finance
- IT and systems support
- Legal issues including documentation related to exports and imports
- Environmental and climate issues and safety
- Personnel
- Innovation
- Corporate social responsibility

## 11.8  Supply Chain Challenges Facing Logistics Businesses

Businesses encounter several challenges that must be taken into consideration when analysing and planning a supply or value chain. These include:

### 11.8.1  Continued Growth of e-Commerce

E-commerce continues to grow, and new e-commerce business models emerge based on new approaches to logistics. On-line platforms, combined with the networking effect, open up possibilities for the creation of many new business models resulting in increased competition

associated with disruptive innovation (see Chap. 3). Innovations in e-commerce have transformed high street retailing. This includes click and collect solutions linking e-commerce provision with high street stores.

Amazon has introduced Amazon Hubs as a brand to cover investments in Lockers and relationships with retail locations. Lockers are self-service kiosks where customers can collect and return Amazon parcels at any time. Counters are agreements that Amazon has negotiated with convenience or high street stores where customers can collect Amazon parcels. Once a parcel has been delivered to a Locker or Counter then the Amazon e-commerce platform e-mails a collection barcode to customers.

E-commerce includes an increase in reverse logistics. Customers order goods that they do not want to keep resulting in increased returns. Some e-commerce retailers are identifying customers with exceptionally high return rates and developing strategies to reduce these.

### 11.8.2  Technology Matters

Information technology (IT), including sensors, operational systems and GPS tracking, are playing an increasing role in logistics management and have become core elements in transportation, sorting, storing and tracking technologies. Logistics service companies are capital intensive but are increasingly becoming much more technologically intensive. This includes the collection, management and application of Big Data and the development of new algorithms to manage supply chain logistics.

### 11.8.3  Understanding the Capabilities of Suppliers and Service Partners

Business partners' capabilities are important because logistics service companies are dependent on inter-firm relationships. Of course, their customers—manufacturing or service companies requiring logistic services—are important, but logistics service companies also have suppliers, for example, providers of IT systems and transportation equipment. Actual, or potential, suppliers may introduce innovations that could be important for logistics service companies. Logistics service companies may outsource some functions and often other companies are responsible for the management of part of their supply chain. Managing inter-firm relationships is critical to reduce problems that might undermine the quality of services provided.

### 11.8.4 'Customers as King/Queen'

Service marketing, and management research, has highlighted that customer satisfaction is critical for service businesses and for the quality of the service experience (Chap. 8). Logistics and supply chain management must not impact on the quality of the customer's service experience.

## 11.9  Just-in-Time and Lean Production

Supply chains and logistics are central to the efficient management and delivery of service experiences and of goods. The rationalization principles that were developed in Japan in the 1980s and 1990s have been adopted by manufacturing industries globally. These principles also play an important role in logistics services. Logistics are at the centre of the rationalization approach to enhancing the efficiency of production systems.

Just-in-time approaches to the management of supply chains transformed manufacturing-based value chains. This system is based on the principle that goods or components should not be produced and shipped before demand and need is manifested. A car consists of a complex set of interchangeable modules with customers selecting from a range of options. Customers can order many variations of a car, but car manufacturers do not have to store all components required for all product/good variations. Customized cars are built to order, and this requires the design and

management of just-in-time production processes.

The just-in-time principle challenges supply chain and logistics service providers. They must ensure that a component is available for integration into a good as it is required. Storing goods and components just-in-case they are required ties up capital in components and in storage facilities. A just-in-time approach transfers these costs to suppliers and to their logistics providers.

Just-in-time raises several important questions for logistics and supply chain management including:

1. How much capability and capacity should a logistics service firm have, at what time and at what locations?
2. What happens if the logistics service firm cannot fulfil the demands of the customer (the goods sender)?
3. Who is responsible for the supply—the sender, the receiver or the logistics service company?

Logistics service companies have to innovate to meet just-in-time demands, for example, by identifying new transport modes, introducing new IT systems that can track and manage the delivery process or new forms of employment that can ensure 24-hour delivery. These new forms of employment also include gig-style employment in which 'employees' are self-employed with limited employment rights (see Chap. 6).

Rationalization included the adoption of lean-based production systems and these have been applied to logistics and supply chain services (Arlbjørn et al. 2011; Tortorella et al. 2017). Lean requires a company to explore all procedures identifying redundancies including wasted time, material resources and storing capacity. The focus is on identifying waste and reducing costs. Nevertheless, these rationalization efforts must also focus on customer satisfaction. Lean involves the design of production and delivery procedures focusing on balancing investment with waste reduction. This is a strategy based on optimization combined with customer needs involving prices and delivery options. A logistics and supply chain should adopt lean principles combined with contingency planning.

Supply chains may be differentiated or variegated; some customers require standardized and rationalized services whilst others expect customization including flexibility in the logistics system (Arlbjørn et al. 2011). The latter implies that logistics services, to a lesser degree, are no longer ad hoc services that are sold on a day-to-day basis, but instead logistics providers develop longer term relationships with their customers enabling them to invest in the creation of flexible supply chain systems (Tortorella et al. 2017).

Lean supply chains are difficult to establish (Tortorella et al. 2017). Logistics services companies have many different customers with different demands and satisfaction levels. Supply and logistics include many different processes and related tasks that may be difficult to identify, analyse and change. Often a logistics service provider only takes responsible for one part of a supply chain process. The challenge is that the creation of a total lean supply chain is dependent on a company working with many different organizations.

**Case: Lenovo—Supply Chain Complexity, Management and Risk Reduction through AI**
Global value chains are becoming increasingly complex as companies continue to apply and develop complex spatial divisions of labour resulting in the continual fragmentation of supply chains. Longer supply chains tend to be much more complex and are more difficult to manage. To enhance decision-making companies are incorporating artificial intelligence (AI) into the management of their supply chains.

IBM has developed a Supply Chains Insights program that is based on the application of AI to identify operational cost reductions that will enhance incremental revenue accumulation. Lenovo, the PC manufacturer, joined IBMs Watson™ Supply Chain Fast Start program to complete an analysis of its supply chain using IBM Supply Chain Insights. This took five weeks.

The outcome was an analysis that enabled Lenovo to optimize decision-making including the identification of cost savings and up to a 95% increase in Lenovo's reactions to supply chain disruptions with associated reductions in risk.

The context for Lenovo was the on-going commoditization of the PC market leading to a reduction in profit margins. To enhance Lenovo's ability to compete it is essential that it orchestrates its global supply chain effectively with a focus on cost-effectiveness. Lenovo's supply chain contained many nodes, and each was generating significant quantities of data every day. This data stream contained important information that Lenovo could use to enhance supply chain management. Nevertheless, the problem was the volume and velocity of this data stream. IBM's application of AI to the analysis of this data stream enabled Lenovo rapidly to identify disruptions in any link in the supply chain and to calculate the financial implications. It also ensured that Lenovo could engage in strategies that would mitigate the impacts of any disruptions. Part of this approach enabled Lenovo to introduce new approaches to production including 'available to promise' (ATP). The company is now able to precisely estimate deliveries to clients in real time. This adds an additional dimension to Lenovo's ability to compete in a highly competitive market.

## 11.10 Wrapping Up

This chapter has highlighted that logistics services, supply chain analysis and management play a critical role in the international economy and in global value chains. Logistics, and the management of supply chains, are important capital-intensive services and they are services that have become saturated with big data and data analytics. Supply chain failure results in significant disruption and such disruption usually is caused by the complex interplay between companies and infrastructure systems that underpin logistics systems. Supply chains and logistics play a key role in underpinning or facilitating internationalization, including the internationalization of service businesses (see Chap. 10) and also manufacturing companies. The latter includes flows of data, money, people and expertise and it is to this topic that we now turn our attention.

The on-going fragmentation of global value chains has been supported by innovations in transportation infrastructure, including ports, airports and containerization and logistics. Developments in approaches to logistics play an important role in the emergence of new business models (see Chap. 14) and in facilitating flows of raw materials, people, expertise and goods between places. Logistics is supported by global financial services including the insurance industry, but also leasing companies that finance the purchase of aircraft and merchant vessels. There are many different types of supply chain and each type requires a different type of logistics solutions including supply chains that transport customized products compared to those involved in transporting standardized goods. Logistics has always been a capital-intensive industry, but there has been an increase in the expert intensity of this sector. Big data from embedded sensors combined with AI is playing an increasingly important role in the management of logistics service functions.

**Learning Outcomes**

- Logistics and supply chain services have become critical for the competitiveness of client companies and for the management and organization of global value chains.
- Any disruptions to the infrastructure that supports logistics services, or to logistics processes, has major consequences.
- Supply and value chains have become much more complex.
- Supply and value chains have become more digitalized.
- The application of radio frequency identification (RFIDs) to supply chains enables further streamlining and inventory optimization.
- Logistics and supply chain services are increasingly outsourced to specialized service providers—both 3PL and 4PL.

- Logistics services play a key role in catalysing internationalization including the on-going fragmentation of GVC/GPN.
- To enhance decision-making companies are incorporating AI into the management of their supply chains.
- Logistics are at the centre of the rationalization approach, that emerged in Japan in the 1980s, to enhance the efficiency of production systems.

**References**

Arlbjørn, J. S., Freytag, P., & de Haas, H. (2011). Service Supply Chain Management. *International Journal of Physical Distribution and Logistics Management, 44*(3), 277–295.
Beale, P. (2005). *England's Mail: Two Millennia of Letter Writing*. Tempus: Stroud.
Billing, C. A., & Bryson, J. R. (2019). Heritage and Satellite Manufacturing: Firm-Level Competitiveness and the Management of Risk in Global Production Networks. *Economic Geography, 95*(5), 423–44.1.
Council of Logistics Management. (1998). Retrieved August 11, 2019, from http://www.clm1.org/mission.html.
Grawe, S. J., Daugherty, P. J., & Dant, R. P. (2012). Logistics Service Providers and Their Customers: Gaining Commitment through Organizational Implants. *Journal of Business Logistics, 33*(1), 50–63.
Harvey, D. (1990). *The Condition of Postmodernity: An Enquiry into the Origins of Cultural Change*. Cambridge, MA: Blackwell.
Hertz, S., & Alfredsson, M. (2003). Strategic Development of Third Party Logistics Providers. *Industrial Marketing Management, 32*(2), 139–149.
Huemer, L. (2012). Unchained from the Chain. *Journal of Business Research, 65*(2), 258–264.
Hugos, M. H. (2011). *Essentials of Supply Chain Management*. New York: Wiley.
Langley, C. J., Coley, J. J., Gibson, B. J., Novack, R. A., & Bardi, E. J. (2008). *Managing Supply Chain; A Logistics Approach*. Nashville, TN: South-Western College Publications.
Lusch, R. (2011). Reframing Supply Chain Management: A Service-Dominant-Logic Perspective. *Journal of Supply Chain Management, 47*(1), 14–18.
Massey, D. (1994). *Space, Place, and Gender*. Minneapolis: University of Minnesota Press.
Minter, A. (2013). *Junkyard Planet: Travels in the Billion-Dollar Trash Trade*. New York: Bloomsbury Press.
Mokyr, J. (2009). *The Enlightened Economy: Britain and the Industrial Revolution: 1700–1850*. London: Penguin.

Porter, M. (1998). *Competitive Advantage*. New York: Free Press.

Potter, A., & Mason, R. (2015). How Has Logistics Come to Exert Such a Key Role in the Performance of Economics, Society and Policy Making in the 21st Century? In J. Bryson & P. Daniels (Eds.), *Handbook of Service Business*. Cheltenham: Edward Elgar.

Simchi-Levi, D., Kaminsky, P., & Simchi-Levi, E. (2008). *Designing and Managing the Supply Chain: Concepts, Strategies and Case Studies*. New York: McGraw Hill.

Skjøtt-Larsen, T. (2000). Third-Party Logics - from an Interorganisational Point of View. *International Journal of Physical Distribution and Logistics Management, 30*(2), 112–123.

Soinio, J., Tanskane, K., & Finne, M. (2012). How Logistics-Service Providers Can Develop Value Added Services for SMEs: A Dyadic Perspective. *The International Journal of Logistics Management, 23*(1), 31–49.

Stone, B. (2013). *The Everything Store: Jeff Bezos and the Age of Amazon*. London: Bantam Press.

Sundbo, J. (2011). Extended Value Chain Innovation. In J. Sundbo & M. Toivonen (Eds.), *User-Based Innovation in Services*. Cheltenham: Edward Elgar.

Tan, W. J., & Enderwick, P. (2006). Managing Threats in the Global Era: The Impact and Response to SARS. *Thunderbird International Business Review, 48*, 515–536.

Tortorella, G., Miorando, R., & Marodi, G. (2017). Lean Supply Chain Management: Empirical Research on Practices, Contexts and Performance. *International Journal of Production Economics, 193*(C 11), 98–112.

UPS. (2016). Retrieved August 11, 2019, from https://www.ups.com/content/us/en/bussol/browse/article/what-is-logistics.html.

Yao, J. (2011). Decision Optimization Analysis on Supply Chain Resource Integration in Fourth Party Logistics. *Journal of Manufacturing Systems, 29*(4), 121–129.

## Further Reading

Kakhi, M. D., & Gargeya, V. B. (2019). Information Systems for Supply Chain Management: A Systematic Literature Analysis. *International Journal of Production Research, 57*(15–16), 5318–5339.

Stark, A. (2019). *Supply Chain Management*. Waltham Abbey, Essex: ED-Tech Press.

Sweeny, E., Grant, D. B., & Mangan, D. J. (2018). Strategic Adoption of Logistics and Supply Chain Management. *International Journal of Operations and Production Management, 38*(3), 852–873.

## Useful Websites

http://www.more-for-small-business.com/value-chain-analysis.html.

https://www.ups.com/content/us/en/bussol/browse/article/what-is-logistics.html.

http://www.clm1.org/.

http://www.supplychainedge.com/the-edge-blog/the-five-main-supply-chain-challenges-companies-face-today/.

http://www.swlearning.com/quant/coyle/seventh_edition/coyle.html.

https://www.ibm.com/case-studies/lenovo-watson-customer-engagement-supply-chain.Odi cusa atur?

# Servitization and Manufacturing Companies

**12**

**Key Themes**

- What role do services play within manufacturing firms and their goods?
- Service businesses within manufacturing companies
- Defining and exploring servitization
- Challenges of servitization and the service relationship in manufacturing
- Alternative strategies
- Research traditions and challenges within management, marketing and operations

Maintaining good service relationships with customers is one of the factors that has led manufacturers to focus more on the contribution services make to the production and sale of manufactured goods. Manufacturing companies purchase services to improve production and sales processes; however, they also sell services directly to customers. This has led to the development and application of a service-informed approach to the sale of manufactured goods. This creates new challenges, not least the challenge of adopting and developing a service culture by manufacturing companies. New strategies and tactics must be developed to overcome these challenges.

Reading manufacturing businesses now requires understanding how service tasks are

incorporated into the business models and operational processes required to produce physical goods. This includes understanding the transformation of some goods into services and the development of additional services that are attached to or embedded into manufactured goods. In this chapter, we consider the ways in which services have been incorporated into the operational processes that support manufacturing and product/good-related services. This includes the provision of consultancy services, design and development services, retail and distribution services, financial services, logistics services, installation and setup services, management and operating services, maintenance and support services and disposal and conversion services (Mastrogiacomo et al. 2019). The focus of this chapter is on understanding the emergence of material product-service systems and the challenges related to their organization and management.

This chapter is in five parts. Following the introduction, various types and degrees of servitization are explored. Then the challenges facing manufacturing companies as they adopt servitization are identified and explained. This leads to a discussion of alternatives to servitization such as deservitization, standardization and productization. Finally, three dominant business perspectives developed to explore servitization are reviewed to understand the problems and challenges managers in manufacturing companies

**Electronic Supplementary Material** The online version of this chapter (https://doi.org/10.1007/978-3-030-52060-1_12) contains supplementary material, which is available to authorized users.

face as they develop and apply service-led approaches to the realization of material goods.

## 12.1   Servitizing in Manufacturing Companies

To highlight the role services play in manufacturing, Brax and Visintin (2017, p. 17), along with many others, explore the Xerox Corporation. They noted that in 2013 over 84% of this corporation's total revenues came from selling contracted services including equipment maintenance, consumable supplies and finance and that since 2007 there had been a 12% increase in the proportion services accounted for of total revenues. Xerox is often cited in the business and management literature as an extreme example of how manufacturers are redefining their core offerings by moving from selling goods to selling product-service systems. In this case, a manufacturing company, Xerox, is selling printing/copying services rather than printers and reprographic machines.

Another example is Lego, the Danish toy manufacturer. Lego is well-known for selling construction sets consisting of plastic bricks and components. This company has developed a range of services and experiences which are designed to develop and create relationships with customers. Legoland theme parks have been established in Denmark, the UK, Germany, Japan, Malaysia, Dubai and the US, and parks are being developed in New York, South Korea and Shanghai. The Lego®VIP program was developed for customers over 18 years old. Members collect VIP points by shopping in stores or online and by completing surveys, watching videos, visiting the Lego Facebook page or by recommending friends to join the programme. The Lego Ideas initiative has been designed to encourage consumers to develop and share new Lego designs with the company. This is an interactive process in which creators are encouraged to enter competitions and to vote for designs created by other Lego consumers. Lego no longer just wants consumers to purchase a box of Lego, but instead tries to develop longer-term relationships. This type of relationship building is a form of end-user innovation in which consumers become incorporated into Lego's research and development programme.

Other large manufacturing firms that have adopted service-informed business models include Ericsson, IBM and GE (Sjödin et al. 2019), Rolls-Royce, Alstom Transport, Caterpillar (Baines and Lightfoot 2013), General Motors, Apple, Volkswagen, Johnson and Johnson (Gebauer et al. 2012) and Vestas (Møller 2018). For example, Møller (2018) identified that in 2016, revenue from selling services by one of the world's largest wind turbine manufacturers, Vestas, exceeded revenues from designing and fabricating wind turbines. Sjödin et al. (2019) explored 50 small, medium and large Swedish manufacturing companies that were providing different types of advanced services to customers. Using Fuzzy-set Qualitative Comparative Analysis (Fs/QCA) they analysed the relationship between the conditions and outcomes of servitization identifying three servitization strategies which improved the financial performance of these firms.

The adoption and development of service strategies by manufacturing companies appears to be a significant trend (Rabetino et al. 2018). Brax and Visintin (2017) explored a series of studies that identified the importance of this trend and this included a survey that identified that 30% of manufacturing companies had adopted servitization strategies. They also noted that 16% of the turnover of European manufacturing companies was derived from selling services (Brax and Visintin 2017). In 2019, Mastrogiacomo et al. undertook an analysis of 190,407 companies with more than 50 employees and identified that, on average, 38% were servitized (Table 12.1)

This phenomenon of manufacturing companies shifting to selling goods and services has been given different labels and has been explored from different perspectives. In 1988, Vandermerwe and Rada published the first article that highlighted the on-going process of what they termed the "servitization of business" (Vandermerwe and Rada 1988). Other labels used to describe this phenomenon include service

**Table 12.1**  Extent of servitization by country

| Country | % Servitized manufacturing firms |
|---|---|
| UK | 56 |
| USA | 53 |
| Finland | 44 |
| Germany | 39 |
| China | 38 |
| South Africa | 37 |
| France | 36 |
| India | 27 |
| Vietnam | 27 |
| Brazil | 24 |
| **All** | 38% |

Source: After Mastrogiacomo et al. (2019)
Note: Based on the analysis of a sample of 190,407 companies with more than 50 employees. Of these, 72,780 were servitized companies and 113,861 pure manufacturing companies

infusion (Brax 2005), transforming towards solution business models (Storbacka et al. 2013), service transformations or transitions, the services duality and the rise of the manuservice economy (Bryson and Daniels 2010). All these labels indicate that there has been a shift towards selling service solutions or product-service systems rather than goods.

The phenomenon observed by Vandermerwe and Rada was that services had become increasingly important for manufacturing companies and their management teams. Selling services enhances corporate competitiveness as part of a process of developing longer-term relationships with customers. Physical goods could be converted into services. In this case, a company no longer transfers ownership of a good to a consumer but sells services that are accessed via the good. This includes airlines paying for engine power by the hour rather than owning aviation engines. The key point is that manufacturing companies should not focus on producing either goods or services, but they should sell bundles of services and goods 'with services in the lead role' (Vandermerwe and Rada 1988, p. 314).

Vandermerwe and Rada highlighted the complex relationships that exist, and which have always existed, between goods and services. Manufacturers have always produced services that are related to their goods, for example, pro-

viding maintenance and repair services. The delivery, or co-creation of services, is also reliant on manufactured goods. There are virtually no pure goods or services. Services almost always include some 'hard' good-like features, including, for example, the meals we eat at restaurants or music downloaded to smartphones. Conversely, goods are embedded in services. A bicycle or car comes with warranty and maintenance services. What Vandamerwe and Randa noted, however, is that the service aspects of goods have become much more central to manufacturing companies. Many of the operations undertaken by customers when purchasing a good, for example, having a car serviced, can be transformed into systematic services provided by manufacturers. In this case, cars can be purchased outright, can be purchased with attached services or can be leased with embedded service packages. An increasing amount of added value created by manufacturing firms is produced through the production and co-creation of product-related services.

Perhaps the key is the switch from manufacturers predominately developing, designing and fabricating goods towards using a goods *plus* services approach to business models that are based on the creation and provision of complex '"bundles" consisting of customer-focused *combinations of goods, services, support, self-service, and knowledge*' (Vandermerwe and Rada 1988, p. 316). For example, a good such as an expensive bicycle comes with embedded maintenance services and information concerning where and how to use the bicycle including information about cycleways, maps and signs. In this case, bundles of services are performed by many different actors sometimes in collaboration with the manufacturer in the form of a service ecosystem which supports a manufactured good. An excellent example are smartphones. These can be purchased outright or leased as part of a service contract that includes a bundle of services and a phone, but consumers can purchase cases and also additional software and content. In other areas, for example, Xerox printing / copying service, the manufacturer offers packages of services on their own or an integrated product-service system or solution-oriented value proposition.

Manufacturing companies have been refocusing their attention on the downstream elements of value chains to try to extract value from operations, tasks and activities that were formerly the customer's responsibility. In doing so, some argue that they offer 'capabilities' related to the use of a good, such as the capability of printing or transporting (Baines and Lightfoot 2013). By offering services, manufacturers alter the emphasis in their business models from just selling goods to assisting customers to maximize the values provided by the services and linked values that can be delivered by the good (Baines et al. 2007). For example, car manufacturers may sell additional services which enhance customers' capabilities to drive cars safely and in a more environmentally sustainable manner by offering different combinations of hardware and software solutions or bundles. Selling a good to a customer creates one moment of profit realization compared to selling a good with embedded services or selling a good as a service. The latter provides manufacturers with a series of potential moments to engage with customers and each is a possible profit generation moment. In addition, by expanding usage and offering product/good-service systems, manufacturers can ensure that customers are updated with the latest solutions.

To Vandermerwe and Rada the shift towards servitization was driven by customers. Customers are more knowledgeable with increased technological and financial resources. They have become more critical and demanding requiring more information and knowledge about goods and services. This shift has been driven by technological and economic developments. There are many and complex factors that encourage or force companies to adopt servitization strategies. In particular, the pressure to remain competitive by responding to customers' requirements. Yet it is often difficult for manufacturing companies to appropriate the benefits that come from adopting a service-led approach as they must balance the tensions between their existing manufacturing culture and the creation of a more service-informed culture.

Servitization represents a new business logic (Skålén and Edvardsson 2016) that has profound implications for how companies consider their business models, how they build their organizations, their business culture and how management and employees come to deal with customers. A service-led good strategy requires that manufacturing companies must build their business models around the application of service-informed logic to their goods and processes developing a service-informed approach to customer interactions. The services provided by a good become the central feature of a company's business model. The organization must be turned upside down so that value is not just equated with the sale of goods, but with the use and the values created in collaboration with customers. A service culture must be inculcated to ensure that employees are committed to developing and adopting this approach.

## 12.2   Defining Servitization

It is important to clearly define the servitization process. To Baines et al. (2009a) servitization is 'the innovation of a manufacturer's capabilities and processes to move from selling goods, to selling integrated product-service offerings that deliver value in use' (p. 512). This definition can be developed by exploring Kohtamäki et al. (2018) who suggest that servitization represents a change in business model towards a product-service-system (PSS). They note that 'We consider servitization as a transition in business models from goods to PSS, where goods and services are bundled to generate higher use-value, pricing is based on value, and capabilities support customer-dominant orientation' (p. 3). Servitization is a process that impacts both a company's strategy or business model and operations.

These definitions build on the classical distinction between goods and services. Let us briefly consider this distinction and how it is applied in this context. A good (which is 'something you can drop on your foot') is usually defined as a material thing that can be owned by someone and sold on to someone else. By contrast, a service has been described as an intangible social or economic activity that does not lead to ownership of a material thing (Baines et al. 2009b). This distinction is implicit in Hill's seminal definition of services that states that a service is a process operating on a person or good. In this definition, 'a service is defined as a change in the condition of a person, or a good belonging to some economic unit, which is brought about as the result of the activity of some other economic unit, with the agreement of the former person or economic unit' (Hill 1977, p. 318). It is important to note that ownership of a service is not included in this definition. A service is a change in some form of state or condition that does not have to be associated with ownership of a physical good.

Similarly, the service marketing literature has outlined certain 'service characteristics' which may be used to define and identify services from physical goods. These include services as being characterized by intangibility, heterogeneity, inseparability and perishability (Zeithaml et al. 1985). This implies that a service is something that cannot be sensed or touched in the same way as a good, or circulated and recirculated in the marketplace (see also Gadrey and Delaunay 1992) (also see Chap. 1, section 1.13).

These distinctions are nevertheless quite academic and partly problematic because goods and services are so closely intertwined and dependent on one another. Digitization continues to transform services and manufactured goods. These distinctions are used in the servitization literature to highlight business transformations that are shifting manufacturers from a good- to a product-service focus. It is important to recognize that the distinction between manufacturing and services reflects an old way of considering production systems (Daniels and Bryson 2002). Manufacturing and services are hybridizing leading to the creation of new product-service and service-product combinations or bundles. Rather than outlining a distinction between these two sectors, the servitization literature outlines a new approach to doing business in which new dimensions, especially the use-aspects of goods and services, are incorporated into the business models of manufacturing companies.

Similar to the servitization literature, Vargo and Lusch (2004) have argued for a distinction to be made between operand resources (raw materials and goods) and operant resources (skills and knowledge). This distinction indicates that a shift has occurred in the approach to doing business. They contend that there has been a shift in the economy as a whole towards emphasizing operant resources, and how these perform and interact on operand resources. Vargo and Lusch make a broader claim that all economies are best described as service economies where value is co-created by numerous ('multiple') actors (Vargo and Lusch 2008) (see Chap. 2).

Initially, the debate on services focused on the provision of service by service firms. Subsequently, the servitization debate has highlighted the importance of exploring the application of service-led or service-informed approaches by manufacturing companies. Here it is important to recognize that very few manufacturing firms are only engaged in the production of manufactured goods; all manufactured goods have service tasks embedded in their production processes and the majority are involved in the creation and co-creation of services. Manufacturers now have to think like service firms and to pay much more attention to the service aspects of their operations, marketing and innovation processes.

It is important to note that there are, however, different levels of commitment to services by manufacturing companies. Some manufacturers create a limited number of services that are intended to support customers in a good's use and maintenance, for example, when it needs to be repaired. Nevertheless, customers continue to be responsible for decisions regarding when a good should be serviced including purchasing and installing spare parts. Not long ago it was usual for consumers to return devices such as radios, tape recorders and other electrical household appliances for repair to the store where they were purchased. In this case, it was the store which was responsible for providing these product-related services, but customers were responsible for making decisions regarding servicing and repairs. For goods under warranty, the risks were shared between customers and manufacturers.

In the case of a modern, digitized car, the service systems are more advanced as they are embedded in the good. The responsibilities and risks are distributed between many actors contributing to the delivery and functioning of the car as an integrated transportation system providing a service—movement. It is often the car dealer's responsibility to contact customers regarding servicing that must be paid for. Many cars will alert drivers regarding the timing of the next service. Customers who fail to act on this information may forgo some rights. The service system, or service ecosystem, that is wrapped around and embedded within a car becomes more complex when a car is leased. Contracts between the various parties involved in a product-service system, including possible financial partners and sub-suppliers, can grow ever more complex. This complexity intensifies with more complex technologies, including goods that are part of an Internet of Things (IoT). The product-service system becomes much more sophisticated and complicated with roles, risks and responsibilities distributed amongst multiple actors.

To clarify these various degrees of complexity, there have been attempts to identify and separate different types of product-service systems (Mastrogiacomo et al. 2019). An important and much cited example is Tukker's (2004) in which a distinction is made between eight archetypes belonging to three overall categories of service business in manufacturing. These categories are (a) product-oriented, (b) use-oriented and (c) result-oriented services (Table 12.2). This type of analysis highlights the distinction between three types of services: customer services, product services and service as product (Mathieu 2001).

There is a continuum of ways to incorporate service-based business transactions into manufacturing. At one end of this continuum is the application of very simple services and, at the other end, the transformation of a good into a service-based delivery system involving no exchange in ownership of a manufactured good. Baines and Lightfoot (2013) have suggested a simpler approach to categorizing different

**Table 12.2** Eight categories of service business in manufacturing companies

| Product-oriented services | • Product-related, when a service is required for a product to be used.<br>• Advice and consultancy, such as advice on logistics and organizational structure. |
|---|---|
| Use-oriented services | • Product lease, when a customer pays a fee for leasing a product but responsibility for repair rests with the owner.<br>• Product renting and sharing, when several individuals rent a product at different times.<br>• Product renting and pooling which is the same as the previous type except that renters have simultaneous use. |
| Result-oriented services | • Activity management/outsourcing, when a company outsources an activity but conducts quality control.<br>• Pay per service unit when customers pay for the output of a product rather than the product itself.<br>• Functional results when the customer pays for the results independently of the products used to produce the result. |

Source: Developed from Tukker (2004)

degrees of servitization. They distinguish between base services, intermediate services and advanced services. Their interest primarily lies in describing the competitive advantages and challenges related to the provision of advanced product-service offerings. Base service provision includes equipment, spare parts and warranties. Intermediate services include activities such as maintenance, overhauling and delivery. Advanced services include customer-support agreements, revenue through-use contracts and rental agreements. Customers receive 'capability delivered through the performance of the product' from accessing advanced services. The shift towards advanced services would normally imply a more linear economic model (following sequences of generation, deployment and executions) and longer and extended life cycles with longer service contracts, because it involves more planning and commitment.

To enhance understanding of the provision of advanced services, or complex product-service systems by manufacturing companies, it is important to consider the differences between competence versus capability. Advanced services would, according to Baines and Lightfoot, focus on capabilities related to use, such as transportation. The difference between these two terms is not easy to capture since the literature sometimes uses them interchangeably. Competence tends to denote the qualifications required to perform a task to create a desired result, such as when a car manufacturer delivers a car that functions according to expectations. Capability is a broader concept concerning knowledge, competency, support structures and networks that are required to produce certain outcomes. In the context of servitization, competence tends to have a product-focus and capability a user-focus. In other words, competence concerns the provider sphere and capabilities the user sphere. Thus, a hospital may have the competence to treat patients and, in addition, it may also have the ability to deliver capabilities that produce health outcomes, for example, knowledge, competences, support structures and networks. Thus, the provision of advanced services by manufacturing firms involves delivering this capability to users/customers.

In their analysis of advanced services, Baines and Lightfoot (2013) explore railways. The advanced services which are delivered to a train operator include the capability to transport passengers. The company contracts with a train manufacturer to deliver this capability instead of purchasing trains and delivering the entire service itself. This implies that a railway is based on a number of contracts and interactions to ensure quality, the distribution of responsibilities and risks, to ensure demand through time tabling, provide extra services (such as selling food and drink on trains) and supporting services (such as consultancy on rules and regulations) and being available for discussions and negotiations about capabilities. The key point here is that the focus is on the capabilities involved in train transportation systems which are delivered by manufacturers to customers and are sold on to passengers. Previously, a train operator's focus was perhaps more focused on the competencies required to provide train services on time by using the required resources and skills. However, the broader focus on receiving capabilities from manufacturers means that there is room for change and service improvement over time.

To summarize, the servitization approach, understood as a business model, involves a shift in manufacturers from selling goods (such as bicycles, cars, trains, computers or printers), as the main outcome of a business exchange, to delivering user capabilities (the users' capability to print documents, the municipality's capability to deliver movement, the end-users' capability to move but using a bicycle). This represents a shift in emphasis from the provider's ability to produce a given good in a competent way to enabling users to perform tasks by means of a set of goods and services.

Advanced servitization can lead to longer-term contracts between producers and customers. Purchasing a good is a single commercial transaction while a product-service system extends the life cycle of the commercial relationship between the producer and the consumer. Implementing an advanced product-service system in a manufacturing company requires greater planning efforts, more complicated contracts, a more linear approach to generating, deploying and executing services given the complexity of the system, and longer service delivery life cycles (Fig. 12.1). Improving and updating the various technologies and services that are important for delivering outcomes is usually part of a service contract. There may be a risk of customer lock-in to a service system.

Advanced servitization can be applied to providers of traditional services. Teachers, rather than delivering a piece of teaching, deliver the capability of learning. They deliver a set of goods and services relevant to the students' learning capacity. Health organizations deliver the capability of health stressing the patients' ability to take care of their own bodies and value creation rather than the provision of a specific treatment.

## 12.3  Challenges of Servitization

With developments in new technologies, and new market structures, manufacturers need to deliver new service solutions. Nevertheless, it is chal-

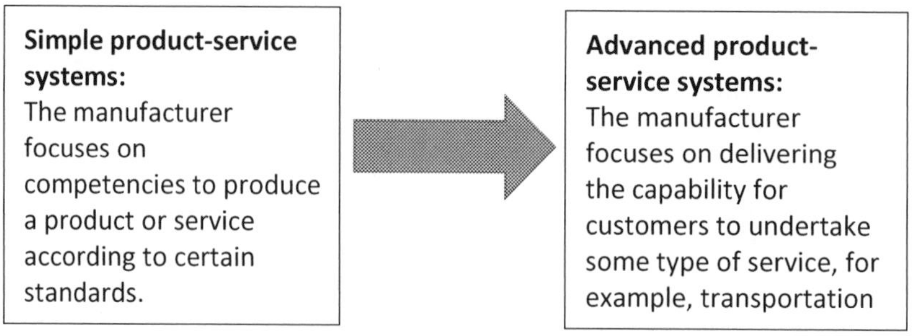

| Simple product-service systems:<br>The manufacturer focuses on competencies to produce a product or service according to certain standards. | → | Advanced product-service systems:<br>The manufacturer focuses on delivering the capability for customers to undertake some type of service, for example, transportation |

**Fig. 12.1** The changing focus of manufacturers from simple to advanced product-service systems. (Source: Authors' own)

lenging for a company to reap the benefits that come from servitization. This has been termed the 'service paradox' (Gebauer et al. 2005) in which the introduction of servitization by a manufacturing company leads to increasing revenues but decreasing profits. One explanation for this service paradox is that it is difficult for manufacturers to create synergies between manufacturing production systems and services and to calculate the product-service prices required to cover the costs related to the co-creation of services (Kowalkowski et al. 2017).

One set of problems concerns cognitive barriers that result in manufacturing companies not being motivated to embrace adding services to their business models (Gebauer et al. 2005). A key issue is that companies focused on product/good fabrication have a manufacturing culture based around product-orientated traditions. The good is the central focus of their business model and linked operations. The focus is on improving goods and their production processes to reduce costs and increase functionality. It is a significant challenge to apply service logic to a well-established manufacturing company.

Cognitive barriers also affect organizational choices. At the centre of manufacturing culture is the factory and a concern with economies of scale. Production processes are centralized to achieve scale and enhance efficiency (Baines and Lightfoot 2013). For a manufacturer, services can appear to be too intangible and challenging when they are applied to a hardware and engineering culture operating within a factory system. A manufacturing-orientated company will be

product-centric focusing on the realization of goods to meet customer needs. Nevertheless, manufacturing production systems are complex and capital intensive and the sunk costs embedded in these systems makes change difficult.

A service culture, by contrast, is customer-centric with a focus on service co-creation and delivery. For manufacturing companies, the shift towards more service-orientated business models involves developing different ways to create value and different approaches to production. The company's focus must now be on how customers create value from the services they use and on maintaining relationships with customers. Developing solutions to these new service elements within a value chain increases the number of activities that management must oversee, and this can have negative consequences on production management.

Two other cognitive barriers have been identified by Gebauer et al. (2005). First, manufacturers may fail to recognize the economic potential of services, and, therefore, they pay insufficient attention to the creation of services. The second concerns the economic risks associated with services. There is a general risk affiliated with transitioning towards a more service-informed manufacturing business. This risk is related to a shift that is beyond an existing management team's core competence. It requires investment in new skills and new technologies. New capabilities are needed to increase the intensity of customer/producer service relationships.

Another risk stems from a manufacturer's need to gain insights into customers' value chains and operations to understand where and what services may be embedded in which process and product. Customers may, however, resist this as they might have concerns with a manufacturer passing sensitive information on to other customers and companies. Furthermore, manufacturers must open up their value chains enabling existing and potential customer to engage in the co-creation of service-product experiences. Services need to be developed through interactions and exchanges of sensitive information between manufacturers and their customers. For example, a train manufacturer must understand railway operational procedures and systems to ensure that trains are designed and fabricated to meet user needs. Train manufacturers must engage in a dialogue with railway operators and both parties must accept the risks connected with exchanging information about business processes. Gebauer et al. concluded that to overcome the 'service paradox', and to ensure the successful introduction of service business to manufacturing companies, then the barriers to servitization must be addressed. Solutions include increasing service awareness, accepting the risks of extending a company's activities to include service business and believing in the economic potential of services (Gebauer et al. 2005). This suggests that there are learning and trust aspects involved that take time to resolve.

As a result of these challenges, and this service paradox, there is a non-linear relationship between servitization and performance (Kohtamäki et al. 2013). Often there is no direct connection between increasing services and increasing profits. It takes time before manufacturers learn how to generate additional profits from providing services or from converting goods into products that deliver services.

The literature has focused on various ways in which manufacturers respond to these challenges. One conclusion is that there is not one but many ways to achieve a positive outcome. Thus, there is 'equiefficiency' in the sense that there are many pathways to success. There is a need for more contextual and historical understandings of service businesses within manufacturing companies rather than searching for one model that

might produce optimal results (Bryson and Daniels 2010). For example, more attention must be paid to best practice in the application of servitization through historical, institutional and contextual research. Sometimes servitization is depicted in an overly simplistic way to try to persuade managers to adopt this approach. Servitization, however, is not a well-defined process and it is difficult for managers to foresee or control outcomes. One option is to adopt a more flexible approach to the factors influencing servitization (Sjödin et al. 2019) or to explore variations in the ways in which servitization can be performed (cf. also Brax and Visintin 2017).

One topic of interest is how service businesses in manufacturing companies can be managed and governed. Again, there is not one but several solutions to this challenge. Some manufacturers apply formal governance strategies, including contracts, intended to capture value from servitization especially when the risk of losing customers is high. Based on a sample of 50 Swedish manufacturing firms (small, medium and large) Sjödin et al. (2019) noted that there are different conditional factors for the adoption of servitization that can be combined in different ways. These include service innovation abilities, customer costs related to switching to other providers, attractiveness of alternative solutions and the use of explicit contracts. Three successful governance strategies were identified which improve a company's financial performance under different conditions. The first involves pursuing strategies based on innovation but driven by a concern with customer retention by limiting the attractiveness of alternative options. The second is relational governance emphasizing innovation, openness and trust but ensuring that switching costs remain high and the application of contracts low. The third strategy is a market-based governance strategy including formal contracts when there are alternative options and with low switching costs.

The implication is that the road to servitization is not straightforward; there are many alternative pathways. The selection of the most appropriate pathway reflects the types of goods produced by a manufacturing company and the existing market structure. Managers must consider how various situational factors can be combined into a strategy that improves financial performance and enhances competitiveness and sustainability.

A related way to explain the difficulties of creating service business within manufacturing companies is through the lens of 'practice'. Practices are purposeful socially recognized routine behaviours produced through everyday actions and bound together by mental models, understandings and materials. They are intertwined with everyday experiences and tacit knowledge and they are difficult to manage in a linear way or mobilize for certain organizational ideas or outcomes. In research on strategy-as-practice, attempts have been made to uncover the real strategic practices and strategizing in organizations rather than assuming that strategies govern action. In the servitization literature a discussion around the notion of practice has been initiated (Kohtamäki et al. 2018) to investigate and understand the real practices of servitization. But limited research has been undertaken on this topic. In this approach, research needs to investigate how manufacturing practices already provide a mechanism for servitization, and which servitization practices already exist within a manufacturing company that can be further developed and sustained. Service practices almost always exist in manufacturing companies. Manufacturers interact with customers attempting to understand customer problems. In many manufacturing companies, service-oriented personnel are already employed, for example, in marketing and sales, who might have the potential to play a more central role. Practice-based research is important in this context. This type of research reveals the messy realities of the everyday activities of practitioners. This approach could be used to identify existing practices that could be modified or strengthened to encourage servitization. Manufacturers seeking to promote servitization must identify and explore their existing mechanisms, practices and experiences and how these relate to servitization.

Servitization is a difficult business transformation process. It is often implied, however, that this process is a conscious and strategic process

under management control. This process is sometimes described as linear with discrete stages. Some of the early research on strategy developed a process and practice perspective (e.g. Henry Mitzberg). This highlighted that strategy is an iterative and chaotic process often including a process of 'way-finding' (Chia and Holt 2006) and this could well be the case with servitization. In this regard, Kowalkowski et al. (2012) identified a process of 'service infusion' drawing upon Lindblom's notion of disjointed incrementalism to characterize the process of service infusion. By this they meant that servitization strategies were not entirely deliberate with a particular goal in mind. Rather that these strategies emerged within firms. They explored BT industries, a leading manufacturer of warehouse trucks. BT industries experienced a decline in customer loyalty. One response was to develop more services including renting warehouses. Kowalkowski et al. (2012) concluded from this case study that this company's service strategies were emergent and disjointed. This contrasted with this company's approach to goods which included top down planning with clear goals and subsequent evaluation. Yet in services the process was neither one of abrupt change towards servitization with clear explicit goals, nor one of logical incrementalism where management designed the process and remained in control. Instead the process was much more illogical and incoherent. Over time, as managers became more experienced with managing services strategies these became more coherent and organized. Kowalkowski et al. (2012) developed the concept of agile incrementalism to denote how organizations must continuously deal with ambiguity and uncertainty, but in a responsive way.

Practice-based and process-based understandings of service-businesses within manufacturing companies emphasize that managers and employees must experiment with solutions, make sense of service business and develop actions. This is an incremental learning process as a manufacturing-orientated culture and strategy is transformed to one that appreciates the management, organization, delivery and integration of services into product-based business models.

Some authors have drawn attention to the 'microfoundations' of servitization, for example, manufacturers must develop individual tactics to overcome resistance to servitization (Lenka et al. 2018) including entrepreneurial tactics that trickle down to individual employees. The micro foundation movement in business research emphasizes how macro-phenomena needs to be translated into action formation activities at the micro-level to enable action. Servitization is thus understood as a macro-phenomenon, or a mega-trend at the societal level, which is dependent on actors developing tactics and strategies at the micro-level before servitization can be realized.

## 12.4   Other Developments and the Service-Manufacturing Relationship

Other phenomena identified and explored by researchers include service reduction (deservitization), standardization of services and productization. For some companies, servitization might be a preferred strategy in an attempt to retain customers whilst there might be no economic benefits for other firms. Importantly, deservitization can be linked to industry development. For example, some firms start out as high-tech firms delivering complicated technologies. In the beginning, they are dependent on a series of services to improve processes and to assist customers in the adoption of new technologies. These companies use knowledge services given high levels of uncertainty and the requirement to generate knowledge about technical changes and how markets develop. Nevertheless, as the technology and market matures and technology becomes easier to forecast and manage, there is a reduction in the need to incorporate services into customer delivery systems leading to deservitization (Kowalkowski et al. 2017).

Another possible counter-evolution is delivering services in a more standardized and 'manufactured' way (cf. Levitt 1972). As was explored in Chap. 5, Levitt (1972) has developed a product-line approach to service co-creation and delivery. In this account, services need to become like

goods, and this includes the industrialization of service production systems including the capabilities required to produce and sell services. Services must become manufactured like material goods. There are three processes at work. First, manufacturing is experiencing a process of servitization. Second, service providers are shifting towards an emphasis on services as a process involving the mass production or manufacture of service products. As Levitt (1972, pp. 51–52) stated:

> Once service-industry executives and the creators of customer-service programs begin seriously to think of themselves as actually manufacturing a product, they will begin to think like product manufacturers. They will ask: What technologies and systems are employable here? How can things be designed so we can use machines instead of people, systems instead of serendipity? Instead of thinking about better and more training of their customer-service representatives, insurance agents, branch bank managers, or salesmen "out there," they will think about how to eliminate or supplement them.

This involves the application of technological solutions to service delivery systems that are substituting labour with capital investment, people with algorithms, high street shops with e-commerce platforms and, in some cases, service workers with robots.

Productization is a third alternative development trend. It is described in the literature as changing a service offer by 'adding tangible products to core services or by decomposing service components into combinable modules' (Leoni 2015). Services can be more integrated with technologies such as digital technology and services can be sub-divided into small units and each can be sold separately. Both strategies, integration with technology and modularization, are intertwined as both require more sophisticated descriptions of the service and the establishment of service delivery standards. For example, computer-based or media-based services can be described in terms of speed or in terms of different modules that can be added to the service. A hotel service can be modularized based on the number of 'products' that may be added to the hotel room. In a fully automated hotel, all services are embedded in a material structure—a good. Productization becomes a way to make services more marketable and tradable.

Another evolution that blurs the boundaries between services and manufacturing concerns the increasing use of services in production and the dynamics that this entails (Daniels and Bryson 2002). Daniels and Bryson highlight that services have always been used in manufacturing processes, for example, in administrative tasks including book-keeping, procurement, marketing and human resources. Today manufacturing companies are dependent on an increasing array of knowledge-intensive business service firms that provide intermediate inputs into client production processes. Some manufacturing companies become providers of service solutions by outsourcing manufacturing production, whilst others may move in the opposite direction, that is, focus on the core business of producing goods and outsourcing all administrative and service tasks. The use of information and communication technologies in production, design, research and marketing also makes the distinction between services and manufacturing less obvious. Generally, one may end up seeing, on the one hand, manufacturing companies moving more into services and, on the other hand, service companies moving more into manufacturing.

Economies are restructuring. One consequence is that the distinction between manufacturing and service firms is being challenged as service firms embrace some of the characteristics associated with manufacturing and manufacturing companies become more service orientated. The focus needs to shift away from research and management approaches highlighting differences between manufacturing and services to an approach that acknowledges that production is a process that blends manufacturing and service tasks together producing hybrid products.

With inspiration from Daniels and Bryson (2002), we argue that the concept of 'service' is important, though perhaps not so much because it denotes a sector, but because it describes a particular approach to business operations, marketing and innovation based on the management of 'service relationships' and on 'service-orientated'

business models. All companies, services and manufacturing, develop different approaches to creating and managing service relationships with their customers. These service relationships are important; differentiation between firms is founded on the nature and quality of service relationships rather than just on product-based differentiation. Goods can be copied but service relationships are much more inimitable. The importance of service relationships deserves special attention by managers. Services as product, and product as services, has increasing weight and importance in national and regional economies and needs to be explored in a systematic manner. The issue of service relationships revolves around how manufacturing and service companies develop relationships with their customers. According to Daniels and Bryson, academics, policymakers and businesses should stop talking and writing about manufacturing and services as sectors, and instead focus more generally on production. In this case, the challenge is on understanding how economic actors—manufacturing and service companies, all organizations—develop service relationships.

## 12.5 Perspectives on Servitization Relevant for Management

The change in business perspective towards an increasing emphasis on services, or service relationships and service business models, has, in the service marketing literature, been treated more broadly as a change in business logic that is relevant to all societal sectors. Thus, a discussion has revolved around 'service logic' and 'service dominant logic' and how such logics can be adopted and appropriated by service businesses and manufacturing companies. This led to a more interactional and relational approach to value creation than had previously been the case in the marketing literature that was based on service relationships. Thus, in this case, the focus is not on the service sector per se, but rather on understanding and adopting an emerging new institutional logic (Skålén and Edvardsson 2016) which becomes increasingly important in society and thus must be adopted by all organizations. An institutional logic is defined as the basic assumptions and beliefs that drive business action, and which tend to affect business actors more generally. The S-L perspective has further led some authors to formulate an alternative customer dominant logic perspective (CDL) (Heinonen and Strandvik 2015). This focuses on customers' logics, activities, and experiences and how customers use service elements in their lives and businesses. This posits that the key aspect of a service relationship is how firms can be involved in their customers' lives rather than the other way around. This stretches service relationships even further.

Changing the logic or way of thinking towards an enhanced emphasis on the service relationship entails at least three sets of management challenges for manufacturing companies. First, there is a strategy challenge which includes formulating strategies for stretching their activities along the supply chain and beyond to develop new advanced services for their customers. The type of servitization that is required, and what barriers and drivers exist, is dependent on product/good type, company size and the degree of innovativeness. There is not one model; manufacturing companies must find their own governance and management strategies to gain control over this process and how far they want to go.

Secondly, there is the challenge of sustaining service management and service innovation approaches, which may already be present, but seriously underdeveloped in a manufacturing company. Managers must deal with innovation in new service-oriented ways by involving 'ordinary' employees and including experiences from service encounters (see Chap. 7). Service innovation is seldom based on R&D and thus management innovation strategies must be combined with inputs from service employees. Executing innovation strategies within a loosely coupled system of interactions between management, employees and customers becomes a central challenge. Furthermore, for manufacturers with a product-centric approach it will be a challenge to adopt and develop more interactive and customer-centric service processes.

Thirdly, manufacturers need to consider if they want to adopt services as their dominant business logic with service delivery becoming their most important economic, or value creation activity. The service marketing literature is not especially helpful in explaining how a company should adopt this type of service-led strategy. The service-dominant logic literature explains how value is always co-created by many societal actors, but not how this process occurs. This is an important omission. The service logic literature explains in a more specific way how value is facilitated by providers, created by users through value-in-use and possibly co-created with providers. The customer dominant logic literature emphasizes that providers must gain access and achieve understanding of customers' value creation processes. Overall, this research suggests that the service relationship, or service-orientated business models, becomes an overriding logic and challenge for all firms, both in manufacturing and in services. This has consequences for how employees and managers direct their attention towards service relationships and managing customer needs.

## 12.6 Wrapping Up

Manufacturing and services have often been separated as two distinct sectors. Nevertheless, the borderline between these sectors is becoming increasingly blurred. Manufacturing companies use services in their production or operational processes, and they sell services related to their core goods. Services become increasingly standardized and are dependent on goods as carriers of services. Both manufacturing and service companies often expand their organizations to offer combinations of products/goods and services, or product/service bundles. For manufacturers, this implies that a different organizational culture is required founded on the creation and management of service relationships with customers. Services can play a minor or a major role. They play a minor role when manufacturing companies just sell physical goods. Services play a more prominent role when manufacturers offer educational programmes, training, repair services or maintenance. Finally, manufacturers can offer advanced services. This includes Xerox providing print services rather than selling printers, IBM or Microsoft providing licenses to access cloud-based computer software or when Rolls-Royce offers TotalCare services including power by the hour packages rather than selling aviation engines (see Chap. 14, section 14.2).

Manufacturing companies developing servitization approaches to value creation must adopt aspects of service management. This includes a more loosely coupled organization, a less R&D-intensive organization and an emphasis on company strategy and strategizing informed by inputs from frontline employees. Manufacturing businesses involved in service co-creation and delivery must highlight the importance of service management and customer-focused service relationships. At the same time, manufacturing culture does not simply disappear. Manufacturing culture is also affected both positively and negatively. A manufacturing firm must rethink their goods as providers of service experiences and must place service relationships at the centre of their operational processes and business models.

The service marketing literature highlights that service as a concept, process and value creator must be considered as a business logic that is applicable to all economic sectors. In this logic, value is said to be determined by the beneficiary/customer rather than being embedded in goods. Providers do not deliver value but offer value propositions or facilitate value for customers. This logic has been described in the literature as a broad societal logic where actors are broad generic actors (Heinonen and Strandvik 2015), and as a specific business logic that has implications for how goods and services are managed and marketed. In the latter case, it becomes relevant for understanding and managing different service models or customer service relationships. The business and management literature suggests that there are many different pathways towards applying such models and that these pathways are not institutionally determined. Actors can develop and negotiate different servitization models and approaches and apply them to their

existing business models, operations and goods. The outcome will be a shift towards a service-informed production process. The conclusion is that there is not one approach, but many different pathways towards developing a service-orientated business approach within manufacturing. Every company must select the pathway(s) that best meets the needs of its goods, market sector and existing operational procedures and business models.

**Learning Outcomes**

- Servitization involves manufacturing companies increasingly producing bundles of customer-focused combinations of goods and services.
- Some manufacturing companies produce a limited scope of basic services which are critical to their production processes. Other companies adopt a fully fledged advanced approach to services. This shifts the focus of their business activities towards more complex product-service systems and changes their core business towards providing capabilities for customers.
- Servitization entails a service paradox: while there is an increase in revenue, it appears to be more difficult for manufacturers to immediately benefit from an increase in profits.
- The service approach, or 'logic', is not replacing but supplementing manufacturers' existing production processes.
- No single optimal model for implementing a service approach in manufacturing companies exists. The servitization pathway that is selected by a manufacturing company is context dependent related to product, process and sector.

# References

Baines, T., & Lightfoot, H. (2013). *Made to Serve: How Manufacturers Can Compete Through Servitization and Product–Service Systems*. Chichester: Wiley.

Baines, T. S., Lightfoot, H. W., Evans, S., Neely, A., Greenough, R., Peppard, J., & Wilson, H. (2007). State-of-the-Art in Product-Service Systems. *Proceedings of the Institution of Mechanical Engineers Part B-Journal of Engineering Manufacture, 221*(10), 1543–1552.

Baines, T., Lightfoot, H., Peppard, J., Johnson, M., Tiwari, A., Shehab, E., & Swink, M. (2009a). Towards an Operations Strategy for Product-Centric Servitization. *International Journal of Operations & Production Management, 29*(5), 494–519.

Baines, T. S., Lightfoot, H. W., Benedettini, O., & Kay, J. M. (2009b). The Servitization of Manufacturing: A Review of Literature and Reflection on Future. *Journal of Manufacturing Technology Management, 20*(5), 547–567.

Brax, S. (2005). A Manufacturer Becoming Service Provider – Challenges and a Paradox. *Managing Service Quality, 15*(2), 142–155.

Brax, S. A., & Visintin, F. (2017). Meta-Model of Servitization: The Integrative Profiling Approach. *Industrial Marketing Management, 60*, 17–32.

Bryson, J. R., & Daniels, P. W. (2010). Service Worlds: The "Services Duality" and the Rise of the "Manuservice" Economy. In P. Maglio, C. Kieliszewski, & J. Spohrer (Eds.), *Handbook of Service Science* (Service Science: Research and Innovations in the Service Economy). Boston: Springer.

Chia, R., & Holt, R. (2006). Strategy as Practical Coping: A Heideggerian Perspective. *Organization Studies, 27*(5), 635–655.

Daniels, P. W., & Bryson, J. R. (2002). Manufacturing Services and Servicing Manufacturing: Knowledge-Based Cities and Changing Forms of Production. *Urban Studies, 39*(5–6), 977–991.

Gadrey, J., & Delaunay, J.-C. (1992). *Services in Economic Thought: Three Centuries of Debate*. Boston: Kluwer.

Gebauer, H., Fleisch, E., & Friedli, T. (2005). Overcoming the Service Paradox in Manufacturing Companies. *European Management Journal, 23*(1), 14–26.

Gebauer, H., Ren, G. J., Valtakoski, A., & Reynoso, J. (2012). Service-Driven Manufacturing Provision, Evolution and Financial Impact of Services in Industrial Firms. *Journal of Service Management, 23*(1), 120–136.

Heinonen, K., & Strandvik, T. (2015). Customer-Dominant Logic: Foundations and Implications. *Journal of Services Marketing, 29*(6–7), 472–484.

Hill, T. P. (1977). On Goods and Services. *Review of Income and Wealth, 23*(4), 315–338.

Kohtamäki, M., Partanen, J., Parida, V., & Wincent, J. (2013). Non-linear Relationship between Industrial Service Offering and Sales Growth: The Moderating Role of Network Capabilities. *Industrial Marketing Management, 42*(8), 1374–1385.

Kohtamäki, M., Baines, T., Rabetino, R., & Bigdeli, A. Z. (Eds.). (2018). *Practices and Tools for Servitization. Managing Service Transition*. Cham: Palgrave Macmillan.

Kowalkowski, C., Kindstrom, D., Alejandro, T. B., Brege, S., & Biggemann, S. (2012). Service Infusion as Agile Incrementalism in Action. *Journal of Business Research, 65*(6), 765–772.

Kowalkowski, C., Gebauer, H., Kamp, B., & Parry, G. (2017). Servitization and Deservitization: Overview, Concepts, and Definitions. *Industrial Marketing Management, 60*, 4–10.

Lenka, S., Parida, V., Sjödin, D. R., & Wincent, J. (2018). Exploring the Microfoundations of Servitization: How Individual Actions Overcome Organizational Resistance. *Journal of Business Research, 88*, 328–336.

Leoni, L. (2015). *Servitization and Productization: Two Faces of the Same Coin?* Paper Presented at the 25th Annual RESER Conference – Innovative Services in the 21st Century, Copenhagen.

Levitt, T. (1972). Production-Line Approach to Service. *Harvard Business Review, 50*(5), 41–52.

Mastrogiacomo, L., Barravecchia, F., & Franceschini, F. (2019). A Worldwide Survey on Manufacturing Servitization. *International Journal of Advanced Manufacturing Technology, 103*, 3927–3942.

Mathieu, V. (2001). Service Strategies within the Manufacturing Sector: Benefits, Costs and Partnership. *International Journal of Service Industry Management, 12*(5), 451–475.

Møller, J. K. (2018). Service Infusion in Manufacturing and Corporate Strategies in the Service Solutions Market – Driving Forces and Components. In A. Scupola & L. Fuglsang (Eds.), *Services, Experiences and Innovation: Integrating and Extending Research*. Cheltenham: Edward Elgar.

Rabetino, R., Harmsen, W., Kohtamaki, M., & Sihvonen, J. (2018). Structuring Servitization-Related Research. *International Journal of Operations & Production Management, 38*(2), 350–371.

Sjödin, D., Parida, V., & Kohtamäki, M. (2019). Relational Governance Strategies for Advanced Service Provision: Multiple Paths to Superior Financial Performance in Servitization. *Journal of Business Research, 101*, 906–915.

Skålén, P., & Edvardsson, B. (2016). Transforming from the Goods to the Service-Dominant Logic. *Marketing Theory, 16*(1), 101–121.

Storbacka, K., Windahl, C., Nenonen, S. and Salonen, A. (2013). Solution business models: Transformation along four continua. *Industrial Marketing Management, 42*(5), 705–716. doi:10.1016/j.indmarman.2013.05.008.

Tukker, A. (2004). Eight Types of Product-Service System: Eight Ways to Sustainability? Experiences from SusProNet. *Business Strategy and the Environment, 13*(4), 246–260.

Vandermerwe, S., & Rada, J. (1988). Servitization of Business: Adding Value by Adding Services. *European Management Journal, 6*(4), 314–324.

Vargo, S. L., & Lusch, R. F. (2004). Evolving to a New Dominant Logic for Marketing. *Journal of Marketing, 68*(1), 1–17.

Vargo, S. L., & Lusch, R. F. (2008). Service-Dominant Logic: Continuing the Evolution. *Journal of the Academy of Marketing Science, 36*(1), 1–10.

Zeithaml, V. A., Parasuraman, A., & Berry, L. L. (1985). Problems and Strategies in Services Marketing. *Journal of Marketing, 49*(2), 33–46.

## Further Reading

Baines, T., & Lightfoot, H. (2013). *Made to Serve: How Manufacturers Can Compete Through Servitization and Product–Service Systems*. Chichester: Wiley.
Bryson, J. R., & Daniels, P. W. (2010). Service Worlds: The "Services Duality" and the Rise of the "Manuservice" Economy. In P. Maglio, C. Kieliszewski, & J. Spohrer (Eds.), *Handbook of Service Science. Service Science: Research and Innovations in the Service Economy*. Boston, MA: Springer.
Daniels, P. W., & Bryson, J. R. (2002). Manufacturing Services and Servicing Manufacturing: Knowledge-Based Cities and Changing Forms of Production. *Urban Studies, 39*(5–6), 977–991.
Gebauer, H., Fleisch, E., & Friedli, T. (2005). Overcoming the Service Paradox in Manufacturing Companies. *European Management Journal, 23*(1), 14–26.

## Useful Websites

http://andyneely.blogspot.com/2013/11/what-is-servitization.html.
https://www.emeraldgrouppublishing.com/realworldresearch/strategy_growth/what-is-servitization-of-manufacturing.htm.
https://implementconsultinggroup.com/servitisation/.

# Measuring Company Performance and Customer Satisfaction

13

**Key Themes**

- What measurement instruments have been developed to control and manage service businesses?
- How are measurement tools used by service firms?
- Measurement tools
- Measuring service performance
- Measuring customer satisfaction and marketing
- Benchmarking
- Innovation capability measure

Measurement plays a critical role in the everyday management of service businesses and in the development, implementation and adaptation of both strategy and operations. It also plays an important role in monitoring and enhancing the quality of the service experience and in the co-creation of service innovations. Measurement plays an important role in underpinning and informing the everyday and strategic management of service businesses. Reading a business is part of a strategic approach to management in which a firm continually observes the business to monitor and evaluate the relationships between strategy, operations and the production of value, or outcomes. This involves identifying areas for improvement that could lead to adjustments to

routines or everyday practices. This is a process of strategic reflexivity in which reading, including measurement, is a continual process supporting management practices.

Each chapter in this book contributes to understanding the ways in which service businesses develop and apply tools that are designed to measure performance, innovation and the evolution of the business. Nevertheless, it is important to focus on the ways in which service businesses develop and apply approaches to measurement as part of everyday business practices. This chapter explores the application of approaches to measurement and evaluation by service businesses. These include approaches to measuring service firms' key performance, particularly production performance, customer satisfaction and innovation capabilities. This chapter engages with the debates explored in Chap. 5 on service operations and productivity, Chap. 7 on service innovation and Chap. 8 on customer satisfaction by exploring operational measurement tools and explaining them in detail.

These company performance measurements are intended to measure failure and problems in service production and delivery, for example, how to handle queuing problems and complaints, but also the measurement of efficiency in production and delivery systems. The costs related to an increase in performance are also part of some business approaches to measurement. Running a service business is not just a matter of improving

**Electronic Supplementary Material** The online version of this chapter (https://doi.org/10.1007/978-3-030-52060-1_13) contains supplementary material, which is available to authorized users.

performance as the cost of any alteration must also be taken into consideration; service businesses must be profitable and sustainable. It is important to appreciate that measurement involves both marketing, including a focus on customers, and operations. On the one hand, quantified marketing and customer measurements are often explored in marketing textbooks (e.g. Palmer 2005; Lovelock and Wirtz 2011; Hollesen 2015) and these are mostly directed towards measuring customer satisfaction. On the other hand, production performance measurements tend to be explored in service operations textbooks (e.g. Wright and Race 2004; Johnston and Clark 2005).

This chapter will first present and discuss core instruments for measuring production performance. This is followed by a discussion of service quality, customer satisfaction and marketing performance measures. Finally, this chapter explores measurement tools intended to explore firms' innovation capabilities.

## 13.1   Measuring Production Performance

### 13.1.1  Capacity Planning and Yield Management

Services are traditionally considered to be labour intensive and this restricts the ability of firms to produce and deliver a certain amount of services at a given time. If a service firm cannot fulfil demand, then it loses business leading to dissatisfied customers. If a firm has unutilized overcapacity, then it also loses money as this overcapacity involves additional costs including salaries and other costs related to under-employed staff. It is difficult to balance service delivery with customer demand given variations in demand and it may be difficult to predict current and future demand. Therefore, the challenge for service businesses involves balancing decisions regarding capacity and utilization with actual and potential customer demand. Pricing is important and can be a means to regulate demand and this might enable a firm to balance capacity with

demand. Systematic approaches and tools to investigate and regulate the relationships between capacity and demand have been developed (Belobaba 1989; Adenso-Diaz and Gonzáles-Torres 2002). This approach has been conceptualized as a process of yield management (Kimes 1989; Berman 2005) or a process by which measurement and operational delivery tries to allocate capacity to certain type of customers at a given time. This section explores problems related to capacity planning and yield management including a discussion of measurement.

Capacity planning involves addressing alterations in service demand throughout the day and the week. This is particularly relevant for service businesses that absolutely must be produced at the moment of consumption and are unable to be stored. These services include restaurants, hotels, transportation services, call centres and medical clinics. Capacity planning is also relevant for lawyers and accountants, for example. Here it may be possible for firms to apply flexible approaches to staff management to try to equalize employee workloads. One implication being that accountants work exceptionally long hours towards the end of a tax or financial year as accounts need to be audited and approved.

Capacity must be planned, and the first step includes measuring demand, for example, counting the number of customers every hour or every day. Statistics and demand curves can then be created to inform operational decisions. One example is provided in Fig. 13.1 which highlights a peak in demand within a call centre.

In this example, there are several peaks making it difficult for a service business to optimize the service delivery process. Here the challenge involves developing an answer to the question: how many call centre operators should be employed per hour? The first observation is that customer demand peaks around lunch time—12:00–13:00. Call centre operators must work during this time and their lunch times must be scheduled around the lunchtime peak. There are relatively few calls during the first and last hour and thus call centre capacity can be reduced. This level of customer demand variation makes it difficult for a call centre to develop an optimum

**Fig. 13.1** Enquiries per hour in a call centre (number of calls per hour). (Source: Authors' own)

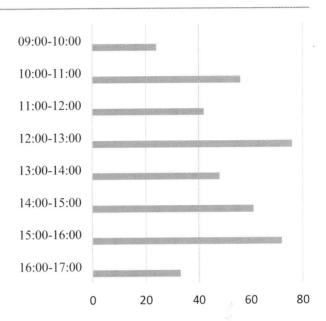

solution. There are perhaps three options for the operator:

1. Employ more staff during the peaks. This might be difficult given the problems of persuading employees to work for 60 minutes and then to take an unpaid break.
2. Link call centres together ensuring that over-capacity at one centre can be transferred automatically to the next available centre.
3. Ensure that some customers are dealt with by automated systems by filtering out customers who could be dealt with by some form of automated system.
4. Estimate the average demand during the day, but employees must expect extremely busy periods and times during which there is limited demand.

The key issue is to monitor demand and to employ call centre operatives on relatively flexible contracts. Call centre operatives need to meet key performance indicators including response times and the average time required to deal with each customer. There is thus a clear focus on productivity combined with the quality of the service experience (see Chaps. 5 and 8). An alternative strategy is to engage in nudges intended to try to persuade customers to change their behaviours, and to use the call centre during times of reduced average demand. This can be achieved by informing customers of waiting times and, during key demand peaks, trying to persuade them to engage with the company at another time or via another service delivery channel, for example, a chatbot.

Where there is a direct price for a service, for example, the number of guests in a restaurant then customers' behaviour can be influenced by price differentiation. The price can be reduced during hours or days with limited demand and increased during periods of peak demand. This leads to 'happy hours' with reduced prices in bars during the late afternoon and differentiated prices on flight travel and hotel rooms based on demand variations. Online retailers apply data analytics to predict demand altering prices to maximize profit as part of process of dynamic pricing known as surge pricing, demand pricing or time-based pricing. Pricing algorithms have been developed that challenge the relationship between product pricing, customer value and the pricing of competitor products (see Chap. 5, Sect. 5.3.2). Innovations in revenue management pricing systems have enabled companies, particularly in the hospitality and leisure industries, to link demand with alterations in pricing. This has led to dynamic pricing in which a provider instantly alters the pricing of a service or good as demand alters. Thus, prices will fall if there is a reduction in demand and will increase during times of peak demand. The integration of artificial intelligence with algorithmic pricing programmes has replaced human decision-making with automated systems that monitor demand and supply to facilitate dynamic pricing.

Dynamic pricing is one approach to yield management, or the process by which firms maximize revenue, through production planning. The aim is to reduce delivery costs by optimization focused on minimizing overcapacity as much as possible and increasing prices as much as possible. The latter is restricted by the customers' willingness to pay; they may, for example, engage in comparator pricing seeking the least cost approach. Which price customers are willing to pay and at which time can be calculated theoretically, but is very difficult to measure in practice? Competitors also alter prices regularly to optimize yields. A service company may engage in pricing experiments by lowering and increasing prices at different hours during the day or over a week and then measure impacts on customer demand and revenues including the ratio between costs of service delivery and profitability. Service businesses can also ask customers about how much they might be willing to pay for services at different times. This may be a more laborious process. Such measurements can only be applied reasonably and only for services that are paid directly including airplane tickets and hotel rooms. Developments in dynamic pricing, using algorithmic pricing programmes, have transformed the ways in which online service businesses manage the relationship between price, demand and operations. A service might be provided free as it is included as part of a much more complex service package, for example, an online or telephone ticket service for booking tickets to some event. In this case, a price experiment regarding the delivery of this type of service will not measure customers' reactions to waiting times. A survey might, however, be developed to assess the waiting times that different customer segments would find acceptable.

Another technique for increasing revenue involves reducing the price of a service. This might be a single service that is paid for, or it might involve a service that is included as part of a larger service packet or bundle. That will reduce profit levels per customer, but it might also create an increased tolerance for longer service delivery waiting times because customers perceive that they are purchasing a discounted service and the expectation is that this will involve longer waiting times. A service firm can, therefore, decrease demand, particularly during periods of peak demand, and reduce delivery costs related to a reduction in delivery capacity. The aim is to try to spread demand, avoiding peaks, resulting in a reduction in service delivery costs. This is an optimization process.

Several effects must be taken into consideration and assessed in calculating the preconditions for, and revenue effects of, changing service delivery capacity. These preconditions and effects are:

- Customers' price and waiting tolerance, and changes in that caused by other service companies' offers
- The costs of expanding capacity, or saved costs by reducing capacity
- Lost revenue from customers leaving the firm permanently in response to an increase in waiting times. This results in an erosion of a firm's client base and a reduction in customer loyalty
- The administrative costs of managing a differentiated price system

Many of the capacity problems can be overcome by digitizing service delivery processes (Wirtz et al. 2018). Self-serviced IT systems have much greater capacity compared to labour-intensive systems, and peak loads are normally not a problem. Furthermore, such capital-intensive systems are much cheaper as they have reduced variable costs. They come with other advantages including reductions in the costs of obtaining and analysing detailed knowledge about every service transaction. Such systems produce a continual stream of data and data analytics can be applied to identify patterns to inform operational decisions. This highlights the enhanced importance of big data and the ability of service firms to monitor and modify service delivery. Nevertheless, not all services can be digitized including, for example, restaurant meals and live theatrical performances.

For services where capacity is difficult and expensive to alter, for example, hotel rooms and airplane seats, companies have developed a system based on overbooking. They sell more beds and seats than they have on the understanding that not all people will arrive. The advantage of this is a full utilization of capacity and thereby increased revenue. In addition, a service company may even benefit from selling the same room or seat twice as those who fail to utilize the service may still have to pay, for example, a hotel room or a flight reservation. This approach only works when the exact number of predicated non-arrivals occurs. If the number of non-arrivals is less than predicted, then the service company is in difficulty. They have more customers than capacity. A calculation is then made regarding losing customers, decreased customer satisfaction and loyalty. One solution is to pay compensation (e.g. airline companies) or to transfer customers to a competitor. All this adds additional costs that must be weighed against the increased income obtained by selling all seats or rooms and perhaps occasionally obtaining double payment. The management of services involved in overbooking requires measurement of the following variables:

- The probability of the number of customers who will not show up at a given time and place.
- The costs of procuring alternative services for customers including paying exemplary damages.
- The combined value of lost customers, customer satisfaction and loyalty including possible impacts on public relations. Furthermore, overbooking creates complaints and often results in aggressive behaviour to employees from customers who have booked and paid to receive a service but are unable to obtain this at the specified time and place. Employees may react by working to rule impacting on produc-

tivity, an increase in absences related to sickness and enhanced labour turnover. The financial impacts may be difficult to measure, but these wider impacts must be taken into consideration in the design of service businesses that adopt overbooking strategies. These businesses must also balance the tension between business efficiency, customer satisfaction and responsible business behaviour.

### 13.1.2  Queue and Waiting Measures and Management

There is a continuum of service businesses. On the one side, are capital-intensive businesses that apply technological solutions to cope with balancing supply and demand. On the other hand, are labour-intensive businesses in which it is difficult to avoid queues and waiting lines emerging during times of peak demand, for example, self-service restaurants, call centres, car rentals and retail. A service company can investigate when and how such queues and waiting lines emerge. Techniques can be developed to make queuing more acceptable for customers reducing customer dissatisfaction levels. This was especially the case during Covid-19 when socially distancing had to be applied to the management of retail demand.

People do not want to wait in line in queues. They become stressed and dissatisfied and may decide to purchase services from another provider. Sometimes people turn around and leave when they see a queue, for example, in a supermarket or restaurant. Nevertheless, queuing frequently cannot be avoided.

It is important for a service company to explore acceptable customer queuing times. The company should attempt to reduce waiting time to this level, but this increases the costs of service delivery. For example, opening another supermarket checkout involves transferring an employee from one task to another. Furthermore, different customers will have different perceptions regarding acceptable waiting times. It is difficult to avoid the negative impacts of queuing and this involves both optimizing service delivery systems combined with queue management. On the one hand, the service business must balance customer dissatisfaction with increased costs. On the other hand, queues provide an opportunity to engage with customers and to provide distractions that might enhance sales.

A service business can measure and calculate when queuing occurs and acceptable customer waiting times. This can be measured when queues occur including how many people are waiting and for how long. A queue, for example, in a supermarket or at a hotel reception, can be monitored and additional employees deployed to deal with peak demand, or technological solutions developed, for example, automated check in procedures at a hotel. For digitized services, an algorithm can be developed that automatically monitors demand and supply and tries to optimize delivery. In both cases, it is important to monitor when people leave the queue without completing a service transaction. This is a major problem for e-commerce retailers as customers select items and add them to their baskets, but never complete the transaction. All service businesses involving customer queuing must develop an appropriate approach to measuring and managing queues and in enhancing the customer experience of queuing.

There are theoretical and mathematical queuing models that can calculate when queues occur and waiting times. Let us consider one example based on calculating queue waiting times at supermarket check out counters. The probability of a customer waiting in a queue is:

$$Pw = \frac{m \times n}{c}$$

$Pw$ = Probability of waiting
$m$ = Average number of minutes it takes to serve one customer
$n$ = Average number of customers per minute
$c$ = Number of counters

An example is as follows. One counter is open ($c$) and it takes 2 minutes to serve one customer ($m$) and 3 customers arrive every minute ($n$):

$$Pw = \frac{2 \times 3}{1} = 6$$

Customers will continue to wait, and the waiting line will expand exponentially. Six counters would be required to avoid queues forming. Redundant capacity will occur if more than six counters are provided.

This calculation is about balancing cost by increasing capacity by opening more service lines versus loss of revenue as customers decide to leave a queue and perhaps obtain services from a competitor. This relationship between queue waiting, capacity and the identification of a balance point can be graphed (Fig. 13.2). Optimal capacity occurs where the missing income curve and the additional cost curve intersect.

There is a formula for calculating when an extension in capacity is profitable when the cost of extending the capacity is less than the missed income:

$$\frac{a}{b \times N} < 1$$

When the reduction of waiting time exceeds missed customer income by customers deciding to leave the queue:

$$(c \times N) > (b \times N)$$

$a$ = Marginal cost of capacity expansion (e.g. opening an additional supermarket check-out counter)
$b$ = Missing income per customer leaving the company
$c$ = The marginal reduction of waiting time per customer (e.g. less waiting time in counter queue)
$N$ = Number of customers having their waiting times reduced

There is an important distinction to be made between actual versus perceived queuing time. Customers waiting to be served require companies to try to manipulate actual time by altering customers' perceptions of the actual length of time that they have spent queuing. These techniques involve distractions to try to ensure that those waiting ignore the actual amount of time spent waiting and instead are distracted by some experience. This

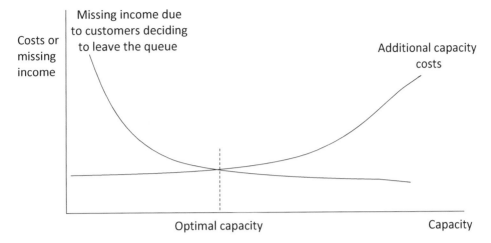

**Fig. 13.2** Determining the balance point between queue waiting and capacity. (Source: Authors' own)

includes companies trying to increase customers' tolerance for waiting by deploying a number of psychological mechanisms including:

- Management of waiting numbers
  A customer can be provided with a number ensuring that they no longer need to stand in line. This enhances the customer experience and waiting may become more comfortable and therefore acceptable. In a telephone queue, the service company may offer to return the customer's call whilst retaining their place in the queue.
- Reducing customer sight lines as they queue
  This involves ensuring that a queue does not take the form of a single long line but is designed to restrict customer sight lines. This may reduce the perceived length of the queue.
- Information provision
  Service businesses must manage customer expectations regarding queuing. Part of this task involves providing information regarding waiting times. This type of information provision may increase customer tolerance levels encouraging customers to continue to queue. Information provision makes people feel safer and more in control. Nevertheless, notification of very long waiting times will encourage customers to leave the queue.
- Entertainment
  Provision of entertainment, for example, music or visuals on screens, whilst people

wait may make them overlook the time spent queuing. In this case, entertainment is designed to distract or divert customers' attention from the experience of queuing. However, it might also distract as people may leave the queue to avoid the entertainment. This type of diversion also involves placing merchandise adjacent to the queue and signage. For some service businesses, queues provide an opportunity to engage with customers as they represent an unusual time when customers face the same direction. This provides an important opportunity to communicate messages to customers.

- Provision of complaint personnel
  Employees may 'work' the queue to distract customers from the queuing experience by diverting their attention. In this case, customers may complain about the length of time spent queuing to employees. The danger is that this type of employment is not attractive as the role involves the management of unhappy customers. This type of human interaction between service providers and customers may also be used to educate customers to reduce service delivery times. At airports, employees inform customers in queues about preparations they should make before reaching a check-in point.

The key issue for a service firm is to balance the cost of service delivery, as measured by staffing levels, against loss of income as frustrated customers decide to leave the queue without completing transactions. One solution is to hire part-time assistants to cover peak times. This is only a partial solution as such employees may be less experienced and will perhaps work at a slower rate compared to full-time employees.

### 13.1.3 Balanced Scorecards

One of the most important generic instruments that has been used to measure company performance over the last decades has been the balanced scorecard approach (Kaplan and Norton 1996). This approach has also been applied to services. A balanced scorecard approach tries to develop a holistic account of an organization ensuring that productivity enhancement occurs across an organization. The balanced scorecard is a tool to measure how close a company comes to implementing its strategies and business goals. Several quantitative measures and several qualitative assessments are included and placed in a matrix. A balanced scorecard is not a single index summarizing all variables, but rather it is a series of measures of the important factors or goals which best reflects a company's strategy and business goals. The first step is, therefore, to define which factors or variables should be included in a firm's balanced scorecard. Kaplan and Norton (1996) identified four performance areas which should be included:

1. Financial performance
2. Customer relations
3. Internal business processes
4. Innovation, learning and growth

Within these four areas a single company can define which variables and factors it wants to include. The balanced scorecard approach is a tool that supports a company by providing a set of measures that management can use to assess how far a firm is meeting its stated goals. It is not a type of scientific prediction index that will lead to theoretically pre-defined and guar-

anteed results. The selection of variables and factors should be decided carefully based on the identification of which factors are most critical for the company's business success. These factors should be measurable, either quantitatively or as a qualitative description of the state of the company. The metrics included within a balanced scorecard must be identified using a SMART approach. They must be Specific, Measurable, Achievable, Realistic and Timely. They must not include aspects of business performance that cannot be measured, and the SMART metrics must be closely aligned with a company's strategic plan. It is worth noting that this approach should not dominate the everyday management of a business as critical processes might not be fully reflected in a set of quantifiable measures. Thus, it is important to remember that not everything can be measured used SMART metrics.

The factors included in a balanced scorecard reflect different operational processes and stakeholder interests. All companies must satisfy owners, customers and employees. Sometimes these three different types of stakeholder group can be satisfied by a company performing across the same set of SMART metrics, but often there may be divergent interests leading to conflict. Different factors and variables in the balanced scorecard approach promote different stakeholders' interests. A company then must decide which factors are the most important to be included. That is why it is meaningless to combine all factors in one index. Creating a single index would be possible, but it would hide more than it would reveal (Table 13.1).

A balanced scorecard can be created for individual employees and managers to measure their individual performance or, for managers, their department's performance. The measurement results can be used to discuss and adjust employees' and managers' tasks and work performance. These alterations should be designed to ensure that the company comes closer to realizing its strategic and business goals. Safari (2016) developed a measurement tool that quantitatively can measure individuals' and teams' performance. The tool is based on identifying

**Table 13.1**  Balanced scorecard example: An IT service company's targets and measures for a given period

| Performance area | Strategic goal | Measure | Target |
|---|---|---|---|
| Financial performance | Saving costs | Expenses as % of the budget | 90% |
| | Initiatives to save costs | Number of suggestions for cost savings | 2 per employee |
| | Use a specific cost sheet to obtain an overview of the costs | Number of employees using the sheet | 75% |
| Customer relations | Identify customer needs | Number of new customer needs reported to the innovation and development department | 2 per employee |
| | Increased efficiency in saving customer problems using hotlines | Reduced answer time | Answering time reduced by 10% |
| | Increase customer satisfaction | Customer satisfaction survey | >15% increased customer satisfaction |
| Internal business processes | Provide a reliable IT architecture | Number of service calls related to IT architecture | >5% reduction of these calls |
| | Action regarding software training and knowledge base | Number of inquiries for new training activities | >1 per employee |
| | Employees handling own stress and work environment situation | Work satisfaction survey | >10% increased satisfaction score |
| | Reduction of internal procedure failures | Number of reported failures | >20% reduction |
| Innovation, learning and growth | Leader training development with mutual exchange of experiences | Leaders attending internal training courses | >30% of the leaders attending |
| | Innovative ideas | Number of ideas for innovations from employees | >20 ideas |
| | Investment in innovation projects | Investment in new innovation projects | >100,000 € |
| | Information from projects stored in a learning database | Number of experiences from projects stored | >50 |

Source: Authors' own

and setting target goals which are predefined for a period and an employee. The tool is an index that measures whether the employee, within a designated period, has under- or over-performed. These target goals are expressed in measurable SMART terms. Table 13.2 is an example of how this type of approach, known as a credit grid, is created for an employee involved in personal customer handling in a retail bank. The credits are measured as the number of work tasks fulfilled over a period. For example, if an employee, within a designated period, has agreed 180 loan applications and the agreed goal was 150 then there is a credit of +30 and an over-performance of 20%. The credit points of all work tasks are then summarized creating the

employee's total credit points for a designated period. This calculation might be used to calculate bonuses recognizing over-performance.

Such individual performance measures are widely applied by service companies to provide SMART measures to support salary systems. It can motivate employees and managers to enhance performance but within the parameters set by the company's strategy. Such systems have, however, been criticized by employees and trade unions for being very Tayloristic (cf. Frederick Taylor's famous industrial employee management system) and related to enhanced employee stress levels, illness and attrition. They might also be considered as an approach in which employees are very closely monitored

**Table 13.2** Individual performance credit point grid for a bank employee

| Performance category | Activity | Credit points |
|---|---|---|
| Payment-personal banking | Bill payment | 5 |
| | Personal loan payment | −10 |
| | Credit card payment | 8 |
| | Mortgage payment | 22 |
| Investigation-personal account | Pre-authorized payment | 2 |
| | Charge-back | −5 |
| | Monthly statement review | 15 |
| Errors/defects, returns, reworks) | | −25 |
| TOTAL | | 12 |

Source: After: Safari (2016, p. 215)

**Table 13.3** Examples of service quality improvement costs

| Internal costs | External costs | Quality measurement costs |
|---|---|---|
| Reorganizing service processes. Facility downtime. Higher employee turnover. Loss of productivity. | Service guarantees. Possible loss of income from customers who leave because of service changes. | Time and money spent on quality investigations. Employees spending time on providing information for quality measurement. |

Source: Authors' own

and appraised. It is important that a company does not become too distracted by SMART measures. The key issue is overall performance including the relationship between service delivery costs and profitability. There is another critical issue to consider. This is the provision of services that differentiate one company from another and perhaps one service worker from another. There are many aspects of service employment and service co-creation that are perhaps impossible to measure (see Chaps. 8 and 9). These more intangible aspects must not be overlooked as they perhaps underpin performance measured by any SMART metrics.

## 13.2 Measuring Quality, Marketing Performance and Customer Satisfaction

Customer satisfaction and sales performance are connected to the concept of service quality. Consequently, their measurement is often conceptualized as measures of service quality. Service quality and customer satisfaction are central to marketing practice and theory. Sustainable competitive advantage within service businesses is founded upon delivering high quality services creating satisfied customers. Customer satisfaction is related to customer retention and loyalty and underpins profitability, market share and the relationship between investment and return. Service quality is also related to cost and profit (see Chap. 8 and the quality of service experiences). Improving service quality may increase service delivery costs and perhaps the key issue is the relationship between additional costs versus any increase in revenue. Service quality can also be considered as part of an analysis of competitors' processes and products. A service firm should perhaps not provide a quality that is better than competitors, at least not if this difference is not reflected in higher prices. Such considerations must be reflected in measures of service quality and customer satisfaction.

There are many costs related to the enhancement of service quality. These are both tangible, or easy-to-measure, and more intangible costs and related impacts. In Table 13.3 some of these potential additional costs are considered.

In this section we explore some of the most common measurement instruments of service quality and customer satisfaction.

### 13.2.1 Dimensions in Measuring Service Quality and Customer Satisfaction

Before measurement, service quality must be defined operationally or, in other words, a framework must be developed enabling a company to measure quality quantitatively. The first decision

**Table 13.4**  Service quality dimensions and how they can be measured

| Dimension | |
|---|---|
| Construction quality | How the service is constructed and produced? Services and deliveries must be specified and any reduction in quality reflects deviations from the specified quality. *Example: Airplanes should not be delayed. Measured from arrival times.* |
| Process quality | Employees' attitudes and behaviour in customer interactions or customers' experience of the firm's website. *Example: Maximum 10% of customer calls to the firm's hotline should lead to customers not receiving a satisfactory answer to his/her problem. Measured by a short questionnaire and recording of telephone conversations (qualitative measurement).* |
| Result quality | The customer is generally satisfied with the service. *Example: Is the customer satisfied with the insurance he/she has and the insurance company? Measured by general customer surveys.* |
| Relative quality | Customers' satisfaction with the services with price taken into consideration. How customers assess this service firm and its services compared to competitors? *Example: Car repairs. Is the repair/ service including customer handling and information about pricing and what has been repaired satisfactory? Is the price fair? Would the customer prefer to use an alternative provider? Measured by questionnaire to customers or measuring the proportion of repeat customers.* |

Source: Authors' own

**Table 13.5**  Business services: Stakeholders in customer firms

| Stakeholder | |
|---|---|
| The contract holder | The customer, a firm, commissions, contracts and pays for a service that they have decided to outsource. The general manager is responsible for the firm's business model including balancing quality over cost. |
| The purchaser | Often the service contract is negotiated and administered by a departmental manager, or a specialist procurement function within a firm. The decision is one about balancing risk versus cost. |
| The user | Customers, in other words the firm's employees, use the service, for example, the canteen or personnel administration. They want the best service, for example, quality food at an affordable price. |
| Customer of the company that has outsourced the function/ task/ activity. | Customers of the firm that have outsourced the service also experience the outputs of these business services, for example, the cleanliness of an office or the service quality of a call centre. |

Source: Authors' own

that must be made concerns what a company wants to measure. There are choices here. A company can measure the quality and satisfaction of a single service, service quality and satisfaction of a customer or customer attitudes towards the service firm—or all of these. Measurement instruments have been developed that measure different aspects of quality and customer satisfaction (Table 13.4).

A decision needs to be made regarding the most appropriate individual to assess service quality. Sometimes the customer cannot be easily

identified, for example, in the provision of business services. Business service providers, including the provision of outsourced work canteens, office cleaning, or call centres or personnel administration (including pay and pensions), have many possible different stakeholders (Table 13.5). The selection of which group to include in any assessment of service quality is a difficult decision; all stakeholders' satisfaction and quality assessments are important for customer firms and for providers of outsourced business services.

A debate needs to occur regarding the definition of each dimension included in any measurement of service quality. A service firm will not be able to assess all quality dimensions and should not attempt to do so as the rewards will not reflect costs, including time, of this type of appraisal. A service firm should, therefore, only attempt to measure and enhance quality up to an optimal point defined by the point at which income from improved service quality exceeds the costs of

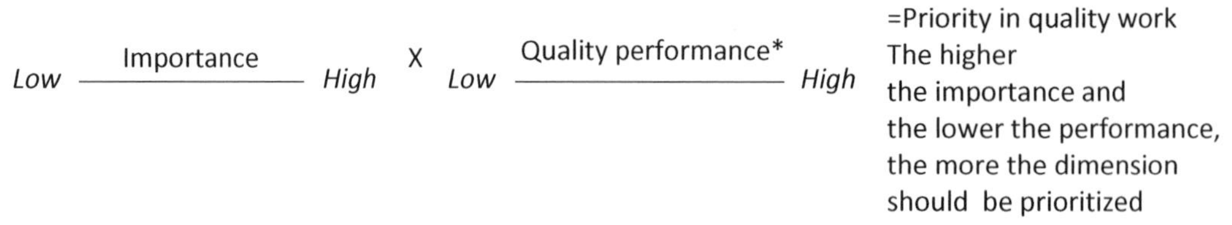

Low ——— Importance ——— High    X    Low ——— Quality performance* ——— High    =Priority in quality work
The higher
the importance and
the lower the performance,
the more the dimension
should be prioritized

**Fig. 13.3** Priority in service quality work: Each quality dimension.
Note: * In customer assessment and possibly objective measures (e.g. waiting time); perhaps compared to competitors' performance. (Source: Authors' own)

improving quality (Chap. 8). This can be calculated when a firm knows the additional expenditure required to enhance quality and is then able to calculate the impacts on profitability. Any attempt to enhance quality must balance the importance of each measure of service quality against performance (Fig. 13.3).

## 13.2.2 Mapping Service Quality and Customer Satisfaction

Many methods and tools for measuring service quality and customer satisfaction exist (see also Forsyth 1999; Bourne and Neely 2003; Franceschini et al. 2009). In is important to appreciate the interrelationships between service quality and customer satisfaction. Both customer satisfaction and service quality are multidimensional constructs requiring similar measures (Sureshchandar et al. 2002). In the following we explore the most important and widely used measurement instruments.

**Total Service Quality Indexes**
Different indexes that combine service quality dimensions can be constructed. In Table 13.6 an example of such an index of service quality is provided which includes the importance of each indicator and performance for a provider of broadband services. The index includes economic performance and employee satisfaction (which is important for customers' experience of the service encounter (cf. Chap. 8)).

**The Service Journey**
This is an instrument to systematically assess how a typical customer experiences service delivery

with all the touch points that they might have with a service firm. This experience is seen as a journey during which the customer becomes aware of the problem which the service will solve, to the solution of this problem or, in the worst-case scenario, there is perhaps no solution. The customer's journey can be drawn as a model using a blueprint technique (Bitner et al. 2008). This tool can be applied by a service firm to understand and re-design the service delivery system. It can be used as a framework to formulate questions in customer surveys and to collect experiences from employees about each customer touch point. Customers can also be asked to experience the journey in a laboratory-like situation. Figure 13.4 is an illustrative example of such a service journey model based on a railway company. At each touch point the customer can be satisfied, which brings them closer to becoming a satisfied loyal customer, or they can be dissatisfied encouraging them to find an alternative mode of transportation.

**Surveys**
Service firms often use standardized surveys to ask customers about service quality. We all have experienced several such surveys. They typically ask actual customers to comment on a series of concrete and detailed points, often just after the service has been delivered (Fig. 13.5).

These questionnaires can be varied in many ways. They are either given to customers at the end of the service delivery process or sent to customers after the service event has concluded either by e-mail or via smartphones. A problem is the reliability of these customer surveys. People receive many service quality questionnaires and there are low response rates. There is a risk that only the most dissatisfied customers respond, and

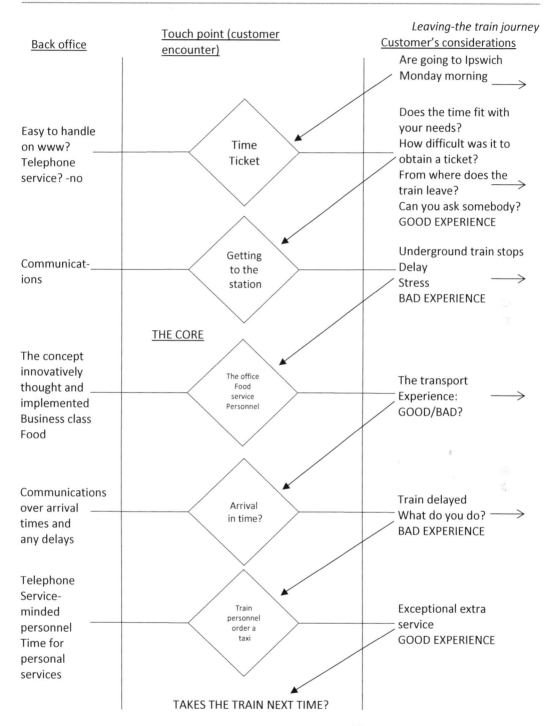

**Fig. 13.4** Service journey with touchpoints. Example a train journey from London to Ipswich. (Source: Authors' own)

**Table 13.6**  Total quality index for a broadband provider

| Weight (importance) | | Indicators | | Performance measured points |
|---|---|---|---|---|
| y1 | 30 | Economy | Achieved budget total | a1 |
| | | | Return for the year | a2 |
| | | | Change in value from last year | a3 |
| | | | Income per employee | a4 |
| y2 | 45 | Service | Installation precision, time delays | b1 |
| | | | Fault in deliveries, numbers | b2 |
| | | | Corporate image vs other providers | b3 |
| | | | Customer service centre, number of enquiries | b4 |
| | | | Customer service centre, waiting time | b5 |
| | | | Online service centre, number of enquiries | b6 |
| | | | Number of faults reported by customers | b7 |
| | | | Customer complaints, number | b8 |
| y3 | 25 | Employee satisfaction | Number of work accidents | c1 |
| | | | Support from supervisor (qualitative measure) | c2 |
| | | | Team spirit (qualitative measure) | c3 |
| | | | Sick leave days per working hour | c4 |

Source: Adapted and Developed from Edvardsson, Thomasson and Øvretveit (1994, p. 189)
Note: Index values = $[y1 \times (\sum a1 - a4)] + [y2 \times (\sum b1 - b8)] + [y3 \times (\sum c1 - c4)]$

perhaps the over-satisfied, extremely loyal, customers are also more likely to respond.

## Web-Based Satisfaction Scoring Platforms

There exist many Web-based review platforms where people can evaluate service quality and service experiences, both quantitatively via standard questions based on categories and qualitatively by providing comments (see also Chaps. 3, 4 and 11 for digitalisation tendencies in services). These may be provided on the service provider's website, or via a third-party platform. Often service firms are given overall scores enabling potential clients to compare one provider with another. These third-party review platforms include TripAdvisor for hotels and restaurants and Trustpilot for customer services.

These platforms are business models in their own right generating revenue from linking customers with service providers (see Chap. 3). It is important that the revenue-based nature of these operations is considered in any assessment of their ability to provide an independent assessment of the quality of a service firm's products. Customers provide feedback on service providers for free and the review platforms play an increas-

ingly important role in influencing consumer decision-making. Customers can easily access and explore these online reviews to compare with different levels of service quality provided by different firms.

These review platforms do not provide a completely objective and balanced review of service quality. There are problems with response bias as well as the possibilities of false or fake reviews. False reviews might be provided by employees of the service provider or by rival companies. Often service firms are able to comment on individual reviews and these responses may influence customer assessments.

## Focus Groups

A focus group is a qualitative method intended to obtain information about customers' impressions of a service firm's service quality. A service firm can invite a small number of customers, preferably about eight to ten, to discuss service quality and their experiences of a firm. The customers are, for example, asked to discuss some good and some bad service experiences with this service firm and perhaps to compare with other service experiences that were extremely good or extremely bad. A focus group should develop

Extremely unsatisfied                                                                Extremely satisfied

| 1 | 2 | 3 | 4 | 5 | 6 | 7 | 8 | 9 | 10 |

Assess the following (extremeley unsatisfied to extremely satisfied):

1. The reservation process

2. Start of the rental

      a. Waiting time before you reached the counter

      b. Helpfulness of our staff

      c. The explanation of charges and fees you received

3. The vehicle

      a. The make and model of vehicle you received

      b. The cleanliness of the vehicle

4. Vehicle return

      a. The signage to the return location

      b. Waiting time to be served

      c. The helpfulness of our agent

      d. Your charges were as expected

(General question: extremely unlikely to extremely likely)

5. Based on this rental, how likely are you to recommend XX to a friend or colleague?

Extremely unlikely                                                                   Extremely likely

| 1 | 2 | 3 | 4 | 5 | 6 | 7 | 8 | 9 | 10 |

**Fig. 13.5** Example of a service quality and customer satisfaction questionnaire: Car rental company XX. Note: All questions should be answered on a scale from 1 to 10. (Source: Authors' own)

into a conversation amongst customers and during this discussion the customers influence and often determine the structure of the conversation. The focus group organizer is only able to guide or shape the discussion rather than completely control it. Focus groups are recorded and transcribed and then analysed using qualitative approaches based on coding and the identification of key themes.

The advantage of a focus group discussion compared to a standardized survey is that a service firm can acquire a detailed understanding of quality problems including identifying customers' criteria for good service quality. There is always the possibility that quality issues not identified by the service firm emerge during focus group discussions.

**Critical Incidents and Service Quality**

Critical incidents are events or occurrences where a service delivery fails in some way or some problem is avoided. All service firms should identify, monitor and explore critical incidents as they occur during the service co-creation process.

Employees involved in an event must provide a detailed account of the incident. A firm must explore the origins of any potential service quality failure and learn to avoid them. A critical incident could, for example, involve an accountancy firm failing to identify an account irregularity, or failing to meet an expected deadline. Some critical incidents are so critical that they threaten the continued existence of the service business.

Critical incidents must be considered as the outcome of a set of processes which must be analysed to identify what, where and how the problem emerged. This involves a process of tracing back the processes and the ways in which they worked to produce a critical incident in service delivery. The key point of the critical incidence approach is to identify what occurred to ensure that any possible reoccurrence can be avoided. This might involve alterations to employee training combined with adaptations to everyday service delivery routines, or everyday practices.

## Benchmarking

Often a service firm, or a department within a service firm (e.g. a bank branch), is measured and benchmarked against other similar service firms or departments. Benchmarking against other service firms, particularly competitors, is intended to challenge a service firm's existing services to enhance service quality. A key issue is to highlight, develop and refine differentiation in the marketplace by product and process. Benchmarking can be used as the basis for quality improvements and to optimize service quality. The service quality of a service firm should meet that of comparable competitors but should not be significantly higher. This is to highlight the importance of product and process segmentation by price and quality. The balance between price and quality determines profitability.

Benchmarking the internal departments of a service business is intended to inspire, encourage and sometimes force each department to enhance their service quality and customer satisfaction rates. This should be undertaken without increasing costs. Productivity within each department could also increase through benchmarking.

## SERVQUAL

A much-used benchmarking measure of relative service quality, or the service quality of a service firm in relation to its competitors, is the SERVQUAL scale. This was developed by Parasuraman, Zeithaml and Berry (1988). This scale measures service gaps, for example, where a service firm provides a lower or higher perceived service quality than its competitors.

The SERVQUAL scale is based on a survey requesting customers to provide details about their experiences of a service firm. Customers are asked to provide feedback on a series of service quality and customer satisfaction variables. The SERVQUAL method is divided into two measures. First, an expectation section which measures how important each variable is for the customer. Second, a perception section which measures how the customer assesses this service firm's performance against each variable. This tool is constructed to measure service quality gaps or how the perception of the actual quality lives up to the interviewees' expectations. The actual service quality may be lower, similar or higher than customer expectations. A third measure might be added, namely how customers assess competitors' services compared to the service firm under examination. This could be achieved by asking interviewees to indicate their perception of competitors' service quality (the B-score column in Table 13.7).

The SERVQUAL tool as it was developed by, Parasuraman, Zeithaml and Berry (1988), includes five dimensions (Table 13.7). On each dimension, several variables are measured, and the interviewee is asked to assess each variable on a 7-point scale where 1 is 'strongly disagree' and 7 is 'strongly agree'. The interviewee should answer questions regarding their expectation of the service in general and then explore their actual perceptions. Each answer is scored from 1 to 7. A service firm can then calculate the gap between each service variable in terms of the relationship between expected and perceived outcomes. This highlights whether the perceived quality variable was given a higher or lower score compared to customer expectations. A total quality score gap can then be calculated.

**Table 13.7** SERVQUAL: Dimensions, variables and scores

| Expectations to XY (any *service field*, e.g. banking, cleaning) companies | A.Score (1–7) *How important is this?* | Perceptions of ZW's service (any *company* within the chosen service field) | B.Score (1–7) *How does ZW perform?* | Gap score B–A |
|---|---|---|---|---|
| *Tangibles* | | | | |
| v1 XY firms should have up-to-date equipment | A1 | ZW has up-to-date equipment | B1 | B1–A1 |
| v2 XY firms' physical facilities should be visually appealing | A2 | ZW's physical facilities are visually appealing | B2 | B2–A2 |
| v3 XY firms' employees should be well dressed and appear well dressed | A3 | ZW's employees are well dressed and appear well dressed. | B3 | B3–A3 |
| v4 The appearance of the physical facilities of XY firm should be in keeping with the type of services provided | A4 | The appearance of ZW's physical facilities is in keeping with the type of services provided | B4 | B4–A3 |
| *Reliability* | | | | |
| v5 When XY firms promise to do something in a certain time, they should do so | A5 | When ZW promises to do some-thing in a certain time, they do so | B5 | B5–A5 |
| v6 When customers have problems, a XY firm should show a sincere interest in solving them | A6 | When you have problems, ZW shows a sincere interest in solving them | B6 | B6–A6 |
| v7 XY firms should perform the service right the first time | A7 | ZW performs the service right the first time | B7 | B7–A7 |
| v8 XY firms should provide their services at the time they promised | A8 | ZW provides their services at the time they promised | B8 | B8–A8 |
| v9 XY firms should keep their records accurately | A9 | ZW keeps their records accurately | B9 | B9–A9 |
| *Responsiveness* | | | | |
| v10 Employees of XY firms should tell customers when services will be performed | A10 | Employees of ZW tell customers when services will be performed | B10 | B10–A10 |
| v11 Employees of XY firms should give prompt services to customers | A11 | Employees of ZW firm give prompt services to customers | B11 | B11–A11 |
| v12 Employees of XY firms will always be willing to help customers | A12 | Employees of ZW firm are always willing to help customers | B12 | B12–A12 |
| v13 Employees of XY firm will never be too busy to respond to customer requests | A13 | Employees of ZW are never too busy to respond to customer requests | B13 | B13–A13 |
| *Assurance* | | | | |
| v14 Customers should be able to trust employees of XY firm | A14 | You can trust employees of ZW | B14 | B14–A14 |
| v15 Customers should be able to feel safe in their transactions with XY firms | A15 | You feel safe in your transactions with ZW | B15 | B15–A15 |
| v16 XY firms' employees should be polite | A16 | ZW's employees are polite | B16 | B16–A16 |
| v17 XY firms' employees should get adequate support from their employers to do their jobs well | A17 | Employees get adequate support from ZW to do their jobs well | B17 | B17–A17 |
| *Empathy* | | | | |

(continued)

**Table 13.7** (continued)

| Expectations to XY (any *service field*, e.g. banking, cleaning) companies | A.Score (1–7) *How important is this?* | Perceptions of ZW's service (any *company* within the chosen service field) | B.Score (1–7) *How does ZW perform?* | Gap score B–A |
|---|---|---|---|---|
| v18 XY firms should be expected to give customers individual attention<br>v19 Employees of XY firms should be expected to give customers individual attention<br>V20 Employees of XY firms should be expected to know what the needs of their customers are<br>v21 XY firms should be expected to have their customers' best interests at heart<br>v22 XY firms should be expected to have operating hours convenient to all their customers | A18<br>A19<br>A20<br>A21<br>A22 | ZW gives you individual attention<br>Employees of ZW give you individual attention<br>Employees of ZW do know what your needs are<br>ZW does have your best interests at heart<br>ZW have operating hours convenient to all their customers | B18<br>B19<br>B20<br>B21<br>B22 | B18–A18<br>B19–A19<br>B20–A20<br>B21–A21<br>B22–A22 |
| **Total score** | $\sum$ A1–22 | | $\sum$ B1–22 | $\sum$ [(B1–22)–(A1–22)] |

Source: Authors' own

It is not only the size of the gaps between expectations and perceptions that are important. The results must also be seen in relation to the size of the expectation score. In principle, interviewees are free to expect that a service firm provides the highest service quality on all variables; however, they are supposed to provide realistic expectations. Another problem with SERVQUAL is that price is absent from the analysis of the appraisal of service quality. A service firm, applying the SERVQUAL scale to improve service quality, may fail to retain or attract customers because of price differences between competitor products. There is a risk that, despite improved service quality with perhaps the same pricing, customers decide to purchase from another firm offering similar services, but at a lower price. An ideal scale should also ask customers about pricing and the relationship between expectations and perceptions.

## 13.3 Innovation Capability Measures

Service innovation is important for the development of service firms (Chap. 7), and also for manufacturing companies (Chap. 12). It is more difficult to measure service firms' innovation capabilities compared to measuring manufacturing firms' technological innovation capabilities. Service innovation often does not involve research and development (R&D) activities and technological investments. R&D innovation usually involves significant capital and revenue investment and a formal innovation process which is relatively easy to measure. Service innovation capability is a complex phenomenon that amongst other variables includes employees' entrepreneurship, management systems, customer interaction, co-creation of innovation with customers, service processes and a series of other factors that are difficult to measure. An ideal measure of service innovation capability does not exist.

Sundbo (2017) has developed a quantitative measurement instrument that identifies inputs to and outcomes of innovation processes. This instrument was developed based on a literature review and was tested using two cases. The conclusion was that it was impossible to construct a single measure—an index—of service innovation capabilities. The challenge is that so many different factors influence a firm's service innovation capabilities. The result of the test was that some variables can be measured in companies, and combined the measures are able to provide an estimation of a service firm's innovative capability. The factors included in this approach are divided into input factors (factors that determine innovation) and outcome factors (measures of the result of the innovation effort). The factors, and suggestions for quantitative measures, include the following:

**Input Factors**
These are investments in either money or time and time can be converted into an indicator of cost or a measure of financial value.

- *Working hours within the firm* (at all levels and including all activities, such as interacting with customers in co-creation activities, converted into a measure of financial value).
- *External advice and knowledge procurement* (both of which can be expensive, e.g. consultancy or paid research).
- *Expenditure on technology and other materials.*
- *Public support* (income, e.g. public grants or free advice provided).
- *Network benefits* (e.g. competitors who are also collaborators, representatives from the value chain and others from networks; inputs from network activities are normally free; however, the firm's time used in network activities should be deducted).

**Outcome Factors**
Four types of outcome factors were identified as important:

1. Income and growth
   (a) *Turnover* (more sales—increased turnover).
   (b) *Profit* (either positive or negative).
2. Employee factors
   (a) *More employees* (an indicator of growth—may be a power factor for departmental managers).
   (b) *Productivity increase.*
   (c) *Employee motivation and competence* (more satisfied and efficient employees).
   (d) *Employee entrepreneurship* (employees more engaged in innovation activities).
3. Customer/market factors
   (a) *Increased service quality and customer satisfaction.*
   (b) *Branding and PR* (the firm becomes better known by the market because of the innovation).
   (c) *Penetration into new markets* (a new service product launched in a new market can result in firms being able to sell other services in that market).
4. Strategic/business model factors
   (a) *Organizational learning* (the firm learns how to innovate more effectively and efficiently).
   (b) *Changed strategy* (the firm may change to a more appropriate strategy because of the innovation).
   (c) *New networks* (if the innovation required relationships to be formed with new external actors, then these can be a future innovation resource).

The conclusion is that not many instruments have been developed to measure service companies' innovation capabilities and it is difficult to construct a simple measure. Nevertheless, a multi-dimensional measurement framework can be developed.

## 13.4 Wrapping Up

There are two types of services. On the one hand, there are services that are customized and co-created between a service provider and consumer. These are labour-intensive services that are highly customized service experiences. On the other hand, there are standardized services that are increasingly extremely capital intensive rather than labour intensive. There is an on-going process by which services are becoming increasingly digitized and automated.

Measuring the quality of a co-created highly customized service experience is difficult. The primary measure is based on the scale of repeat business. It is important that the measurement of service quality and customer experiences is not an end in itself. The aim of all investments in the measurement of service businesses must be a focus on service quality enhancement. It must be accepted that there are some aspects of a service experience that are more about emotions, feelings and perceptions and these are difficult to measure and compare. There is also the added difficulty in that a service experience is a very immediate experience and perceptions of the experience may fade with time. An important question is when and how to measure service quality and customer satisfaction? Measurement of the service outcome will not enable a service provider to modify the service process to enhance quality and customer satisfaction. Too much measurement during the service delivery process may interfere and perhaps undermine service quality. A further complication is the relationship between service quality and customer satisfaction. All service firms need to develop an approach that develops a solution to balancing the interrelationships between price, quality, value and expectation. This is critical as it is this relationship that plays an important role in the long-term viability of service businesses and their continued ability to compete.

**Learning Outcomes**

- Many tools to measure service company performance, service quality and customer satisfaction exist.
- Before measuring, service quality must be defined operationally or, in other words, a framework must be developed enabling a company to measure quality quantitatively.
- Customer satisfaction and service quality are complex multi-dimensional constructs.

- SERVQUAL is one of the most used instruments. There might be difficulties in using SERVQUAL because it does not measure the effect of price.
- Mapping the service journey is another widely used instrument.
- Queue handling is one of the areas where most measurement instruments have been developed.
- Very few tools have been developed to measure service firms' innovation capabilities.

# References

Adenso-Diaz, B., & Gonzáles-Torres, P. (2002). A Capacity Management Model in Service Industries. *International Journal of Service Industry Management, 13*(3), 286–302.

Belobaba, P. (1989). Application of a Probabilistic Decision Model to Airline Seat Inventory Control. *Operations Research, 37*(2), 183–197.

Berman, B. (2005). Applying Yield Management Pricing to Your Service Business. *Business Horizons, 48,* 169–179.

Bitner, M., Ostrom, A., & Morgan, F. (2008). Service Blueprinting: A Practical Technique for Service Innovation. *California Management Review, 50*(3), 66–94.

Bourne, M., & Neely, A. (2003). Implementing Performance Measurement Systems: A Literature Review. *International Journal of Business Performance Management, 5*(1), 1–24.

Edvardsson, B., Thomasson, B., & Øvretveit, J. (1994). *Quality of Service*. London: McGrawHill.

Forsyth, P. (1999). *Marketing Professional Services*. London: Kogan Page.

Franceschini, F., Galetto, M., & Turina, E. (2009). Service Quality Monitoring by Performance Indicators: A Proposal for a Structured Methodology. *International Journal of Services Operations Management, 5*(2), 251–273.

Hollesen, S. (2015). *Marketing Management*. Harlow: Pearson.

Johnston, R., & Clark, G. (2005). *Service Operations Management*. Harlow: Prentice-Hall.

Kaplan, R., & Norton, D. (1996). *Balanced Scorecard*. Boston: Harvard Business School Press.

Kimes, S. (1989). Yield Management: A Tool for Capacity-Constrained Service Firms. *Journal of Operations Management, 8*(4), 348–363.

Lovelock, C., & Wirtz, J. (2011). *Services Marketing*. Boston: Prentice Hall.

Palmer, A. (2005). *Principles of Services Marketing*. Maidenhead: McGrawHill.

Parasuraman, A., Zeithaml, V. A., & Berry, L. (1988). SERVQUAL: A Multiple Item Scale for Measuring Customer Perceptions of Service Quality. *Journal of Retailing, 64*(1), 14–40.

Safari, A. (2016). A New Quantitative-Based Performance Management Framework for Service Operations. *Knowledge and Process Management, 23*(4), 307–319.

Sundbo, J. (2017). Quantitative Measurement Instruments: A Case of Developing a Method for Measuring Innovation in Service Firms. In F. Sørensen & F. Lapenta (Eds.), *Research Methods in Service Innovation*. Cheltenham: Edward Elgar.

Sureshchandar, G. S., Rajendran, C., & Anantharaman, R. N. (2002). The Relationship between Service Quality and Customer Satisfaction – A Factor Specific Approach. *Journal of Services Marketing, 16*(4), 363–379.

Wirtz, J., Patterson, P., Kunz, W., Gruber, T., Lu, V. N., Paluch, S., & Martins, A. (2018). Brave New World: Service Robots in the Frontline. *Journal of Service Management, 29*(5), 907–931.

Wright, J. N., & Race, P. (2004). *The Management of Service Operations*. London: Thomson.

Hauser, J., & Katz, G. (1998). Metrics: You Are What You Measure! *European Management Journal, 16*(5), 517–528.

Hope, C., & Mühlemann, A. (1997). *Service Operations Management*. Hemel Hempstead: Prentice Hall.

Iacobucci, D., Ostrom, A., Braig, B., & Bezjian-Avery, A. (1996). A Canonic Model of Consumer Evaluations and Theoretical Bases of Expectations. In *Advances in Services Marketing and Management* (Vol. 5, pp. 1–44). Greenwich, CT: JAI Press.

Klassen, K., & Rohleder, T. (2002). Demand and Capacity Management Decisions in Services. *International Journal of Operations & Production Management, 22*(5), 527–548.

Information Resources Management Association. (2018). *Operations and Service Management: Concepts, Methodologies, Tools, and Applications*. Hershey, PA: IGI Global.

Taylor, F. (1947). *Scientific Management*. New York: Harper & Brothers.

## Further Reading

Fitzsimmons, J., & Fitzsimmons, M. (2006). *Service Management. Operations, Strategy, Information Technology*. New York: McGraw-Hill.

## Useful Websites

https://www.smartsheet.com/balanced-scorecard-examples-and-templates.

https://www.slideshare.net/rockpulkit/servqual-model.

# Reading and Managing Service Businesses: An Integrated Case Study Approach

# 14

**Key Themes**

- How do different business activity systems interact within and between service businesses?
- How is value created and what types of value are created by service businesses?
- Case study-based approaches to reading and managing service businesses
- Developing an integrated approach to service businesses
- Hybrid manufacturing or selling products as services: Rolls-Royce and the Flowserve Corporation
- TikTok and platform-based services
- Zara, design, supply chains and logistics
- Reading the Dubai city-region as a service space
- Retail malls and service experiences: reading The Dubai Mall

Service businesses exist to create value and value-in-use through the sale of products and services and various combinations of products and services. Multiple values are created through this process including profit or economic rents and surplus value, but also social, community and individual benefits. The service-dominant logic approach (see Chap. 2) emphasizes that value is

created by beneficiaries and co-created by multiple actors that in some way influences beneficiaries. This is a complex process involving intra- and inter-organizational collaborations.

This book has developed an integrated or systematic approach to reading and managing service businesses. Our intention has been to identify and explore all the key activity systems, or domains, that are important for understanding the creation of value by service businesses. Our object of study is service businesses rather than some element or processes within service businesses. Each chapter has focussed on one process, or business activity system, that plays a critical role in service businesses, but also the ways this process is positioned within the wider context of service businesses. Each process is part of a more complex system of systems or set of interlocking business activity systems that, working together, transform inputs into all types of value.

This chapter is very different from the preceding chapters. Our intent in this chapter is not to focus on a business process or activity system, but rather to highlight how different processes work together within service businesses to create value. This approach is based on case studies. The aim is not to develop extremely detailed case studies as these rapidly become outdated. The purpose of this final chapter is to provide a nested-based approach to understanding service business. The aim is to develop integrated case studies that reflect some of the complexities of

**Electronic Supplementary Material** The online version of this chapter (https://doi.org/10.1007/978-3-030-52060-1_14) contains supplementary material, which is available to authorized users.

J. R. Bryson et al., *Service Management*, https://doi.org/10.1007/978-3-030-52060-1_14

managing and organizing service businesses. Innovation and heterogeneity are core central themes that cut across these case studies. Our integrated approach to case studies is perhaps more indicative compared to the more conventional approaches adopted in other books. It is indicative of the complexity of service businesses and the inter-organizational relationships that sit behind the co-creation of service experiences and service values. This chapter is intended to stimulate questions and a debate over the integration of the themes and topics explored in this book.

This chapter has three aims. First, to begin to develop integrated approaches to service businesses by exploring five cases. These are: Rolls-Royce, Flowserve, TikTok, Inditex (including Zara) and Dubai. The last case, Dubai, represents a different approach as in this analysis we develop a broader perspective on the development of a city-region and the role service businesses play within city-regions. In this account, we explore three dimensions of Dubai: as a service economy, as a location for service spaces—The Dubai Mall—and of service businesses. Here the challenge is to explore the ways in which an observer can 'read' a city-region as a service space and can read a particular servicescape—a shopping mall.

Second, the intent is not to develop complete case studies, but for these cases to be the starting point for further analysis and debate. Here it is important that readers of this book update these cases and are also able to add to them based on their own interests in particular aspects of service business. Third, to provide a mix of different styles of case study. These include more academic-style case studies to individual readings of city-regions and of service spaces.

## 14.1  Case Studies and Service Business

In developing this book, we engaged in a discussion regarding the importance, or unimportance, of using case studies to inform the analysis of service businesses. This discussion began with a debate regarding the definition of service business. This included:

1. The cultural attributes of service work/employment. What is the nature of a manufacturing job versus a service job? The technical aspects of employment including skills and training.
2. The need to explore different types of service and manufacturing businesses including public services. This should include an account of pure services and manufactured goods as well as hybrid combinations.
3. A service is a quality that is realized in the future. There is temporality to the service experience as the same person might experience the same service in a different way depending on the location and time of the experience. A good is more standardized but will also be experienced by consumers in different ways. Service providers try to standardize services, but their interpretation by consumers will be different depending on mood, time, expectation, experience and background.
4. Differences between the business model approaches developed and managed by different service business firms including capital- versus labour-intensive approaches.
5. A service firm is a business and there must be an emphasis placed on the nature of the service that is provided to customers, the quality and nature of the service experience, but it is important that the analysis also explores profit and risk versus reward. There is also an interesting relationship between the nature of the service experience that is created and the reward—quality and cost versus profitability.
6. There are three dimensions or characteristics of services: experiences; the operational delivery of intangibles or service experiences and outputs and the on-going blurring of the boundaries between goods and services.

This book was intended to develop an integrated approach to understanding the challenges and problems of running service businesses. This was an account of what works but also of what does not work. This includes identifying generic issues and then aspects of service business that apply to specific sectors or types of services. There are two types of case studies included in this book. First, short explanatory cases that are integrated into the earlier chapters. Second, more developed case studies of firms, or more integrated case studies, which are the type developed in this chapter.

There are three problems in using case studies. The first involves the selection of the cases and discussions on how representative these cases should be. This must also include a discussion on the orientation taken in the account of a case. Should the case be written from the perspective of the service consumers, service employees, managers, owners or all of these stakeholders? This is an important issue for understanding service businesses. Yesterday, one of the authors of this book had an interesting service experience. His car identified a potential problem with tyre pressure. This required a visit to a recently opened garage for the first time. This was the closest garage and he was away from home. The mechanics identified that the wheel had a screw embedded within the tyre and that they would try to make a repair. If this attempt failed, then two replacement tyres would be required. It took 20 minutes to repair the tyre and this garage provided this service for free. For the garage, this free service was the first stage in a journey of relationship building with a possible future customer and for the 'customer' that was an unexpected, but high-quality service experience. This is a brief vignette of a service experience from the point of view of the customer rather than a more formal company case study. But understanding service businesses involves both appreciating the quality of the experience and how it is produced and co-created.

Second, a company case study is an account of a firm as it operated in the past. Thus, case studies provide academics and their students with a historical account of firms. This is problematic as businesses are in a continual process of becoming—of change, modification and innovation. New routines emerge and existing routines change. A case study might be of a very special business—one that is inimitable. Such case studies are interesting but raise questions about applying learning from one case to another. This raises questions about the role case studies play

in understanding economic activities and the management of service businesses.

Third, a single case of a firm must come with a set of health warning. All firms will project a corporate narrative that might balance corporate social responsivity with employment opportunities and profitability. The challenge is to ensure that a case study draws upon many sources of evidence to ensure that the case is rigorous and robust. There is a real danger that a case study is presented as unique and exceptional (Tokatli 2015) or that it highlights one aspect of a firm's activities over many others. In this book, we have adopted an unusual approach to exploring firms. This integrated approach explores as many aspects of service business as possible. The conventional approach would be to focus on the internationalization of service businesses or the marketing of service businesses. This is to focus on one business task or process rather than on understanding the complexity of tasks, and the blend of tasks, involved in creating value-in-use through the co-creation of services.

There are many types of case studies including industry, firm, subunit of a firm (branch, international aspects), city-region or city. There are many styles of case studies or approaches to creating case studies and many of these are rather formulaic. Here the aim is to raise questions regarding the development of a more integrated approach to understanding and managing service businesses by identifying relationships between different business processes.

## 14.2   Manufacturing as Service: From Rolls-Royce to the Flowserve Corporation

The delivery of a service provides an opportunity for firms to develop relationships with consumers. These can be relationships that are formed during face-to-face encounters or that are mediated by information and communication technologies. The relational element that is central to a service production process represents a relational asset that may provide a firm with a competitive advantage in the marketplace. The manufacture and sale of a standard good that is not wrapped around with services provides limited opportunities for producers to develop long-term relationships with consumers. Relational assets are not owned by a company, but they are available to a firm and can be managed and developed. Such assets include customers, suppliers (parts, raw materials, finance) and strategic partners. Relational assets are formed around dyadic relationships based on face-to-face contacts, direct experience, reputation and ultimately trust. This type of relationship-focussed strategy enhances the inimitability of a firm's competitiveness strategy. Customers purchasing a good may be transformed into captive consumers of a set of supporting services making it difficult for this relationship to be broken or copied by competitors.

To create value, relational assets can be translated into customer-connecting and non-customer-connecting processes and this classification mirrors the distinction made between product-supporting services and production-supporting services (Chap. 2). It would perhaps be conceptually beneficial to alter the former to include people and customers by changing the description of this process to product/customer-supporting services. The argument is that firms selling goods have limited opportunities to develop relational assets whilst firms providing product/customer-supporting services have much greater opportunities. Relational assets represent an important opportunity for firms to develop new product/good and service bundles that could be sold to existing consumers. Developing and exploiting relational assets, however, require firms to learn and develop new competencies. It also implies that employees and firms must be sensitive to service quality, service experience as well as the creation of value-in-use.

The starting point for this analysis is manufacturers who have begun to convert their products to services. This topic was explored in Chap. 12 when we explored services within manufacturing firms or the blurring of the boundaries between manufactured goods and services. Hybrid production systems and hybrid products have been developed by all types of small and large firms. All production systems involve the hybridization or blending of service tasks with manufacturing tasks. A manufacturing firm has within it many different types of service workers performing service tasks including finance, human resource management and procurement. Service firms are unable to create services without manufactured goods. Some companies have developed complex hybridized good/service product bundles that blur the boundaries between goods and services. These are products in which a physical good has been transformed into a service through the development of a service-led business model. It is useful to explore two case studies of firms that have developed hybrid manufacturing systems or product service systems and are involved in the creation of hybrid goods: Rolls-Royce engines and an American manufacturer of industrial pumps.

## 14.2.1 Rolls-Royce

Rolls-Royce is one of the most frequently cited examples of a firm that has shifted towards a service-based business model. In the financial year 2017–2018, 50% of this firm's revenues were derived from the delivery of services and 50% from selling equipment (Rolls-Royce 2018, p. 18). In 1987, Rolls-Royce 'supported our engines in service by offering repair and overhaul arrangements which often failed to align our interests with those of our customers' (Rolls-Royce 2007, p. 14). At this time, services were considered as a supporting set of functions rather than as an integral element within the firm's business model. Since 1987, Rolls-Royce has transformed itself into a provider of power rather than a provider of engines. This transformation has occurred in the firm's core market segments ranging from civil aviation to defence aerospace and marine engines. Central to this transformation is the firm's installed base of engines that provides significant opportunities for on-going growth in the delivery of product-based services. By 2018, 90% of the current Rolls-Royce widebody fleet of engines were covered by TotalCare service agreements (Rolls-Royce 2018).

The transformation of Rolls-Royce into a company that provides services has involved the company in developing:

> comprehensive through-life service arrangements in each of our business sectors. These align our interests with those of our customers and enable us to add value through the application of our skills and knowledge of the product. In 2007, underlying aftermarket service revenues grew by nine per cent and represented 55 per cent of Group sales. This growth has been achieved partly as a result of the introduction of new products, but also because our ownership of intellectual property enables us to turn data into information that adds value to our customers. (Rolls-Royce 2007, p. 14)

A good example of this shift is the mission ready management solutions (MRMS®) package developed by Rolls-Royce. MRMS® provides the military with customized solutions that include total support packages and 'Power by the Hour'®. With the latter package, major airline and defence customers pay a fixed warranty and operation fee for the hours that an engine runs. Contract performance is measured against the performance of the fleet and in terms of ready for issue engine availability.

Rolls-Royce offers three types of service solution. First, TotalCare is based upon an agreed rate per engine flying hour enabling customers to engage in accurate financial forecasting. This package is designed for airline fleet and it transfers the technical and financial aspects of fleet maintenance from customers to the service supplier. At the same time, it converts Rolls-Royce into a service provider or more precisely into a provider of hybrid products or product/good service systems. Second, CorporateCare is intended for corporate and business jet customers and is designed to ensure that aircraft are available when required and also may result in increased residual value. Third, MRMS® is targeted at defence customers providing them with engine management and maintenance ensuring 24/7 operational capability. These types of hybrid products have transformed Rolls-Royce from a company that designs and manufactures engines to a provider of turnkey engine power

(Table 14.1). To maximize profitability, Rolls-Royce must now focus on the effective management of an extended manufacturing value chain or its hybrid production system. This includes the design and development of engines, installation, after-sales maintenance, repair and overall services and parts availability and management.

This service-informed business model has advantages for both Rolls-Royce and its customers. On the one hand, Rolls-Royce is able to develop a long-term relationship with customers providing the company with a relatively secure and predictable flow of revenue for the provision of services. These types of service agreements lock customers into long-term relationships with service providers. On the other hand, customers know that 'power' is available when needed and are also able to predict the costs of accessing power. Engine reliability is critical for customers as any downtime not only results in significant costs including loss of revenue, but also damages the relationship between an airline and its customers.

## 14.2.2   Flowserve Corporation: An American Manufacturer of Industrial Pumps

Companies that provide machine tools and parts that are an integral part of a customer's production system must compete on the quality of the product combined with service and reliability. The Flowserve Corporation is an American company specializing in the design, manufacture, marketing and servicing of flow-handling equipment. This company sells engineered pumps, precision mechanical seals, valves and a range of related services to the petroleum, chemical and power industries.

Flowserve can trace its origins back to 1872 and, like all manufacturing companies, it has had to cope with intensified competition. Since 1997, this company has focussed on core areas and has also engaged in a cost-cutting programme that has involved transferring the production of pumps from a high-cost plant located in Belgium to two

**Table 14.1** The transformation of Rolls-Royce from a provider of goods to a provider of hybrid products

| Good | | | | Service |
|---|---|---|---|---|
| Delivery of engine | ⟶ | | | Delivery of power |
| *Traditional support* | *Enhanced support* | *Advanced support* | *Total support* | *Extended support* |
| Spare parts Repair and overhaul | Data and forecasting services Technical and logistics support Customer training | Comprehensive package integrating elements of basic and enhanced support Spares, including repair and overall contracts | Complete, availability-based services. Can cover all aircraft or some aircraft activities Configuration management and reliability enhancements covered | Partnered capability Turnkey service Non-propulsion-related support solutions |
| *Customer responsibility* | ⟶ | | | *Service provider responsibility* |

Source: Authors' own

factories in the Netherlands and also opened a valve production plant in Bangalore.

The manufacture and sale of pumps and valves responds to periods of economic growth and decline and related profitability and this is influenced by macro-economic trends. Flowserve realized that the service and repair of existing equipment amongst its captive customers was an activity that was not subject to cyclical downturns. In 1997, the company established a Service Repair Division that focussed on providing services to already installed equipment. According to Flowserve's then Chief Executive Officer, Bernard Rethore:

we saw an opportunity to give new emphasis and focus to the service business so that we'd go beyond just manufacturing and what had been done before by each company in repair and maintenance and get into the service business in a whole new way. (Rethore and Greer 1999)

The service division became the Flow Solution Division in early 1999 creating a single, world-class vehicle for the delivery of integrated services. This division operates from a network of 75 service and quick response centres to provide 24/7 customer support. The company has also produced smart sealing products containing built-in microprocessors and equipment-monitoring software.

Flowserve has become a cradle-to-grave company that not only designs and manufactures flow-handling equipment, but also provides

long-term services. The company has realized that one of its most important assets is existing installed equipment and this is now seen as an important captive market. The company's then Chief Operating Officer, C. Scott Greer, noted that the supply chain was shifting and one example of this shift

is evidenced in the service aspect of our business. Traditionally, our customers had done much of their own service while we supplied the parts. Many of these customers are starting to say, Wait, we want to move upstream to get closer to the consumer, identify products that differentiate us. We're going to let the maintenance of pumps and valves go to those people who are the experts." I think you're going to see, because of this basic change in focus, double-digit growth in our service business. You should think of Flowserve as a "cradle-to-grave" type of company. We're focussing on the entire life cycle of the product. (Rethore and Greer 1999)

A good example of this 'cradle-to-grave' approach has been the introduction of ten-year standard warranties for some of the company's products. This provides customers with a long-term relationship with Flowserve based around the provision of original equipment manufacturer produced spare parts, guaranteed Flowserve field and shop maintenance, a reduced risk of downtime and protection from the costs associated with the failure of a piece of flow-handling equipment.

Flowserve has developed from a manufacturing firm to a company that sells products and services by utilizing 'our LifeCycle Advantage program to establish fee-based contracts to manage customers' aftermarket requirements. These programs provide an opportunity to manage the customer's installed base and expand the business relationship with the customer' (Flowserve 2018, p.7). These LifeCycle services are designed around a customer's specific key performance indicators (KPIs) and are intended to ensure that customers focus on those areas that require improvement including equipment performance, energy audits, optimization to improve asset utilization, simplified procurement and on-site training.

## 14.3  TikTok and Platform-Based Service Businesses

Rolls-Royce and Flowserve are manufacturing firms that have innovated through the development of new service-oriented business models. Platform-based businesses provide a very different approach to developing and managing a service business. Many of these are based on multi-sided service business models (see Chap. 3) that provide free services linked to advertising revenue. Such multi-sided platform-based business models include Facebook, Google and Twitter. The majority of these international platform-based businesses have been established by American companies. In 2017, TikTok was one of the very few Chinese apps to successfully enter Western markets. In 2018, TikTok was the most downloaded application from Apple's App Store.

TikTok is perhaps an unusual app that is part of the strange world of social media dance routines and viral pranks. It is an app that targets teenagers. In China, apps like TikTok became extremely popular with younger people spending considerable periods of time using social media. This led to the Chinese government insisting that from June 2019 short-video apps, including TikTok, would need to include a 'youth mode' that would permit parents to control their children's use of the app. TikTok enables users to share short 15-second videos of themselves lip-syncing or dancing to songs. Popular subjects for lip-syncing on TikTok are TLC, the American girl group, Tyler The Creator, the rapper and Narendra Modi, the prime minister of India. These videos include special effects and filters. Users can also reply to a TikTok post and create collaborative videos including responses to challenges. TikTok's owner, Bytedance, is one of the very few Chinese technology companies to develop a platform-based product that has been extremely successful outside China. The app applies artificial intelligence to identify users' preferences and interests to provide a targeted customized user feed. The TikTok app was initially introduced in China under the brand name Douyin in September 2016. In 2017, Bytedance released the app to core international markets under the brand name TikTok.

There are two important questions to explore regarding the transformation of Douyin into an international platform-based service. First, how did TikTok internationalize? The difficulty with platform-based service businesses is that they encounter high barriers to entry based on networking effects (see Chap. 4) that lock consumers into existing providers of social media. For Bytedance, introducing TikTok to Western markets was challenging as Western consumers already had messaging apps. The challenge was how to embed TikTok in existing Western social media platforms. The solution was for Bytedance to acquire Musical.ly for around $1bn and to merge this company's social media platform with its own video service.

Musical.ly was a start-up company based in Singapore, but with an office located in Santa Monica, California, that allowed users to create short lip-syncing and comedy videos. The Musical.ly app was already popular amongst American teenagers. TikTok merged with Musical.ly on 2 August 2018 and existing accounts and data were consolidated into one app under the brand TikTok. This meant that users of Musical.ly did not have to download TikTok as the Musical.ly app was automatically updated to TikTok. By 2019, TikTok had over 300 million users outside China including 5 million in the UK and 120 million in India. In comparison, Snapchat had around 210 million users and Twitter only 145 million monetizable users. The growth of TikTok highlights the importance of placing an app on the smartphones of millions of possible users. Existing smartphone apps and operating systems may lock users into a particular combination of apps. The challenge is to develop an approach that tries to ensure that a new app overcomes any existing networking effects.

Second, TikTok has been downloaded by over 110 million Americans and these users are mostly young. The app targets children from age 13. In September 2019, concerns were raised over Bytedance using TikTok to further China's foreign defence policy through censoring material. This concern included discussions on TikTok as a potential counter-intelligence threat and as an app that could be used to influence US election outcomes. By November 2019, TikTok's non-Chinese user data was not stored in China, but before February 2019, US user data might have been stored in China. There is another concern, which is the potential for the app to become a tool used by paedophiles. Regulators in the US and Europe have begun to consider TikTok and Bytedance has been trying to self-regulate the app. Nevertheless, Bytedance is trying to negotiate the regularity frameworks that are emerging and intended to ensure that apps do not harm consumers.

There is an interesting geopolitical problem facing platform-based businesses like TikTok. This includes the different data regulatory regimes existing in China compared to other national economies. TikTok has to try to balance these different systems. At the moment, the company is beginning to enhance its multi-sided business model by increasing revenue from targeted advertising. Nevertheless, the key risk remains that it might become impossible for a company like TikTok to continue to provide services to customers based in China and elsewhere.

Bytedance has a series of country-specific advantages including access to Chinese consumers that can be involved in the co-creation of new products. It also has access to large quantities of big data enabling it to develop novel approaches to the application of social media platforms to generate new forms of data-related value. The company also has firm-based advantages including its information and knowledge base and the ability to create social media platforms. Nevertheless, the internationalization of TikTok required Bytedance to acquire another company's ownership-specific advantages. One strategy adopted by companies formed in emerging markets is to blend their country-specific advantages with another company's ownership-specific advantages through mergers and acquisitions or the establishment of some form of joint venture (see Chap. 10). The acquisition is often an established company based in a developed market economy.

## 14.4   Zara: Design, Retail and Logistics

TikTok is a twenty-first century platform-based business based on algorithms. The interface between the consumer and service provider is mediated through a computer program and smartphones. Zara, the retail company owned by the Spanish company Inditex, is a very different type of service company producing a very different style of service experience and related values.

Inditex is one of the world's largest fashion retailers that owns eight retail brands (Zara, Zara Home, Pull&Bear, Massimo Dutti, Bershka, Stradivarius, Oysho and Uterqüe). It sells fashion collections in 202 markets and by the end of 2018 had a network of 7490 stores located in 96 markets and was selling fashion online in 96 markets. Inditex continues to expand its retail network at a time when many retailers are failing or restructuring in response to competition from low-cost platform-based retailers. During 2018, Inditex focused on enhancing the company's sales footprint including opening more and larger stores combined with an integrated approach to the shopping experience based on blending store and online retail experiences. Customers can shift between retail channels combining the strengths and weaknesses of both. Between 2012 and 2018, Zara's store sizes, on average, increased by 50%

from 1452 m² to 2184 m². The shopping experience was enhanced by the addition of new services including Click & Collect, self-service checkouts, automated online order pick-up points and same-day delivery in 12 cities and next-day in 8 markets.

Zara has been extensively studied by academics (Tokatli 2008, 2015; Tokatli and Kizilgun 2009, 2010). For Zara, it is important to read the media and academic accounts of this firm with care. It is also important to appreciate the ways in which Inditex has created a corporate narrative. In one critical reading of Zara, Tokatli argues that 'so many observers have been getting the case of Zara wrong' (2015, p. 642). In this account, Tokatli argues that Inditex is a global retailer that relies on thousands of suppliers all over the world and that Inditex 'is a key driver of globalization' (2015, p. 642) defined as being reliant on an extensive network of contract manufacturers. There is no question that Zara is a complex, successful and interesting firm. It is also a firm that plays an important role in the everyday lives of its consumers. Fashion is partly about dreams, fantasies, identities and service experiences.

Zara's business model is based on integrating retail and online service experiences with an in-house design team, in-house manufacturing and logistics and outsourced manufacturing and logistics. The business model blends an internalization with an externalization or outsourcing strategy. This is important as Zara's success relies on design, marketing, retailing, manufacturing, the management of a complex supply chain and logistics. Thus, its business model blends different systems together. The blend and the approach provide Zara, and the other Inditex brands, with distinct competitive advantage. Let us consider the different elements of this approach.

First, Zara employs over 700 designers (Inditex 2018). Each brand has a purchasing, sales and pattern-design team focusing on identifying new fashions and designing and developing a fashion collection. The designs mirror fashion trends in relatively real time by observing trends as they emerge in key markets. Zara tends to follow rather than to make new fashions. Zara's designs are fabricated in its own factories and

across an external supply chain. The design and fabrication processes are dynamic, focusing on creating fast fashion. Combining the in-house design team with the supply chain and logistics support enables Zara to provide its stores and online retail platforms with a continual stream of new products that arrive offline and online twice per week.

In 2018, Inditex's design teams created over 75,000 stock keeping units (SKU). These were marketed through the stores, but also by the creation of 373 fashion stories providing customers with an audio-visual experience of a sample of the company's products. These fashion stories are a form of virtual but carefully curated service experience combining many narrative threads to encourage consumers to appreciate the company's new clothing designs. The design teams support a proximity-orientated manufacturing model that tries to ensure that Zara is able to design, fabricate and transfer new products to the appropriate sales channel as rapidly as possible. The supply chain in 2018 included 1866 suppliers and 7235 factories.

Second, Zara's logistics are based on a centralized distribution model in which all products, irrespective of where they are produced, are transported to the company's central logistics platform located in Spain. From this platform, product bundles are selected and transported to the appropriate location and sales channel. The logistics business model (see Chap. 11 on logistics) is based on the principle that the average length of time to transport merchandize from the distribution centres to a store is 36 hours for Europe and a maximum of 48 hours for Asia and the Americas. Logistics and the logistics platform play an important role in the Inditex business model. Radio-frequency identification (RFID) tags are being applied to all brands enabling each Inditex brand to track every garment in real time (see Chap. 11). RFID plays an important role in the company's online-offline stock management system enabling customers to access products irrespective of their location.

Inditex continually innovates to remain competitive and successful and also to increase productivity. There are challenges. In June 2019,

Inditex's Indian partner, Tata, decided to establish its own extreme fast fashion retail chain in India. Tata had managed Zara's stores in India for nearly a decade. Tata will use the local Indian supply chain that was part of Inditex's Indian supply chain. Hennes & Mauritz (H&M), the Swedish multinational clothing-retail company and another Zara competitor, has also negotiated contracts with two of India's largest online retailers—Myntra and Jabong.

The Inditex business model is an excellent example of an integrated approach to developing and managing a service business based on the sale of fast fashion. This integrated approach to design and logistics, combined with localized manufacturing, enables the company to reduce its exposure to excess stock. In comparison, H&M has problems with stock control resulting in discounting that is reflected in profit margins. There is an additional problem. Inditex invested over $500 million in its stores between 2012 and 2014 whilst H&M failed to invest in its stores. The quality of Inditex's retail space, and related service experiences, has encouraged consumers to spend more. For both these retailers, perhaps there are two major threats. First, the onward growth of discount fashion retailers including Primark and TK Maxx, which provide consumers with fashionable but competitively priced clothing. Second, online-only retailers (ASOS, Boohoo, Zalando) are able to sell fashionable clothing targeted at younger consumers for as little as £5 combined with free delivery.

Mixed marketing channels, including blending online and in-store provision, provided retailers with an ability to respond to lockdown related to Covid-19. Primark, for example, the provider of low-cost fast fashion, had focused on in-store sales but had failed to develop an online store. This meant that the company experienced a complete collapse in sales during the Covid-19 lockdown period. Nevertheless, for companies like Zara, Primark and H&M, there is another threat. This is the emergence of the slow fashion movement that is against fast fashion, and mixed material clothing, on environmental and sustainability grounds (Bryson and Vanchan 2020).

## 14.5   Dubai

Consumption, and consumer behaviour, is embedded in place with consumer decisions influenced by place-based associations and influences. These influences stretch between places. It is important to develop a place-based understanding or a regional understanding of service economies. It is to this that we now turn our attention. In this case, we explore a city-region as a complex service space focusing on reading Dubai as a service space that is saturated with service firms and service experiences. This case study is intended to provide an overview of a complex city-region service economy. The style of this analysis is deliberately informal and avoids the more formulaic approach that is found in most business/management case studies.

### 14.5.1   Unravelling the 'Dubai Intertwingularity': Reading the City-Regions

This is a reading of Dubai written by one of the authors of this book during an extended visit to this city-region. In this account, understanding Dubai involves both an exercise in developing an academic analysis of this city-region, and Dubai as a service experience. Let us commence a reading of Dubai. I am here in Dubai for ten days. I am an academic interested in service businesses in place and across space. As a student of place and space, it is important to experience many different places to try to understand the on-going evolution of the international economy. Most of my time in Dubai is spent in a strange solitary occupation. I am writing a book, this book. One chapter of this book, Chap. 10, will be written here rather than in Europe along with two sections of this chapter—Chap. 14. Writing is always influenced by the place in which a text is written. The chapter I am working on is exploring the internationalization of service businesses; Dubai is an excellent place to reflect on this topic and also on Dubai as a service space.

Dubai makes me think of many things. I want to explore two of these. First, how does one read a city-region? or how to read a place like Dubai? At the centre of the analysis of city-regions is heterogeneity and a complex interplay between place, space and a concatenation of spatial and sometimes aspatial processes. A city-region also has its own special or distinctive 'essence' and the use of this term highlights that many aspects of a city-region cannot be measured but perhaps can only be experienced (Bryson et al. 2018). Reading a city-region is partly an exercise in trying to capture an appreciation of the essence of a place.

There is another way of considering a city-region. This is to argue that urbanization is a process that includes on-going transformations in the intensity of a place. Central to this process is the speeding up of the interconnections that exist within a place—flows of people, goods, information—combined with an ever spatially spreading web of connections to other places. Dubai is very much a place of connections—from a place that attracts leisure, business and educational tourists to the role played by Dubai International Airport as a transfer hub. Reading Dubai is an exercise in identifying and understanding a complex interconnected web of local and international flows— of people, money, information, data, goods, but set within the context of appreciating the essence of this place and its ever-changing intensity. Central to these flows, for Dubai, are flows of people. There are many such flows. Some are very temporary—from airport transfers to short holidays—and some involve much longer but still temporary visits. People pass through this place with varying degrees of intensity. There are temporary visitors who are here for a few hours as they transfer between flights, and visitors who come to Dubai to work, for education, health and tourism.

Second, in 2013, Dubai established the Dubai Knowledge Park. This place-based intervention was intended to build upon Dubai's centrality as an important international hub. This park is a free trade zone, not for physical goods, but for people, for service workers. It is a human resource management, professional learning and educational free trade zone that specializes in providing facilities for corporate training. This is an exercise in applied integrated economic development. It attracts training providers and trainees—both generate a set of complex place-based local economic multipliers including airport landing fees and expenditure in hotels, including a hotel room tax, and in kiosks or smaller retail outlets. This Knowledge Park includes the 'International Centre for Culinary Arts' and the 'Eton Institute' (EI). The latter provides language training and assessment, including teacher training, in over 160 languages. EI has no relationship with the other Eton, Eton College (UK), apart from the shared name. The other Eton was founded in 1440 by King Henry VI as the 'Kynge's College of Our Ladye of Eton besyde Windesore'.

Names have many meanings—as simple identifiers but also as signs with signifiers and signifieds. A signifier is the physical form of a sign while a signified is the meaning or idea expressed by a sign (Rusten et al. 2007). Applying a name that has developed a complex signified over centuries to another activity, function or organization is an exercise in trying to transfer a signified from one organization to another. This might be accidental or be planned. It is a complex process, as it tries to link one reputation with another on the assumption that readers of this sign will appreciate the association and their decision-making will be influenced. It fails when readers do not make or understand the association or see through the exercise in sign transfer.

Place-making, city-region making, is an exercise in the creation and projection of a place-based brand or identity. Thus, the essence and intensity of Dubai is connected to the shaping of the Dubai city-region brand. This is a very complex brand that includes many interconnected layers of meaning and also involves transferring signifieds. It is also a brand that is read, interpreted and misinterpreted. This is the case for all 'signs'; a process of translation and distortion occurs between a sign and the reader(s). This means that reading a city-region is partly an exercise in reading the ways in which a place's brand has been developed, created and evolved, but is also interpreted and perceived. It is also important to appreciate the diversity of readings and experiences as people from very different backgrounds try to read a place. This can be a shallow reading as people rapidly pass through a place, while for some this is an exercise in reading and engaging with a place as an exercise in everyday living.

A visit to The Dubai Mall—the second largest shopping centre in the world that is also adjacent to the tallest building and includes the Dubai Fountain, the world's largest choreographed fountain system—is an experience in viewing and reading service experiences. This mall also includes the Dubai Dino, a genuine Diplodocus fossil, that comes from the Dana Quarry, Wyoming, US Reading city-regions is also an exercise in understanding and reading theatre. The Dubai Mall is a carefully crafted theatrical service experience. It also highlights the relationship between lifestyle and climate. Here, the mall is a place for walking, strolling, eating, entertainment—like all malls, but it is also an air-conditioned place.

This reading of Dubai as a city-region was inspired by fieldwork undertaken at the Dubai Fountain and The Dubai Mall. This initial reading of Dubai emphasized that there are many different ways to read Dubai, but all readings must include an account of theatre, spectacle and the construction of a place-based identity, a brand and a collection of linked signs. There is another way of reading Dubai. This is as a complex concatenation of flows of all types. Dubai is, if anything, at the centre of a web of interconnected flows; it is a place at the centre of a whirlwind of flows. Like all places, there are intra-city-region flows including flows of cars, lorries and buses. These flows of vehicles represent many things. At one level, they are flows of pollution producing localized air quality problems. At another level, each vehicular movement reflects a flow of people, of expertise, of information, of knowledge of employees and of families. Some vehicles are transporting raw materials—sand for construction in a sea of sand—and finished products.

A visit to the local supermarket at Silicon Oasis highlights one aspect of the complex set of global flows that link Dubai with elsewhere. A supermarket can be read in the same way that one should try to read a city. Let me take one exam-

ple. A pizza was on sale; a culinary form that was developed in Italy. But this pizza is not Italian, rather more Italian-style as this is a German pizza that was 'Made in Germany: from local and imported ingredients'. This is a German version of an Italian product transported and sold in Dubai. This is an excellent example of the geography of food and the space of flows that have evolved forming new food-related global commodity chains or global production networks. The internationalization of food that was on display partly reflects those living in Dubai from elsewhere, but it also reflects the internationalization of food.

This food example is one very narrow reading of the space of flows that is Dubai. There are more important flows than Italian-style pizza from Germany. Dubai's economic history reflects the on-going evolution of places that are positioned as international hubs; places in which spaces of flows come together. Dubai is a 'concatenation' of flows. This is an understatement of the complexity of these flows. A concatenation is a term that describes the action of linking things together in a series, or the condition of being linked in such a way. This is not Dubai, and this is not an adequate analysis of the on-going internationalization of spaces of service flows. There is a much better word. Dubai is an intertwingularity.

The term intertwingularity was introduced by Ted Nelson in a book published in 1974 on computers. In the second edition of this book he noted that hierarchical and sequential structures are often artificial (1987). Perhaps these represent the identification of 'false' patterns or a distorted sequential view of socio-economic-cultural-political processes. Intertwingularity is not generally emphasized as one of the primary characteristics of socio-economic processes and of the developing global economy. And, yet an international business is best described as an intertwingularity and globalization is one of the archetypal intertwingularities. But, what does this mean? To Nelson, an intertwingularity describes the complexity of the interrelations of human knowledge. In this account, the emphasis is placed on a complex array of interlinked and networked cross-connections of human knowledge that are intertwingled. Nevertheless, intertwingularity highlights the complex weaving together of processes of all types—it is a reflection on the interconnectedness of everything. Perhaps the most complex intertwingularities emerge in the interactions between place, space and the socio-economy—interactions within and between city-regions. Reading a city-region is an exercise in unravelling and exploring intra- and inter-regional intertwingularities.

The concept of intertwingularity has not been applied in any rigorous way to city-regions. But a city-region, like Dubai, is an intertwingularity of flows, of interlinked and networked cross-connections, that link this place in complex and often unimagined ways to other places. There are many aspects to Dubai as an intertwingularity. Understanding the economic history, or economic geography, of this place is an exercise in the unravelling of many intertwingularities that are layered upon one another with complex interconnections. The recent history of Dubai commenced with the discovery of oil in 1966 and the development of a city-region constructed on the development of a new oil-based intertwingularity. In this case, this involved investment in oil-related infrastructure including port facilities. This transformed this place and began to alter the interconnections between Dubai and the rest of the world—a new intertwingularity emerged and evolved based on flows of people, money and oil. The word 'evolved' highlights that the creation of a place-based, spatially connected intertwingularity is a dynamic process.

From the mid-1990s, Dubai began to attract an inflow of foreign direct investment (FDI). An increase in oil prices provided Dubai with the finance to invest in local and international infrastructure. This was forward-thinking strategic planning based on the appreciation that Dubai's oil stock was limited. The long-term resilience of Dubai required a transition from an economy that was constructed upon an oil-based intertwingularity to one based on flows of people, information and knowledge—an economy increasingly based on services. This was a transition from an economy based on the extraction of a liquid, to

one based on the attraction and retention of people and firms. A new intertwingularity for this place had been imagined.

This new intertwingularity can be perhaps traced back to the initial decision to develop Dubai airport. This commenced in 1959 with the construction of a 1800 m runway. Dubai International Airport is now a major regional and international hub. It is the busiest airport in the world for international passenger traffic and the sixth most important cargo airport. If anything, Dubai's current economy is constructed upon an aviation intertwingularity. Over 90,000 people are employed by the airport supporting an additional 400,000+ jobs elsewhere in the Dubai economy. An analysis of the impact of the airport on the Dubai economy is revealing. In 2013, this aviation intertwingularity contributed US$26.7 billion to the Dubai economy. This represents the airport's 'core' impact that added US$16.5 billion to Dubai combined with an additional US$10.2 billion from tourism—another type of intertwingularity, but this time of tourists and related tourism infrastructure. This analysis of the airport's economic impacts revealed that the combined economic impact of the airport was equivalent to 26.7% of Dubai's total gross domestic product (GDP) creating 416,500 jobs or 21% of Dubai's total employment (Oxford Economics 2014). This report attempted to look into the future. The predication was that the direct, indirect, induced and tourism gross value added (GVA) impact of aviation on Dubai will rise from 26.7% of Dubai's GDP in 2013 to 37.5% by 2020 and to 44.7% by 2030. This is quite some aviation intertwingularity.

The aviation intertwingularity that has developed with Dubai at the centre of a complex web of people and cargo flows is the foundation for another set of service-led intertwingularities. These include a retail intertwingularity, and a leisure and entertainment intertwingularity as Dubai attracts investment in water, amusement and theme parks. There is also another process at work—the emergence and development of different forms of FDI-led intertwingularities. In 1985, Dubai established the Jebel Ali free economic zone to attract FDI. This has become the largest free zone in the world. Building on this, Dubai has developed free economic zones across the city-region that are intended to specialize in particular activities. These include Dubai Internet City, Dubai Media City, Dubai Maritime City, Silicon Oasis and the Dubai International Academic City (DIAC). The Silicon Oasis strategy is intended to transform this place, this part of Dubai, into a major international centre for advanced electronic innovation, design and development. The free economic benefits that are available for businesses establishing at Silicon Oasis include 100% foreign ownership, 100% repatriation of capital, zero income tax, zero corporate taxation, no import or export taxes, low cost of operations and stable and clear regulations.

Dubai is an important place, it is an exciting place, it is a fascinating place. A stroll through Dubai airport represents one way of reading Dubai—as a place that is increasingly a complex intertwingularity of flows of people and money. These flows commenced with oil and then aviation. The investment in aviation infrastructure reflected the development of a new aviation-centred intertwingularity. This was the first stage in the on-going transformation of this place from desert, to oil-based economy to the complex intertwingularity of this place's service-led economy. Oil flows were replaced with people flows combined with flows of FDI; money and people flow together—they are intertwingled. Initially, these people flows were encouraged by strategies designed to attract tourists and flows of FDI.

More recently, there has been an important addition. This has been the development of Dubai International Academic City (DIAC), launched in April 2007. This is a strategy intended to enhance this city-region's reputation as an international higher education centre. Another form of intertwingularity is forming—an educational and research intertwingularity that is attracting universities from around the world to come to Dubai. There are three new flows linked to this initiative—of education-related FDI—money, of academics and support staff and of students. One of these flows is one that links Birmingham, UK, to Dubai, with the establishment of the University

of Birmingham Dubai campus. There are other flows linked to DIAC—of ideas, knowledge and reputation. DIAC will attract students from around the world to study here. These flows of students will contribute to Dubai's evolving intertwingularity. On graduation some may stay in this region and some will go but return eventually. Some may make decisions from afar that produce new flows of people and finance that will become embedded in this place.

The challenge is 'how to read a city-region?' There are many such readings—as theatre, spectacle, as a site for governance, as a place of intra- and inter-flows, as a site for work and play—of lifestyles, livelihood and liveability. Nevertheless, Dubai, if it is anything, is best understood as an evolving intertwingularity of intertwingularities. There are many different types of service space in Dubai, but perhaps some of the most visible are retail spaces and it is to these that we now turn our attention.

## 14.5.2   Reading the Dubai Mall: Service Spaces, Experience Spaces and Strolling Spaces

The Dubai Mall is many things—a substantial piece of real estate—for property development and investment, an engineered space, a brand, a service space, an experience space, a working space and often a comparatively low-wage space. This is quite some mall, but it is still only the second-largest mall in the world. Visiting a mall is a lesson in global flows of fast-moving consumer products—from food to cosmetics to fashion—and in people flows from across the world. Every year more than 80 million visitors stroll through this place, and in one year this was the most visited building on this planet.

This mall has 3.77 million sq. ft. of lettable space and over 1300 retail outlets including two anchor department stores, Bloomingdale's and Galeries Lafayette. A visit to The Dubai Mall comes with opportunities for some serious shopping and eating. There are over 200 food outlets. A ten-minute stroll in each store would amount to a visit of over 10.4 days, but these are

24-hour days! But we are in luck as this mall is open from 10 am to midnight—14 hours, 7 days a week. This means my ten-minute visit to each store will take me 17.8 days, but I will need time to eat, and sleep. The Dubai Mall provides everything the mall explorer could want—from charging stations, to a porter service and a sleeping pod lounge.

There are many aspects to this mall. There is shopping, eating, strolling and entertainment. The mall includes the Dubai Aquarium & Underwater Zoo with a 270-degree walkthrough tunnel; the VR Park for virtual reality; KidZania® an 'edutainment' experience targeted at children; the Reel Cinemas megaplex; the Olympic-sized Dubai Ice Rink, Dino the Dinosaur and the Waterfall. The Dubai Mall is part of a much larger property development intended to attract shoppers and tourists seeking experiences. This mall is part of the large-scale, mixed-use Downtown Dubai development. This is a 2 km² development that includes the tallest building in the world, Burj Khalifa, the Dubai Fountain—the world's largest choreographed fountain system, and The Dubai Mall. There is no question that this is a cosmopolitan place, a theatrical place, a servicescape and an experience scape.

There are many sides to Downtown Dubai. On the one hand, there is the fountain. This is a piece of America that will always be Dubai. It was designed by WET Design, the Californian company that designs water features across the US including Las Vegas. The fountain is a transposition of Las Vegas to Dubai. Alternatively, the Burj Khalifa comes alive at night with a dramatic lighting show. The lighting was designed by Jonathan Speirs, co-founder of Speirs + Major, a UK lighting design consultancy. The design of Downtown Dubai is a lesson in the internationalization of architectural and related design services, but it is also a lesson in the complex bundle of service inputs that are required to create servicescapes and service experiences. Both the fountain and the lighting show reveal another side to this place—free entertainment for all.

How do we read The Dubai Mall? Perhaps, in the same way as we read a city-region (Bryson et al. 2018), but a mall is a microcosm. It is a place that is simultaneously real and artificial, a carefully crafted and designed retail and experience space, but a private space and also a monitored space. A space of cameras—a safe and secure place. This is a place of contrasts. I strolled through the mall on a Saturday at 7 pm and again at 10 pm. There were many experiences—from the aquarium to watching ice skating. I stood by one of the entrances, waiting and watching many people—mainly couples—enter and leave this crafted space. This was a concentrated space of flows. One thing was apparent, very few strollers leaving this mall had any indication that they had shopped. But it was Saturday night. There were very few carrying shopping bags but remember that this is also an entertainment and eating place.

There are two points to consider about this place of many potential service experiences. First, retail habits are changing; visits to shopping malls are less frequent, but of longer duration and involve travel over greater distances. The retail mix within large shopping centres is changing; ten years ago, food and drink outlets would account for 5% of outlets but today developers aim for at least 20% (The Dubai Mall is over 13%). This highlights the on-going transformation of shopping centres into leisure spaces that are saturated with service experiences, or just food (Bryson and Daniels 2015).

Second, one reading of retail is about the decline of the high street and of the shopping mall as e-commerce continues to transform the retail sector. It is interesting to note that the rise and decline of the high-street shop has occurred over a relatively short time. Shops, as we know them, only emerged in the later part of the seventeenth century. Prior to this, goods were purchased from temporary stalls set up in marketplaces or from 'shops' without glass windows. Instead, they were protected outside working hours by window-shutters that were let down and when open, supported on posts, for the display of goods. The word 'shop' only emerged as a verb with the meaning of going to purchase goods in the mid-eighteenth century (1764); prior to this the term meant to expose goods for sale or a workshop. The rise of e-commerce is partly behind the shift away from shopping to consume goods to shopping to consume service experiences. Shopping malls have become places to explore products that are then purchased online, perhaps click and collected, but too often returned.

Malls are places designed to encourage us to consume. Within the confines of The Dubai Mall, the tourist can gaze and consume a variety of different landscapes, entertainments and shops. Malls are spaces in which to see and to be seen (Bryson et al., 2004). 'Consumers' can enter the world of the mall and pretend that they have just shopped or are just about to shop or consume. They can gaze, stroll and be gazed upon consuming the space rather than relating to the mall as a place of consumption (Shields 1989). This is a form of resistance that implies that the psycho-geographers that design malls may have been too successful. Consumers of mall space increasingly consider a mall to be a real rather than a form of artificial public space. The public street, or the square, has been translocated into a form of enclosed, private place—a private place masquerading as a public place.

Reading a mall is an exercise in reading life. Strolling through the mall are shop assistants, entertainment creators, cleaners, security guards, mall guides and couples, families, and friends; all strangers who come together to explore this very carefully designed and designer-enclosed place. The whole world comes to The Dubai Mall, but what do visitors take away? Presents, products, food and memories of service experiences; memories of a time spent in a place of theatre, a place of over 1500 shops and of Dino the Dinosaur.

## 14.6   Wrapping Up

This chapter has explored services through the development of an integrated approach to service business. This approach has been to identify interrelationships between different activity systems within service businesses reflecting the development of a nested-based approach to understanding service business. This is a nested approach as one business activity system depends on other activity systems. Thus, Zara functions by combining design and manufacturing with logistics and the management of a large chain of stores and related retail channels. The aim has not been to develop extremely detailed case studies as these rapidly become outdated.

The analysis has focussed on three types of cases: company, city-region and servicespace. A case study approach should always come with a caveat regarding the selection of the cases. A key question is how representative are these cases? In this chapter, the strategy has been to select very different cases. This includes manufacturing firms that have become more service-orientated to platform-based businesses. The location of the cases includes the UK, the US China, Spain and Dubai, and this was deliberate to reflect businesses from different national settings.

The initial focus was on exploring the blurring of the boundaries between manufacturing and services. On the one hand, Rolls-Royce is a high-technology manufacturing firm focused on research and development and the creation of innovative solutions to the provision of power systems. It is also a company that increasingly sells services. Thus, Roll-Royce is an excellent example of the Services Duality (Chap. 2) in which companies combine production- and product-related services. On the other hand, Flowserve highlights that all types of products can be converted into services. Industrial pumps play an important role in industrial production, but they tend to be largely invisible. There is, for example, no well-developed social science literature on the manufacture of industrial pumps.

TikTok is an important example of a Chinese social media service platform that has successfully entered Western markets. This is unusual. The TikTok case highlights some of the specificities of platform-based business models. It draws attention to how Chinese firms are able to use mergers and acquisitions to acquire resources facilitating internationalization.

Inditex highlights the interconnections between different business functions or tasks required to create service retail experiences. The analysis of one of Inditex's subsidiaries, Zara, engages with the discussion in Chap. 7 on the assimilation perspective and service innovation in which service innovation cannot be separated or isolated from technological innovation. Zara is simultaneously a design firm, a manufacturer, a manager of a complex external supply chain, a logistics manager, a creator of retail service experiences and a manager of online retail experiences. It is a service firm, a manufacturing company, a logistics operator as well as being a company based around data analytics.

This approach concluded with a reading of one type of complex service space—the Dubai city-region. This shifted the analysis from companies to reading city-regions. It is important to appreciate that all businesses are situated in place and that geographical location matters in many ways. Location influences products and services, but also the ways in which a firm orientates itself to national and international markets. The Dubai account highlights the complexity of city-region economies combined with an appreciation of dynamics or the evolution of regional economies.

The final case focussed on a very complex and highly designed service space—The Dubai Mall. Malls are designed to encourage consumption and are perhaps one of the most contrived service spaces on this planet. Reading The Dubai Mall places many individual service businesses in the wider context of the mall. This, The Dubai Mall, is the location for retail outlets owned by Inditex, including Zara. In September 2019, Zara opened a new flagship store in The Dubai Mall. This was the first Zara store to showcase Zara's new shopping concept including self-service checkouts, automated collection points for online orders and a smart fitting-room management system. The Dubai Mall, if it is anything, is an excellent example of the on-going transformation of the service economy. In this case, the transformation includes a transition from the shopping mall as primarily an enclosed high street designed to encourage consumption to a theatrical space in which service experiences are co-created.

**Learning Outcomes**

- The limitations and advantages of a case study approach.
- The importance of adopting and developing an integrated approach to understanding service business.
- Reading city-regions as service spaces.
- Reading shopping malls as service spaces and as spaces of theatre and service experiences.
- The blurring of the boundaries between products and services.
- Platform-based service business models.
- The complexity of organizing and managing international retail service businesses.

## References

Bryson, J. R., Andres, L., & Mulhall, R. (Eds.). (2018). *A Research Agenda for Regeneration Economies: Reading City-Regions.* Cheltenham: Edward Elgar.

Bryson, J. R., & Daniels, P. W. (2015). Service Business: Growth, Innovation, Competitiveness. In J. R. Bryson & P. W. Daniels (Eds.), *Handbook of Service Business: Management, Marketing, Innovation and Internationalisation.* Cheltenham: Edward Elgar.

Bryson, J. R., & Vanchan, V. (2020). Covid-19 and Alternative Conceptualisations of Value and Risk in GPN Research. *Tijdschrift voor Economische en Sociale Geografie,* 111(3), 530–542.

Bryson, J. R., Daniels, P. W., & Warf, B. (2004). *Service Worlds: People, Organizations, Technologies.* Routledge: London.

Flowserve. (2018). *Think Beyond: Annual Report.* Irving, TX: Flowserve.

Inditex. (2018). *Annual Report.* Madrid: Inditex.

Nelson, T. (1987). *Computer Lib/Dream Machines* (Rev. ed.). Redmond, WA: Tempus Books.

Oxford Economics. (2014). Quantifying the Economic Impact of Aviation in Dubai: A report for Emirates and Dubai Airports, Oxford Economics. http://www.dubaiairports.ae/docs/default-source/Publications/oxford_economics_quantifying_the_economic_impact_of_aviation_in_dubai_november_2014_final(1)cc4dc38b5d08685a9b2fff000058806b.pdf?sfvrsn=0, accessed 3 October 2019.

Rethore, B.G. and Greer, C.S. (1999). Flowserve Corporation, *The Wall Street Transcript,* 17 November 1999, available at https://www.twst.com/interview/bernard-g-rethore-flowserve-corporation-fls, accessed 3 October 2020

Rolls-Royce. (2007). *Annual Report 2007: A Global Business*. London: Rolls-Royce.

Rolls-Royce. (2018). *Annual Report, 2018: Pioneers of Power*. London: Rolls-Royce.

Rusten, G., Bryson, J. R., & Aarflot, U. (2007). Places through Product and Products through Places: Industrial Design and Spatial Symbols as Sources of Competitiveness. *Norwegian Journal of Geography, 61*(3), 133–144.

Shields, R. (1989). Social Spatialization and the Built Environment: The West Edmonton Mall. *Environment and Planning D, Society and Space, 7*(2), 147–164.

Tokatli, N. (2008). Global Sourcing: Insights from the Global Clothing Industry – The Case of Zara, a Fast Fashion Retailer. *Journal of Economic Geography, 8*(1), 21–38.

Tokatli, N. (2015). Single-Firm Case Studies in Economic Geography: Some Methodological Reflections on the Case of Zara. *Journal of Economic Geography, 15*(3), 631–647.

Tokatli, N., & Kizilgun, O. (2009). From Manufacturing Garments for Ready-to-Wear to Designing Collections for Fast Fashion: The Changing Role of Suppliers in the Clothing Industry. *Environment and Planning A, 41*(1), 146–162.

Tokatli, N., & Kizilgun, O. (2010). Coping with the Changing Rules of the Game in the Global Textiles and Apparel Industries: Evidence from Turkey and Morocco. *Journal of Economic Geography, 10*(2), 209–229.

## Further Reading

Bryson, J. R., Andres, L., & Mulhall, R. (Eds.). (2018). *A Research Agenda for Regeneration Economies: Reading City-Regions*. Cheltenham: Edward Elgar.

Tokatli, N. (2015). Single-Firm Case Studies in Economic Geography: Some Methodological Reflections on the Case of Zara. *Journal of Economic Geography, 15*(3), 631–647.

## Useful Websites

https://thedubaimall.com/.
https://www.flowserve.com/en.
https://www.rolls-royce.com/.
https://www.businessofapps.com/data/tik-tok-statistics/.
https://www.inditex.com/.

# Index

Printed in the United States
By Bookmasters